# French Generals
of the Great War

# French Generals of the Great War

## Leading the Way

Jonathan Krause and William Philpott

Pen & Sword
**MILITARY**

First published in Great Britain in 2023 by
Pen & Sword Military
An imprint of
Pen & Sword Books Ltd
Yorkshire – Philadelphia

Copyright © Jonathan Krause and William Philpott 2023

ISBN 978 1 78159 252 6

The right of Jonathan Krause and William Philpott to be identified as Authors of this work has been asserted by them in accordance with the Copyright, Designs and Patents Act 1988.

A CIP catalogue record for this book is
available from the British Library.

All rights reserved. No part of this book may be reproduced or transmitted in any form or by any means, electronic or mechanical including photocopying, recording or by any information storage and retrieval system, without permission from the Publisher in writing.

Typeset by Mac Style
Printed in the UK by CPI Group (UK) Ltd, Croydon, CR0 4YY.

Pen & Sword Books Limited incorporates the imprints of Atlas, Archaeology, Aviation, Discovery, Family History, Fiction, History, Maritime, Military, Military Classics, Politics, Select, Transport, True Crime, Air World, Frontline Publishing, Leo Cooper, Remember When, Seaforth Publishing, The Praetorian Press, Wharncliffe Local History, Wharncliffe Transport, Wharncliffe True Crime and White Owl.

For a complete list of Pen & Sword titles please contact

**PEN & SWORD BOOKS LIMITED**
47 Church Street, Barnsley, South Yorkshire, S70 2AS, England
E-mail: enquiries@pen-and-sword.co.uk
Website: www.pen-and-sword.co.uk

Or

**PEN AND SWORD BOOKS**
1950 Lawrence Rd, Havertown, PA 19083, USA
E-mail: Uspen-and-sword@casematepublishers.com
Website: www.penandswordbooks.com

# Contents

| | |
|---|---|
| *List of Abbreviations in Text and Footnotes* | vi |
| *Notes on Contributors* | vii |
| *Preface* | ix |
| **Introduction** Leadership and Learning, *by* William Philpott and Jonathan Krause | 1 |
| **Chapter 1** Joseph Joffre: Strategist of Mass War, *by* William Philpott | 23 |
| **Chapter 2** Ferdinand Foch: Master of Strategy, *by* Michael Neiberg | 48 |
| **Chapter 3** Philippe Pétain: The Soldiers' General, *by* Jonathan Krause | 64 |
| **Chapter 4** Robert Nivelle: A Formula for Failure, *by* Paul Strong | 83 |
| **Chapter 5** Marie-Émile Fayolle: The Forgotten Marshal of France, *by* William Philpott | 106 |
| **Chapter 6** Fernand de Langle de Cary: A Pragmatic Survivor, *by* Simon House | 130 |
| **Chapter 7** Paul Maistre: Missing in Action, *by* William Philpott | 147 |
| **Chapter 8** Pierre Roques: A Political General, *by* Simon House | 165 |
| **Chapter 9** Marie-Eugène Debeney: A Fighting Professor, *by* William Philpott | 185 |
| **Chapter 10** Charles Mangin: 'This Devil of a Man', *by* Tim Gale | 206 |
| **Chapter 11** Maurice Gamelin: A Successful Apprenticeship, *by* Martin Alexander | 226 |
| **Chapter 12** Jean-Baptiste Estienne: Father of the Tanks, *by* Tim Gale | 240 |
| *Bibliographical Note* | 256 |
| *Notes* | 259 |
| *Index* | 302 |

# List of Abbreviations in Text and Footnotes

| | |
|---|---|
| AFGG | *Les Armées françaises dans la grande guerre* (Paris: Imprimerie Nationale, 11 tomes in 105 vols, 1922–1937) (French official history of the war) |
| AS | *Artillerie spéciale* (tank corps) |
| BC | *brigade de chasseurs* (chasseur light infantry brigade) |
| BCP/A | *bataillon de chasseurs à pied/alpins* (light infantry/mountain battalion) |
| BI | *brigade d'infanterie* (infantry brigade) |
| CA | *corps d'armée* (army corps) |
| CAC | *corps d'armée colonial* (colonial army corps) |
| CSG | *Conseil supérieur de guerre* (higher war council) |
| DI | *division d'infanterie* (infantry division) |
| DIC | *division d'infanterie coloniale* (colonial infantry division) |
| DSA | *Direction de service automobile* (transport service) |
| ESG | *École supérieure de guerre* (French army staff college) |
| GAN/C/E/R | *Groupe d'armées du nord/du centre/de l'est/ de réserve* (army group north/centre/east/reserve) |
| GQG | *Grand quartier général* (army general headquarters) |
| JMO | *journal de marche et opérations* (unit war diary) |
| RFV | *Région fortifiée de Verdun* (Verdun fortified region) |
| RI | *régiment d'infanterie* (infantry regiment) |
| SHD | *Service historique de la défense*, Vincennes (defence historical service – French military archives) |

# Notes on Contributors

**Martin S. Alexander** is Emeritus Professor of International Relations, Aberystwyth University. He held posts at Yale, the US Naval War College, Salford University and the Sorbonne. He has published extensively on French defence policy, doctrine and wars from 1914–66, including a study of Maurice Gamelin as French army chief of staff, *The Republic in Danger: General Maurice Gamelin and the Politics of French Defence, 1933–1940* (1993). He is currently writing a book about the French army's performance in 1940.

**Tim Gale** completed his doctorate on the French army's tank force in the Department of War Studies, King's College London. He has published two studies of French tank operations, *The French Army's Tank Force and Armoured Warfare in the Great War: The* Artillerie spéciale (2013) and *French Tanks of the Great War: Development, Tactics and Operations* (2016). He is Secretary General of the British Commission for Military History.

**Simon J. House** completed his doctorate on the 1914 Battle of the Ardennes in the Department of War Studies, King's College London, after retiring from a career in the telecommunications business. It was subsequently published as *Lost Opportunity: The Battle of the Ardennes, 22 August 1914* (2017).

**Jonathan Krause** completed his doctorate on the French army's tactical development during 1915 in the Department of War Studies, King's College London. It was subsequently published as *Early Trench Tactics in the French Army: The Second Battle of Artois, May–June 1915* (2013). He has held teaching posts at the RAF College, Cranwell, King's College London and Oxford and Wolverhampton universities. He is currently writing a comparative study of anticolonial rebellions during the First World War arising from an AHRC funded early career research fellowship, 'Rebellion and Mobilization in French and German Colonies, 1914–1918'.

**Michael S. Neiberg** is Professor of History and Chair of War Studies at the United States Army War College in Carlisle, Pennsylvania. His published work specializes on the First and Second World Wars in global context. The *Wall*

*Street Journal* named his *Dance of the Furies: Europe and the Outbreak of World War I* (2011) one of five best books about that war. His latest book is *When France Fell: The Vichy Crisis and the Fate of the Anglo-American Relationship* (2021). In 2017 he was awarded the *Médaille d'or du rayonnement culturel* from *La Renaissance française*, an organization founded by President Raymond Poincaré in 1915 to keep French culture alive during the First World War.

**William Philpott** is Professor of the History of Warfare in the Department of War Studies, King's College London. In a thirty-year career he has published extensively on the First World War, with a focus on strategy, operations and Anglo-French relations. His book, *Bloody Victory: The Sacrifice on the Somme and the Making of the Twentieth Century* (2009) won the Society for Army Historical Research's Templer Prize and the World War 1 Historical Association's Norman B. Tomlinson Jr book prize. *Attrition: Fighting the First World War* (2014) was a *Wall Street Journal* book of the year. He is President of the British Commission for Military History.

**Paul E. Strong** is a senior historian at the UK's Defence Wargaming Centre, specializing in wargame design, scenario development, and wargame adjudication. He co-authored *Artillery in the Great War* (2011) and co-edited *Women in War: From Home Front to the Front Line* (2012). Recently his published work has focused on the role of the Royal Navy's Western Approaches Tactical Unit during the Second World War, and the future role of artificial intelligence in the Royal Navy.

# Preface

This volume presents the first collective study of French senior commanders of the First World War. The editors have chosen individuals from all levels of command: better known senior figures responsible for strategic leadership, Foch, Joffre, Pétain and Nivelle; important mid-level field commanders, de Langle de Cary, Fayolle, Maistre, Mangin and Debeney; and more junior yet significant individuals, Roques, Estienne and Gamelin, who exemplify traits of the wartime French army. The generals selected are studied in the contexts of warfare that is adapting to the industrialization of the battlefield and mass mobilization, and of an army that is rapidly modernizing when faced with the challenges presented on the Western Front. The studies show how commanders learn, perform, progress and on occasion fail to meet those challenges. Collectively, the study offers a more positive interpretation of command ability and military performance than used to be customary when studying First World War command, sitting squarely within the genre of literature that argues for effective learning and appropriate practice evolving in the crucible of modern warfare between 1914 and 1918.

One later generation general, André Bourachot, has cautioned, 'The key players of that era…are inevitably put on trial by the tender conscience of our era. The military – especially the generals – all receive the same pitiless sentence of posthumous infamy, now that it is too late to condemn them in their own lifetime.'[1] In fact, with a couple of exceptions, French generals are not so vilified as their English counterparts: excepting the most senior leaders they are largely overlooked in the extensive French historiography of the First World War, that concentrates predominantly upon the common soldiers' experience, or the battles that were fought. Although biographies of individuals exist, French commanders await systematic investigation. The decisions they took and the doctrine and experience that guided these are a rich ground for historical investigation. An extensive archive exists in the wartime army's records held at the *Service historique de la défense* in Vincennes, and it is hoped that this collection will encourage the sort of scrutiny that has been given to British and more recently German command and commanders during the war. Although a collective biography can only present a small sample from the hundreds of individuals who held positions of responsibility in the French army, the editors hope that the commanders surveyed here represent the range, ability and achievements of the men who led France and her allies to victory and that these essays will go some way towards correcting Bourachot's blanket impression of military command. These studies will rehabilitate men who, although not without human faults, rose to the professional challenges that mass war with new tools and novel methods presented.

The volume's contributors are established experts on the history of the twentieth-century French army, whose work in recent years has started to assess the nature and achievements of that army in the First World War systematically for the first time. The volume arises from the work of the First World War Operations Research Group in the Department of War Studies, King's College London, which has been engaged in the comparative study of First World War armies for a number of years. The editors would like to thank the members of that group for their engagement with the material presented in this volume, as well as the members of the Institute of Historical Research's military history research seminar that has provided a forum in which to present and discuss early drafts of some of these chapters. Above all, we would like to thank our editors at Pen & Sword, Richard Harding and Harriet Fielding, for their continued support and patience during the lengthy preparation of this work.

# Introduction: Leadership and Learning

## William Philpott and Jonathan Krause

At the enquiry into the fall of the fortress on Maubeuge in September 1914 the defence council for General Henri Fournier and his subordinates had cautioned the jury of seven successful wartime commanders, 'beware, you are the "horizon blue" judging the "red trousers". Your experience, you who are the victors, is it not due to the mistakes of others?' To which the president of the jury, General Paul Maistre, had murmured in acknowledgement and admission, 'and also our own'.[1] Such self-awareness, evincing understanding of the possibilities and limitations of warfare between 1914 and 1918, should stand as a leitmotif for studying command and commanders in this war and more generally. In recent decades this has increasingly become the norm, although French commanders remain shadowy figures, and the French army's adaptation to modern warfare had received far less scrutiny than that of their British ally and German enemy. This volume assesses the efforts, errors and achievements of twelve French generals in a war in which they played leading roles as theoreticians and practitioners; and secured a victory that drew on their collective professional skills, as well as the efforts and sacrifices of the soldiers they led. The studies suggest that all commanders had strengths and weaknesses: also, that the challenges of a new style of warfare were evident and surmountable given the right intellectual training and a practical approach.

Ever since politicians, poets and a generation of historians mounted a collective assault on the reputations of Britain's wartime commanders in the middle decades of the twentieth century a veritable war of words has been waged to condemn or rehabilitate Britain's First World War generals. Although popular understanding generally lags behind academic evaluation, in the twenty-first century military historians have moved towards a consensus that, while there were serious failures and harsh learning experiences as part of the process, the British army and its commanders adapted effectively to the demands of mass industrialized warfare between 1915 and 1918. In this re-examination many key figures, from commanders-in-chief Sir John French and Sir Douglas Haig, through army commanders down to army corps and divisional commanders, have been assessed.[2] In contrast, the French army's

2  French Generals of the Great War

wartime leaders are, largely, either caricatures or unknowns. The studies in this volume, of twelve figures who occupied command positions at all levels during the war, some famous – even infamous – and some more obscure, offer for the first time a systematic assessment of the commanders and command style of arguably the most modern and effective First World War army.[3]

French First World War generalship has never generated the intensive analysis that British generalship has attracted, nor even the level of interest that is shown to German command. This appears strange given the French army's predominant role in the Western Front campaign, as well as French leadership of the coalition.[4] In France there has been no great controversy over their military leaders, although at the turn of the century a few popular historians tried to condemn some key figures in the same way that British generals had been vilified.[5] Rather than attempting a balanced assessment of their subjects as military leaders, such 'butchers and bunglers' genre studies emphasized notorious incidents and high casualties (inevitable in a mass war of attrition).[6] The French army, and on the whole the French people, still hold their wartime leaders in high regard, even if they remain figures of lore rather than historical substance.[7] Certainly the principal leaders, Joseph Joffre, Philippe Pétain and Ferdinand Foch, have been the subject of biographies, but in Joffre's case never and in Foch's not for many years in English.[8] Pétain's notorious second career as head of France's Second World War Vichy regime attracts more interest than his earlier illustrious military career.[9] Systematic scholarly work on these principals is only now starting to appear, although (perhaps to engage an English-language readership) it focuses on their leadership of the allied coalition rather than their command styles.[10] Similarly, the army that they commanded is only now starting to emerge from the historical shadows to which an excessive focus on British military performance has assigned it.[11] There is much still to learn about the men who led the French army and the army that they led.

\* \* \*

President Raymond Poincaré pithily condemned in August 1914 'the school of military thought more inclined to enthusiasm than caution' that had imbued French general staff thinking, an impression that has coloured subsequent historiography.[12] In 1988 Douglas Porch contributed a chapter on the French army to an influential volume on military effectiveness in the First World War. His verdict was damning: 'the French adapted badly to the trench deadlock. … French commanders attempted to rush events…. The general historical verdict on the French Army in the First Word War is that it put in a courageous but unintelligent performance.'[13] In his defence, Porch had little material on which to base his evaluation. His own study of the pre-war army's lacklustre preparations furnished the intellectual framework for his assessment, while available secondary sources were limited.[14] Porch essentially concluded that pre-war errors (which were more accurately a lack of decisions) were indicative of systemic problems that persisted well into the war, until Pétain took command. In Porch's unbalanced analysis Joffre is castigated while Foch is all but ignored as figures who shaped the ethos and performance of the army. Recent reassessment of First World War armies as learning organizations suggests that Porch's judgment lacks depth and nuance. Certainly, as the chapters in this collection elucidate, the French army had problems before and at the start of the war (as did all armies). It clearly had much to learn, but it would adapt more rapidly and successfully than is supposed.

Essentially, First World War armies were engaging with a periodic military conundrum: how to balance firepower with shock action at a time of changing military technologies. Tactics were in flux after long-range, quick-firing weaponry – rifles, machine guns and field artillery – was adopted in the early years of the century and armies had to adapt doctrines to fighting on a firepower-dominated battlefield. French doctrine was evolving alongside that of other armies as they tried to integrate the infantry assault with the artillery barrage,[15] although the nuanced solutions adopted are too often caricatured as a simplistic and quasi-suicidal '*offensive à outrance*' – overreliance on the bayonet and moral forces rather than firepower.[16] At the emergent operational level of war the French army was grappling with the problem of controlling higher formations – army corps and armies – that would be deployed once war was declared. In an era of mass conscript armies that could mobilize a huge pool of trained reserves, the development of campaigns was hard to predict. Such were the challenges that pre-war theoreticians such as Foch and Colonel Louis de Grandmaison grappled with, although with no real outcome – 'historians' they were, as Porch has classified them,[17] because they studied history as a means for understanding and better engaging with warfare, rather than because they expected that history would repeat itself on the contemporary battlefield. Foch for one had anticipated the likely operational outcome when mass forces were pitched against one another:

> the armies have outgrown the brains of the people who direct them. I do not believe there is any man big enough to control these millions. They will stumble about then sit down helplessly in front of each other, thinking only of their means of communication to supply these vast hordes, who must eat.[18]

The fact that a new infantry tactical regulation drawn up by Grandmaison was promulgated in April 1914 suggests that these divisive doctrinal debates were reaching a conclusion.[19] However, introducing a new doctrine is not the same as re-educating an army. French reservists' training schedules meant that a majority of the soldiers deployed in July and August 1914 had been trained in the earlier 1897 doctrine. Fortuitously for Germany if not for France, Germany invaded France at a time when the army was in the grip of doctrinal change and structural reform (as had happened previously in 1870 and was to happen once again in 1940), a momentary but potentially decisive advantage.[20]

French tactical doctrine privileged suppressive fire from the famous *soixante-quinze* – the quick-firing 75mm field gun first deployed in 1897 that heralded the firepower revolution – that would allow the infantry to cross the killing zone and close with the enemy. *Élan* or spirit, that elusive moral force, would in part compensate for the prevalence of material on the battlefield, not least the advent of the machine gun: these the French army deployed in the same numbers as the German in 1914, but individually in a localized fire-support role, rather than en masse to control ground as was German practice. This is not to say that pre-war Joffre neglected the need for heavier artillery. Modern heavy howitzers were demanded regularly from a succession of rapidly changing war ministers. Politics and finance prevented the delivery of such guns in large numbers, but those that Joffre's army deployed in 1914 were the equal of their enemy's weapons. Where the French erred was in their disposition. Held back under army command rather than pushed forwards under divisional control, in the first huge and bloody battles along the French frontier quick-firing howitzers were not used for close fire-support in the way that German field howitzers, which were integral to infantry division artillery establishments, were.[21] This (among a complexity of factors) helps to explain initial German victories in the encounter battles of August 1914 (although by the time the enemy's infantry came up against dug-in French defenders in Lorraine in early September progress was less assured and more costly). It also suggests that it became apparent early on that this would be an artilleryman's war.[22]

It was not simply doctrine, but its implementation that was at fault. In the first battles on the frontiers operational concepts were poorly grasped by senior officers: Pierre Roques's failings as a corps commander in the Battle of the Ardennes and Pierre Ruffey's lacklustre performance as Third Army commander in the same battle, for which he was relieved of his command, are good examples.[23] The resulting purge of superannuated or undynamic officers from the army's high command by Joffre was obviously necessary.[24] Certain senior officers such as Roques and Fourth Army commander Fernand de Langle de Cary, whose performance had been at best mediocre, survived the cull (perhaps because they had strong political support) and would be given a chance to prove themselves in the defensive battles that followed. But this shake-up of the highest ranks cleared the way for others, generals and colonels who had proved more adept either as commanders or staff officers, to take their first step on the promotion ladder.

\* \* \*

Although it was bested in its early encounter battles the French army did not collapse. Mass armies are resilient: there were more than enough trained reservists in French depots to replace early losses before the next big battle on the Marne. Unlike his opponent General Helmuth von Moltke the younger, Joffre had not used his second-line reserve divisions, over one-third of his strength, in the front line and many remained in hand for the second phase of the campaign. In late August the French army was able to rally and give a better account of itself on the defensive: in the Battle of Guise and in the fighting retreat to the Marne; defending the Grand Couronné at Nancy; and at Verdun, the right-flank pivot on which Joffre would hang his counter stroke on the left wing, the Battle of the Marne, in early September. The fact that Joffre could redeploy forces from east to west and strike back with altogether greater ferocity and effect come September is itself evidence of the French army as a thinking organization; one that had the potential to adapt more rapidly and effectively to the actual circumstances of the industrialized battlefield than the inelastic German enemy or the 'small war' minded (and organized) British ally.

While France's commander-in-chief proved flexible and dynamic when meeting the practical and operational challenges arising from German invasion, like all other generals in 1914 he could not gainsay the fundamental nature of the war that Europe faced once mass armies with plentiful reserves were committed against each other. The tactical nature of the war the French army was facing emerged in September along the Aisne front where the first trench battles were fought. As well as being a static positional war tactically, it would become an attritional one operationally: armies and doctrines would have to adapt to these dual determinants of modern warfare. Once the space for outflanking was filled with redeployed formations during October's 'race to the sea' and the opposing trench lines came to rest on the Channel coast, the central operational challenge presented itself: how to exhaust the enemy's reserves to such a point that a decisive military result could be attained. This should be clearly distinguished from the tactical battlefield challenge of how to fight in and conquer fortified field defences. In October and November, Foch conducted the first battle of attrition, the First Battle of Ypres, as both sides threw in their last fresh reserves in a struggle to hold or break the defensive line. The Germans could not find fresh forces to shatter the thinly held allied line into which Foch parsimoniously fed penny-packets of reserves at the points and moments of acute crisis. One lesson was being suggested. Infantry should be used sparingly, to contest ground but not to buy it at heavy cost in the face of concentrated firepower, as the enemy were demonstrating in their massed assaults on dug-in firing lines. This was a straightforward and key principle of modern warfare, but one that armies would take time to inculcate.

The processes by which the armies which Foch directed and opposed conducted that gruelling battle, cycling infantry formations in and out of the line to exhaust each other in their turn, were essentially the processes of warfare for the next four years. Over that period the tactical methods, the technological and material base of warfare, the systems of operational command and control and the very nature of battle would all change. What would not change immediately, however, would be ideas of the 'right' way of warfare. There persisted for too long (in many civilian and some military minds throughout the war and beyond) an obsession with positional objectives and ground, the geographical outputs of battle – taking trenches, capturing villages, breaking through defensive lines into open country – that sat uneasily with the straightforward Napoleonic principle of finding, fixing and destroying the enemy's forces, the military outputs. Two of these the enemy had already addressed: the German army was to be found in the trenches opposite where it had fixed itself. Destroying it would of course be a matter of time; how much time depended on whether it could be annihilated – 1914's battles suggested that it could not – or whether it would need to be ground down through systematic attrition. By 1916 the determining principle of allied military strategy had become 'the destruction of the German and Austrian armies',[25] although halfway through the war the means and methods to do so effectively, diminishing the inevitable reciprocal damage, were still falling into place. Trench tactics were starting to be effective, although the modern operational precepts needed to translate localized tactical success into strategic outcomes were still being conceptualized. By the middle of 1917 the French army had closed this 'operational gap' and would demonstrate, once the opportunity arose, that they had the methods and skill to break their enemy on the battlefield.

Generals always try to fight their battles on favourable ground. In that the enemy started the 1915 Western Front campaign with a real advantage that presented the French high command with a specific tactical challenge. In retreat the German army had chosen its positions, commanding heights that overlooked the allied lines in many places, and challenged their enemy to push them off: to that extent ground had not lost its significance as a tactical objective. These crests and plateaus would be the epicentres of battle for the next three years: the Passchendaele and Messines ridges around Ypres, Vimy ridge in Artois, the Thiepval ridge north of the river Somme, the Chemin des Dames above the river Aisne, and the heights around the strategic fortress of

Verdun. In winter and spring 1914–15 the hills of Notre-Dame-de-Lorette in Artois, the Hartmannswillerkopf and Le Linge in the Vosges, the Butte de Vauquois and Les Éparges on either flank of the Verdun salient were the locations of early localized struggles for commanding viewpoints. This was gruelling, costly and unproductive warfare, but essential. Breaking the enemy's defensive line, with a view to resuming a war of movement, proved no more achievable an objective in early engagements. In Champagne over the winter de Langle de Cary's Fourth Army fought its first close-range fights for Perthes-lès-Hurlus, Tahure and Souain, fortified villages and hills whose names would become notorious from the army's official communiqués.

These relatively fruitless fights were the French army's early battle schools. As reports of bloody failures and false starts began pouring into divisional, army corps, army and eventually general headquarters the sheer magnitude of the problem started to become apparent. Such battles presented localized tactical problems, and from this wealth of experience came the first inklings of how to tackle a wired trench network fortified with machine-gun positions and supported by rapid-firing artillery. Lessons learned regarding trench construction, the best use for different weapons (each calibre of artillery piece and different type of shell fulfilled nuanced roles), and how to maintain the impetus of an attack were collated into the French army's first coherent doctrine for trench warfare published in April 1915: *Buts et conditions d'une offensive d'ensemble* (Note 5779). Updated in summer 1915 and again in 1916, this document would form the theoretical foundations for French trench tactics for the rest of the war. Without the bloody failures of late 1914 and early 1915 a functional tactical doctrine could not have formed.[26]

During 1915 the army was in the process of transformation. A new design of uniform had been sanctioned shortly before the outbreak of war – the 'horizon blue' army would replace the blue-tunicked and red-trousered infantry of 1914 – although it was not only uniforms but equipment and methods that would define the modernized French army. Heavy guns of advanced design existed in small numbers and would be manufactured in greater numbers to enable the army to compete materially by late summer 1916, by which time appropriate tactical doctrine had been developed to coordinate artillery and infantry action. Concurrently, new munitions were developed to increase the effectiveness of a bombardment. In the interim obsolescent heavy fortress artillery pieces that had to be reregistered after every shot had to be pressed into service to support offensive operations, dictating the slow, steady pace of battle during the first phase of the war. The emphasis was on destructive barrages designed to smash the enemy's field defences before the infantry attacked, hence Pétain's famous adage, 'the artillery conquers, the infantry occupies'. The '75s' had proved devastating in open warfare but relatively ineffective against dug-in troops.

They would be relegated thereafter to a close infantry support role, firing creeping barrages to cover an infantry advance, gas shells to neutralize enemy defensive positions, or high-explosive and shrapnel shells to break up enemy attacks.[27] The infantry themselves would become modern soldiers – grenades, rifle-grenades, Chauchat light-machine guns, 37mm trench cannons and trench mortars enhanced their firepower and 'Adrian' steel helmets completed the *poilus*' new look. This redesign manifested a resolution of the pre-war doctrinal debates between advocates of firepower and élan. In time, Joffre's infantry would regain élan (if they ever lost it), but they would also have their own integrated tactical firepower, and heavier and better artillery support to enable them to fight effectively on an entrenched battlefield. The final novel elements of the modern tactical weapons system, aircraft and tanks, cutting-edge technologies at the time, were developed through 1915 and in 1916 and 1917 respectively started to change the way the French army fought its battles. France had an early technological lead in both – in aircraft thanks to Pierre Roques – but they would have to be incorporated into the army's order of battle and doctrinal methods adapted to integrate them with the other arms.[28] General Jean-Baptiste Estienne, a pre-war artillery theorist destined to be the father of the French tank, emerged as the sort of dynamic technocratic officer who could not only conceive the means to fight positional warfare effectively, but also showed the drive to get things done within France's bureaucratic administrative systems.

\* \* \*

Appropriate tactics had to be matched with precise operational methods, which would take one-and-a-half years of trial and error, and a further year of misadventure, before they became standardized. When the trench stalemate set in many commanders, including Joffre, believed trenches were a temporary phenomenon, the equivalent of 'winter quarters', and it only required an attack of sufficient scale and intensity to overthrow the German army's field fortifications and return to mobile warfare. This problem persisted until 1918, although the enemy's defensive refinements in response to steady allied offensive tactical improvements meant that it would offer a dynamic, constantly adapting challenge. As Jonathan Boff has suggested when analysing the outcome of the 1918 campaign, it was less a case of finding the correct 'recipe' for victory, more of adopting a pragmatic problem-solving approach to the complexities of warfare based on experience.[29] Successful French commanders achieved this, but also grounded their learning in military history and theory – it is significant that a group of pre-war staff college professors were the army's senior leaders come 1918.

The greater operational problem, defeating the German army, was a different level of challenge. Partly this was an issue of coordinating and leading the coalition, Joffre's primary task in 1915 and 1916.[30] Partly it was a matter of resources, something else Joffre focused on in the first year of stalemate as he importuned the French war ministry for manpower and guns and munitions. Partly it was a question of developing and deploying appropriate military technologies. Partly it was a matter of planning and preparing the right sort of operations to progress the strategic objective of liberating occupied French soil, which *Grand quartier général*'s (GQG) staff wrestled with. But above all it was a matter of execution, which placed faith in army and army corps commanders' ability to apply emergent doctrine properly and to deliver results on the battlefield. While there were certainly localized successes, no one would dispute that in 1915 French operations were executed with more determination than skill. Yet the early campaigns in Artois and Champagne, undeniably costly compared with those which came later, were at least productive in terms of ideas and experience. Commanders faced novel, yet solvable, military challenges and several of the generals studied in this volume – Pétain, Marie-Émile Fayolle, Robert Nivelle, Charles Mangin and Maistre – made names for themselves as successful army corps and divisional commanders in these early offensives.

The first year of trench warfare presented tactical and operational problems: how to take and hold enemy defensive positions and how to manage the large and complex military formations that sustained prolonged offensives – armies divided into army corps with attached supporting arms. Taking enemy defences was a matter of bringing sufficient firepower to bear to suppress the defence. This was a simple principle quickly learned, even if early in the war there was insufficient firepower to attack more than a very limited section of the enemy's defences at any one time, and techniques of counter-battery fire to suppress the enemy's supporting artillery were as yet rudimentary. Integrating a fire-plan with infantry objectives required managerial skills and good communications – command was becoming a desk exercise suitable to the technically minded soldier rather than an outdoor pursuit for the traditional leader of men. As 1915 went on generals would have to incorporate new support weapons such as aircraft and gas into their 'weapons systems', while their infantry would be adapting to fighting with mortars, hand- and rifle-grenades, light-machine guns and trench cannons, as well as new types of bombardment such as the 'lifting' and 'creeping' barrages that were being trialled in the field. Although such techniques were rudimentary in 1915, even then if properly planned and adequately resourced such complex battles were likely to succeed, at least in their first phase before the enemy could deploy reserves. 'Breaking in' to the enemy's defences was never really a problem.[31]

Breaking through was another challenge entirely, and an operational false start. 'Breakthrough', an ill-defined and perhaps specious conception, is an idea still bandied about by detractors of First World War commanders as if it were a military aberration, with little grasp of context and intention. It was certainly a fluctuating concept at the time, its method and potential outcomes altering with time and place. As an abstract concept it involved forcing forces through the enemy's fixed defences into open country – itself a two-part process of 'breaking in' and then 'breaking out' – with the expectation that such a breach could be exploited with fresh reserves of infantry and more mobile cavalry (assuming of course that the enemy had no reserves to close it). Yet a breach might be local and tactical, on a short section of front, which could be contained by flanking fire, or strategic, on too wide a front for the enemy to contain it. For example, the Moroccan Division's dash onto the Vimy ridge in May 1915 at the start of the Second Battle of Artois was merely a tactical breach that was contained and squeezed out.[32] In contrast, the Second Army's breakthrough in Champagne in late September was a wide breach of the first enemy position (essentially a 'break in'), which was thereafter confronted by a second position through which narrow tactical breaches were forced. As on the Vimy ridge, these were contained, heavy losses being inflicted on the now concentrated French forces in the process. Any threat to break through to threaten the enemy's lateral railway communications was thereby nullified. Second Artois gave false hope that the solution to the stalemate was to be found in effective assault tactics. Second Champagne indicated that this was an operational dead end, in comparison with the simultaneous Third Battle of Artois in which Tenth Army's *grignotage* – literally 'nibbling' at the successive German defences – achieved steady but less showy progress through the German defences.

Holding captured trenches against enemy counter attacks also proved difficult. If rushed an attack would often collapse in confusion, with a breakdown in command and control making consolidation difficult. The primitive nature of battlefield communications did not allow revision once an operation was underway, or rapid reaction should it go awry. Attacking formations were at their most vulnerable to a well-organized counter attack at this point. Moreover, exploiting a success was problematic in the face of an alert enemy. Often it was not the first planned attack but the second more hastily improvised follow-up that ended in disaster: the second phase of the Champagne offensive, in which French reserves were thrown repeatedly against narrow breaches in the enemy's second-line defences and cut to pieces by unsilenced artillery and machine-gun fire, is a classic example.

What 1915's operations demonstrated, above all, was that as well as sufficient firepower system, steadiness and sustainability were essential for progress and results in positional warfare, principles emphasized in Foch's seminal December 1915 doctrinal paper, 'Lessons from Our Last Attacks'.[33] The first was a matter of technology and technique, the other three issues of organization and leadership. System required appropriate planning, command, control and communications by high command; steadiness involved strong junior leadership, effective training and high morale among the troops; sustainability depended on increasingly sophisticated logistics to supply men to the fight and the resources with which they lived and fought.

Such methods dictated a measured, repetitive operational tempo, but extended siege warfare seemed undynamic and ill-suited to French élan and prevailing political imperatives to liberate occupied French soil quickly. Foch, who had directed the battles in Artois, deduced that 'breaking through' was an operational chimera as long as the enemy had rearward lines of trenches and the reserves to man them. Battle was inexorably becoming deeper as defensive tactics adapted to more effective assault methods, and so the way to conduct operations effectively was to fight and defeat the enemy's reserves within his fixed defences where they could be targeted by massed firepower rather than to attempt to force him to fight in the open. Such a controlled battle – a 'scientific battle' in Foch's formation – would have a slower tempo and be more resource intensive, would require careful command and control and would sacrifice spectacular advances, but it would economize French infantrymen's lives and by tying down his reserves negate the enemy's power to respond dynamically.[34]

\* \* \*

This method would be put to the test in the French army's next major offensive that Foch would direct, the Battle of the Somme. Although the army began the 1916 campaign with appropriate tactical and operational methods, operational goals remained elusive. As Fayolle, who was to lead Sixth Army in the battle, identified as the Somme offensive was being planned: 'Do they hope to break through? I do not think so. Then what is the point of this battle? Attrition they say. Fighting to wear down the enemy. Hum! That is hardly enough.'[35] Moreover, offensive operations at this point in the war presented a peculiar challenge:

> If there are so many defensive positions, there will need to be as many battles, succeeding each other as rapidly possible. Each one needs to be organized anew, with a new artillery preparation. If one goes too quickly, one risks a check. If one goes too slowly, then the enemy has time to construct successive defensive lines. That is the problem, and it is extremely difficult.[36]

Moreover, at GQG there was still an emphasis on breaking through. The *rupture* of the enemy's front – essentially collapsing a long section of the German line rather than forcing a narrow breach – remained an operational goal. But expectations were on a cusp. GQG offered two alternative scenarios just before the offensive commenced: 'the enemy's front will give way to our pressure in a few days along the whole sector of the attack [leading to] a rupture of the front by surprise…or [it will be] a hard and long battle whose denouement will be the attrition of the enemy's forces that he can deploy in this theatre'.[37]

Foch and Fayolle were unconvinced of the possibility of a quick *rupture* and prepared and fought accordingly. (Haig was not and his army suffered the consequences on 1 July 1916.)[38] The four-and-a-half month Somme offensive exerted steady, sustained pressure on the German defence, wearing down the enemy's reserves. After two-and-a-half months of continuous effort Fayolle's troops would eventually penetrate the final line of German field defences on the Somme, at Bouchavesnes on 12 September 1916. It was a hollow triumph that promised much and delivered nothing – another narrow breach that was sealed before French reserves could be brought up to exploit it.[39] This should have put paid to any lingering belief that the solution to the stalemate was breaking through into open country; new commander-in-chief Nivelle was to make one final, disastrous attempt in spring 1917, however. Significantly, something else had been confirmed from this experience. Foch chose after the war to have his statue erected at Bouchavesnes, and General Marie-Eugène Debeney, who had been a corps commander in that sector at the time and was to unveil it, hinted at the significance of the Somme in his public oration. It had been

> the first of the great mass battles, in which we asserted our tactical superiority over the enemy…. After the Somme [Foch] began to abandon the simplistic idea of obtaining success by breaking a short section of the enemy's front, replacing it with the more fruitful idea, which was to give us victory, of progressively dislocating the various sectors of the front.[40]

During September Foch had trialled a new operational process – successive but limited strikes with four allied armies all along the enemy front that would by the end of the month bring the German defence to crisis point.[41] Rather than the forward-thrusting battle that Fayolle had been obliged to fight despite its tactical and logistical difficulties, Foch was looking in future to use repeated heavy but limited blows to smash the German defence along the lines which it held, exploiting laterally rather than pressing forwards against stiffening resistance. This, along with improved communications and greater resources, would allow him in time to mount a quick-tempo, wide battle as an alternative to the slow, deep operations of 1916.

The system that would bring rewards within two years was emerging. During the offensive French troops had shown their steadiness under the control of methodical field commanders who planned their attacks with precision and care: several of these, including Debeney and Maistre, would be commanding armies in 1918. Maurice Gamelin, a brigadier on the Somme and a rising star, would by then be commanding a division. Despite the muddy anti-climax to the battle after autumn rains set in, the army was to end the Somme offensive with high morale, confident that it could now take on and master its enemy. Similar improvement was happening in the later phase of the Battle of Verdun under Nivelle's direction.

Sustainability had proved more difficult in battles that lasted months, but solutions were developing. Battle had become material-intensive, and the tyranny of logistics had to be addressed. At Verdun, where battle continued at greater or lesser intensity for most of the year, supply and reinforcement was organized by Pétain along the famous *voie sacrée* that cycled men and munitions into the defensive battle at a steady rate. When on the offensive a similar road-train system had to be organized: during the Somme offensive along the Amiens–Proyart road along which at the height of the battle trucks passed at a faster rate than along the *voie sacrée*.[42] This was supplemented by a network of narrow-gauge railways which supplied the heavy guns on which the artillery-centred offensive method depended. Objectives were determined by what artillery support could accomplish. This saved lives, but since guns and shells were not limitless, it also inevitably limited the ambition of an offensive, particularly in its later stages. Foch had recognized before the campaign started that the army lacked the guns and munitions required to force a victory in 1916, and he was proved correct.[43] Nevertheless, this final piece of the operational jigsaw was falling into place by the end of the year. Expanding industrial productivity would sustain more frequent and ambitious attacks in later years; a light railway-based communications system behind the whole front would allow operations to be shifted rapidly from one sector to another.

In the Battle of the Somme – with the exception of Verdun the longest, biggest and most costly battle fought by the French army between 1915 and 1918 yet largely forgotten as a feat of French arms – the trench-warfare tactics of 1915 were proved and refined. Combined-arms warfare, with precise coordination between artillery barrages and infantry assaults, came into its own. Modern-style infantry infiltration tactics enabled the enemy's pulverized defences to be rapidly seized and consolidated. Heavily armed infantry squads were able to subdue unsilenced enemy defences and to drive off the enemy's inevitable counter attacks with their own integral firepower. Air superiority and close air support became elements of battle. Counter-battery fire against the enemy's guns became increasingly sophisticated – this was a particular obsession of Fayolle, the former professor of Artillery tactics – and the principle of neutralizing rather than destructive fire started to be adopted.[44]

While Fayolle demonstrated how artillery-centric tactics combined with methodical operations could take on and defeat the German army while systematically reducing the enemy's field defences, elsewhere the army was fighting a more existential battle. The army's resilience and the nation's morale were staked on the defence of the fortress of Verdun, which lasted from February to December 1916. After the initial shock when the front lines were rapidly overwhelmed and Fort Douaumont captured at the end of February, the defence consolidated, logistics were organized to supply the voracious battle and the customary pattern of attritional operations – intermittent set-piece attacks separated by phases of steady *grignotage* – ensued until October. The credit for this went to Pétain, who Joffre appointed to organize the defence of the fortress. There were moments of crisis for the French defence – in early June when Fort Vaux fell for example – but overall the defence was well managed and well led. Lives were to be economized through the adoption of Petain's *noria* (waterwheel) system which cycled reserves into and out of the battle at a speed which preserved the integrity and fighting capacity of military formations. Many divisional and corps generals took their turns in the furnace of Verdun, including Debeney, Maistre, Charles Mangin and Nivelle (commanding III *corps d'armée* before he replaced Pétain in command of Second Army in May). The latter pair would be the men whose reputations were made by Verdun – they sustained the defence through July, August and September as the Somme battle raged, and ended the struggle at Verdun with a series of powerful set-piece counter attacks from October to December that recaptured forts Douaumont and Vaux. Nivelle was to boast loudly that he had discovered a new way to fight battles but, as Fayolle wrote dismissively after visiting Verdun, this was in fact simply the French army's way, his own way, 'the methods used on the Somme reconfigured by Mangin'.[45]

The generals who would end the war in 1918 emerged from the battles of 1916: Foch would be supreme allied commander; Pétain was in command of the French army; Fayolle, was his principal army group commander, joined in the summer by Maistre; Debeney and Mangin were France's most offensively-minded army commanders; Gamelin was a dynamic divisional commander. The career success of such men suggests that a new sort of general emerged from the proving ground of the trenches. France's new breed of commanders were masters of tactics and technologies as well as logistics, had staff training and a grasp of what was possible on the industrialized battlefield, and often had a past as a military educator; they were generals who were able to lead their men in battle while running their commands in a dynamic, business-like fashion. Other generals, who had kept their commands after Joffre's 1914 purge, slipped from the higher echelons of the army. De Langle de Cary and Roques were both recalled from active command. Perhaps unfairly, Joffre himself would also go. By that point he had not only laid the tactical and operational groundwork for victory but had also brought forward the commanders who would achieve it.

\* \* \*

The year of Verdun and the Somme had been difficult for France. Although the 1916 campaign ended on a high note at Verdun after the German army had been bled white in its turn on the Somme, France was growing war weary. Although the balance of advantage in the trench stalemate had shifted, the lines had not, and a strategic decision still seemed some way off. At the end of the most gruelling year of the war the human cost seemed too high. Politicians sought an easier option: France it seemed needed a quick victory rather than slow, grinding attrition and Nivelle's method seemed to offer this. Therefore, in December 1916 Joffre, who could only advocate more of the same, would be promoted out of any operational responsibility and Nivelle would be tasked with breaking the German army once and for all. This was a matter of politics rather than strategy – like the other belligerents, France was entering a difficult year in which governments were unstable and army and people would have to be remobilized behind the war effort – but it proved a rash experiment that damaged the army and arguably set back progress significantly. The efficacy of Joffre and Foch's methods had not been demonstrated: Nivelle was in post before the enemy's strategic retreat to the Hindenburg Line in spring 1917 acknowledged the punishment that had been meted out to them on the Somme. But this withdrawal would also disrupt Nivelle's preparations for a large-scale spring offensive. The truth, Fayolle recognized, was that there was 'a desire to lower the Somme to make Verdun shine with a brighter light'.[46] This was politics, which was always a problem for French commanders-in-chief.[47] Whether it was sound policy remained to be tested.

The operational debate, with antecedents going back to mid-1915, had always been over the relative merits of breaking the German lines and defeating them quickly in open warfare, or steadily wearing down the enemy's reserves within their defensive positions. Nivelle and Mangin's final victories at Verdun were actually impressive examples of the latter but did not represent a new way of war. Howsoever Nivelle represented it to France's political leaders anxious for a formula for victory, tactics for capturing the enemy's defences were not translatable into an operational method for manoeuvre warfare. It is, nevertheless, arguable that had Nivelle's offensive been launched in February as intended, and on the scale originally envisaged, it might have struck a powerful enough blow to knock the still-reeling German army over. To that extent Nivelle's plan conformed to Joffre's strategy of a rapid and overwhelming follow up to 1916's attrition. Where Joffre and Nivelle differed was over operational method. Nivelle judged that the tactics that had brought success in the later stages of the Battle of Verdun could be scaled up, and their pace accelerated, to break the German lines. Nivelle rejected the methodical artillery-intensive tactics which had brought Mangin and Fayolle success in 1916 in favour of a more speculative attempt to rush the successive German positions – in essence a reversion to 'breakthrough' operations, but against much deeper and stronger German field defences than those that had contained 1915's attacks. The essential dilemma of tactics and operations was repeating itself: how to balance the systematic reduction of the enemy's field defences with the need for dynamic progress to 'rupture' the defence. A balance had to be struck between mass, the weight of firepower and the strength of the infantry assault, and tempo, the speed of advance against a defence that would inevitably solidify once the operation commenced. One possible facilitator was technological. Nivelle would commit tanks in a French offensive for the first time, believing that they would compensate for a reduced concentration of artillery fire as well as give added impetus to the assault. While the theory was plausible, there were not yet enough tanks available and they were an untried weapons system at this point in the war. Nivelle's subordinates could see the flaws in his method, and on the eve of the offensive they advised the French government to cancel it. But a new and shaky government could not risk a military crisis and the offensive was allowed to go ahead.[48]

While not a complete disaster, Nivelle's offensive fell far short of what he had promised the government and his own soldiers – a result in forty-eight hours (an over-confident promise that he had toned down as the date approached). The mechanically unreliable tanks were not a great success; logistics that relied on a rapid pace of advance broke down; once again the German second position checked the assault and the offensive ground to a cold, soggy halt under heavy spring rain. Its legacy was a return to 1916-style *grignotage* in the Chemin des Dames sector. The rank and file expressed their dissatisfaction with their commander and his methods in a series of mutinies concentrated in rear of the now-attritional battle being waged to take the ridge. Steadiness would need to be restored. Nivelle was replaced by Pétain, a 'soldiers' general', who restored military discipline by responding to the troops' grievances, and reshaped the army's doctrine and methods to better reflect what was possible on the battlefield. Debeney was appointed his chief of staff. Foch, whose responsibilities had been reduced after the Somme, returned to the centre of things as chief of the general staff in Paris, the government's principal strategic and technical advisor. Fayolle was promoted to command an army group and

Mangin was removed from army command, replaced by Maistre. The Artois–Somme team were back in control and their system would prevail.

\* \* \*

Nivelle's offensive had demonstrated the naivety of trying to scale-up effective tactics to achieve operational and strategic results. Notwithstanding, by 1917 offensive battles could be fought and won with proportionate losses if properly planned and prepared. Shock action would not be abandoned, but refined thereafter to fit circumstances, as the French army restored its morale. Indeed, by the end of the year, having lost all the strategic high ground along the front, the enemy's positions in the west had become untenable – this was one reason why Germany was forced to go on the offensive in 1918. The French army could fight successful battles (as increasingly could their British allies) and German morale was wilting under an intensive sustained assault. It remained to apply this combined-arms method appropriately to deliver the *coup de grâce*.

In writing about the French army's adaptation to modern warfare there has been a tendency to emphasize Pétain's contribution over Foch's. Pétain certainly had a great influence over tactics, doctrine and training; Foch's input was at a higher level. He developed the operational systems used by the French army, changing warfare as well as war fighting. The origins of the controlled all-arms battle can be seen in Foch's 'scientific' system of late 1915 and 1916 and it would manifest in his offensive campaign in 1918. Petain's armies, whose commanders had learned their profession in Foch's battles, would employ such a system. When it came to strategy, Pétain advocated patience and preparation – usually shorthanded in his statement that France should 'wait for the Americans and the tanks' – but not passivity. Operationally, he reverted to the methods he and Fayolle had learned on the Vimy ridge during 1915, as army corps and divisional commanders respectively. The principle that 'the artillery conquers, the infantry occupies' prevailed, to which adage might be added 'the tanks and aircraft support'. After Nivelle's failure offensives became shorter, methodical and instrumental. In two (now largely forgotten) meticulously prepared set-piece 'bite and hold' offensives in late summer and autumn 1917, mounted to capture the symbolic and tactically significant objectives of the Verdun heights and the Chemin de Dames, Pétain's commanders showcased what was now possible using the army's material-intensive methods. In particular, Maistre's masterpiece, the October 1917 Battle of Malmaison which blasted the Germans off the Chemin des Dames in a matter of days, demonstrated French offensive methods' efficacy. Vital ground could be seized if objectives were limited, and heavy casualties inflicted on the enemy with relatively light losses to the attackers.[49] Pétain's battles combined thorough preparation and training of the troops with realistic objectives and limited ambition. As well as beating the enemy, they were designed to restore the *esprit de corps* of France's weary and querulous troops following the mutinies. France could approach 1918 with well-led and trained troops, confident in themselves and of ultimate victory. Such confidence, matched as it was with skill, would be needed as the war reached its climax and battle was rejoined with an intensity not seen since 1914.

In Foch, who would be appointed allied supreme commander in March 1918, France found a military genius who could use operations for strategic ends, finally closing the operational gap that had compromised military strategy since 1915. The origins of Foch's *bataille générale*, which broke the German army in a few months once the allies resumed the offensive in summer 1918, can be traced back to the later stages of the Somme offensive, in which Foch had intensified the attritional pressure on the German army with a series of powerful, coordinated but limited strokes in the hope that it would finally break. After the battle he had noted that the Somme had been 'a battle which worked, always victorious, beating the Germans, pushing them back. We should continue in this vein as far as we can, denying them any freedom of action and opportunity, continue to beat them.'[50] However, on the Somme the rate of attrition had been insufficient to break the German army in a single campaign: to beat the enemy required 'army-sized actions geared towards consistent tactical and strategic objectives', and a large space in which to operate.[51] More resources, which would allow repeated blows all along the front, and an arm for rapid exploitation (Foch suggested tanks or armoured cars) were the missing material aspects of this offensive system.[52] These would be available by 1918. Being confident that the armies under his direction could deliver powerful and effective blows at relatively short notice all along the front – a matter of skill and armament – Foch could then concentrate allied forces towards a strategic objective, the destruction of the German army through a process of cumulative attrition. 'Everyone into the battle', Foch was accustomed to exclaiming, an epigram that hinted at the scale of his ambition. Speed and coordination were also vital. The successive and rapidly sequenced blows struck by the French and allied armies under his direction in summer and autumn 1918 were geared towards a subtle object, 'to embarrass the enemy in the utilization of his reserves and not allow him sufficient time to fill up his units'.[53] Each individual blow, of similar size to a set-piece operation of 1916 or 1917, but limited in depth, took a chunk out of the German order of battle – perhaps it was still *grignotage*, but taking much larger bites. Accumulating success could be measured in ground gained (much of it surrendered when lateral exploitation made hastily improvised German defensive positions untenable) and growing numbers of prisoners and guns captured. Faster-tempo operations, utilizing rapidly infiltrating infantry supported by light tanks, could now penetrate effectively to the enemy's gun-line and beyond, something that had not been possible at the operational pace of earlier years, although this still fell short of modern manoeuvre warfare. Foch never tried to break through the German lines, but he pushed them back at a steady if unspectacular pace for three months (averaging less than a mile a day over the course of the campaign), exploiting local opportunities when these arose. Eventually, with few reserves to oppose the allied advance, the German army capitulated. Attrition, with just enough manoeuvre, brought the war to a relatively swift end, just as Foch had predicted at the end of 1916.[54]

\* \* \*

The army that secured this victory was able to develop effective commanders. Results were rewarded with promotion, failure with so-called *limogéage* (being sent to Limoges, the base depot to which sacked general officers were posted for reassignment on their disgrace). The French army had only two general officer ranks, *général de brigade* and *général de division*. This gave a relatively flat command structure and allowed commanders to be promoted or demoted according to achievement rather than seniority. Promotion to senior command would be provisional, with a general given time to learn and show aptitude in a role before 'acting' rank – *à titre temporaire* in French – would become substantive. The system also allowed demotions, restorations and sideways shifts within the topmost commands. For example, *Général de division* Charles Mangin commanded a division in 1914, a corps in 1916 and an army in 1917, before *limogéage* for his part in Nivelle's offensive. In December 1917 he was given a second chance, reappointed to army corps command and then raised to army command in June 1918. Others rose rapidly above former superiors, notably Foch who went from army corps through army to provisional army group commander in 1914.

Two groups of officers can be identified among the senior commanders who rose to the top in wartime, for convenience distinguished as 'professors' and 'soldiers' – although often a successful commander would demonstrate aptitude in both dimensions. A number of pre-war staff college teachers were in the highest positions in the army by 1918: Foch, Pétain, Fayolle, Maistre, Debeney, and several others commanding armies or in senior staff positions. Often these men would have experience in senior staff positions preceding or alternating with field command. For example, Debeney began the war as a staff officer in First Army, then commanded a division, army corps and army before becoming Pétain's chief of staff at GQG in 1917, returning to army command in 1918. The soldiers might lack staff experience but would have proved themselves in field commands. Many such men came from the pre-war

Colonial army, bringing experience in imperial campaigning to the Western Front. Joffre, Nivelle, Mangin, de Langle de Cary and many others – one army group and five army commanders in 1918 – can be numbered among the colonials. A certain rivalry existed between these men and their metropolitan army comrades. Fayolle complained bitterly of the operational naivety of the 'colonial blockheads' after Nivelle and Mangin's elevation (by a newly appointed 'colonial' war minister, General Hubert Lyautey).[55]

Fayolle's outburst was indicative of the scourge of politics that beset the French army even in wartime. Before the war political views or supposed antirepublican leanings would have impacted on promotion prospects following the notorious Dreyfus affair and the attempted republicanisation of the army under war minister General Louis André (1900–1904) that followed. Secret dossiers on officers were compiled in the *affaire des fiches*, and careers were advanced or curtailed as a result.[56] In particular, Catholic officers such as Foch, Fayolle and Nöel de Curières de Castelnau had their career advancement slowed. Although the *affaire* was short lived, its legacy was lasting. In the ensuing years republican officers continued to be advanced. Joffre, for example, was seen as a compromise but politically reliable choice for army chief of staff.[57] Republicanism enabled the careers of certain army commanders during the war, Maurice Sarrail of Third Army being the prime example. However, in wartime suspicion of conservative, Catholic officers seems to have been set aside once France united in a political *union sacrée* against the invader. An army commander in August 1914, de Castelnau was to serve as GQG chief of staff and as an army group commander during the war, and Foch and Fayolle's late careers also prospered. Even the best generals might fall foul of changes in the political wind, however: Foch's temporary demotion at the end of 1916 is the best example. Some senior leaders benefitted from political connections and service in the war ministry, Roques, who had served with Joffre in the engineering directorate of the war ministry before the war, being a good example. Although a lacklustre army corps commander, Joffre promoted him to army command in early 1915 and he would continue his career as minister of war in Paris the next year. Two other 1918 army commanders, and Pétain's last chief of staff, Edmond Buat, had held appointments in the war ministry early in the war. Buat owed his promotion to politics. He replaced François Anthoine, in 1914 Second Army chief of staff and in 1917 First Army commander in the Battle of Flanders (Third Battle of Ypres). Anthoine had earned the hostility of premier Georges Clemenceau and generalissimo Foch, who forced Pétain to replace him in July 1918.[58] Other generals had to learn to play politics. Estienne, the founder of the army's tank arm, the *Artillerie spéciale*, struggled with military bureaucracy to bring his idea to realization.

\* \* \*

It is customary to talk of a 'learning process' in British military operations between 1915 and 1918. A parallel learning process was taking place alongside them, in the French army, always somewhat ahead of the curve relative to their ally, and increasingly effective against their enemy. By late summer 1916 they were the dominant army on the Western Front, and by 1918, under Foch's direction, tactical–operational effectiveness would be matched to strategic success.[59] This progress and achievement owes much to the increasing effectiveness of command, which showed an adaptiveness and willingness to innovate in novel and challenging military circumstances. The roots of victory on the Western Front lay in France's commanders translating tactical skill and operational science – the management of higher formations, army corps and armies, in warfare – into effective operational art.

When it came to commanding the French army as it liberated national soil, Foch was *primus inter pares*. Yet what he achieved would not have been possible without subordinates who understood the army's methods and could put them into practice with speed and skill. Partly these tactics and operational methods were Foch's, conceived and honed when conducting the offensives in Artois and on the Somme; partly they were Pétain's and Fayolle's, whose lessons were learned on Foch's battlefields. The strategy that brought victory was essentially Foch's, although its key principles harked back to Joffre's period of command. Many of the men who delivered the victory in the field were their acolytes, from the days when these professors had lectured at the *École supérieure de guerre* (ESG) together before the war. As Debeney, who had lectured at the ESG before 1914 and was appointed to command it when it reopened afterwards later testified, open-minded teaching underpinned the success of the wartime army. Often criticized for inculcating the wrong doctrine in the minds of its pupils, in fact the very intensity and range of doctrinal debate at the ESG served a different purpose – to produce intellectual officers who could work through problems rather than a doctrinaire officer corps.[60] To that extent soldiers such as Nivelle, Gamelin, de Castelnau and Anthoine who had passed through the ESG were also professors. In the war of innovation and rapid adaptation they encountered, this gave the thinking French army a distinct advantage over the more dogmatic Germans. When asked by his American liaison officer why so many ESG professors had prospered in command, Foch himself explained:

> to teach a doctrine successfully, you have got to be absolutely sure it is right. This means profound study and a long meditation upon all the objections advanced against it. Once sure, you can proceed with confidence and you carry conviction with your pupils. The men who had taught at the *Ecole de*

*Guerre* went through this process. The early disasters of the conflict could not shake their faith in our doctrine. They continued to apply it and we finally won.[61]

These pupils were the hundreds of successful French generals who cannot be considered in this volume; men who made individual contributions to a collective success but whose identities have faded into historical obscurity.

Of course, the process of fighting and winning a war was not – could not be – smooth or faultless, as its facilitators were well aware. Commenting on Maistre's interjection at the enquiry into General Fournier's conduct quoted at the start of this introduction, his biographer acknowledged that Maistre and his fellows 'knew very well that the art of war had to be prepared at the war school, but it had to adapt to circumstances, to men, to material, to logistics and that in a war lasting more than four years it needed to be modified, perfected, errors corrected constantly'.[62] The French army could do this since many of its leaders were pre-war thinkers or teachers and their pupils had clearly learned their lessons well. In a matter of a few years an educated, well-led and adaptive army rose to the challenges of a new type of war and the imperative of liberating *la patrie*. Debeney remembered from his own staff college training that his teachers had emphasized that the next war would be won by the more intelligent army.[63] Excepting the shock of 1914, Porch's verdict that it was an 'unintelligent' performance does not stand up to scrutiny. The errors of 1914 might be excused: Fournier, who spent the war in a German prisoner of war camp rather than relearning his trade, was acquitted. Those who sat in judgement upon him perhaps appreciated that they had started in a similar position but had the opportunity to learn from experience, to understand, to adapt and to prosper. Theirs was a victory won by intelligent soldiers, taught by fighting professors.

# Chapter 1

# Joseph Joffre: Strategist of Mass War

## William Philpott

If any one man could be said to have developed and implemented the strategy and methods that led to victory in the First World War, that man would be Joseph Jacques Césaire Joffre. Joffre dominated the first half of the war, although try as he might he could never live up to his imperial name: republican France would tolerate no military dictator, even at a time of acute national crisis. Yet for a while Joffre probably had more power than any Frenchman since Napoleon III. His responsibilities grew as the war evolved and became more complex. In 1914 he commanded the army that checked the German invasion of France. From 1915 he served as France's strategic director and increasingly as the allies' strategic coordinator. In that role he presided over the large-scale, costly battles in Artois and the Champagne in 1915 and at Verdun and on the Somme in 1916 that epitomize attritional, industrialized warfare. After the Somme offensive he was rewarded with a marshal's baton but moved aside in favour of a more dynamic younger leader, General Robert Nivelle.

Because his command was truncated, Joffre's reputation will always be compromised by the 'butcher's bill' of the first three years of war. Early on Winston Churchill damned him for the 'blood test' he imposed upon the British and French armies, without any real grasp of the nature of the war Joffre was obliged to wage.[1] That criticism has stuck, although it needs to be tempered with a proper appreciation of the tasks that Joffre faced and how effectively he responded to them. Joffre was confronted with a new sort of warfare in which the mass mobilization of manpower and resources interrelated with the impact of industrial technologies on the battlespace. There were tactical and operational challenges to address, but in mass warfare new strategic paradigms also emerged that were difficult to engage and, crucially, hard to accept. Always subject to intense political scrutiny, Joffre's star waned in 1916 since he was unable to deliver a quick, decisive military victory, the outdated paradigm of warfare that his political masters still countenanced. By then, however, he had laid the foundations for France's liberation and for the allies' military victory: a properly equipped and effective French army, an appropriate attritional strategy and close coordination with allied forces. Thereafter he remained, informally, a strategic adviser to the government – France's national saviour could not be tossed aside lightly – looking on as his acolytes completed the war he had designed and engaged. The failed Nivelle experiment, which reversed many of the gains Joffre had made in 1916, did not alter the fundamental track upon which he had set French and coalition strategy.

\* \* \*

Born in 1852, Joffre was the son of a cooper from the Pyrenees, whose high intelligence won him a place at the *École polytechnique*. His studies were interrupted by the 1870–1 war with Prussia, in which he served in the artillery. After graduating he joined the engineers. As a young captain he supervised construction work in France's new frontier fortress barrier, designed to keep the Germans out in future. Thereafter he built fortifications and railways in France's colonies in Indo-China and Africa, seeking active service where possible, until fortuitous circumstances – he commanded a flying column that captured Timbuktu in 1894, snatching victory from the jaws of defeat – brought him national recognition. Returning to France, Joffre served in staff posts in the war ministry and various provincial commands, rising eventually to command II *corps d'armée* (CA). By 1910 he was a member of the *Conseil supérieur de la guerre* (CSG) and the army's director of supply and communications. A solid republican, in 1911 Joffre was appointed, as the politically uncontroversial compromise candidate, to be Chief of the General Staff of the army and commander-in-chief designate in the event of war.[2]

Joffre had three principal tasks in the war ministry, which reflected those he would assume in wartime: to plan the next war with Germany, to prepare his army to fight it, and to strengthen links with France's potential military collaborators, Russia and Great Britain. Arguably he did the first better than the other two, although the seeds of the French army's long-term success as well as of its short-term reverse can be seen in doctrinal and practical developments that occurred while Joffre was chief of staff.

Plan XVII, Joffre's plan for a counter offensive against German armies which were expected to invade France across their common frontier and by way of south-east Belgium, was a pragmatic response to the strategic realities of the day. With his active front-line forces outnumbered significantly, Joffre would deploy four armies behind France's frontiers and await the German advance, probing for a weak spot to counterattack with a fifth army held in reserve for that purpose. Such a strategy might dislocate the German advance in its first phase and save France from another invasion. It was a rational plan (and rather more subtle than those historians who see the French army as committed to a misjudged policy of *offensive à outrance* give Joffre credit for), but its weaknesses – essentially ones of execution – were to be exposed when battle was joined.

An appropriate and flexible battle plan would only partly mitigate the facts that France's army was significantly outnumbered by Germany's and she was reliant on allied support. It might buy space and time for this assistance to make its weight felt. Russia in the east was France's real and more dependable ally, but how quickly and how powerfully the Tsar's army could strike to relieve pressure on France was always uncertain. Under the terms of the defensive military convention signed between France and Russia in 1899, French staff officers worked before 1914 to assess and improve the military effectiveness of the large but unwieldy Russian army. Joffre took steps after his appointment as chief of the general staff to accelerate the mobilization and engagement of Russia's forces in the event of a general war, an initiative that would pay off in August 1914 (and might have proved decisive had Russia's armies proved more militarily effective).[3] Joffre himself attended Russian army manoeuvres in 1913, and while the Russian troops impressed – 'the men seemed vigorous and carefully drilled' – the higher command and their understanding of warfare did not.[4] The judgement was probably derived from a report on the Russian army drawn up by Joffre's staff officer, Henri Berthelot, which offered a similar assessment. His observation, 'The Russians seem, in all the decisions of their high command, to attach a predominate importance to the occupation of terrain which results in fixing them to the ground and transforms an apparent resolute offensive into a defence entirely subordinated to events…. In the offensive there is too great a tendency to conserve reserves', was a lesson that would be learned the hard way by French commanders.[5] All this is evidence that Joffre conceived the coming war as a multi-front continent-wide struggle.

Great Britain, with her small but well-equipped regular army organized into the British Expeditionary Force (BEF), could in the short term offer relatively meagre but more direct and rapid military support. However, with no formal alliance between Britain and France this aid was not a given and it was as a longer-term insurance policy in the event of an indecisive first campaign that Britain and her empire might be of real value to France.[6] Joffre's pre-war contacts with the British general staff were to facilitate the BEF's quick deployment to France, as well as to ensure that it could operate effectively alongside the French should it come.[7] This 'mentoring' of the British army, while by no means complete when war broke out, prefigured the way the French army would work with allied forces throughout the war. Joffre himself failed to establish a personal rapport with the BEF's commander, Field Marshal Sir John French: they had been due to meet at the French army's 1914 manoeuvres, but war intervened. While French was a strong supporter of the continental commitment of British forces, he was less wedded to the general staff plan worked out before 1914 of dispatching the BEF to support the French left wing directly and immediately, partly because his forces might fall under foreign command.[8] This would weaken cooperation in the field significantly as early encounters strained the nascent Anglo-French military alliance. Joffre always conceived France's strategy in terms of maximizing alliance strength and coordination – that was the only way to contain and defeat Germany – and his coalition conception of warfare was to persist and to prove vital in wartime.

When it came to preparing his own army, this was a work in progress when hostilities commenced. Although he identified weaknesses in intellectual and practical preparation, institutional weakness, budgetary constraints and political opposition prevented Joffre updating French field-service doctrine or addressing the army's shortage of heavy artillery, its lack of training facilities and outdated uniforms in time.[9] While new doctrine had been promulgated over the winter of 1913–14, there had been insufficient time for the army to absorb and implement it in the training regime and this came out in its indifferent military performance in early encounter battles. In 1914, Joffre was obliged to campaign with an army that had not been fully prepared, materially or doctrinally, as well as allies whose assistance was conditional and uncertain, and he would have to address evident deficiencies in the maelstrom of war rather than in the relatively benign if frustrating conditions of peacetime.

\* \* \*

Military performance is of course a relative concept. There were good reasons why Joffre's armies performed poorly relative to their German enemies in August 1914; and other reasons why they were able to reverse this early misfortune rapidly and counterattack with effect within a month. Joffre's incomplete preparations were tested when his counter offensive failed to find the invading German armies' weak point. In truth, an underestimation of the strength of invading German forces (which better attention to intelligence gathered by the Belgian army might have redressed) meant that such a weak point was not there to be found.[10] Probing attacks all along the frontier were checked, and when Joffre's reserve Fourth Army was launched on 22 August through the Ardennes against the hinge of the German sweep through Belgium it crashed headlong into a German reserve army. In the battle that ensued German command-and-control proved more dynamic. While there were local opportunities for French commanders to exploit, these were missed; where opposing forces came to grips German tactics generally prevailed.[11]

Doctrinal ambiguity, lacklustre operational command and weak tactics – and, it should not be forgotten, superior German strength – resulted in defeat in the Battle of the Frontiers. More damning, this was the bloodiest moment of the war for the French army, due partly to the scale of the engagement, but also to inept French leadership. Joffre responded with decision and determination, wielding an axe on the deadwood of peacetime leaders and rapidly raising up talented senior officers who had demonstrated calmness and initiative in the field or, it should be noted, at field headquarters where many critical decisions had to be taken at moments of acute stress. Two army commanders and perhaps as many as ninety other generals were sacked.[12] Many future leaders, men such as Ferdinand Foch, Philippe Pétain and Paul Maistre, received their first promotion at this point, and were to justify their step-up in the following weeks.

German forces had deployed in unexpectedly large numbers: unlike Joffre who held second-line reserve divisions back from active operations in the first weeks of war for refresher training or supporting tasks, Germany used reserve units alongside active formations to increase her front-line fighting strength from the start. By late August these forces were sweeping round the open left flank of the Anglo-French armies, touching on Amiens at their extreme right. This was a more existential threat: Joffre had to buy enough time to reorganize his forces, rethink his strategy and reverse his army's fortunes.

Despite strong political criticism, Joffre was not removed from his command at this time of acute military crisis, as his protégé – and at this point Joffre's principal aide de camp at *Grand quartier général* (GQG) – Maurice Gamelin, would be in May 1940. War minister Adolphe Messimy (who had appointed Joffre in 1911), who had protested against Joffre stripping the Paris garrison to reinforce his frontline forces and tried to order him to reinforce it, was replaced instead, and Joffre was given the chance to redeem himself (although General Joseph Galliéni, who would prove another thorn in Joffre's side, was appointed to command the defence of Paris at the same time).[13] At this point Joffre's personality and experience came into its own (in contrast to that of his opposite number Helmuth von Moltke the younger, who would experience a nervous collapse under the strain of command within a few weeks). Often characterized as stolid, determined but slow-witted, such steadiness and shrewdness were positive attributes at a time of acute crisis. President Raymond Poincaré was wont to describe his commander-in chief as having the stomach of an ostrich [and] who sleeps like a child.[14] Phlegmatic and focused, Joffre would think carefully and then act decisively, understanding from his earlier responsibilities as a logistician the capabilities and limitations of the forces at his and the enemy's disposal. While he relied on a team of dynamic, favoured young staff officers, dubbed the 'Young Turks' by his detractors, to execute his intentions, the ideas were all his own.[15]

In a fortnight Joffre would disengage his armies, redeploy his forces, strengthen his grip on the BEF's wayward commander, re-engage and repulse the enemy. This was a demonstration of leadership and operational control worthy of a great captain: not without justification, if with some hyperbole, the second phase of the campaign became known as the 'miracle of the Marne'. After ordering retreat from the frontiers, Joffre's guiding principle was to regroup and counter attack. When, where and how would be settled over the next few days. First, the experienced railway logistician consulted his director of communications, to ascertain how fast troops could be redeployed from the right to the vulnerable left wing. On the basis of this calculation, he determined the line on which he would halt and counterattack the enemy in due course – the line of the river Seine, east of Paris.[16] While he assembled a new army of redeployed and uncommitted reserve formations east of Paris, his subordinates disengaged the pursuing enemy in a number of strong delaying actions: Le Cateau, Guise, the defence of the Meuse crossings, the defence of the Grand Couronne at Nancy. He anchored the eastern end of the French line on the fortress of Verdun and formed another new army – the Ninth Army under Foch – to strengthen the centre of the French line. This line would have to hold while Michel Maunoury's Sixth Army and the Fifth Army under its new commander General Louis Franchet d'Esperey, supported by the BEF, engaged the German right wing as it swept in front of Paris. France's allies were also shaping up and easing the pressure on Joffre's armies. Active Russian operations in East Prussia obliged the redeployment of two German army corps eastwards; the Belgian army besieged in Antwerp was tying down two more; and the BEF, after some show of reluctance on the part of its commander, was pledged to support any French counter attack. In an emotional encounter on 5 September at British headquarters in which Joffre called upon French's sense of honour, Sir John promised his support and the BEF was reintegrated into the allied line.[17]

The counter attack began on 6 September. The hard-pressed French centre held, the German right wing was outmanoeuvred, and von Moltke undertook his own strategic withdrawal to the Aisne heights, where German forces would remain entrenched until 1917. This successful riposte, the Battle of the Marne, saved France and consolidated Joffre's reputation as an imperturbable fighting general. But it postponed a quick, decisive end to the war, and therein lay the seeds of Joffre's own decline and fall. A cult of personality developed among French soldiers and civilians, who idolized Joffre as France's saviour; although further success would be needed to sustain such a reputation. Try as he might, for the rest of the 1914 campaign during which his army sought to turn the Germans' open flank Joffre could not find the elusive weak point and decisively defeat the invader. He discovered his own weak points: the difficulty of coordinating France's effort with those of her allies (both strategically with the Russians far away in the east and operationally with the British army in France); his army's inadequate resources, particularly in heavy artillery; and the political pressure that had to be borne by an unsuccessful commander. He took steps to address each before the year was out. Although more reactive than pro-active when it came to events on the Eastern Front, Joffre monitored the Russians' actions closely and would increasingly factor Russian needs into his broader strategic assessments.[18] To better control the disparate allied forces on the left wing – to which he would later attribute the failure of his plan to turn the German flank – he raised Foch a step further to coordinate French, British and Belgian operations around Ypres and on the river Yser, and designated him his potential successor.[19] He met the British war minister, Field Marshal Lord Herbert Kitchener, to try to accelerate the deployment of British troops to France, with limited success, the start of a difficult and sometimes confrontational relationship with his British opposite number.[20] His hopes to have the British commander-in-chief or chief of staff replaced, early signs that he felt that he should control rather than coordinate with allied forces, came to nothing.[21] He ordered an extensive heavy artillery and munitions programme at the end of September, although it would be well into 1916 before French industry could fulfil it and subsequent orders; in the interim he fell back on redeploying obsolescent fortress artillery pieces to support the siege-style operations that set in over the winter.

Although Joffre ended 1914 with a high reputation and strong popular support, his position would always be vulnerable. One French divisional staff officer, reflecting on his first vision of the commander-in-chief in early 1916 after the battle of Verdun had started, remembered 'his heavy, solid frame, badly dressed in red trousers and a 1914-style black dolman, but also his striking calm and impassivity, and his silence which gave an impression of assurance and justified the soubriquet "unbreakable rock".' He recollected how popular Joffre remained with the nation, while noting that politicians were starting to lose faith in him by that point. In the military the men and junior officers had great confidence in and strong affection for him. However, while aware of Joffre's merits, in the higher ranks there was little empathy: 'one was not drawn to him like other great chiefs; one did not feel one had his confidence, but feared him'. This was largely a consequence of the '*limogé*' system: its victims were stirring up trouble for the commander-in-chief in Paris.[22] Such a nuanced assessment was typical. Joffre was a strong character with a powerful reputation, but he was more respected than loved.

\* \* \*

In February 1915, in another context, British Chancellor of the Exchequer, David Lloyd George, had affirmed that 'this is an engineer's war'.[23] Joffre was an engineer by training, as coincidentally was Kitchener. Joffre had been struck by President Armand Fallières's comment when he had been nominated chief of staff, 'In my opinion war has really become an engineering art'. Joffre reflected in his memoirs: 'I have often thought of this remark, because it seems to me profoundly true. It is not enough in these days to have merely military genius; it has to be supplemented by a sense of organization capable of combining and employing the numerous means which science and industry and progress now place at the service of an army. …a great war of masses…brought to light the immense complication of all the many elements which had their place in the struggle.'[24] This applied to manoeuvring troops across France in 1914's mass battles; also to the strategic conduct of war between mass armies sustained by the resources of mobilized empires which was Joffre's new challenge. Not only the war in France, which to Joffre always remained the principal and potentially decisive theatre, but its wider European and global aspects (now that the Ottoman Empire had joined the war on the enemy's side) would now engage the war's directors.[25] Faced with trench stalemate and the need to rethink strategy, Joffre would come into his own.

At the turn of 1915 both Joffre and Kitchener would assess the strategic balance. Their rudimentary statistical analysis enabled both men to conclude that the allies possessed a preponderant advantage in manpower and material capacity that would in time decide the war in their favour. How long that would take, and what to do while that capacity was being mobilized, tested planners and strained inter-allied relations in the first phase of the trench war. Kitchener remains most famous for raising men – this aligned with his perception that the allies were facing a long war of attrition, 'to the last breath and the last horse'.[26] But it would take the best part of two years before Kitchener's armies were raised, equipped and deployed and they would become a bone of contention as Joffre pressed a more active offensive strategy in France to placate French politicians and succour the Russians. Joffre had more pressing need to produce guns and shells for his own army, without which 1915 would turn out to be a year of trials and disappointment. From this the army which he led at least learned much about how to fight modern war effectively. It was becoming clear that France faced a costly war of attrition, although Joffre remained confident that the allies' superior manpower and economic resources would eventually bring victory. He was also determined to ensure that France's allies shared fairly the sacrifice in the common cause.

Much would change on the battlefield in 1915 as tactics adapted to trenches, although in France and Flanders at least those trenches would remain roughly where they were as operations and strategy took time to adapt to the realities of material-intensive mass warfare: *materialschlact* as the Germans called it. Tactical progress, an iterative process between the armies in the field and GQG, is discussed at various places in this volume so will not be reprised here:

suffice it to say that come 1916 Joffre would have an army far more suited, both materially and doctrinally, to fighting in the new conditions. Meanwhile, however, operational misconceptions and strategic imperatives had inflicted heavy and perhaps unnecessary losses on that army.

Effective conduct of operations would depend on addressing the weaknesses identified in 1914. These would not be resolved quickly, although the pressing need to drive the enemy from French soil obliged Joffre to take the offensive. Over the winter of 1914–15 localized operations in the Champagne had identified some basic tactical principles for fighting trench warfare, although the artillery and munitions needed to wage it dynamically on a large scale were lacking. Division commander Marie-Émile Fayolle noted the crux of Joffre's operational challenge presented at a briefing of senior commanders in the spring:

> [Joffre] talks straightforwardly about the opening of the second phase of the war. We must wait because we do not have enough munitions, and to rebuild formations and create reserves. The time for making a breach is approaching and there must be units to push through it, he said. That suggests there will be an attempt to break through somewhere, but when? And what will the troops on other sectors of the front do? That's the terrible problem.

The commander-in-chief was not inspiring: 'Heavy, low voiced, poorly dressed, hardly an orator, no bearing, poor posture'.[27]

Joffre is accountable for the three phases of offensive operations on the Western Front in 1915, in the Champagne over the winter, in Artois in the spring and in Artois and the Champagne in the autumn, in which French and British forces sought to achieve the operational fallacy of 'breakthrough' – piercing the enemy's fortified defensive line and threatening his communications, thereby restoring mobility to warfare. If this strategy had worked it promised to liberate much of occupied France, so its political–strategic aim made sense. However, with resources only partially mobilized, and with the relative tactical advantage lying with the defence at this early point in the war, the consequences were counterproductive: huge loss of life and no substantive progress in liberating France. Joffre himself later attested that nothing was impossible for French soldiers 'on condition that they feel themselves commanded by capable officers who have proved themselves worthy of their confidence'.[28] Unfortunately, 1915's experience began to undermine that confidence, which would manifest in disaffection and mutinies later in the war.

That being said, Joffre and his armies could not afford the luxury of sitting idle while the enemy seized the initiative elsewhere. Moreover, France's allies were engaged in their own struggles and French and coalition policies had to be reconciled. Russia seemed panicky. An anxious telegram from Russian commander-in-chief Grand Duke Nicholas sparked the British response that would, much against Joffre's wishes, drag France into the Dardanelles campaign by the end of April. Then Russia proved lightweight. Over the course of the year successive heavy Russian defeats and retreats in Poland would cancel out Russia's success against Austro-Hungarian forces in 1914 and oblige Joffre to attack in an attempt to tie down German forces on the Western Front in order to relieve pressure on the Russians. The autumn offensive had this grander strategic rationale as much as an expectation that Germany's armies could be beaten at that point in what Joffre later called 'the war of stabilization' during which forces and resources were too evenly matched for a decision.[29]

When it came to coalition management, Joffre's responsibilities had shifted from directing allied field commanders to negotiating with other allied strategists. A direct telegraph link from GQG to Russian headquarters allowed him to liaise with Grand Duke Nicholas, commanding in the east, although whether this was used to do much more than exchange information is uncertain. Joffre's relationship with Kitchener was both more immediate and more fraught with tension, not least because Kitchener had his own ideas on strategy as well as control of the coalition's principal manpower reserve, the New Armies he was raising potentially to reinforce the Western Front. When that would be, and whether that would be timely, preoccupied Joffre for the first half of the year as British attentions, and with them some military reserves promised for the Western Front, shifted to the Near East: it might yet be too late in Joffre's anxious estimation, and he used French war minister Alexander Millerand as his proxy to try to force Kitchener's hand in the spring.[30] Kitchener, who felt that the war would remain stalemated until he had raised a mass British army, preferred to focus British effort during 1915 on the Dardanelles campaign against Turkey, in Joffre's estimation an 'affair [that] appeared to me, from its very principle, to be constructed on a very uncertain basis. ...which, though of modest proportions at the outset, threatened to carry us much further than we should desire.'[31] For Joffre 'the matter of secondary operations was a source of constant thought; but, to my mind, the advantages they offered were almost always theoretical, while the dangers they presented were real and present.'[32] Yet Kitchener made sending more British troops to France conditional on success on the battlefield.

Since the Anglo-French offensive in Artois in May and June 1915 had mixed results the impasse persisted into the summer. The British attack failed, largely owing to a lack of munitions, while the French offensive was initially successful before bogging down in close-range trench fighting. The initial penetration of the enemy's front opposite the Vimy ridge taught a false lesson that the German defences could be broken, which Joffre would aim to do in the autumn offensive in the Champagne, with bloody yet ineffective results. By then Joffre had improved coordination with the British. In July Kitchener had agreed to send the New Armies he was raising to France and, pressed by Russia for a relief offensive in the west, had consented to British participation in the autumn offensive, at Loos (which would have equally frustrating results). Meanwhile the Dardanelles campaign had grown but still ground on inconclusively, proving Joffre's judgment to be sound. Ultimately his political troubles at home convinced him to divert a French army to the Near East to end the Dardanelles distraction once and for all. It was not to be, as Bulgaria's entry into the war on the Central Powers' side obliged that this army be diverted to the Greek port of Salonika in a confused, tardy, and ultimately ineffective attempt to succour Serbia. This represented the ultimate failure of French Balkan diplomacy, that after bringing Italy into the war on the allied side in May had hoped to muster the smaller Balkan states to the allied cause. It brought down René Viviani's government, something that would not have upset Joffre in the least.

Joffre's problems with French politicians had grown during 1915 as he failed to make obvious progress towards defeating the Germans. Moreover, with many parliamentarians mobilized into the army there were potential spies in the military camp in a republic whose generals and politicians had little respect for each other.[33] Joffre's 1914 victories had bought him some time, but could he sustain his position in the long term? While war minister Millerand remained in post he had a strong advocate in government, and was able to push his agenda for building up the army's armaments and munitions in the early months of 1915 – in his memoirs he was not shy to blame this deficiency on the government's pre-war parsimony.[34] At the time, however, after parliament reconvened after a hiatus in 1914, the Chamber of Deputies' army commission was actively trying to apportion blame to the man who led the pre-war army.[35] Influential members of parliament briefed against Joffre, notably the vice-president of the Senate army commission Paul Doumer, civilian secretary to Galliéni, who was actively scheming to have his boss replace Joffre.[36] Joffre resisted forcefully political interference within the *zone des armées* in which martial law held sway, while civilian politicians feared Joffre's pretensions to military dictatorship. Things came to a head when in July Joffre dismissed republican Third Army commander Maurice Sarrail, ostensibly on grounds of his indifferent military performance, but undoubtedly also because he had been receiving parliamentary deputies including Doumer at his headquarters and had been touted as a possible successor to Joffre.[37] The resulting hoo-ha, the *affaire* Sarrail, was only resolved when Sarrail was appointed to command the new *Armée de l'orient* to reinforce the Dardanelles.

When Sarrail's army was precipitately deployed to Salonika the political crisis that ensued owing to the government's lack of foresight actually led to a strengthening of Joffre's authority. In December the new premier Aristide Briand confirmed his position as commander-in-chief responsible for French strategy in all theatres, and coordinating strategy with France's allies.[38] His stature among France's allies was growing: in September he made an official visit to the Italian front, and in late October he became the first and only French general to address a British war council meeting.[39] However, with the new government, in which Galliéni was nominated minister of war, endorsement of Joffre's strategic authority came with caveats. Joffre was obliged to reconstruct his headquarters staff and take General Nöel de Curières de Castelnau as his chief of staff. Joffre later suggested that this was his decision, endorsed by the minister of war.[40] In fact Galliéni had been determined since taking office to assert ministerial authority over the high command and had identified de Castelnau as his preferred choice for shaking up Joffre's staff.[41]

The 1915 fighting emphasized what General Marie-Eugène Debeney would call 'the tyranny of material'. Joffre's freedom of action was constrained by 'the preponderance of material manifested in the unbelievable spectacle of millions of men obliged to face off during two terrible, murderous years for what exactly? The moment when they had increased material to meet modern requirements.'[42] If Joffre's performance is judged primarily on battlefield events, there is some justification for the criticisms that developed during the year and have persisted. He had forced his armies onto the offensive for understandable political and military reasons when they were still inadequately equipped and trained, and as a consequence the reputation he had won in 1914 would start to diminish. Yet the wider war had developed along lines that conformed to his overall perception. More material was needed certainly, but better coordination was essential, through focused coalition leadership and an agreed plan; diversion of effort from the main theatres would have to be controlled, and with his enhanced authority the French commander-in-chief would have to impose his vision on politicians, allies and subordinates if more was to be achieved in 1916.

\* \* \*

Of necessity, the offensive would continue – the situations in France and of the wider war dictated this – but in 1916 Joffre's role would be eased and more effective as allies were more amenable and his own army was better led, equipped and prepared to engage and defeat the enemy. Joffre's immediate objective was to seize the initiative, to be proactive rather than reactive now that he had mustered the forces and developed the techniques for taking on and beating the enemy and was deploying the material resources on which these depended. He was aware that it was potentially a lengthy and costly process

– on the Western Front in 1916 'the race between our offensive matériel and the German defensive organizations, both of which increased in strength with every week that passed', would continue to play out[43] – and so he factored attrition into his plan for the coming campaign. Joffre's strategic vision of the unfolding war was presented at a conference held at GQG in Chantilly from 6–8 December. He advocated coordinated military effort, intensified attrition, and concerted pressure on the enemy's defence until it broke. The military representatives at the conference agreed on a single objective for 1916, 'the destruction of the German and Austrian armies', and to that end each allied army would take the offensive on their own front when ready at some time and place yet to be determined.[44] This principle was easy to agree, the practicalities harder to implement. To defeat Germany and her allies would require time and effort, but how much time and whose effort were matters of opinion and debate between Joffre and the other allied commanders as the strategy took on more concrete form, and the enemy engaged its own offensive plans, dislocating allied preparations in each theatre.

As the year started, Joffre hoped that it might be the year of decision, although as the months passed he scaled down his expectations along with his ambitions: the campaign might not end the war, but it would at least shift the balance of the war in the allies' favour. For Joffre it was a matter of when and where and on what scale battles would take place; for the allied army commanders a question of how they would be conducted. Over the months that followed the Chantilly agreement the attack was delayed and whittled down such that the so-called General Allied Offensive when it was engaged in summer 1916 fell significantly short of Joffre's ambitions: the enemy and allies saw to that.

At Chantilly it had been proposed that the main offensive was to be preceded by an attritional phase, that Joffre expected would be carried out by the two armies that had not suffered heavy casualties in 1915, the British and Italian. General Sir Douglas Haig, the incoming British commander-in-chief who had not represented the British army at Chantilly, demurred; essentially, as Joffre rightly surmised, because British politicians would not sanction more costly yet apparently indecisive battles after the recent Battle of Loos that had cost Sir John French his job. Coordinating with the British would be a day-to-day challenge. It would seem Haig and Joffre's relationship started well. Sixteen months into his role, Joffre made a good impression at British headquarters. John Charteris, Haig's director of intelligence,

> was introduced officially to General Joffre, and had a few minutes' talk. He is pleased at the change at G.H.Q., though he does not know [Haig] personally. There never was anyone less like the ordinary conception of a

great soldier, than Joffre. He is a very big person, very placid in appearance, almost benevolent, slow in his movements and in his speech, and has remarkable eyes – very steady and still. He keeps his eyes fixed on you all the time you are with him, not glaring or unfriendly, but just as if he were determined that no change of expression should pass unnoticed. ...He said I was the first of the new G.H.Q. Staff to visit him, and presented me with one of the pipes of which he keeps a stock to give favoured visitors.[45]

During the early weeks of 1916, Joffre and Haig negotiated a compromise. Joffre would not insist on a preliminary and separate British attritional operation and Haig's army would support a French attack astride the river Somme rather than mounting an operation in Flanders towards the Belgian coast. Yet although place was soon agreed, time and scale remained points of contention through the spring and early summer as the Battle of Verdun, which began in late February and was to carry on at varying degrees of intensity until December, sapped French strength and diverted British resources. Haig agreed to take over more of the line, reducing the troops available for the joint offensive on the Somme, and argued for delay to train his inexperienced citizen army. French reserves were committed to the defence of Verdun, reducing French forces for the Somme offensive from three to a single army, such that by the summer the French were to support a British attack. The demands of such negotiations took their toll on the commanders' relationship. On his part, Haig was becoming more confident and assertive with his French colleague, who he referred to somewhat contemptuously as 'the old man'.[46] By April Haig (whose evaluations of French colleagues generally stressed their faults) was carping that Joffre 'signs anything which is put in front of him now and is really past his work, if indeed he ever knew anything practical about tactics as distinct from strategy. Joffre was an engineer.'[47] Foch, the army group commander charged with preparing and running the offensive, argued that the army now had neither the manpower nor material to push for a decision and that the offensive should be postponed until 1917. Joffre demurred, judging that it was better for his army to be on the offensive rather than to use up its resources in the morale-sapping Verdun sector.[48]

The Italians were willing, but not entirely ready or very able. On first acquaintance, Joffre judged the Italian commander-in-chief, General Luigi Cadorna, 'very self-possessed and well-informed in modern warfare.' However, since they were as yet only at war with Austria–Hungary that limited the Italians' strategic utility, while the mountainous terrain in which they were having to fight restricted their tactical effectiveness especially as political decisions had left the army short of equipment and not yet fully mobilized.[49] Therefore, the Italian spring offensive when it came – the Fifth Battle of the Isonzo, somewhat hurried as Joffre pressed Cadorna to engage the enemy to take some pressure off his own army at Verdun – was short lived and ineffective. When in mid-May the Austrians struck back in the 'strafexpedition' (punishment offensive), rather than standing ready to assist France the Italians were now calling for relief themselves.[50] The most they could organize to support the offensive on the Somme was a limited counter attack in the Trentino.[51]

Being only formally at war with Austria–Hungary at this time, the Italians could not bring pressure on the main enemy, the Germans. Therefore, Joffre relied on the Russians to second French and British efforts on the Western Front. At Chantilly the Russian representative had tabled an alternative plan sponsored by the Russian chief of staff, General Mikhail Alexeieff, for a concerted attack on Austria-Hungary from three sides – southern Russia, Salonika and Italy. While Joffre's strategy prevailed at the conference, in the event, rather than engaging the Germans Alexeieff defaulted to the easier option of fighting the Austrians. From the start, Joffre had always accepted that it was necessary to wait until Russia was ready before launching a general offensive, and he was prepared to delay it from spring to summer to maximize Russian participation. For his part, Alexeieff was loyal to the principle of combined action agreed at Chantilly, but had to adapt his preparations to circumstances. In the spring the worsening situation at Verdun obliged Joffre to press Alexeieff for premature action. Russian forces launched hasty and ultimately unsuccessful attacks on the German lines on the Eastern Front in late March (Battle of Lake Naroch). True to the spirt of the Chantilly agreement, Alexeieff then advanced the date of the main Russian offensive to early June to relieve pressure on the Italians. That it did. General Alexsei Brusilov's blow was the most powerful yet struck by allied forces and it smashed in a lengthy section of the Austrians' front, obliging the Germans to redeploy reserves southwards. Thereafter, however, Alexeieff chose to reinforce success rather than extend his offensive northwards against the Germans' lines in the east,[52] perhaps missing an opportunity to make the decisive blow that would overstretch and collapse the Central Powers' defence. As the General Allied Offensive prepared the principle of cooperation held firm, but when it came to fighting battles, self-interest prevailed.

This applied to the French front as well, where Joffre had to meet the German offensive at Verdun that commenced towards the end of February. Joffre responded with his usual calm, appointing Pétain to organize the defence of the vital fortress, thereby containing the immediate threat. Yet as it dragged on that battle would both compromise the Chantilly agreement and provoke another political crisis. Joffre came under intense parliamentary criticism as the battle developed. He was accused of having weakened the fortress's defences dangerously, a charge originally levelled at him by nationalist deputy Colonel Emile Driant, whose heroic death in the front line at Verdun on 22 February

38  French Generals of the Great War

added piquancy to the charge.[53] The battle put great strain on the commander-in-chief, but he did not let it show. When he met him for the first time, behind the Verdun lines in mid-March, press officer Henri Bordeaux painted a pen-portrait of Joffre:

> the generalissimo…tall and bulky, wearing an ancient, faded uniform: red breeches, black tunic, red kepi with a double braid of oak leaves. Is he corpulent, avuncular, childlike or gripped by his inner thought process? He looks over his interlocutor rather than fixing him with his gentle, occasionally sparkling, blue eyes. His face is adorned with a thick white moustache. He sits at the table opposite General Maistre, and what a contrast there is between the calm of the one and the nervous gestures of the other who commands the most threatened sector and lives in constant anxiety. … This Joffre is perhaps an astonishing man.[54]

While Verdun held, the situation showed little sign of improvement. Pétain proved a solid defensive commander, but pessimistic about the prospects of holding the fortress or counterattacking. He was promoted out of direct responsibly in May and the more dynamic III CA commander General Robert Nivelle took over Second Army with responsibility for the day-to-day defence of the fortress (with repercussions for Joffre's own situation by the end of the year). War minister Galliéni's criticisms of Joffre had focused on the conduct of operations rather than his strategic competence. With his resignation owing to declining health in March – bowing out with a final stinging report on the commander-in-chief to the cabinet – and replacement by General Pierre Roques, a former general staff colleague and army commander, Joffre might have expected a period of relative calm. Yet parliamentary criticism persisted, culminating in a secret session of the Chamber of Deputies convoked at the start of June to discuss the conduct of the war generally and Joffre's more particular responsibility for events at Verdun. With Roques and prime minister Briand speaking strongly in his defence, Joffre survived the vote of confidence comfortably.[55] Although it was clear that his strategy remained on sufferance.[56] In early July there was a further Senate secret session on the conduct of the war, but since by then French troops had achieved a smashing victory south of the river Somme, the greatest since 1914, Briand's government comfortably survived a vote of confidence.[57] Joffre's offensive strategy would be allowed to run its course during the summer and autumn, although politicians would be watching him closely.

As Verdun drew increasingly on French reserves through the spring a relief offensive became a priority. Haig was disinclined to attack before his raw troops were trained and therefore negotiations over the timing and nature of the joint offensive dragged into May while the political wolves continued to circle; eventually although reluctantly he capitulated to Joffre's entreaties as he was growing increasingly anxious about the French army's staying power.[58] When it was finally launched at the end of June the offensive on the Western Front was much reduced in scope from Joffre's original ambition, partly due to the attrition of the French army at Verdun. Indeed, Joffre himself had slowly come to accept that the general offensive was unlikely to produce a quick victory, and shortly before it commenced had ordered an expanded munitions programme for 1917. But by the time Haig's army attacked on the Somme on 1 July 1916 with French support, the Russians and Italians were engaging the Habsburg army and there was hope that a sustained campaign of attrition could break the enemy once and for all, that summer or the following year.

Joffre's task in the spring had been to bring about the General Allied Offensive that he had initiated: as Haig rightly recognized, 'General Joffre…alone knew the situation fully' and was in a position judge the timing and nature of the offensive.[59] He succeeded, bringing the December 1915 agreement in principle to a practicable, if less ambitious and poorly focused, offensive that would roll out across the various allied theatres of war between June and September. He ensured that allied military leaders remained committed to the plan, accepting that each had to adapt their contribution to their own army's military situation. He finessed political concerns once again. He exerted himself to ensure that operations in Russia and Italy were prepared to coincide with an Anglo-French offensive in the west. But the months of strain took their toll: 'the old man looked tired' and appeared uncertain when he met Haig on the eve of the opening of the Battle of the Somme.[60] Indeed, he was. While hoping that Verdun had inflicted enough damage on the Germans to allow a real victory, he was well aware that the Somme might default to another long battle of attrition;[61] and that France's allies would have to be kept to the task should that turn out to be the case.

\* \* \*

The Somme offensive began very well for the French army; much less so for Haig's inexperienced troops, who in Joffre's straightforward judgement had failed because of basic tactical errors. 'The causes of this check are to be found in poor artillery preparation, and the failure of the forward waves to mop-up the enemy's trenches when they passed through', which allowed the enemy to emerge from their dug-outs, to cut off the first wave and repulse the second, he noted on 2 July: 'The English do not yet have "the way".'[62] These contrasting fortunes provoked an almighty row between Joffre and Haig on 3 July over how to continue the battle.[63] The upshot was that Joffre passed responsibility for coordinating the joint offensive to Foch, with a directive to *'entrainer'* the British forces – support them, get them to fight and to teach them how to fight.[64] He himself would focus on coordinating the two battles now underway on the Western Front and integrating French effort with that of the other allied armies.

While after some success in early July the Somme offensive slowed significantly – the Germans did at least turn their focus from attacking at Verdun to defending on the Somme as the battle defaulted to the routine of mutual attrition – the wider war situation improved over July and August. The Russians continued to make progress and in early August Cadorna launched the Italian army's offensive – the Sixth Battle of the Isonzo – and struck the heaviest blow yet against the Austrians' defences, capturing the town of Gorizia. The General Allied Offensive was now, in Joffre's later estimation, bearing fruit, and the grip needed to be tightened on the enemy.[65] With French forces fully committed that was up to the British and the Russians. On the Somme Fayolle's Sixth Army continued to advance steadily between the British army's right wing and the Somme river valley, but after picking up tempo in mid-July Haig's advance had stalled on the Thiepval ridge. Joffre judged that British methods continued to be at fault and were causing unnecessarily high casualties, resulting in political pressure to scale back offensive operations. Foch was directed to get that battle going again and in mid-August Joffre reasserted his authority with the British commander-in-chief after some weeks of disengagement.[66] Following a lunch at Haig's headquarters on 12 August, to which Poincaré and Joffre were invited to meet King George V, the president with royal support insisted to Haig on the need to renew the attack soon and with more vigour, to which Haig seemed to agree.[67] Yet Haig would not be hurried – he was waiting, among other things, for a new 'wonder weapon', the tank, to be available – and Joffre became increasingly frustrated and overbearing in the way he treated the British commander-in-chief.[68] To compensate, Joffre increasingly committed French reserves in the hope that the dual pressure on the Somme and at Verdun would break the German army's power of resistance. His own subordinates were also becoming fractious. Foch and Fayolle were arguing about how best to continue the battle and Joffre had to step in to resolve their disagreement.[69] Pétain and Nivelle were also airing their differences about the conduct of the battle at Verdun, that needed reconciling.[70]

Joffre had bigger matters to consider. The war was taking another strategic turn with Romania finally joining the allies, and he strove to reinvigorate allied effort to coincide with Romania's declaration of war. By mid-September Joffre's grand vision seemed to be falling into shape. On the Somme the French army expanded its offensive, General Alfred Micheler's Tenth Army extending the battle southwards on 4 September before Sixth Army delivered a series of powerful blows that advanced the line several kilometres between 12 and 26 September (and broke up the largest German counter attack in the battle with ease in between), inflicting heavy casualties. The British attack was finally renewed with vigour on 15 September in the battle of Flers–Courcelette, followed by several much more effective set-piece assaults culminating in the capture of Thiepval village on 27 September.[71] Attrition seemed to be working and the German defence was nearing breaking point, manifested in the replacement of the chief of the general staff, Erich von Falkenhayn, with the Eastern Front duumvirate Paul von Hindenburg and Erich Ludendorff at the end of August. In an impressive show of coordination, on 14 September the Italians attacked once more on the Isonzo front shortly after the allied forces at Salonika renewed their offensive begun in early August that had been disrupted by a Bulgarian counter offensive. However, the latter provoked disputes between Sarrail and the commander of the Italian forces in the theatre, General Petiti, and his subordinate General Victor Cordonnier who commanded the French forces, that would divert Joffre's attention while he had better things to do. His renewed entreaties to have Sarrail removed were rejected by the government, with Cordonnier being recalled instead.[72]

In the east Romania declared war on Austria–Hungary on 27 August (and Germany on Romania and Italy on Germany the day after), but rather than proving the proverbial straw that would break the camel's back Romania's intervention threw grit into Joffre's now well-oiled allied military machine. While Romania brought twenty-three divisions to the allied side, the commanders were unfamiliar with the new type of war being waged and the troops were poorly equipped. Their advance against the Austrians petered out in mid-September and they soon faced a powerful concentration of Central Powers' forces led by the recently disgraced Falkenhayn that took the war into Romanian territory and conquered most of it by the end of the year. Immediately Joffre recognized the need to induct the Romanians in modern warfare, a mission he assigned to his 1914 operations director Henri Berthelot.[73] But he was reluctant to send them guns that were needed for the battles he was conducting himself. More disruptive for Joffre's strategy, Romania's poor performance obliged Alexeieff to suspend the Russian offensive and divert troops to their aid; and the Russian chief of staff also started to complain of the support he was receiving from his western allies.[74]

As the initiative in the east and at Salonika was lost the Western Front offensive also bogged down as winter set in. On the Somme the new German command organized a more effective defence in depth that would, with the onset of autumn rain and the exhaustion of the allies' own reserves and munitions stocks, take most of the momentum out of Foch's advance, although it would continue to creep forwards with increasingly meagre results until mid-November. Joffre switched his attention elsewhere, allocating Nivelle the resources to launch a long-demanded counter attack to retake the lost forts at

Verdun, which resulted in a stunning victory at the end of October (at least compared with events on the Somme by that time) and brought Second Army's commander wide acclaim and political support.

Joffre was expecting to continue his strategy of attrition in the coming campaign, but it was not to be. Facing another year of war, Joffre convened the allies' military leaders at Chantilly once again, on 15 November. Here he offered a scaled-up version of the December 1915 plan to capitalize upon the damage the General Allied Offensive had clearly inflicted on the enemy's forces, representing that a concerted and powerful blow early in 1917 would complete the work of destroying the enemy's military capacity before the summer was out. The allied generals agreed. Pressure would be maintained over the winter while each allied front was prepared for a coordinated offense that would be launched by the middle of February. In the Balkans an offensive would be made from Salonika and the Russo-Romanian front to knock out Bulgaria.[75] However, Joffre would not receive the free rein he had in 1915. On the same day a political conference met in Paris and strong objections were raised to continuing a strategy of attrition, not least by the British delegation dominated by war minister and soon-to-be prime minister Lloyd George. When Joffre met the politicians the next day to present the military agreement, political endorsement was deferred.[76] Soon afterwards Briand's ministry came under pressure as the situation in Romania worsened and another secret session of the Chamber of Deputies was called. To save his own position the premier chose to sacrifice his commander-in-chief. To cut a long story short, it was initially proposed (by Roques himself) to restrict Joffre's directing powers to the Western Front and to hand Roques and the war ministry strategic authority. This idea was rejected, although it was decided to restructure Joffre's GQG staff once again. An alternative suggestion that Nivelle be made commander-in-chief in France and Joffre reassigned as principal strategic advisor to the government had been mooted and this would ultimately be adopted once Briand had survived a vote of confidence in the secret session (during which Joffre's position and action were heavily criticized). Briand appealed directly to Joffre's sense of patriotism to accept a change of his functions in order to save the government: for this sacrifice he would get a Marshal's baton, a residence in Paris and an advisory role which would, Briand suggested, allow Joffre to focus on the wider strategic issues of the war rather than the day-to-day minutiae and decisions of a field commander. Joffre could see the writing on the wall and, tired of the fight, acquiesced. Briand could take this capitulation to the secret session and secure his place for a few more months.[77]

The new Marshal of France returned to Paris with misgivings – he was now designated 'general-in-chief' rather than 'commander-in-chief' and the government's decree announcing the change was so worded that he would be 'able to assist' the newly created ministerial war council as 'technical advisor to the government' rather than have any formal responsibly to participate in its deliberations. He felt the government had acted deviously and protested to Poincaré, demanding he have the right to attend council meetings, to give orders to both Nivelle and Sarrail, and to liaise directly with allied commanders. But Briand and Roques's successor as war minister, General Hubert Lyautey, demurred, even rescinding his designation as 'technical advisor'.[78] Joffre's role in future would be one of influence, but with no formal authority.

Joffre had conceived the summer offensive as the means to grip and defeat the Central Powers' armies with a sustained battle of attrition, and by September the strategy seemed to be working. It was (and would continue to be) the right strategy, but at that point in the war execution was problematic and Joffre paid the price.[79] Rather than France's allies taking on and defeating the Germans with help from the French army, as the General Allied Offensive developed the French took on an increasingly heavy burden of fighting on the Western Front, while Joffre struggled to keep his allies up to the mark in the wider war. Despite the relative failure of British arms on 1 July 1916 the French attack was effective enough to justify continuing the Somme offensive, not least because Joffre was bound into a mutual support agreement with France's other allies. Unfortunately, while wearing down the Austrian army the Russians and Italians did not engage directly with the German army, so that burden fell increasingly upon the tiring French army, and it was to this that French politicians increasingly objected, not least because they were guilty by association. Joffre's secondary objective, training-up the British army, seemed to have been achieved: Haig's citizen army was a competent and reliable fighting force by the end of the year. The same could not be said of France's other allies however, the need for Berthelot to take the Romanian army in hand being the prime example. When he met Cadorna in November Joffre arranged for an exchange of officers between the two armies: 'the first step towards working together and cooperating with the Italian army on a single western front. When the two armies have the same methods, when they know each other and mix effectively, they will be better able to work side by side.'[80] The new American ally that was to join in spring 1917 would present a similar challenge. Since Joffre had come to realize that the war would not end in 1916, he needed to ensure that the forces that would continue it were effective enough to take over the burden of fighting from the French, and could work well with them. Joffre's intention to exploit the degradation of the German army decisively by renewing the attritional battle on the Somme early in 1917, extending it in scale, was not to be. Although Briand had lost faith in his commander-in-chief and his strategy, Joffre had retained faith in himself: he had been replaced 'just at the point I was going to gather the fruits of [a year of victories]. The war would have finished a year earlier, before the Americans', he believed.[81] It is a thought-provoking if unverifiable claim. If Joffre had been allowed to continue, and been successful in 1917, a French-led victory before American intervention and the Bolshevik revolution would certainly have created a very different twentieth-century world order to that which emerged in 1918.

\* \* \*

Joffre occupied an office at the *École de guerre* for the remainder of the war, watching it progress but having limited power to influence it. The documentation collated in his personal archive suggests that he followed events in the war assiduously as it developed according to the parameters he had established.[82] On the evidence of his official journal, he met many military and political figures and remained attuned to the turn of events. Yet Bordeaux found him in February 1918 'in a vast, empty office, sitting at his desk without papers, and appearing bored, or dreaming. He is much rejuvenated, blond and rotund, with the honest look of a captain of gendarmerie transfigured either by a thin smile or a malicious peasant look.'[83] He had the satisfaction of watching his successor fail and his acolytes Pétain and Foch take control of the army and coalition military strategy and bring the war to a successful outcome following the principles that he had established. A meeting on 6 October with Foch (who was then army chief of staff in Paris and effectively technical advisor to the government) that he recorded shows that Foch continued to respect his 'wisdom and experience'.[84] They were agreed on military strategy and that its main parameters should follow those Joffre had set earlier in the war – 'the formula of the Somme, a battle in which one brings all means to bear that one pursues in the hope of overstretching the enemy's powers of resistance, without exhausting our own effort. Attacks of the same type on other fronts will accentuate this effect.'[85] As allied generalissimo in 1918 Foch would pursue this plan to a successful outcome.

Although Foch was the coming man, Joffre remained a figurehead and a 'default option' in allied relations. He was chosen to participate in the French mission to the United States after that nation entered the war in spring 1917. The great general whose reputation preceded him was feted across the Atlantic. While in the States he presented proposals for creating an American army to fight in France. He was also able to establish a working relationship with the commander of the American Expeditionary Forces, General John Pershing, and thereafter he was consulted on how to develop the command relationship between the French and American armies.[86] Politicians often looked to him for guidance, especially on questions of inter-allied relations. Indeed, when the prospect of appointing an allied generalissimo was mooted towards the end of 1917 his name was canvassed, as a man known to and respected by all the allied commanders.[87] It was not to be. 'Where is Joffre's sang froid', Poincaré opined as the allies' lines in Picardy were stove in in March 1918.[88] But then the responsibility to coordinate went to the aggressive Foch rather than the phlegmatic Joffre, with the latter's endorsement.[89] The idea that he be appointed to lead the allied expeditionary forces in Siberia in summer 1918 came to nothing. Once again it was a question of politics: French premier and war minister Georges Clemenceau probably vetoed the idea after Foch had suggested that the mission needed a Frenchman 'of the first order' to lead such a sensitive inter-allied venture.[90]

After the war, as a marshal Joffre remained on active duty and in 1920 was appointed a member of the reconstituted CSG where he worked alongside many of the commanders who he had appointed in wartime (including Nivelle) dealing with France's post-war security problems.[91] Extensive public and international honours included election to the *Académie française*, the country's leading intellectual institution, in spring 1918.[92] A soldier rather than a man of letters, Joffre was initially hesitant, yet welcomed the opportunity to celebrate the achievements of the army.[93] In his investiture speech he took care to praise both the *poilus* he had led and, perhaps for the first time, the staff officers who had directed the war to a successful outcome.[94] He would secure a place of honour riding alongside Foch in France's victory parade on Bastille Day 1919; but not without difficulty. Foch suggested he accompany an allied contingent. Poincaré (who perhaps lacked any sense of irony) proposed that he ride with the head of the Chamber of Deputies in front of the ministers. But Joffre, whose journal indicates an exaggerated self-importance, insisted on sharing the place of honour to which Clemenceau, although never a great admirer of his, acquiesced in the face of popular clamour for the marshal to take part.[95] In the 1920s he would write memoirs that would be published posthumously in 1932. This 'vibrant and magisterial treatise on the art of command' gave an insight into the mind of a 'very great man', Debeney judged; one whose calm, languid demeanour cloaked brilliant and deep judgement, tenacity and determination to follow 'his own wide ranging and long-nurtured plan'.[96] Following his death in 1931 France honoured her 1914 saviour with a state funeral. Unlike Foch, however, Joffre does not lie in the pantheon of French heroes at Les Invalides, but in a simple plot next to his wife in his garden at Louveciennes.[97] Place Joffre, directly outside the *École de guerre* in Paris, was named in his honour in 1933, and his equestrian statue was erected there in 1939, shortly before France found herself at war with Germany once again.

\* \* \*

André Bourachot, one of Joffre's many biographers, identifies that he is 'a divisive figure who is either adored or hated.... These superficial extremes seem to be the only two answers that are ever given when questions are asked about this controversial personality.'[98] He is condemned for operational failures (like so many Great War generals). His command record is mixed: he lost and won battles in 1914, engaged his army too hastily in 1915, and successfully contained and counterattacked the enemy in 1916. His principal adversary, von Falkenhayn, has a similar record and was to lose his job a few months before Joffre.

Joffre is largely forgotten or misunderstood as a strategist of modern war, where he deserves much credit. In an initial assessment, this author judged Joffre 'a competent military leader rather than a military genius, courageous but not imaginative'.[99] This is a fair evaluation of his achievements as an army commander and coalition manager. But that assessment needs to be reviewed when his evolving responsibility as the coalition's strategist is factored in. Early on Joffre grasped the nature of the war and the tools and processes needed to fight and to win it. A modern, technical army, ample munitions and materiel, staunch allies properly led and managed. There would be a time lag before these were in place: others had grasped this and urged restraint until circumstances were more propitious – Kitchener in 1915, Foch in 1916. These men had the luxury of relative detachment and lesser responsibility. Joffre had to lead a huge army, and to engage, justify and defend his actions in rapidly shifting military circumstances, in a still unsteady coalition and to an increasingly hostile political leadership. Joffre was a pragmatist, a battler, a survivor. He got his way with allies on most occasions, outmanoeuvred politicians when it mattered and stuck to his determined course in the face of military and political reverses. Arguably, towards the end of 1916 Joffre was in a position to engage and win the war of attrition just as his time ran out: he certainly maintained that opinion while the last two years of the war unrolled.[100] All this does not make Joffre a military genius of course, but it suggests that he was a military colossus; perhaps the archetypal 'flawed colossus'. He controlled the war like no other individual on the allied side and he deserves to be recognized as the war's dominant strategist, who conceived the strategy for liberation and prepared France's army for the victory it would win under his successors by establishing in the first half of the war its doctrinal, material and international foundations, while pulling together a disparate and often fractious coalition during two years of rapid change in warfare.

When Joffre rode alongside Foch in the victory parade along the Champs Elysées in 1919 many spectators wondered who the portly general riding alongside the war's victor was. In the final years of the war Joffre had limited influence on the war policy of a state whose leaders felt that they knew better than the general who had waged a bloody but increasingly effective attritional war for three years. Like many other generals through history he fell victim to factional French politics and so would not get the opportunity to lead France to victory. However, given that strategic policy had been set during his tenure of command and was pursued by his nominated military subordinates thereafter Joffre should be recognized as the strategic lynchpin of France and the allied coalition. Joffre proved himself a steady if stubborn commander, calm in a crisis, determined and resourceful, domineering when he deemed it necessary. He was also wily and combative, surviving in the bear-pit of Third Republican politics for over five years. It is Joffre's misfortune to be associated with pre-war military deficiencies and the trials and errors of 1914–1916 – these are very obvious from his memoirs, which carefully explain the way he approached war-making – rather than France's and the allied coalition's later success whose foundations were laid during Joffre's period of command. He was as worthy a marshal of France as those others who were promoted to that rank, capable of the higher leadership which world war demanded and quite able to play politicians at their own game. His own circumstances were more difficult than those he passed on to his successors. While robbed of due recognition as the strategist of victory, Joffre would always remain the victor of the Marne, France's deliverer in the difficult early months of war. Above all others he deserves the plaudit 'architect of victory' even though Foch would be 'the man who won the war'.

Chapter 2

# Ferdinand Foch: Master of Strategy

## Michael Neiberg

The most publicized photograph of Ferdinand Foch in 1914 shows a proud, confident man in the prime of his career with his chest thrust out and his eyes full of self-assurance. He fits the description John Dos Passos later wrote of him as a 'strutting game cock of a man with gray blue eyes and an abundant grizzled mustache.'[1] Foch had ample reason for his self-confidence. He had begun the war as the commander of XX *corps d'armée* (CA), one of the elite large formations of the French army. That army corps was the spearhead of Second Army's attack into Lorraine in mid-August 1914. Despite its initial success, the XX CA met its match on the heights of Morhange where the Germans badly bloodied it before it retreated to the safety of France's frontier fortifications. Although his immediate superior, General Noël de de Curières de Castelnau, blamed the setback on Foch disobeying his orders, commander-in-chief General Joseph Joffre was impressed with Foch's aggressiveness and promoted him to command the newly formed Ninth Army. Foch then held the critical defensive sector of the French line during the Battle of the Marne in September, receiving some of the credit for the miraculous French victory there.[2]

Four years later, photographs of Foch show a man who looks as if he has aged two decades or more. Then serving as 'generalissimo' overseeing strategy for all the allied armies, Foch had shouldered a burden of tremendous responsibility. With a small staff and poorly defined powers, he had to persuade or convince the heads of the French, British, American, and Italian armies to adhere to his general strategic direction. He also had to find ways to keep meddling politicians from four nations out of his business as he tried to bring the most destructive war in human history to a successful close on the battlefield.

If he appeared decades older on the outside, he had also aged on the inside, although he had lost none of his self-confidence. He and his wife had suffered personal tragedy; their only son and only son-in-law were killed in action right at the start of the war, on the same day, 22 August 1914, a day of battle from one end of the front to the other on which the army suffered its heaviest casualties of the conflict. Intellectually, the aggressive army corps commander of 1914 who had believed in the cult of the offensive and had relied on the power of French *élan* to win battles had changed his perspectives by 1918. The Foch of 1918 better understood the limits of élan. He saw more clearly than he had in 1914 the importance of the industrial, human, and coalition aspects war. In these four years he had risen to a position that had not even existed when the First World War began.

His career was proof that commanders who best adapted to the rapidly changing military and political contexts of war could prosper. The road from corps commander to generalissimo was not, of course, without bumps along the way. Before the war, Foch had been one of the advocates of the *offensive à outrance*, the 'offensive to the utmost'. As an instructor at the French Staff College, the *École supérieure de guerre* (ESG) from 1895 to 1901 he had taught this dedication to the offensive to a generation of officers; although in the light of reflection he would moderate his gung ho turn-of-the-century staff college teachings to a more pragmatic stance that tried to integrate material and moral factors in the conduct of war. In the first weeks of the war, Foch put those principles into practice, at tremendous human cost. Although he was not alone in failing to appreciate just how much new military technology would force a reconsideration of pre-war thinking, Foch shares the responsibility for sending waves of infantry against solid German positions well defended by wire, machine guns, and artillery in 1915, although not without learning important lessons from these early engagements.

The 1915 offensives in Artois that Foch oversaw as an army group commander have nearly vanished from the history books. Foch said virtually nothing about them in his memoirs, a silence that speaks volumes. He did, however, admit that the offensives 'clearly demonstrated the insufficiency of our means of attack, above all in heavy artillery.'[3] In his defence, while Foch had pushed his subordinates to keep the offensive going, he insisted that they only do so where and when artillery preparation gave attacks a reasonable chance of success.[4] Still, there is no escaping the conclusion that the 1915 offensives were terribly bloody without producing any operational or strategic gain to justify the costs. The French calculated that the offensives cost France 30,386 men killed, 110,725 wounded, and another 50,686 missing for gains that Robert Doughty appropriately called 'miniscule'.[5]

But if Foch, like others, was still learning how to master the operational level in the war's early phase, he had learned valuable lessons in coalition management. After what Joffre perceived as the British failure to hold and defend the critical French industrial city of Lille, he needed a man he could trust to guide the battles in the northern sector. Joffre gave Foch the unenviable assignment of directing the joint Franco-British-Belgian campaign on the Yser river and around the town of Ypres in Belgium in October 1914. Although the French had the most men in the sector, Foch was in fact junior in rank to the British commander, Field Marshal Sir John French, and the Belgian commander, King Albert. In this crucible, Foch managed to hold together the armies of three nations and prevent a German breakthrough. Foch later said that having to direct an alliance battle was the most difficult task a general could face. Having done so, he supposedly quipped, made him lose some of his respect for Napoleon, most of whose major victories had come against coalitions.[6]

Still, the experience on the Yser and at Ypres proved fundamental to Foch's future success. Douglas Haig remembered Foch's courage there four years later when he supported Foch to become the supreme allied commander.[7] The operations in Flanders gave Foch a keen insight into the workings of a coalition as well as a deep look into the strategic mindset of his British allies. No other allied commander had had such an experience before 1917. It made Foch the logical choice to command the allied armies in 1918. As Elizabeth Greenhalgh concluded, the Ypres and Yser battles 'gained him considerable credit with the Allies, credit that he later cashed in under even more desperate circumstances in 1918'.[8]

The early years of the war taught Foch lessons at the operational level that he later translated at the strategic. Foch had, like most members of his generation, failed to foresee how brutally the awesome power of defensive warfare would force a re-evaluation of some common principles of war. Nevertheless, Foch, to his credit, applied himself to learning what generals needed to do. He supposedly once remarked to a colleague 'I have only one merit. I have forgotten what I taught and what I learned.'[9] Almost uniquely among the senior leaders of 1914, Foch had the intellectual ability to go back to the drawing board and discard some of the ideas that had once been so central to his career. This author of two pre-war books on tactics and former professor of military theory at the French staff college went back to school. To understand why, we need to understand something more about Foch the man.

\* \* \*

Foch's background was similar to that of many French generals. He was Catholic at a time when the anticlerical French Third Republic was severing ties between church and state; he was conservative at a time when the leaders of the republic were wary of the association between senior officers and reactionary groups; and he was from the provinces (the Pyrenees and later Brittany, to be precise) when power was becoming ever more centralized in Paris. As such, like many of his peers, he was an outsider to France's political system.

Yet Foch managed to survive the political maelstrom that grew even more intense in the wake of the seismic Dreyfus Affair at the turn of the century.

Like most of the officers who survived with their careers intact, Foch learned to keep his political convictions more or less to himself. He did not publicly choose sides in the Dreyfus Affair, although it is hard to imagine Foch supporting the Jewish and Alsatian Alfred Dreyfus against the army he loved. Despite his care to remain politically neutral, he was not shy about publicly professing his Catholic faith. Foch believed, probably correctly, that his Catholicism had resulted in his being passed over for the most prestigious assignments and being sent to postings far from the political hothouse of Paris.

In 1907, Foch learned that he had been passed over for command of the ESG. Rumours had spread that Foch's personnel file listed him as politically unreliable. Furious with the charge and with having been passed over for a job he desperately wanted, Foch sent copies of his books of military theory to the French prime minister, Georges Clemenceau. Foch then demanded a meeting with Clemenceau to get an explanation for the decision, although he had every reason to believe he would not get a fair hearing. Clemenceau and Foch were in almost every way opposites. The prime minister was a veteran of the political infighting of Paris. He had been a staunch critic of both the Catholic church and the army, and he had passionately defended the rights of Alfred Dreyfus. Nevertheless, impressed by Foch's thinking and chutzpah, Clemenceau gave him command of the ESG. It was the start of a roller coaster relationship between two future titans of France.

The posting at the ESG gave Foch time to think about strategy and warfare. He read and taught Clausewitz, praising the Prussian thinker for his insights on the links between war and politics. Operating in the hothouse environment of the capital of scandal-riven Third Republic France forced Foch into regular contact with politicians. Although Foch never fully trusted politicians and avoided them whenever he could, his insights into people such as Clemenceau proved useful later in life. The ESG also allowed Foch to get the measure of a generation of French senior officers.

Being in the capital also gave him the invaluable experience of meeting and working with his British counterparts. None of those counterparts proved as important to Foch as Sir Henry Wilson.[10] An Anglo-Irish soldier and skilled political operator, Wilson and Foch first met in 1909, at a time when the growing assertiveness of Germany had begun to worry both British and French officials. Wilson and Foch struck up a close friendship based upon mutual admiration and the overlap of their professional needs. At one point, Wilson is supposed to have introduced Foch to a British colleague by telling him, 'Mark my words. This fellow is going to command the Allied armies when the big war comes on.'[11] The story may be apocryphal, but the friendship was real. Wilson attended the wedding of Foch's daughter and in 1922 Foch rushed to London to be a pall bearer upon hearing that two IRA assassins had killed Wilson. He led Wilson's widow out of the funeral service on his arm.

Personal contacts gave him insight into the British; a lifetime of study gave him insight into the Germans. Foch never asked for a posting outside metropolitan France, even while Joseph Joffre, Joseph Gallieni, Hubert Lyautey, and virtually all the fast-rising members of the French officer corps were making names for themselves in France's colonies. Foch had entered the army as a private in 1870 during the Franco-Prussian War and had seen with his own eyes the damage that the war had done to his beloved France. He later recalled the walls of his barracks in Paris still being covered in blood when he arrived. While the blood was likely attributable to the civil war known as the Paris Commune rather than the Prussians, Foch never stopped seeing Germany as France's essential security problem.

Thus, instead of seeking glory in the empire, Foch remained focused on Germany and the nature of a future Franco-German war. He read deeply in French translations of the major German theorists, and he understood and internalized Clausewitz better than his German opponents did.[12] When the war began, he showed the keenest sense of all of the allied generals for divining what the Germans would do next. Time and time again, he found himself countermanding orders or overruling senior subordinates because their vision of the coming battle conflicted with his own. More often than not, he proved to be correct about German intentions, even if, as during 1915, he could not always design the most appropriate response.

Taken together, these qualities made Foch an almost ideal candidate for senior positions. Joffre recognized in him a rare intellect and a source of nearly boundless energy. Foch was also well served by his chief of staff and alter ego, Maxime Weygand, a hard-working and dedicated officer whom Foch first selected simply because he was the most senior officer on a list of available candidates. Weygand was Belgian by birth and, while even he never knew who his biological parents were, they were well-connected enough to land him a slot at the French military academy at St Cyr. Weygand repaid that generosity by dedicating his life to France which, from 1914 to 1918, meant a complete devotion to liberating France from German occupation. He and Foch proved an effective and efficient team.

Over time Foch gained the respect of his British allies. Foch and Haig never developed a warm and trusting friendship like Foch's with Wilson, but Foch and Haig understood one another well enough. They argued and disagreed when their visions of strategy and operations diverged, but they shared a mutual respect that kept the relationship functional.

In September 1914, following a car accident, Joffre tried to have Foch named his successor in the event of Joffre's death or incapacitation. Although the politicians recognized Foch's abilities they demurred, possibly because of abiding concerns about Foch's political leanings. Although Foch tried to stay out of the political arena during the early years of the war, once the guns fell silent his tense relationship with French politicians would quickly re-emerge.

\* \* \*

As with most operations in 1915, Foch's offensives had been too costly with little to show for the casualties. Foch had, however, begun the intellectual exercise of reviewing his own conduct of the war to date (as well as that of the army more broadly) to find out where it had fallen short. At the end of 1915, he wrote a series of memoranda to Joffre in which he stressed that infantry could not gain ground even if, as in the battles in Artois, it had the support of artillery and gas in unprecedented quantities. In the months to come, Foch argued, France should 'renounce the brutal assault' method of 1914 and 1915 because it had shown itself too costly and ineffective. 'One could be tempted by the idea of eventually transforming attack methods into a violent push', he wrote, but 'we prefer the formula that consists of advancing carefully, methodically, parsimoniously'. The enemy line was no longer just a few trenches, but 'a fortified region both deep and long, covered with repeated obstacles' that no amount of élan would ever break. In other words, more men and more guns alone would not win the war. France and its allies would need new concepts and new doctrines.[13] Foch was far from alone in coming to the conclusion that the war had become a duel of machines, not men, but given his previous attachment to *élan* and *offensive à outrance*, his transformation is noteworthy.

As a result of this intellectual transformation, Foch became one of the leading reformers of the French army. Alongside Generals Henri-Philippe Pétain and Marie-Émile Fayolle, Foch became a member of what Michel Goya calls the 'methodicals', a group of French military leaders looking to vanquish the last remnants of the doctrine of *offensive à outrance*. In its place would come 'scientific warfare' dominated by artillery, aviation, and gas.[14] The new war would also feature what Nick Lloyd has recently called 'offensive in width', a series of blows across the Western Front to prevent the Germans from reinforcing in any one sector.[15] This concept challenged the 'offensive in depth' that had looked for a decisive breakthrough at one single point in the enemy line. Foch, Fayolle, and others had concluded that such a breakthrough was extremely unlikely, but it would take two further costly offensive campaigns before their ideas prevailed.

The reformers needed time to think through and implement their ideas, but the pace of the war did not give them that time. On 6 December 1915, just days after Foch composed his memorandum on future warfare, French and allied military representatives met at Joffre's Chantilly headquarters to agree a strategy for 1916.[16] This contemplated Western Front offensive was to be a joint Franco-British effort, with the French taking the lead. Joffre chose Foch to plan and execute the coming offensive, in large part because of his experience working with British generals. William Philpott noted that 'Only Foch seemed to possess the intellectual apparatus' to understand and conceive of the coming battle, intended to be the largest ever fought.[17] Foch's initial vision for a summer campaign astride the Somme river shows clearly his intellectual journey from the *offensive à outrance* of 1914 to the more careful, studied approach of late 1915. Foch, once a dedicated student of Napoleon, argued against any notion of trying to make the Somme a decisive Napoleonic clash of arms. Instead of becoming another Austerlitz, the Somme would be the beginning of a 'sustained process of beating the German army. Successive French and British attacks, coordinated but not necessarily coincident, would grind down the enemy', allowing for an eventual 'rupture' to take place against a weakened German army.[18]

We will never know how Foch's initial vision for the Somme offensive might have played out because the Germans beat him to the punch. The German army's massive attack at Verdun in late February negated Foch's careful planning. His projected attack force of forty French divisions massed in three armies slowly whittled away as the defence of Verdun required more and more French reinforcements. With the French contribution reduced first to thirty then to twenty-six then to sixteen divisions, Foch saw his role change from commander of a joint operation to a partner in what had become a predominantly British operation. Instead of attacking on a twenty-five-mile wide front, the French would now be responsible for only the eight miles astride the Somme river. In effect, the French had become a diversionary force to what had evolved into (and which would be remembered by posterity as) a British offensive. Strategic purposes had changed as well. Haig and the British sought a rapid break through; the more realistic Foch hoped that a steady, methodical offensive would best serve to help relieve some of the German pressure at Verdun.

Foch accepted the new arrangement for the Somme; given the unfolding catastrophe at Verdun, he could do little else. He would have preferred to delay the offensive until 1917 when the allies had built up their material advantage. By early summer, 1916, the immediate crisis at Verdun had begun to abate but pressure still built for the Somme offensive to begin. Haig resisted such calls, wishing to delay the attack until he felt his young army was ready to fight. As a result, the French army sat largely inactive on the Somme throughout the spring, unable to do anything to help their countrymen at Verdun. Foch felt the frustration of that inactivity acutely.

When the offensive did at last begin at the end of June 1916 it proved to be a study in contrasts. The British army suffered through a litany of failures that left inexperienced infantry badly exposed to the full fury of German machine-gun fire. On 1 July nearly 60,000 British soldiers became casualties, including almost 20,000 dead. While officers at British headquarters did not see the full scope of the casualties and did not see the day's events as a disaster, they could see that the British armies had failed to break through the German lines. Rather than a rupture and pursuit into open country, the British faced a long, tough battle of attrition. In contrast, operations astride the river, planned and directed by Sixth Army commander Fayolle, proceeded 'like clockwork', with the French in an excellent position to exploit their gains.[19] French forces captured 6,000 German prisoners of war, while the much larger British force had captured fewer than 2,000. The French owed their success to a more sophisticated employment of artillery and more skilled infantry tactics, results, no doubt, of the much greater depth of French battlefield experience.[20] Costly the offensives of 1915 surely were, but French experiences in early July 1916 suggest that French generals, led by Foch, had learned at least some of the right lessons. South of the river French forces had secured the critical high ground overlooking the German defences north of the river that they would seek to engage in subsequent phases of the operation.

Nevertheless, Foch's goal had not been to break through German lines, and certainly not to do so alone. He had prepared a battle to break the enemy's power of resistance and orientate his efforts away from Verdun. The Somme was to be a coalition battle and had to be fought as one; that responsibility fell firmly on Foch's shoulders after Joffre and Haig fell out over how to continue operations following the disappointing start in the British sector. Despite the frustrations inherent in a joint campaign, there was a growing level of trust (if not exactly intimacy) between Foch and Haig. In September 1916, British Secretary of State for War David Lloyd George approached Foch looking for answers as to why French forces had performed so much better than British ones. Lloyd George's unhappiness with Haig was well-known; Foch had no trouble divining that the minister sought proof of Haig's incompetence to use in a campaign to remove him from command. Foch refused to take the bait, praising his fellow commander's performance and thereby earning the deep gratitude of not only Haig but the entire British military leadership. Foch knew that a close working relationship with his British military colleagues would be critical to winning the war. This explains the sharp contrast between the patience with which Foch dealt with the British and the sharp annoyance with which he often dealt with his fellow French officers.[21]

Nineteen-sixteen had been a tough year for France. Although the French army had held at Verdun and, after Foch's Somme offensive relieved pressure on the fortress, had even succeeded in recovering some lost ground, it had suffered immense casualties. Losses at the Somme bled the French for no obvious gain. The French official history cites a total casualty figure for the Verdun and Somme campaigns as 579,798; of that figure, 202,567 occurred directly under Foch's watch on the Somme. Although proportionally and absolutely these losses were lighter than the losses for 1914 and 1915, they had, in the eyes of critics, come without changing the strategic picture in France's favour. Despite all the blood and treasure lost, France would have to steel herself for more of the same in 1917.[22] While Foch planned those operations, others were demanding major changes in the French high command.

\* \* \*

On 16 December Foch awoke to find a telegram informing him that he had been relieved of command. Joffre, too, was gone, replaced by the Anglophone and supremely confident General Robert Nivelle. Exactly whose idea it was to remove Foch remains a bit of a mystery. Weygand blamed prime minister Aristide Briand and the politicians in Paris for beginning a 'campaign of disparagement' against Foch based on his presumably poor health.[23] Others, including education minister Paul Painlevé, thought that Joffre, once Foch's close ally, had sacrificed Foch in an ultimately futile attempt to remain in power. Whatever the immediate cause, Nivelle used his new broom to sweep clean. In Nivelle's eyes, Foch was too tightly connected to the falling star of Joffre, no matter what role the latter played in his removal.[24] Nivelle, moreover, preached a doctrine of quickly rupturing the German lines, an operational concept at odds with Foch's methodical offensive doctrine. Although such a promise of rapid victory proved alluring to French politicians, Foch did not buy what Nivelle was selling.

In the first half of 1917, Nivelle gave Foch a series of secondary assignments. They included taking temporary command of the eastern army group while its commander, de Castelnau, went to Russia for staff talks, and preparing contingency plans to thwart a highly unlikely German attack through neutral Switzerland. If in fact poor health had been a problem, this period in exile gave Foch time for a much-needed rest as well as a chance to think. His ideas on the war continued to evolve. He believed that the war would be won or lost only on the Western Front; that the coalition with Great Britain was the *sine qua non* of victory; and that the allies could not hope to win by the kind of spectacular victory Nivelle promised to deliver. Foch watched as the Germans built a new defensive line (the Hindenburg Line) that rendered much of Nivelle's planning worthless. He also watched in frustration as Nivelle stuck to an outdated concept of operations that had failed in the early years of the war.[25]

The series of disasters that befell the army after the failure of Nivelle's offensive proved that Foch had been right but being right gave him no satisfaction. Nivelle's attack on the heights of the Chemin des Dames cost France an estimated 120,000 casualties for no strategic gains. The tragedy stood in marked contrast to Nivelle's unbounded optimism and his nearly unlimited promises of great success. Soon thereafter, thousands of men from the army Foch so loved mutinied, refusing to go on the attack.[26] They were also protesting low pay, poor leadership, and lack of leave. The government relieved Nivelle in mid-May and replaced him with the dour and competent Pétain, who took charge of the situation and brought a badly needed measure of calm to the army.

France needed leadership in this troubled time, and the government turned once again to Foch. In mid-May Painlevé, recently appointed war minister, offered him the position of chief of staff at the war ministry in Paris, a de facto senior military adviser to the government and alternative source of advice to GQG. The arrangement kept the overall command of the army on the Western Front in the hands of the careful and defensive-minded Pétain, but it gave Foch direct influence over strategy and relations with France's allies. In the imaginative words of one recent scholarly assessment, the French government was trying to balance Pétain's ice and Foch's fire.[27] Foch also began to circulate the idea of creating a single, unified command structure to coordinate allied strategy. With the Americans just entering the war and the Russians in the process of collapse, Foch argued that the allied war effort needed a single commander who could set strategy, oversee the management of resources, and ensure proper coordination of effort. It did not require much imagination to see that Foch had himself in mind for this delicate job. Some politicians, including Lloyd George, liked the idea, seeing in it a way to reduce Haig's power without actually taking the politically difficult step of removing him. But most French politicians thought such a role would give too much power to soldiers. They had, after all, spent the last three years reigning in that power. Foch's reputation for anti-republican political ideas, moreover, made him suspect. Those same politicians argued that the overall direction of allied strategy belonged to elected officials, not to the army. They preferred to set strategy through a series of committees chaired by ministers. This method was undoubtedly slower, but it kept power in the hands of the politicians. Many of Foch's fellow generals also objected to his ideas. Some saw the imposition of a supreme commander as an infringement on their own authority. British generals, most significantly Haig, saw constitutional conflicts in yielding authority for the command of national troops to a foreigner. Most importantly, the British opposed the idea on the irrefutable argument that Nivelle's recent show of incompetence on the Chemin des Dames made them reluctant to follow French orders. The

Americans, too, insisted on an independent command despite their lack of familiarity with modern war and their lack of modern staff arrangements. Thus, the idea of a joint command atrophied – for the moment.

In October 1917 a combined German–Austrian force smashed through Italian lines near Caporetto, sending the Italians into headlong retreat and threatening to knock Italy from the coalition. Foch understood immediately that the crisis in Italy had a direct impact on France's ability to wage war and he made it clear that the collapse at Caporetto was precisely the kind of problem that a joint command might have helped to prevent. Now the allies had to mount a major effort to save Italy, despite the obvious problem that French, British, and Italian goals were quite different. The Italians were understandably most interested in salvaging their army and stopping the bleeding; the French wanted to keep Italy alive in order to tie down German units away from the western front; and the British (or at least Lloyd George) saw value in shifting the major thrust of their effort away from the stalemate of Flanders and into another theatre.

Foch, who had studied exactly this contingency in the months previously, personally oversaw an emergency mission to Italy that involved the dispatch of forty-four French artillery batteries and six French infantry divisions. The British sent another five divisions and artillery of their own, meaning that instead of one allied effort to help Italy, there were two national efforts. Foch put his characteristic energy into the Italian problem, personally meeting with senior Italian political and military officials and making suggestions for reforms. The environment was tense, as Foch disagreed with the Italian assessment of the situation and refused to place French troops under Italian command; it was likely, Foch pointedly told General Luigi Cadorna, that Italian troops would have to come under Franco-British command as a precondition of French assistance. Foch urged the Italian government to get rid of the well-connected Cadorna as quickly as possible.[28] Despite these intense disagreements, the morale effect of so senior an allied general devoting himself to the problem of rescuing Italy had a tonic effect, as of course, did the artillery and infantry Foch had brought with him. But Foch remained determined that the Italians should save themselves if they could. Most of the allied reinforcements remained uncommitted as the Italians, now under a new commander that Foch admired, Armando Diaz, stabilized their new front along the river Piave.

Although Foch argued that the Italian problem showed more than ever the need for a unified command, the politicians demurred. At a November meeting in Rapallo, they settled instead for the formation of a Supreme War Council (SWC) with civilians clearly in charge. France's new prime minister, the same Georges Clemenceau who ten years earlier had given Foch command of the ESG, understood clearly how he wanted the SWC to function. At one of its meetings, Foch began to answer a question from Lloyd George only to have Clemenceau publicly berate him with a terse, 'Be quiet. I am the representative of France.'[29] Clemenceau, the man who coined the phrase 'War is too important a business to be left to generals', warned Foch that the generals at the SWC should limit themselves to providing 'technical information' only. Elected officials, not generals, would make the critical decisions. By making his chief of staff, Weygand, French representative on the joint military staff that advised the SWC, Foch at least insured that that advice would be his own.

This clash was one in a long series of public disagreements between Foch and Clemenceau. Despite their differences, however, in late 1917 the two men had much in common. Both wanted to see the war through to the finish without compromise; both supported a firmer direction of the war than that shown by previous governments; and each man saw the other as an important ally. Foch saw Clemenceau as the most determined politician France had to offer, even if he was unscrupulous and did not share Foch's own conservative and Catholic values. For his part, Clemenceau remained worried about Foch's political ambitions (he need not have – Foch had none) but he admired Foch's energy, his drive, and his confidence that France would win the war. For the time being, each man badly needed the other.

\* \* \*

The initial success of the German offensive in March 1918 forced a reconsideration of Foch's plan for a unified command. The Germans appeared to be trying to force a wedge between the French and British armies, thereby threatening the vital communications junction at Amiens.[30] Doing so might force the British to move north to cover the Channel ports while the French moved south to cover Paris, thus creating dangerously exposed flanks. Only a unified command of the sort that Foch had been advocating could prevent such a catastrophe. The SWC formed at Rapallo was, as Foch feared, too slow and too deliberative to make the necessary decisions.

To their credit, Anglo-French political leaders recognized the SWC's weakness and agreed to meet at the town of Doullens on March 26 amid an environment of great panic and consternation. British forces were retreating along the front, French reinforcements were arriving only slowly, and Pétain and Haig were blaming each other for the unfolding disaster. The conferees could hear the sound of artillery fire as they met in the town's Hôtel de Ville. Pétain was despondent, talking of abandoning Paris and openly foreseeing the impending defeat in the field of the allied armies. Haig, one of his biographers asserted, was looking haggard, and appeared to be suffering from 'acute psychological strain'.[31] Foch, by contrast, was energetic and confident, gaining the trust of Clemenceau and even of Pétain. Foch spoke of joint and coalition strategy, winning over the British with promises of French reserves to help shore up British positions. He also had at hand the plan for a unified command and a general, multi-national reserve that he had been advocating for months. Consequently, he emerged from the meeting as 'the only plausible contender' for the position of overall commander, although at that particular meeting he only received authorization to coordinate Anglo-French operations in front of Amiens.[32]

Still, Foch saw clearly that he had met the hour of his destiny. He also appreciated the challenges in front of him. 'Well, you got what you wanted', Clemenceau told him by way of a backhanded congratulation. Foch shot back: 'A fine present…you give me a lost battle and tell me to win it.'[33] Foch knew that defeats would likely continue until he could get a firm grasp on the situation and read German intentions more clearly. He also knew that the Doullens agreement gave him few powers. Furthermore, he knew that he would have to push the independent-minded Americans, who had not had a representative at the Doullens meeting, to follow the general outline of the agreement. A follow-up agreement signed at Beauvais by representatives of the French, British, and American governments on 3 April solved some of these problems by giving Foch 'all the powers necessary for an effective implementation' of allied strategy, although Foch still had no direct influence on the operations and tactics of allied armies whose commanders retained a right of appeal to their governments against any decisions made by the generalissimo.

The next few months posed repeated challenges. The French government fled to Bordeaux in a panic (a move Foch found appalling), and German attacks continued to seize French territory. The Americans continued to assert their political independence even though they followed Foch's overall vision. Still, Foch grew more confident. He knew that the Germans were weakening, and he had begun to divine their overall plan, or rather the absence of such a plan. The German offensives of April, May, and June gained more territory, but they had moved in eccentric directions, meaning that they did not mutually support one another. As a result, Foch knew that they were far less threatening than they appeared. The Germans were, in fact, wasting men and material for tactical, not operational or strategic goals. When David Lloyd George asked him, 'who should I bet on, you or Ludendorff?' Foch replied: 'Me, because Ludendorff's task is much more difficult than mine. He has to beat me, and that he cannot manage. Later, when it is my turn to overthrow him, that's another matter.'[34] Or as Foch told his British liaison officer, Sir Charles Grant, 'I wonder if Ludendorff knows his craft'.[35]

Still, the repeated failures throughout the spring to stop the tide of German success led to calls in the French parliament and inside the army to replace Foch with Pétain. Unlike Foch, Pétain had a reputation as an excellent defensive general. Those on the inside (in both France and Britain) knew, however, that Pétain was far too pessimistic and undiplomatic for the job. Therefore, Clemenceau rose vigorously to Foch's defence in parliament in early July, speaking to a motion of confidence in Foch that passed by 377 votes to 110. Even Clemenceau's strongest political opponent, Aristide Briand, supported Foch.[36]

Foch soon repaid their confidence. His analysis of the situation in early July led him to the conclusion that the next German attack would not come in Flanders, as Haig feared, nor toward Paris, as Pétain feared. Foch concluded that the next German attack (their fifth major offensive of the year) would be toward the rail centre of Reims. When intelligence reports began to confirm that he was right, Foch moved quickly to mass a multi-national army on the western flank of the Marne salient between Soissons and Château-Thierry. He overruled Pétain's preference for a defensive posture and ordered the Tenth Army, commanded by the aggressive Charles Mangin, to cave in the salient once the German offensive had been contained.[37]

The resulting allied triumph in the Second Battle of the Marne, from 14 to 18 July, changed the war almost overnight. Foch had turned the strategic momentum of the war; the allied armies never again fought on the strategic defensive. The way was now clear for Foch to change allied strategy, which he did on 24 July at a meeting of the senior allied commanders. He presented a memorandum to Haig, Pétain, and American commander-in-chief John Pershing that envisioned the battle just concluded as a decisive victory and a turning point in the war. It stated:

> The [allied] armies have arrived at the turning-point of the road. They have recovered in full tide of battle the initiative of operations.... The moment has come to abandon the general defensive attitude forced upon us until now by numerical inferiority and to pass to the offensive.[38]

Foch then surprised his colleagues by announcing that if they acted swiftly they could win the war in 1918. He presented his plan to assume a general offensive despite the fatigue in the allied armies. Successive allied offensives would target key railway lines such as the one linking Nancy to Paris as well as coal and iron mines. The key concept to the plan was to maintain pressure all along the line, simultaneously griding down their forces by a process of cumulative attrition.[39] With the Germans reeling and the Americans arriving in increasing force, the allies had their boots on Germany's throat; Foch was not going to let them get away.

Thereafter, Foch oversaw the series of concerted offensives, starting with the Battle of Amiens on 8 August, that he dubbed the *bataille générale*. He had three overriding principles to guide him. First, allied armies would keep up the pressure all along the line to ensure the operations in width that would keep the Germans off balance. Second, allied offensives would move concentrically in the direction of the main German lines of communications so that they would not repeat the mistake Ludendorff had made earlier in the year. Third, constant pressure would wear down German manpower, material and morale and sap the will to keep fighting. Foch pleaded, cajoled, and begged the allied national commanders to follow his vision, insisting, for example, that the Americans follow up their success at St. Mihiel in mid-September with an offensive into the very difficult terrain of the Meuse–Argonne rather than eccentrically toward Metz, which Pershing strongly favoured.[40] Doing so would support the massive French and British offensives aimed at the centre and north of the enemy's lines.

Foch's vision in late July came to its fruition when the Germans requested an end to hostilities in October. Foch had asked for a liaison officer from the French foreign ministry to help him shape the terms of an armistice, but the government refused. Clemenceau and his foreign minister, Stephen Pichon, envisioned the peace process as two-staged. In the first, military, phase, Foch would set the conditions for the Germans to stop fighting. Then the politicians would step in and shape borders, determine forms of government, and decide on reparations, all matters that they believed did not involve soldiers. Foch, for his part, disagreed, seeing peace as the logical conclusion of war. Nevertheless, he accepted the bifurcation of responsibilities in November, bringing only military officers with him to the armistice negotiations at Compiègne. Foch oversaw the armistice discussions of early November personally in a railway carriage in the famous clearing near Compiègne. He demanded harsh terms from the German delegation, hoping that he could prevent the Germans from resuming hostilities in spring 1919. He also assumed that the harshness of the armistice terms would lay a solid groundwork for Clemenceau and Lloyd George to settle matters with Germany in a final punitive peace treaty.

Clemenceau's determination to keep Foch away from the peace negotiations led Foch to the brink of insubordination. Clemenceau made it clear from the start that Foch's role at the Paris peace conference would be similar to the one he had played on the SWC (which continued in session to draft the allies' peace terms).[41] He would provide technical advice to the civilians but would have no independent strategic voice of his own. Foch was furious, especially amid signs that the Germans were refusing to admit their defeat and, perhaps more disturbingly, that the Americans and British had post-war goals that conflicted with what Foch saw as France's essential security needs.[42] He was also concerned that the leaders of Europe's democracies were not paying sufficient attention to the growing threat of Bolshevism.

Shut out from any formal means of communicating his concerns, Foch reacted by giving interviews to journalists decrying Clemenceau's sacrificing of

France's future. The prime minister, he alleged, was taking far too big a risk by putting his faith in the future willingness of America and Britain to stop a future resurgence of German aggression. Without the cornerstone of an alliance with Russia, Foch argued, France was in fact in a weaker position in 1919 than it had been five years earlier. Foch also began to meddle in politics in the Rhineland, where the French army had an occupation force. Foch encouraged the designs of Rhenish politicians who sought independence from Germany followed by a defensive alliance with France. Lloyd George was absolutely opposed to what he called 'an Alsace–Lorraine in reverse', and Clemenceau fumed at what he saw as Foch's insubordination, threatening to replace Foch with Pétain if such activities continued.[43]

Foch boycotted the signing ceremony for the Treaty of Versailles on 28 June 1919. He famously said of the treaty, 'This is not peace. It is an armistice for twenty years.'[44] He spent the last ten years of his life alternately being celebrated internationally as a great hero and criticizing the terrible security environment the Treaty of Versailles bequeathed to France and Europe. In interviews, memoirs, and public speeches, he lambasted the weakness of Clemenceau, accusing him of cowardice and of having sold out French security. He predicted that the Germans would rearm, form new alliances, and mechanize their army. He further predicted that neither the Treaty of Versailles nor the League of Nations would stop them.[45]

Many years ago, I bought a second-hand copy of Basil Liddell Hart's biography of Foch in a London bookshop. At the end of Liddell Hart's discussion of the Treaty of Versailles, the previous owner of the book had written in blue ink, 'Events have fully justified the judgment of Foch. He was right, and the statesmen wrong. If France controlled the Rhine Germany would not be the menace that it is to world peace today (1938).' While it is debatable that Foch's vision would have led to a long-lasting peace in Europe, this reflection suggests that Foch's political vision was indeed as sharp as his military vision. A century on, scholars still see him as one of the brightest and most perceptive strategists of his age.

Chapter 3

# Philippe Pétain: The Soldiers' General

## Jonathan Krause

Few men in history have been as beloved or as detested as Philippe Pétain; he was both the hero of Verdun and the villain of Vichy. Pétain rose to prominence during the First World War as one of the most beloved and trusted generals in the French army. Soldiers knew that he would look after their best interests and would do his utmost to preserve them from unnecessary, costly attacks. Pétain established this reputation early on in the war, and it would ultimately pave the way for him to become commander-in-chief of the French army following the infamous mutinies of 1917. His immediate efforts to address some of the concerns of the mutineers, as well as his open desire to 'wait for the Americans and the tanks' before resuming the offensive on a large scale were well received by the rank and file and helped bring the French army back from the brink of disorder and collapse. This caution (some would say timidity), however, was not always popular or appropriate. By 1918 Pétain would find his ideas and methodologies less valid than they had previously been. His rise to fame and influence would be overshadowed by the allied General-in-Chief, Ferdinand Foch, whose offensive mind-set would put him and Pétain in conflict as the war progressed through its final year.

\* \* \*

Henri Philippe Pétain was born on 24 April 1856 in the small village of Cauchy-à-la-Tour, near Béthune, in the Pas-de-Calais. Pétain's childhood was not an easy one. His mother died only eighteen months after he was born; his father remarried a little over a year later in 1859.[1] Pétain's stepmother apparently did not get along well with Philippe, and he spent most of his youth living with relatives. It is perhaps unsurprising that he claimed to have lost his Catholic faith in adolescence.

Pétain began his military career at the age of 20, entering St Cyr on 25 October 1876.[2] At enrolment Pétain was listed as ranking 403 out of 412; he would graduate ranked 229 out of 389, far from exceptional.[3] In many ways St Cyr was a formational experience for the future Marshal of France.

During his two years there Pétain would adopt many of the French officer's traditional prejudices including a suspicion of politicians and republicanism. These sentiments would remain with Pétain for the rest of his life. Pétain's first posting was as a *sous-lieutenant* (second lieutenant) to 24ᵉ BCP, elite French light infantry based at Villefranche-sur-Mer. Pétain came from the infantry, and his understanding of and affection for what the British call the 'poor bloody infantry' would have a profound impact on how he approached tactics before, during, and after the Great War. Above all else, Pétain prioritized limiting the casualties suffered by France's brave *poilus*.

Pétain would remain with 24ᵉ BCP for five years. From there he would go on to be a lieutenant in 3ᵉ BCP, from 1883 to 1888, when he left to attend the *École supérieure de guerre* (ESG). Pétain graduated fifty-sixth in his promotion, earning the middling mark of '*bien*'.[4] He was promoted captain, and joined the staff of XV CA based in Marseille. He did not remain there long, however, and bounced around for a couple of years, serving in various regular metropolitan infantry regiments in the Pas-de-Calais and Picardy.[5] In December 1893, he would be given command of a *chasseur* company in 29ᵉ BCP (based at Vincennes), and within a year-and-a-half would be given his first chance to make a name for himself in the French military establishment: in 1895 he was posted to the staff of General Félix Saussier, military governor of Paris, as ordnance officer.[6]

Pétain's time on Saussier's staff did not put him on the fast track. It is possible that this was owing to Pétain's already well-developed sarcasm, which did little to encourage the favourable treatment from superiors necessary for a successful military career. Nevertheless, Pétain continued his slow advancement through the ranks. In 1899, he left Saussier's staff, joining 8ᵉ BCP at Amiens; on 12 July 1900, he was promoted major.[7] Soon after, Pétain was transferred to the *École normale de tir* (Small-arms School) at Châlons.[8] This would be Pétain's first position as an instructor, a role in which he would excel for the rest of his pre-war military career. It was at this time that he began to take a serious interest in tactical doctrine, another field in which he would flourish during the coming war. Pétain took pains to ensure that his students learned to shoot as accurately as possible, and at range. Unfortunately, this time-intensive precision training was completely at odds with what the school's director, Colonel Vonderscherr, had in mind. Instead of Pétain's precision aiming Vonderscherr preferred training riflemen to fire *en masse* (practically in volleys), relying on weight of fire rather than accuracy to stop the well-ordered masses of German infantry that Vonderscherr expected these young riflemen would have to face one day.

Here in microcosm is a snapshot of the wider debate between the advocates of 'firepower' and 'shock' which engulfed the French army in the years before the war (although in reality it was a bit more nuanced than such a distinction allows). Military thinkers at the turn of the twentieth century all understood that advances in technology (quick-firing artillery, machine guns, smokeless powder, etc.) had greatly multiplied the weight of firepower European armies could deploy on the battlefield. The debate, then, was about how an army survives and functions in the face of such an overwhelming weight of fire? Some argued that combat needed to be resolved as quickly as possible, for the longer an infantryman was exposed to modern firepower, the more certain his demise. Thus, bold charges of massed infantry would be the answer. Casualties would still be heavy, but the enemy would be beaten as quickly as possible.

The firepower school felt that a better response was to 'double-down' on firepower; that only by achieving fire superiority over the enemy by concentrated rifle, machine-gun and artillery fire could any attack hope to cross the killing ground. Pétain was firmly in this camp, championing firepower and infantry dispersal.[9] Writing to a colleague in October 1904, he described a series of recent historical examples in which firepower proved dominant on the battlefield. After discussing the dominance of firepower in the South African War (1899–1902), where he argued that there existed an 800-metre killing ground that could not be crossed, Pétain analysed actions from the Russo-Japanese War, which at the time was still raging in Manchuria.[10] He reminded his colleague about the battle of Liao-yang (which had only been fought the month before, in September 1904) in which the Japanese attacked a line of Russian trenches in broad daylight only to be stopped by rifle fire from a distance of some 800 metres.[11] Pétain believed the only sensible way for modern armies to operate was to rely on firepower. The letter ended with typical Pétain scorn by suggesting his colleague re-examine Napoleon's campaigns in Italy from 1796–9. He recommended a few relevant works on the subject, adding at the end 'there is also someone named Clausewitz who has written on the 1796 campaign, the man was neither a fool, nor an idiot'.[12]

Such disdain rarely placed Pétain in people's good graces and, when combined with his entrenched disagreements with Vonderscherr, they led to him being transferred from Châlons rifle school after little more than six months.[13] Despite his personal problems with Vonderscherr, Pétain was noted for his skill as an instructor and would be appointed to the ESG to lecture on infantry tactics in October 1901, just eight months after having left Châlons.[14] That same year Pétain, aged 45, would propose to his lover, Eugénie. The marriage proposal was rejected by her parents on the grounds that Eugénie was only 21 years old (they would eventually marry after the war). Personal life aside, Pétain spent the majority of 1901 to 1914 as an instructor at the ESG (interspersed with intervals spent commanding various units in northeast France, as well as time at the *École de Saumur* – the French army's cavalry school – as professor of infantry tactics).[15] Eventually he would find himself chair, and then director, of the infantry tactics course at the ESG, thereby playing a vital role in educating many of the officers who would command in the Great War.

Nevertheless, this influence would not accelerate his peacetime career. Partly this was owing to his obstinate adherence to a firepower-centric conception of battle; partially it was owing to his growing contempt for many colleagues and superiors. This contempt is exemplified by his actions at the 1913 manoeuvres, the last ones before the First World War broke out – Pétain was then a colonel. After a briefing by his commanding officer, General La Gallet, Pétain addressed the assembled troops and simply said, 'I am certain that General La Gallet has intended, in order to strike your minds more forcibly, to present a synthesis of all the faults which a modern army should no longer commit'.[16] La Gallet's response to this public insult is not recorded. His sentiments, however, were almost certainly in line with those of General Adolphe Guillaumat, military secretary to the War Minister Adolphe Messimy, when he wrote just before the war, 'Pétain will never go beyond [commanding] a division.'[17] Pétain was ageing: he began the war a 58-year-old colonel, just two years from retirement. He would end the war a national hero and future Marshal of France.

\* \* \*

Despite not yet having the rank of brigadier, when the war broke out Pétain was commanding 4 BI at Saint Omer. The brigade joined General Charles Lanrezac's Fifth Army on the far left of the French line, whose bold advance would be compromised by the Germans wide sweeping attack through Belgium, the so-called 'Schlieffen Plan'.[18] Unaware of the scale of this manoeuvre, Fifth Army, supported on its left by the British Expeditionary Force (BEF), marched north from their initial deployment around Mézières towards Namur in Belgium, a march of over 100 kilometres. Fifth Army found itself detached from the rest of the army and isolated. Despite this isolation, and despite having advanced beyond the BEF (thus being completely unsupported), Fifth Army was ordered by commander-in-chief Joseph Joffre to advance yet further and attack the Germans to stall their advance.[19] The attack never happened. Fifth Army, which had moved into position on 19–20 August, was faced the next day with numerically superior German forces and was forced to withdraw on 23 August. After marching to an exposed position Fifth Army would have to fall back to France, hounded by advancing elements of the German army.[20] Pétain recorded some of the events of Fifth Army's 'retreat from Charleroi'. He sorrowfully commented on the great fatigue of the men, who frequently could go no further and collapsed. He noted that 'groups of men begin not getting up after halts, and one is obliged to strike them to make them get up'; this was after marching forty kilometres in the space of a mere twelve hours.[21]

It was during these early, manic days that Pétain began his rise to power. On 28 August he learned that he had been promoted to brigadier, to which news he responded, 'I have just learnt of my promotion to general. It even seems that they want to put me in command of a division. Are they already reduced to using such revolutionary measures?'[22] Pétain would be put in charge of 6 *division d'infanterie* (DI), replacing General Georges Bloch who was one of the many French senior commanders sacked for incompetence by Joffre. Pétain was made commander of 6 DI on 1 September 1914: five days later it would take part in the Battle of the Marne, fighting its way across the Morin rivers as Fifth Army turned on its pursuers. The division would then find itself engaged in early trench battle son the Aisne front.

Having halted the German advance at the Marne, and eventually exhausting any chance to launch a flanking attack after the race to the sea, the French army had no choice but to rest, resupply and reconstitute shattered units; this meant digging trenches to secure static positions. While Pétain had made rapid progress during the opening war of movement, it was in the trench war that he would truly excel. By the time the front line began to settle Pétain was already commanding the recently created XXXIII *corps d'armee* (CA) having been promoted on 23 October.[23] It was an excellent post. The two organic divisions of the corps (70 and 77 DIs) consisted of well-led, elite infantry, including hardened alpine troops and several battalions of *chasseurs*. The corps would be practically a training ground for the command elite in the first phase of the war. Its first commander (Victor d'Urbal) would go on to command Tenth Army, its second and third commanders (Pétain and Marie-Émile Fayolle) would both become Marshals of France.[24]

As part of General Louis Maud'huy's Tenth Army, Pétain's XXXIII CA would take part in the French army's first offensive trench battle in December 1914, the First Battle of Artois. Three battles would be fought in the region over the next twelve months, all of which aimed at capturing the high ground which dominates the region: Vimy ridge and its Notre-Dame-de-Lorette spur. The first battle (16–18 December) was simply a failure. Tenth Army did not have anywhere near the artillery firepower it needed to attack even rudimentary trench defences. Nevertheless, Pétain's contribution still stood out for his innovation of allowing heavy artillery, which was normally controlled by army corps command, to be attached directly to his divisions.[25] This greatly improved the effectiveness of his divisions, as they could quickly plan and revise artillery firing plans, without the bureaucratic inertia of having to obtain approval at corps level. Before the war Pétain had advocated such decentralization; once the war began it would prove an essential component in crafting effective fighting methods.

Tenth Army's second offensive in the Artois region (9 May–18 June) would initially prove far more successful, and was to be a crucial battle in Pétain's career. The battle would be supported with an unprecedented quantity of materiel, 782 field guns and 293 heavy artillery pieces; just fifteen fewer heavy guns than the entire French field army had deployed in August 1914.[26] Pétain's XXXIII CA, chosen to make the main assault on Vimy ridge, was reinforced with the elite Moroccan Division (a formation composed primarily of white colonial troops – as opposed to indigenous Moroccans – and Foreign Legion units of Czechs, Poles, Greeks and Russians). It was allocated additional modern artillery pieces to support the attack, giving the corps significant advantages compared with neighbouring formations. In addition to this material advantage, the corps was gifted with a talented and involved commander. Pétain was meticulous in his oversight of XXXIII CA's preparations, so much so that Basil Liddell Hart would later suggest that Pétain had personally registered every battery himself.[27]

The efforts of a professional and competent commander in charge of highly motivated, elite troops paid off on the opening day of the battle. On 9 May 1915, the Moroccans and the 77 DI advanced four-and-a-half kilometres in an hour-and-a-half, an astonishing advance through fixed trench defences. The divisions would storm Vimy ridge, with advanced units occupying Givenchy-en-Gohelle behind the northern shoulder of the ridge. The advance was so stunning that Michel Goya would later comment that the Moroccans 'gave the impression of marching in open ground'.[28] Unfortunately, the penetration would prove untenable, in large part owing to the failure of neighbouring army corps to advance as quickly as XXXIII CA (Pétain's corps advanced over an open plain, while the neighbouring corps – XXI and XX CAs, also elite formations – had to advance through well-fortified villages or across the heavily defended crest of Notre-Dame-de-Lorette). The Moroccan Division and 77 DI would find themselves isolated, taking fire from both flanks and the rear, and would eventually have to surrender their foothold atop Vimy ridge.[29] Despite repeated assaults on 11 May and from 16–18 June, XXXIII CA would be unable to hold Vimy ridge, which would remain in German hands until 1917 when it was finally conquered by the Canadians.

Pétain's performance and innovation in the first two Artois battles would not go unnoticed. He would be promoted immediately after Second Artois, being given command of Second Army on 21 June 1915.[30] Pétain spent the months between the end of Second Artois on 18 June and the start of the French army's next major offensive in September producing doctrinal works and taking part in the wider debates about the operational methodology of the French army. In essence, Pétain had begun in 1915 to envision the sort of defensive system he would later as commander-in-chief try to force on a French army demoralized and in mutiny. Pétain's influence and attention was not solely felt in the realm of tactics after he took over Second Army; he was also involved in high-level debates about future operations. In late June, not yet two weeks after Second Artois had ended, Joffre summoned Ferdinand Foch, Édouard de Castelnau, and Pétain to discuss how the French army should progress. Despite being the most junior of the group (de Castelnau and Foch had both just been made army group commanders) Pétain put forth his opinions with confidence and conviction. He argued, along with Foch, for a more methodical approach to battle, where the French could capitalize on the initial successes of an attack by launching smaller, discrete offensives. After two or three days the 'battle' would end and a different formation somewhere else along the line would attack.[31] This concept of lateral exploitation, one shared by Foch and Pétain, would eventually prove central to the operational model which the allies used during the final victorious Hundred Days offensive.

Joffre disagreed with Foch and Pétain's cautious approach and was seduced by de Castelnau's argument that Pétain's early successes in Artois proved the French were now tactically superior to the Germans and should press their advantage home. Consequently, a 'breakthrough' battle would be launched by de Castelnau's *Groupe d'armées du centre* (GAC), of which Pétain's Second Army was a part, while Foch's *Groupe d'armées du nord* (GAN) launched an ostensibly diversionary attack in Artois. This would allow Foch to pursue his cautious approach, while giving de Castelnau the opportunity to attempt a breakthrough in the Champagne which, by endangering the German's left-flank communications, might force the Germans to cede large tracts of occupied territory.

Once again, Pétain would command the main strike formation. As before, Pétain's new command would be provided with ample supplies and elite formations, including XX CA and the Moroccan Division. Pétain would not only be responsible for the actions of Second Army but, as adjunct to de Castelnau, would also play a role in crafting the GAC's operational plan for the coming battle.[32] While Pétain's orders for the offensive of 25 September (which would be called the Second Battle of Champagne) are clear and reasonably detailed, they are still orders coming from such a high level that they were much more general than operational orders issued by Pétain when he was head of XXXIII CA. His orders also needed to fit into the ambitious strategic framework laid out by Joffre and de Castelnau, which meant planning a 'breakthrough' battle rather than a more limited, methodical battle, which Pétain would have preferred.

As 25 September approached the French had ample reason to feel confident. They had secured the willing assistance of their British allies, which meant that the Germans would suffer three attacks on the same day on the Western

Front: GAC's attack in Champagne, GAN's in Artois, and a British attack immediately north of the GAN's centred on Loos. GAC's Fourth and Second Armies were supplied with 2,164 artillery pieces, 728 of which were heavy guns, an enormous commitment.[33] More importantly, the French believed that they had found the tactical antidote to the Western Front's trench stalemate, evidenced by Pétain's success in Artois.[34] The results of the battle, however, would fall far short of expectations. Despite the relative success of Second Army, which made an advance of some four kilometres, Fourth Army struggled to advance, as did Tenth Army in Artois. The great September battles would not break the enemy's front, nor would they compel the Germans to retire from the salient they had occupied since 1914, with its apex pointing menacingly at Paris.

After Second Champagne wound down in October, Pétain's Second Army was allowed to pass into general reserve to rest and refit. In theory, Second Army was preparing to launch yet another allied attack, this time across the Somme river, in the spring. As things turned out, however, Pétain would never get the chance to tactically coordinate an offensive operation again.

\* \* \*

For ten months, from 21 February until December 1916, the French and Germans would grapple in an attritional struggle astride the Meuse river in front of the fortress city of Verdun – the longest battle of the First World War. The fortress system at Verdun, under the command of General Frédéric-Georges Herr, suffered a series of devastating attacks by the Germans in late February. The attacks were light in manpower, thus reducing the Germans' exposure to casualties, but enormously heavy in firepower – some one million projectiles including asphyxiating and lachrymatory gas shells were fired. Entire French units were simply wiped out by the initial German bombardment.[35] Despite heroic stands made by isolated pockets of *chasseurs* who held the forward French defence lines, the Germans advanced inexorably, threatening to clear the east bank of the Meuse of French defenders. Losing the right bank would likely mean losing Verdun, as well as significant quantities of guns and materiel which would be overrun as the Germans rapidly advanced. French attempts to stem the tide just resulted in more casualties, and morale began to drop precipitously; some units were keeping machine-gun companies in their rear as insurance against 'those that might forget their duty' to stand and fight.[36] Against this desperate background, Pétain would oversee one of France's most important military victories.

At the time of Verdun Pétain's Second Army was in reserve, resting and refitting after the arduous Champagne offensive. It meant he would be called upon to take over the defence of Verdun and go almost overnight from being just another army commander to becoming a national hero. Sometimes a general gets lucky: Pétain was the immediately available army commander at a moment of crisis, although he was not instantaneously obtainable. When Joffre's order to come to GQG in preparation for Second Army's transfer to the Verdun sector reached Pétain's headquarters at Noailles after 22.00 on 24 February, he was nowhere to be found. Amid panic Pétain's aide-de-camp, Serrigny, ordered a car and drove at breakneck speed to Paris in search of his commanding officer, arriving at a certain Hôtel Terminus near the Gare du Nord around 03.00.[37] After squabbling with the hotel manager (who swore that Pétain was not there) Serrigny was finally shown up to a room outside of which he found Pétain's boots and a pair of woman's slippers (the slippers belonged to Pétain's long-time lover and future wife, Eugénie). Pétain answered Serrigny's knock on the door wearing 'the scantiest of costumes'.[38] Serrigny related the information passed on to him and Pétain convinced him to get a room in the hotel so the two of them could depart together the next morning. After this brief meeting Pétain returned to the dark room from which Serringy heard the sounds of a woman sobbing (presumably worried that she might be disgraced for the compromising situation she had found herself in). In his book on Verdun Pétain would claim that he had expected to be called away to Verdun on the 24th; the circumstances surrounding his being located somewhat undermine this statement.[39]

Pétain and Serrigny made it to GQG by 08.00, met with Joffre, and then proceeded on to the Verdun sector. Pétain officially took command at midnight on 26 February under difficult conditions: the first news Pétain heard upon arrival was of the loss of Fort Douaumont to a handful of German troops who had taken the fort by surprise; not a single man on either side was killed in the bloodless assault.[40] Pétain came at just the right moment and his galvanizing presence had an immediate impact on morale, despite the loss of Douaumont (the facts of which were withheld from the public, who were instead told of a valiant defence which had mown down waves of Germans before finally being overrun). Pétain inspired in the men a sense that they were finally to be properly led; on the first night he had reorganized the command structure of the region, planned a new defensive line and took the artillery firmly in hand to improve their accuracy and efficacy.

In the coming days Pétain would tackle the Verdun sector's greatest weakness: its logistics. Owing to the salient which had formed around Verdun there was only one axis along which goods and reinforcements could travel. Along this axis one railway (*Le Meusien*) and a road came up from Bar-le-Duc to the south. As the railway could only transport some 800 tonnes of materiel a day the road would have to be the main artery along which troops and supplies were fed into the 'Meuse mill'; this road would be transformed under Pétain into the famous *Voie sacrée*, the 'Sacred Way'.[41] The operation of the *Voie sacrée* would be an important step toward the eventual mechanization of logistics which characterizes modern armies. Only automobiles would be allowed to pass along it; troops on foot had to march on either side of the road. Over 4,000 automobiles (lorries and ambulances) would make a total of over 6,000 journeys up the *Voie sacrée* each day, traversing roughly a million miles each week transporting 90,000 men and 50,000 tonnes of supplies; at the height of the battle a lorry passed along the road every 14 seconds.[42] The equivalent of a division's worth of men was dedicated to keeping the road functioning to avoid even momentary delay.[43] So essential was keeping the road open that broken down lorries would simply be shoved off the road to make way for those still working.

Crucial as the *Voie sacrée* was to maintaining a supply of men and materiel in the sector, it was still only part of the logistics effort. Pétain also had to concern himself with the fighting capacity of his men. Respecting the concentrated firepower the Germans had amassed in the Verdun sector, Pétain instituted a reinforcement system called 'Noria': rotating divisions of infantry into and out of the line based roughly on the principle of the water wheel. In Pétain's system divisions of infantry would only be in the front line for a few days (three, perhaps four), before being sent back to rest and refit far behind the lines.[44] Any division which suffered heavy casualties in an attack was immediately relieved, whether it had been in the line for the requisite number of days or not. The system worked exceptionally well in the Verdun sector where even a short stay in trenches utterly drained units' effectives and soldiers' morale.

While 'Noria' underpinned an effective, sustained defence at Verdun, it was a difficult system for the French army to sustain, and it caused enormous friction between Pétain and Joffre. At Chantilly in December 1915, the French and British had agreed to undertake a joint offensive at some point in 1916. This was later arranged to be mounted astride the Somme river. The planned French component of the battle was to be enormous: forty divisions (to the British twenty-five) with more artillery than any army had yet amassed along a single line of battle.[45] As the battle of Verdun progressed, however, the 'Meuse mill' (as the battle was known) began to rapidly chew up the carefully husbanded reserve divisions which would make up the French component of the Somme battle. Pétain made increasingly desperate requests for more men and materiel in May and June; at the same time, he simultaneously urged Joffre to hurry up opening the Somme offensive, despite his doubts that that attack would improve the situation at Verdun.[46]

Joffre did not want to endanger the Verdun sector, but was aghast at the shrinking number of units he had available for the upcoming Somme offensive (in the end the French would have fewer divisions on the Somme in July than the British, although they would come to play an equal role by the battle's end in November).[47] In an attempt to bridge the gap Joffre consented to Pétain's requests for additional men, but capped the number of divisions Pétain was allowed to have at any one time at twenty-six.[48] At the same time Joffre urged Pétain to be more aggressive and to seize the initiative back from the Germans. This was easier said than done. The Germans continued to make gains despite Pétain's efforts to strengthen the sector. On 4 March they captured Douaumont village (which the fort had been named after), taking prisoner a certain Captain Charles de Gaulle in the process.[49] Later that month they expanded the offensive to attack the western heights of the Meuse defences. A month later, still dissatisfied with Pétain's defensive battle, Joffre went to visit Verdun. While there he met General Robert Nivelle, commanding III CA in Second Army, and was struck by his offensiveness.[50] Following their meeting Joffre would urge Pétain to give Nivelle anything he needed to continue counterattacking the Germans. While Pétain tended to be generous with Nivelle, he still saw the battle as fundamentally defensive in nature, and preferred discrete, limited counter attacks to Nivelle's bold and costly rushes. Pétain's caution, and his incessant demands for fresh troops, convinced Joffre to restructure the command arrangements at Verdun. On 19 April, just nine days after he first met Nivelle, Joffre promoted Pétain to command GAC, giving Second Army to Nivelle.[51] This was meant to give Nivelle more independence in launching offensives in the Verdun sector, although in practice Pétain managed to retain a large degree of control over the battle through frequent visits to Nivelle's headquarters.

Under Pétain's leadership the French had weathered the immediate storm at Verdun, although the battle would grind on thereafter in the style of the offensives of the early years of the war. Within a month of the opening of the Somme offensive in July the Germans began to noticeably reduce their presence in the Verdun salient, paving the way for Nivelle's late autumn counter attacks which would eventually recapture Fort Douaumont and much of the ground on the eastern bank of the Meuse lost between February and June.[52] Nivelle's success, built on the back of Pétain's defence of the salient and the Franco-British effort on the Somme, would pave the way for his taking Joffre's place when he was 'promoted' out of being commander-in-chief in December 1916.[53] Nivelle's over-promotion would place the French army on a path towards mutiny, and eventually lead to Pétain taking up command of the French armies in their darkest hour.

\* \* \*

Robert Nivelle found himself commander-in-chief of the French army on the back of a simple message: 'we have the method'. His counter attacks in the Verdun sector, despite being no-more successful than their analogues on the Somme, garnered him significant support because they recaptured the symbolic prizes, forts Douaumont and Vaux. To justify this support, Nivelle had little choice but to launch a major offensive in which his 'proven method' would deliver a crushing defeat of German forces; he declared that 'victory is certain'.[54] If victory could not be achieved in 48 hours, Nivelle promised that the attack would be called off. Nivelle's initial plan was disrupted by the enemy's tactical withdrawal to the Hindenburg Line in March. Details of his revised plan for an attack along the Chemin des Dames leaked to the enemy and the German forces in the area received substantial reinforcements.[55] Despite the clear German foreknowledge of the attack, Nivelle chose to press on. This was against the better judgment of his subordinate commanders, including Pétain, who had recommended to the incoming war minister, Paul Painlevé, that the offensive be stopped.[56]

On 16 April 1917 the Nivelle Offensive began. Instead of destroying the German forces in the open field within 48 hours, the French Fifth and Sixth armies met with mixed results. The high hopes Nivelle had raised among politicians and military leaders in France and Britain had been dashed as the offensive quickly degenerated into another attritional affair. While the Nivelle Offensive had lasted only nine days, the casualties suffered were enormous: 134,000 killed, wounded or missing.[57] April 1917 had cost the French more casualties than any month since November 1914. The impact was hardest felt among the long-suffering *poilus*. It had exposed the illusory goal Nivelle had raised before them: the war would not be won in a single battle. Their frustration would be acted out in one of the largest displays of indiscipline a modern army has ever faced.

As with most instances of mass unrest and indiscipline (civil or military) the causes of the French mutinies were legion. The French rank-and-file had consistently received poor treatment. Their food was poor (hot food was practically non-existent at the front, fresh vegetables were exceedingly rare), rear areas were in a shambles and men were regularly compelled to sleep outdoors during their 'rest'.[58] Leave was infrequent. Combined with the dissatisfaction French soldiers felt with their leadership (that casualties were heavier than necessary) these grievances led to what Denis Rolland has called *'la grève des tranchées'* – the 'trench strike'. 'Mutiny' was never the best word to describe the collective indiscipline that shook the French army in 1917. Very few soldiers were refusing outright to fight on, despite the efforts of pacifists and internationalists to push the soldiery into anti-war actions. Although soldiers could be heard singing *L'Internationale*, it seems more likely that these were simple expressions of discontent expressed in traditional socialist forms, rather than of an intention to desert or rebel.[59] Instead, the 'mutinies' were really a worker's strike, in the great French tradition; soldiers were protesting for better treatment and better leadership.

The exact start date for the French mutinies is impossible to pinpoint. Acts of indiscipline were reported as early as 16 April, but such acts are not uncommon before the launching of a major attack as some soldiers may decide that certain acts of indiscipline might save their lives. Guy Pedroncini cites the disobedience of 20$^e$ RI at Mourmelon-le-Grand in the Champagne sector on 29 April.[60] From there the mutinies would spread to eventually include at least 21,575 mutineers from 121 different regiments, sapping the fighting power of the French army.[61]

It was at this moment that Pétain would rise to be commander-in-chief of the French army. On 29 April, in the wake of the failure of the Nivelle Offensive and calls for his removal, Pétain was promoted from GAC commander to be army chief of staff in Paris, a well-crafted move by Painlevé to gently restrict Nivelle's power without removing him, which might have crushed the already enfeebled morale of the French army. This half-measure proved to be insufficient, however, and Pétain officially replaced Nivelle on 17 May 1917, becoming commander of the French armies in the north and north-east (Pétain would be made commander-in-chief of all French armies, including overseas expeditionary forces, on 17 June).

True to his reputation as a soldiers' general, Pétain focussed on addressing the many legitimate grievances which the *poilus* were raising. He immediately set about improving the soldiers' rations: access to fresh vegetables, better-quality meat and increased regularity of hot food in the trenches, delivered by camouflaged mobile field kitchens.[62] Leave was better organized, with soldiers being guaranteed seven days of home leave every four months, and units were given more time to rest behind the line. Pétain aimed to have 25–50 per cent of all formations resting at any one time: in effect he scaled up Verdun's 'Noria' system and applied it to the whole army.[63] Rear areas were also improved, which meant a vast building programme was begun behind the lines. Of course, all of this would take considerable time before it made a real difference to the lives of disgruntled *poilus*. Longer-term changes would solve the problem, but short-term measures were needed to bring the French army back to fighting readiness.

On 19 May Pétain ordered the cessation of all French attacks, and said that any further attacks would only aim for limited objectives.[64] It was hoped that this would help blunt the mutineers' dissatisfaction and pave the way for the beginning of a reconciliation between commanders and commanded; in practice Pétain's order was not communicated below corps command and had little immediate impact on the situation.[65] Even had Pétain's order been better communicated it would not have been enough to stem the growing indiscipline, which needed to be dealt with swiftly and sternly. In practice, this meant repression. Pétain, looking back on the height of the crisis, said that 'I went further in the repression of serious incidents, I firmly maintained this repression, but did so without forgetting that it was being applied to soldiers who had been with us for three years, and who were "our soldiers"'.[66]

The most feared and resonating aspect of this repression, of course, was the use of capital punishment. Over the course of 1917, 629 soldiers were sentenced to death, including three sergeants and 30 corporals; 428 of these sentences were handed down under Pétain.[67] Not only were more soldiers sentenced to die under Pétain, but they (and all other offenders) were sentenced far more quickly than under Nivelle; Pétain understood that punishment needed to be rapid if it was going to be effective. Of course, receiving a death sentence only rarely resulted in the execution of the soldier in question (this was true in the British and other armies as well). The reasons for this are not surprising. Killing one's own soldiers is not only incredibly difficult, morally, but it does little to further one's war effort. While a small number of soldiers were shot by NCOs without appealing to higher authorities at various points in the war 'as an example' (*pour encourager les autres* to cite Voltaire's famous comment on the execution of British Admiral Byng), few were deliberately executed by the command structure. Of the 428 sentenced to death under Pétain only 75 went through the entire legal process right up to confirmation of sentence by GQG and execution by firing squad.[68]

While quelling the mutinies was undoubtedly Pétain's top priority upon becoming commander-in-chief, he also felt the strong need to reform how the French army operated in the field. Tactical efficacy preoccupied Pétain since he had lectured at the ESG; he had rigorously studied and modified tactical doctrine throughout the war.[69] Upon taking command of the French army tactical precision became even more important for Pétain than previously. Not only was he finally in a position to, in theory, compel the whole army to be as careful and methodical as he had always been, but doing so would be essential to stop the French army collapsing in the face of mutiny. With this in mind Pétain issued a series of tactical–operational directives, which were intended to inculcate appropriate tactical and operational principles through the late-war French army based on the experience and lessons of 1915 and 1916.

On 23 May 1917 the first of these tactical directives (actually 'Directive no. 2') was issued, reorganizing the French system of learning and intelligence.[70] Retraining was to become integrated into the rotation cycle of units into and out of the front line, to ensure that soldiers were kept up to date on the latest tactical developments. As a part of this effort Pétain ordered the creation of the *Section d'instruction* (Instruction Section). The *Section d'instruction* would be staffed with experienced combat officers and technical experts (especially regarding tanks and aeroplanes) whose job would be to constantly revise French small-unit doctrine.[71] Members of the *Section* made regular visits to the front lines and to training grounds to not only learn about the most recent tactical developments, but also to ensure that these developments were being taught throughout the army. The *Section* studied French, German and British battles for evidence of tactical developments, and even liaised with the British army directly to share tactical ideas in a formalized way, which the two armies had not previously done.[72] Ultimately, it was the efforts of the officers in the *Section d'instruction* that made Pétain's more rigorous training and education programmes effective. To deal with larger units Pétain created the *Commission de refonte*, which operated similarly to the *Section d'instruction*. The Commission's first report on high-level tactics would be the framework for the successful battles of late summer and autumn 1917.[73]

The combination of Pétain's repressive measures and improvements in the living conditions of *poilus* with appropriate tactical doctrine eventually got the French army back up on its feet. This was strikingly evidenced on 23 October in the Battle of Malmaison, a short, powerful but limited offensive such as Pétain had promised back in May which retook the long-contested Chemin des Dames sector. Even though casualties were still heavy, the attack captured its objectives and was then halted, making the losses acceptable to French soldiers and hardening their resolve to carry on. As important as was Pétain's success in quelling the mutinies and restoring the French army to a high fighting standard, his other achievements should not be overlooked, especially his role in reshaping French doctrine and in leading the French army to ultimate victory.

Important though these efforts were, they did not always produce the desired results. Pétain's fourth directive, issued in December 1917, was Pétain's attempt to give the French army a coherent model for instituting defence in depth.[74] Since Pétain hoped that the French army would remain on the defensive for much of 1918 and wait for the Americans and the arrival of large numbers of tanks to carry the brunt of the fighting it was necessary for the French to have a working defensive doctrine, modelled loosely after that of the German army.[75] Sound though Pétain's principles were, they proved difficult to implement in a war-weary army. Pétain lamented that 'the length of the war tends to develop 'incuriosity' and laziness [in the troops].... Lessons learned in operations do not spread to units that did not take part in [the operation].'[76] While Pétain's efforts to listen more to frontline troops helped, they failed to convince everyone that his defensive plans were any better than what they had thus far been relying on. This failure to comprehensively impose his new doctrine would have unfortunate consequences when battle was joined in 1918.

In 1918 Pétain's plan was largely conservative, necessitated by the collapse of Russia at the end of 1917. He hoped to continue his 1917 strategy, delaying major attacks until significant numbers of American troops and tanks were available. He understood that the allies were financially, numerically and industrially stronger than Germany; in a war of attrition the allies were bound to win. Once the allies had grown sufficiently strong Pétain hoped to launch an attack into Upper Alsace, a region into which the French had not yet attacked.[77]

On 21 March 1918 the allies' quiet repose was irrevocably shattered when Erich Ludendorff, chief strategist of the German army, launched the first operation in his final desperate attempt to win the war before the arrival of millions of fresh American soldiers made victory impossible. 'Operation Michael', the largest western front offensive since 1914, attacked weakened British positions in an attempt to split the British and French armies. Ludendorff believed that if Germany could force the British into the sea (and thus to the negotiating table), France would quickly follow suit. His assessment of Anglo-French relations was not far off the mark. Despite public expressions of solidarity and cooperation, as well as warm personal feelings for one another, Haig and Pétain found coordinating their response difficult. In the months before Operation Michael General Ferdinand Foch (essentially acting as allied operational coordinator before he had been given that formal responsibility) had tried to coordinate a General Allied Reserve, to be used in case of emergency. Haig flatly refused to release divisions for the reserve as did Pétain, relying instead on a mutual agreement to send each other reinforcements in time of crisis.[78] Both also stymied early efforts to unite the allies' military forces under a single commander, undoubtedly because neither of them had any realistic chance of assuming the post. Haig's army had always been the junior partner in the alliance, and Pétain's well-known pessimism and Anglophobia made him an unlikely candidate.[79]

Haig and Pétain's failure to operate in a truly combined manner would allow Ludendorff a far better chance of success than he would otherwise have had. Even though Pétain would order French troops north after 21 March to support the British – in much larger numbers than initially agreed with Haig – he at the same time issued orders for his reserve armies (under General Marie-Émile Fayolle) to fall back on Paris if the situation worsened.[80] Pétain blamed the British for the desperate situation, in which the two armies were very nearly separated, and openly expressed his belief to politicians that the British would be beaten, and France's defeat would soon follow.[81]

Douglas Haig's account, which has become standard, despite being self-serving and inaccurate, goes as follows.[82] At a meeting of allied generals Pétain openly admitted to his willingness to let the British and French armies be separated, if need be. Haig was furious and immediately after the meeting wired to Henry Wilson, then Chief of the Imperial General Staff, asking him to go promptly to France, 'in order to arrange that General Foch or some other determined General who would fight, would be given supreme control of the operations in France.'[83] Wilson did as Haig requested and after being nominated to coordinate British and French operations in front of Amiens on 26 March, on 3 April 1918 Foch was named General in Chief of the allied armies on the western front. While Haig did in fact support Foch to become General in Chief, Pétain was actually much more proactive in sending French troops to support the British than Haig would later claim. Pétain had readied divisions to be sent north immediately, before Haig even asked for them.[84]

Foch's appointment put Pétain in an awkward position. He was still the commander of the French army, but was de facto subordinate to Foch, a man with whom he had not always agreed. In some ways Pétain was worse off than his peers – Haig and General John Pershing who commanded the American Expeditionary Forces now arriving in numbers on the western front – insofar as he, being French, was not allowed to appeal Foch's decisions, whereas they, as leaders of their nation's armed forces, were. For the most part Pétain followed Foch's lead out of a desire to not cause trouble more than anything else. If he had any serious desire to assert his independence it was undermined when, in the third phase of Ludendorff's offensive, Operation Blücher (27 May–5 June), German forces overwhelmed French defences on the recently liberated Chemin des Dames sector. When in late June he tried to appeal against Foch's instructions he was placed formally under Foch's command by premier Georges Clemenceau.[85]

July 1918 would be a fateful month for the allies. The German offensives had raged for four months, pushing the allies back over hard-won ground, especially in the Somme region. French armies were back on the river Marne, where they had last fought in 1914. The effect on allied morale was understandably grave. Haig remained anxious that the Germans would make a concerted attempt to drive his army back to the ports on the English Channel, exposing Britain to German attacks, economic and otherwise: Ludendorff had planned on doing just that in Operation Georgette (9–29 April), the second phase of his offensive, but French reinforcements had helped check that thrust south of the Ypres salient. Pétain was certain that the Germans would strike again towards Paris, more vulnerable than the capital had been since 1914. Foch, however, saw things differently. He thought the Germans would first attack in and around Reims in an attempt to free up their congested logistical network by capturing a major railway junction. Foch planned to absorb the force of the German attack, minimizing French casualties by essentially evacuating the battlefield before the German thrust, and then to counterattack the right flank of the extended German salient on the Marne, thereby inflicting a serious defeat on Ludendorff's armies and regaining the initiative for the allies. It was a daring plan, and one that required nerve. It nearly failed.

On 15 July, the day after Bastille Day, the German attack opened either side of Reims, where Foch had anticipated it. French losses, even on a thinned-out battlefield, mounted. Fearing the collapse of the French line near Reims, Pétain ordered General Charles Mangin, commanding the Tenth Army which would lead Foch's bold counter-stroke, to halt all preparations for the counter attack and to send troops to reinforce the battered forces around Reims.[86] By sheer chance Foch found himself in a position to countermand the order personally within a few hours of it being issued.[87] Tenth Army's attack went in on 18 July, the Germans were driven from the Marne salient with heavy losses, and Foch was made a Marshal of France as a consequence. From this moment on the allies would hold the initiative, thereafter pushing the Germans back inexorably until the armistice. Pétain would direct France's forces to that victory, although his own role was somewhat circumscribed by the extant command arrangements. Fayolle noted the state of affairs in summer 1918 succinctly:

> Pétain came and spoke to me of his relations with Foch, tense for a while, once more harmonious. Essentially, if Pétain had been left to his own devices we would not have attacked. We owe it all to Foch. It is not that he organized this series of victories, but that he ordered us to fight. It is always the same: Foch says 'attack', Pétain provides the means to do so, drop by drop, and it is I who carries it out.[88]

Pétain certainly clashed often with Foch over the specific details of the counter offensive, if not its broad principles: generally, he was seen as being too pessimistic and reluctant to push too hard the army that he had nurtured through a difficult year. But, Fayolle continued, 'he did everything to give the impression that it was himself who conducted the battle.'[89]

\* \* \*

On armistice day, 11 November 1918, Pétain openly wept. The long slaughter, by which he had been repulsed and which would shape his views for the rest of his life, was finally over. Although made a Marshal of France immediately the war ended, for all his achievements, Pétain would not be crowned with all the glory he felt was his due, even though he lived as a celebrity after the war. Instead, Foch would tour the world and be feted (perhaps justifiably) as the man responsible for the allies' victory. Pétain refused, more than once, to openly ride beside him in the victory parades.

Pétain would, of course, rise to national prominence again in the next European conflagration, as head of the Vichy regime that collaborated with Nazi Germany from 1940 to 1943, and in so doing would win the everlasting ire of his people. It is not the place here to recount and analyse Pétain's second career which has been well treated by his biographers. But it should be noted that it was his leadership of veterans' organizations between the wars that gave him the popular conservative power base on which he could establish his political authority at another moment of national crisis. He ended that short-lived and shameful political experiment as a prisoner convicted of treason, although spared the death penalty owing to his advanced age and his earlier service to France.[90] Charles de Gaulle, who commuted the death sentence, had been one of Pétain's junior officers when he commanded 33ᵉ *régiment d'infanterie* immediately before the war and one of his military assistants between the wars. Ironically, Pétain had sentenced de Gaulle to death for the same offence when he had set up the Free French movement in London. Pétain died in prison on 23 July 1951, aged 95. It was a very sad ending for the career of one of the greatest commanders France has produced.

## Chapter 4

# Robert Nivelle: A Formula for Failure

## Paul Strong

* * *

Robert Nivelle remains one general who is still seen in the historiography of the First World War as a 'butcher and blunderer'. His promotion to supreme command in December 1917 and the intrigue that followed is often portrayed as the result of a power struggle between both allied military headquarters and their political masters, and the failure in April 1917 of the offensive on the Aisne that took his name is often cited as being the direct cause of the mutinies in the French army that followed. Nivelle himself is portrayed as a ruthless and arrogant adherent of the 'cult of the offensive' and a charming imposter who beguiled himself and others into thinking that his operational success at Verdun could be duplicated at the strategic level. While these assumptions are plausible and the strategic failure of the Nivelle Offensive itself is indisputable, the circumstances that contributed to this outcome are more complex than the conventional narrative assumes.

* * *

Robert Nivelle was born in Tulle, a small provincial city in the Corrèze *département* in central France, in 1856, into a military family. His grandfather had fought in Napoleon's campaigns and his father served both in the Crimea and against the Prussians in the Franco-Prussian war. Robert's English mother, Theodora Sparrow, was also from a military family. Nivelle was clearly inspired by stories of his grandfather's adventures and appears to have enjoyed his childhood visits to England.[1] Overall, Robert's education appears to have been excellent, initially qualifying him for either the *École polytechnique* or for St Cyr. Like other intellectually gifted senior wartime leaders, Nivelle opted to complete his education at the more prestigious *École polytechnique* and then, due to his interest in science, dedicated himself to earning a place in the *École d'application de l'artillerie* at Fontainebleau.

Nivelle was initially assigned to the 19$^e$ *régiment d'artillerie* but was soon assigned to take the prestigious horse-artillery course at the *École de cavalerie* in Saumur. Thereafter he served in 1$^e$ *régiment d'artillerie,* before, at the age of thirty-one, Captain Nivelle enrolled at the *École supérieure de guerre*. After graduating near the top of his promotion (but below future army commanders Paul Maistre and Alfred Micheler) he was assigned to a junior staff position in the French colonial garrison in Tunisia in 1889.[2] General Collet described Nivelle when he transferred to the 31ᵉ *régiment d'artillerie* in 1894 as 'a first-class officer who deserves to have an outstanding career'.[3] On a trip to Paris, Nivelle met and married divorcée Clarisse Yung. The young lady's social set was fiercely anti-Dreyfus and Nivelle's romantic instincts saw him tainted by association. As his commanding officer noted, 'Captain Nivelle has not been included in the promotion list for 1900. …Despite this painful disappointment, he has nevertheless continued to fulfil his duties to a high standard. [This officer] should be encouraged.'[4]

In the summer of 1900, Nivelle accepted an assignment to the staff of the French expeditionary force to China, commanded by General Émile Voyron, in which position he showed a talent for diplomacy.[5] On his return to France, Nivelle learned that his wife had died of a rare heart condition. The tragedy made a deep impression on Nivelle and a letter to a colleague suggests that he contemplated suicide.[6] Voyron was surprised when his application to award Nivelle the Légion d'honneur was refused. A disappointed Nivelle accepted a position as the inspector of coastal defences in Corsica. The island's governor was delighted, reporting that 'Nivelle is an officer of great distinction and who deserves greater success in his career than he has seen so far'.[7] Hurtling around Corsica in the first automobile ever seen on the island, re-building defences and conducting training manoeuvres, Nivelle regained his enthusiasm for life and in 1904 courted and married a local widow.

In 1908, Lieutenant-Colonel Nivelle was initially assigned to command the garrison artillery at Oran in Algeria before being made garrison chief of staff. Nivelle rapidly familiarized himself with both local tribes and the colonial units under his command and developed new tactics for getting the most out of the garrison's 75mm field guns. Nivelle's efficiency during the Agadir Crisis brought him new plaudits and his promotion to full colonel was finally approved. Once again, Nivelle had clearly thrived while in a relatively independent role but failed to establish himself in the network of veteran officers with colonial experience.

After a brief sojourn at Vincennes in early 1911, where he was investigating the potential use of aircraft for artillery observation, Nivelle returned to regimental command. Engaging in the tactical doctrinal debates that animated the army in the years before the war, Nivelle outlined his ideas on the coordination of the artillery in support of infantry operations in a short booklet.[8] This document is sometimes presented as evidence of his support for the idea of an *offensive à outrance*, but this narrow interpretation ignores Nivelle's deeper analysis of the tactical challenges of the coming war.

When mobilization came, Nivelle was in command of 5ᵉ *régiment d'artillerie* in VII *corps d'armée* (CA) assigned to the Mulhouse sector in Alsace. In the initial battles Nivelle handled his regiment's guns with consummate skill and showed that the artillery could play a decisive role even when the Germans appeared to have the advantage in indirect fire-support. During September 1914, Nivelle's gunners demonstrated a mastery of counter-battery tactics and night fighting, and decimated unsupported German units in engagements at Puisieux and Montaigu à Ambleny. These actions established Nivelle as an aggressive and daring artillery commander. Contemporaries also remarked on his concern for the welfare of his men and his interest in their ideas. An informal discussion with the astronomer Charles Nordmann, while inspecting his batteries' forward observer positions, led to Nordmann being re-assigned to the task of investigating the potential of sound-ranging as a method for locating German heavy batteries. Nordmann's work laid the foundation for the allies' dominance in this field by 1918.[9] Although a gunner, Nivelle was assigned to command 27 *brigade d'infanterie* (BI) in November 1914. However, just before the Battle of Crouy, his unit was absorbed into 110 BI and Nivelle, sensing an opportunity, lobbied to be assigned to command an all-arms unit made up of battalions from several brigades supported by a *groupe* of 75s. Lacking adequate communications with his batteries, Nivelle sketched out a plan of the battlefield and ordered the gunners to fire a sequence of pre-planned lifts (curtains of fire that usually focused on the enemy trench line) just ahead of where he expected his advancing infantry to be as the attack progressed. This innovative solution was arguably a primitive prototype of what would become the 'creeping barrage'. Unfortunately, the rest of the assault faltered, and the infantry fell back in confusion. Nivelle determined to learn from this failure, noting in his report the paramount importance of improving coordination between the infantry and artillery.[10]

In February 1915, Nivelle was promoted to command 61 *divison d'infanterie* (DI) in General Charles Ebener's XXXV CA. In the summer General Pierre Dubois, commander of Sixth Army, decided to storm the German salient at Quennevières. Although he was aware of the army's ammunition shortage and weakness in heavy artillery, Nivelle argued that, if given sufficient resources, he could break through both the enemy's first and second defensive positions, and requested eight times the usual allocation of artillery to support his attack.[11] 61 DI and 3 *division d'infanterie coloniale* were assigned to the assault. Nivelle commanded the supporting artillery and Ebener coordinated counter-battery fire. The fire-plan combined two days of fire concentrating on destroying the defensive system and cutting barbed wire in front of the German trench line with periods of harassing fire focussed on neutralizing German repair efforts.

Supported by a primitive creeping barrage, the assault, on 6 June 1915, saw initial success but the support fire-plan failed to eliminate the belts of barbed wire protecting the enemy's second position and the attack inevitably faltered. Nivelle, aware of the arrival of German reinforcements and faced with intensive counter attacks, continued to try to take the salient and losses began to mount up. Further attacks on 15 and 16 June fared no better and Nivelle's first experience in offensive command proved to be, at best, a pyrrhic victory. Rémi Hébert, in his analysis of the battle, suggests that the continuation of the action demonstrated many of Nivelle's later character flaws, citing the decision to continue to attack even though more powerful German artillery reserves had been committed to the sector. To be fair to Nivelle, such perseverance was not unusual and Nivelle clearly learnt from the experience, noting after the battle that 'the organization and power of the artillery is the main component in ensuring our success. ...The role of the infantry only commences after the action of the artillery, and the importance of effective [artillery] support continues to be relevant throughout the operation.'[12]

In December 1915, Nivelle took command of III CA, stationed between Péronne and Montdidier south of the river Somme. For the first time, Charles Mangin, then a *Général de brigade*, came under Nivelle's command. In April III CA was assigned to General Philippe Pétain's Second Army in the Verdun sector. Aware that Pétain had a tendency to let others take operational risks while he basked in his reputation for averting catastrophe, commander-in-chief General Joseph Joffre decided to assign him 'aggressive' subordinates that the *Grand quartier général* (GQG) thought were more capable of translating Joffre's demands into action.

Nivelle's orders were to 'seize enemy positions southwest of the Fausse Cote ravine and win back the lost trenches west of Douaumont'. III CA launched a series of successful but costly attacks that secured the Bois de Calliette and positions either side of Forts Vaux and Souville. Joffre was delighted with the aggression shown in these attacks and Nivelle found himself briefing a succession of politicians. Nivelle impressed his audience with his ability to outline both his objectives and his approach to securing them. Nivelle's resolute determination and confident demeanour delighted men who were all too used to being treated like pariahs by military professionals; particularly as he appeared interested in their questions and gave clear and concise answers. Nivelle's success was also an indication of the sad state of civil–military relations in 1916.[13]

Frustrated by Pétain's inability to seize the initiative at Verdun, Joffre promoted him to army group command and gave Nivelle command of Second Army. Denis Rolland contends that Pétain was embittered by the experience of having to hand over operational command at Verdun to Nivelle and made little effort to support his successor. Other historians suggest that Pétain attempted to moderate Nivelle's aggression, but it is notable that the chief of staff of Second Army, Colonel Maurice de Barescut, tended to support Nivelle rather than his old commander. It is also important to note that Nivelle fully supported Pétain's policy of regularly rotating divisions out of the line and improving artillery organization before launching further offensives.[14]

As preparation for the Somme offensive started in earnest, Nivelle began planning to re-take Fort Douaumont, the key to the Verdun defences that had been lost at the end of February. A first attempt on 22 May, with only Mangin's 5 DI taking part, was a costly failure and a few days later Fort Vaux also fell to a German coup de main on 1 June. Nivelle counterattacked on 8 June but the Germans quickly re-took their lost positions and further extended their salient by using their artillery to form corridors of fire through which their infantry could seize isolated objectives.[15] Pétain demanded additional artillery, complaining that the Somme was absorbing reserves needed at Verdun. In contrast, Nivelle remained confident that the situation would be reversed once German reserves were also redeployed.

After the next German assault, on 21 June, Nivelle issued a famous memorandum to Second Army: 'The time is decisive. You will not let them pass, my friends, the country still needs from you this supreme effort. The Army of Verdun will not be intimidated by the artillery and infantry which it has already defied for four months. It will retain its glory intact.' Pétain suggested withdrawing to the right bank of the river Meuse but Joffre and Nivelle disagreed, and enough reserves were found to hold the line. As the Somme offensive began, the Germans made one last desperate attempt to take Fort Souville but this ended in failure after French counter-preparatory fire eliminated many of the German batteries supporting the attack and Mangin's counter attack retook Fleury. The initiative in the Verdun sector had passed to the French.[16] Nivelle was made a *Grand officier* of the Légion d'honneur. The citation read:

> Commanding the past four months an army that has successfully resisted the attacks of a formidable enemy and heroically endured continual hardship... [he has] demonstrated in command, with his leadership, energy and strength of character [characteristics] that have powerfully influenced the development of operations undertaken on the [Western Front] ... [and] having halted the advance of the enemy on an objective that became the moral focus of the campaign, resumed the offensive and foot by foot, by repeated attacks, managed to dominate our opponents on the ground that they themselves had chosen for their decisive effort.[17]

Once it became apparent that the Somme offensive had stalemated, Joffre ordered that Forts Douaumont and Vaux be retaken. With both Joffre and Pétain's support, Nivelle began comprehensive preparations. New GQG instructions on the use of artillery and trench mortars and for improved coordination with the infantry were promulgated based upon experience gained at Verdun and on the Somme.[18] Every unit was fully briefed on the plan. Artillery and air reserves (including numerous observation balloons) were concentrated and new wireless transmitters were issued to forward units to facilitate fire control and flexibility in the barrage. Fort Douaumont was to be bombarded by two 400mm super-heavy railway guns. The final assault by Mangin's XI CA was launched just before dawn on 24 October after a preparatory bombardment lasting four days. Fortuitously, a fog bank concealed the assaulting infantry. A two-wave creeping barrage, by 75s firing 70 metres ahead of the infantry and heavy guns 80 metres beyond the 75s, swept over the German defensive position. Protected by this dual cover, the French infantry overwhelmed the enemy's trenches, taking 6,000 prisoners. Smashed open by the super-heavies, Fort Douaumont fell on schedule. French losses remained heavy – 47,000 in four days of fighting out of 379,000 for the Battle of Verdun as a whole.[19] Such an 'orchestral' approach to the bombardment, using a carefully coordinated and layered barrage that utilized both neutralizing and destructive fires to disrupt the defender's ability to resist the main assault, was becoming ubiquitous by this point in the war: the method was being continuously improved by artillery specialists in all armies, for example Georg Bruchmüller in the German army and Henry Tudor in the British.[20]

Nivelle was delighted by the success of his fire-plan and proposed further attacks. Pétain was reluctant to countenance further operations but Joffre overruled him. A second assault was preceded by three days of bombardment. When the guns fell silent, the Germans commenced their counter-preparatory fire only to find that the French had retained reserve batteries to eliminate any unmasked German artillery positions. The second phase of fire focused on these new targets for a further thirty-six hours before the creeping barrage swept forwards into fog once again. Casualties were heavy, but 12,000 prisoners were taken. Joffre outlined Nivelle's role in his memoirs:

> If history allows me the right to judge the generals operating under me, I assert that the true saviour of Verdun was Nivelle, fortunately assisted by Mangin. …General Pétain, who inherited responsibility for Verdun during a period of chaos, restored order with the help of an excellent staff and with fresh troops. …This was his achievement and I do not underestimate its magnitude.[21]

\* \* \*

When the government were looking for a successor to Joffre in December 1916, their gaze naturally fell on Nivelle who had scored the most recent and striking success. The existing army group commanders were deemed unsuitable: Pétain was judged too pessimistic and contemptuous of politicians; Louis Franchet d'Esperey was considered worn out; Ferdinand Foch was supposedly unfit since he was recovering from a recent car accident; and the devout Nöel de Castelnau was thought 'insufficiently republican'. Of the army commanders, from a politician's perspective, Nivelle appeared to be the one who appeared to have the right combination of talent and aggression. The announcement was greeted with enthusiasm at the front, where Nivelle was seen as a general who delivered results – he was dubbed in one newspaper 'le niveleur' who had levelled the German defences at Verdun.[22] Nivelle himself was initially dismayed by the appointment; when his staff gathered to celebrate his promotion, he remarked 'do not congratulate me, this burden is very heavy'.[23] Nivelle inherited Joffre's plan for the 1917 campaign. The French were to attack between the Somme and the Oise rivers, while the British focused on the sector between Bapaume and Vimy ridge. Before his promotion, Nivelle had informed Joffre that he had reservations about being the army group commander for the proposed offensive. Nevertheless, when it came to it Nivelle understood how to communicate complex plans to busy politicians (including the British). Moreover, his long period in the wilderness before the war meant that he had failed to establish a politically dangerous network of allies in the military. This offered premier Aristide Briand's *Comité de guerre*, which was set up to manage the war at the same time as Nivelle was appointed, the opportunity to make the new commander-in-chief their 'docile instrument';[24] but they failed to realize that this also placed Nivelle in an impossible position. Nivelle had few influential friends and his promotion made him many powerful enemies. With no experience of command at the army group level, he was expected to plan the Entente's spring offensive, coordinate both his fractious subordinates and France's querulous allies, and somehow outwit the *Oberste Heeresleitung* (OHL).

On 5 January 1917, the German Sixth Army's Operations Branch issued an assessment of the options available to the allies called 'The Offensive Options for the Entente'. Based upon an assessment by OHL, the report noted that 'the French and British are preparing the entire lengths of their front for the assault' and outlined the most probable operational objectives that the allies might choose to target during the summer. The report noted that 'the involvement of General Nivelle is a guarantee that the attack will only be launched after careful preparations, down to the smallest detail, have been completed. As a result, there is no possibility that the French–British army will be ready to attack before March 1.'[25]

Their bitter experience of the final battles at Verdun, and on the Somme, had taught the Germans valuable lessons. The defensive systems of 1916 had proved unable to defeat the increasingly sophisticated assault tactics developed by the allies. The solution to the proven effectiveness of both the creeping barrage and the increasingly 'orchestral' approach to artillery fire-planning was to increase the overall depth of the defensive system. As described in 'The Principles of Command in the Defensive Battle in Position Warfare' published in spring 1917,[26] this new defensive doctrine set aside the linear approach of 1914–1916 and substituted a system based upon a series of three defensive layers:[27] an outpost line to slow down and disrupt the enemy offensive and assist in the identification of the main axis of the enemy assault; the main battle-zone, a network of defensive positions, each surrounded by belts of barbed wire situated around a kilometre behind the outpost line:[28] and, out of range of most of the allies' heavy artillery, a final linear position in which the artillery were deployed that served as the jumping-off line for counter-attack units.[29] Over the winter OHL's leaders, Paul von Hindenburg and Erich Ludendorff, made the decision to withdraw the centre of the German front to fresh positions built on these principles, the eponymous Hindenburg Line. All that remained was to select a time for the withdrawal that ensured the complete dislocation of the Entente's plans.

Nivelle arrived at GQG at Chantilly on 14 December 1916 and fortunately made an immediate and positive impression on his new staff. For example, when de Castelnau handed over authority to his old subordinate, Nivelle made a public demonstration of his continuing respect for his former superior.[30] The honeymoon period was not to last. Firstly, Nivelle soon discovered that General Hubert Lyautey, Briand's newly appointed minister of war, had been stripped of many of his predecessor's responsibilities and was as inexperienced as the new commander-in-chief. Secondly, careless promises made to de Castelnau about assigning him command of the main army group in the coming offensive had to be shelved after criticism by Nivelle's own staff. Thirdly, even with Mangin's promotion to command Sixth Army, most of the commanders available for the proposed campaign were unhappy about being subordinated to an officer who had been a mere colonel in 1914. Undaunted, Nivelle threw his energy into perfecting his 'formula' for victory and removing any obstacle to conducting the campaign.

Nivelle believed that his successful but localized counter-offensive tactics could be applied on a strategic scale. Now that France appeared to have sufficient heavy artillery, narrow zones of fire could be used to slice through the German defensive system on a wide front while creeping barrages would cover both the infantry advance and the re-deployment of artillery batteries. A second offensive phase, a decisive rupture of the German line, would commence within forty-eight hours, before the Germans could recover from the first blow, enabling their artillery reserves to be overwhelmed and the entire system to be rolled up by 'audacious lateral exploitation' instead of trying to operate beyond the range of supporting artillery. Assuming that German reserves could be diverted then there appeared to be no reason why 'manoeuvre' and 'decisive battle' could not give France the victory she desperately wanted. In December 1916, an ebullient Nivelle declared 'the experience is conclusive; our method had proved itself'. This over-confident statement would come back to haunt him once the inevitable difficulties of scaling up the 'formula' began to multiply.[31] While there were many tactical and operational innovations in Nivelle's plan,[32] his strategic conception overlooked three vital factors: the difficulty of guaranteeing the secrecy that made success possible; the significant challenge of scaling-up the logistical and planning requirements for an operation involving several armies; and, most importantly, the assumption that the Germans would make no counter-preparations of their own.

Once in command, Nivelle treated his staff with his usual charm and sympathy and even critics such as Jean de Pierrefeu thought him a good leader: 'For my part, I rarely found GQG as benevolent as during his reign. …He was always encouraging towards me…. When my humble task [the Great War equivalent of media operations] was the object of his attention, he never failed to recognize my efforts with a kind word that showed that he had understood.'[33] His dealings with senior subordinates were rather less benign. Nivelle charmed anyone who met him face-to-face but, as de Castelnau quickly discovered, he did not hesitate to scheme for their removal as soon as he perceived that they were a threat to his plan. Nivelle did not have the same level of effortless 'auctoritas' as Joffre and he arguably had no choice but to scheme to get what he wanted. In addition, for political reasons, most commanders of both the armies and army groups responsible for the offensive were replaced after Joffre was side-lined, thereby ensuring that the planning process was completely disrupted.

Lieutenant Colonel Marcel Audemard d'Alençon, Nivelle's *chef de cabinet*, has been assigned a share of the blame for planning deficiencies.[34] A tall and austere character, d'Alençon was not a man who made friends easily. Jean de Pierrefeu, one of our principal sources for the events at GQG in 1917, clearly loathed him, slyly insinuating that, driven by the realization that he was dying, d'Alençon fought any perceived delays to the planning process due to a personal need to see the campaign through to its conclusion.[35] In January 1917, d'Alençon contracted pulmonary congestion during a visit to Italy. He was extremely unwell in April 1917 and was advised to take leave by Nivelle but remained at his post. He survived until September 1917, continuing to serve at GQG after his patron's dismissal. D'Alençon acted as Nivelle's adviser while Colonel Georges Renouard ran the planning team in the Third (Operations) Bureau at GQG.[36] After Pétain, who commanded *Groupe d'armées du centre* (GAC), refused to commit to the overall strategic concept, d'Alençon advised his master to give Alfred Micheler, commanding *Groupe d'armées de reserve*

(GAR), the task of leading the main thrust of the offensive. However, Nivelle did not entirely trust the suave but inherently nervous Micheler and limited his authority. Except for Mangin, Nivelle did not trust any of his subordinates to plan the details of the operation but failed to recognize that the political pressures of his new role precluded any direct involvement by the commander-in-chief.[37]

The government tested their authority over their new appointee by ordering Nivelle to move GQG to Beauvais on 6 January. Soon after a new war minister, Paul Painlevé, forced GQG to move again, to Compiègne on 7 April, to stay close to the new front line after the Germans had withdrawn. Nivelle acquiesced even though the move disrupted his staff's ability to monitor preparations for the pending battle.[38] It is not surprising that Lieutenant Louis Madelin, a staff officer at GQG, described him as vacillating between 'radiating extreme satisfaction' at his new authority and 'appearing overwhelmed and tired'.[39]

Nivelle's choice of the Chemin des Dames as the principal sector for his attack has been heavily criticized by contemporaries and historians but this formidable position was the key to the French section of the Western Front and Nivelle believed that the 'formula' could be applied to the forbidding terrain that overlooked the river Aisne. Nivelle outlined his strategic intentions to his army group commanders, Franchet d'Esperey commanding *Groupe d'armées du nord* (GAN), Micheler and Pétain, at the end of December 1916. The original assault plan focused on two sectors: GAN's First and Third Armies would attack between Canny-sur-Matz and Guiscard and GAR's Fifth and Sixth Armies would take the offensive in the Aisne sector between Reims and the channel from the Aisne to the Oise rivers. Tenth Army, held in reserve, was responsible for operating in the Aisne sector, where a 'rupture' of the German defensive system seemed most practicable, although reserves were to be deployed to support other thrusts if these proved more successful. The whole design was to be assisted by the British, who were to draw the German reserves north with an offensive in front of Arras.

Nivelle faced the same challenge as Joffre, of getting the British commander-in-chief Field Marshal Sir Douglas Haig to conform to his intentions. Nivelle travelled to London to meet the British Prime Minister, David Lloyd George. He assumed that he had gained a powerful ally but instead found that he was to be a pawn in Lloyd George's own plans to neutralize Haig. Even though Haig found Nivelle 'straightforward and soldierly', their meetings were more turbulent than expected. Haig wanted to retain operational independence, particularly as he suspected that Nivelle's offensive might not achieve a decisive rupture in the German defences.[40] In addition, Nivelle's request for an extension of the British front was vehemently resisted, particularly as the British were unhappy about the supporting rail infrastructure and Haig resented being consigned to a supporting role in the proposed offensive. Lloyd George recognized an opportunity when he saw one and with the eager assistance of French politicians initiated a series of secret conversations that led to a plan to give Nivelle formal command authority over Haig. The French noted that the British held a proportionally shorter length of the front and argued that an overall (French) commander on the Western Front made sense. Although he had already established a good working relationship with his British colleague, Nivelle collaborated in the scheme under the assumption that the new structure would function more efficiently. General Sir William Robertson, Chief of the Imperial General Staff in London and a firm supporter of Haig, countered with the observation that Nivelle was not as secure as Joffre and that placing the British army under his command technically placed them under the authority of the politicians in Paris – who had shown little respect for British concerns or interests in the past.[41]

The plot was sprung in Calais in late February. At a conference ostensibly called to discuss railway arrangements, Briand and Lloyd George manipulated the discussion in the hope of forcing a confrontation that might give them an opportunity to remove Haig. GQG had prepared a draft convention for the proposed new command system which Nivelle, who realized that he was being used by the politicians of both sides, only passed on to Haig after the meeting, proffering his apologies. Once Haig and Robertson recovered from their shock at the tone of the document, a compromise was reached that recognized the independence of the commanders of both armies. Nivelle was to have overall strategic direction during the campaign with the caveat that his plans did not jeopardize the safety of the British army.

The relationship between Nivelle and Haig was permanently soured and this 'coordination agreement' between the two armies merely papered over the cracks. While Nivelle fought off a fever, d'Alençon added to the climate of suspicion by sending Haig a missive ordering him to set up a British mission at GQG under Haig's bête noir General Sir Henry Wilson (an experienced liaison officer but a man who had drawn opprobrium for being pro-French and an intriguer). Haig retorted with a message indicating that he considered taking the offensive in Flanders, where he had always wished to mount an independent offensive, as more pressing than the planned offensive. A fresh conference was arranged to resolve the new dispute after it transpired that Haig had threatened to resign and Lloyd George had been summoned to Buckingham Palace to explain his behaviour to the king. Keen to resolve the issue and return to planning his offensive, Nivelle suggested General Hubert Gough as an alternative British commander. This ill-considered intervention did not endear him to the British and Lloyd George, who had run out of political options, was forced into supporting Haig. The London Conference concluded with a new

'Memorandum of Understanding' between the allied commanders establishing the limits of Nivelle's authority. The Calais Agreement would only last for the duration of the offensive. Nivelle publicly stated that he never intended that he wanted Haig to be his subordinate while the latter confirmed that the British army would play its intended role in the spring offensive.

This command crisis had echoes of those that had occurred under Joffre. While the politicians should be held responsible for provoking it, Nivelle himself might be judged complicit. While naturally articulate, he did not show himself to be an astute player when it came to the intricacies of inter-allied politics or civil–military relations. Haig, who had longer and more bitter experience of such intrigues, at least gave him the benefit of the doubt: 'The Calais Conference was a mistake, but it was not Nivelle's fault.'[42]

As soon as Nivelle returned to France he learned that revolution had broken out in Petrograd, ending all hopes of a supporting Russian offensive on the eastern Front in the spring. One element of his plan had collapsed owing to circumstances beyond his control. In addition, his subordinates were still at loggerheads. Micheler and Mangin were proving utterly incompatible, with the former advocating prudence and the latter insisting on a highly aggressive timetable for Sixth Army's assault. Nivelle summoned them both to GQG where Mangin launched into a tirade against Micheler. Nivelle tried to heal the rift by writing to both men asking them to settle their differences, but the argument at GQG had been a public one and the two men were irreconcilable. From this point onwards, Micheler's behaviour veered between sullen acquiescence and outright insubordination.[43]

Then a third and less controllable 'friction', the enemy, threatened the whole offensive plan. In late February 1917, GQG assumed that the Germans were planning to attack in Lorraine or Alsace and as a result failed to note intelligence indications that the Germans were preparing to withdraw from the sectors of front where Nivelle hoped to make his breakthrough. Displeased, on 28 February Franchet d'Esperey travelled to GQG and asked Nivelle if his armies could launch an immediate attack to pre-empt the withdrawal. On 4 March, he put his concerns in writing and suggested either an immediate advance or a delay in the offensive to re-configure the plan. Nivelle's reply suggests that he was bemused by the Germans withdrawal – he could not understand why the Germans would withdraw from positions that were close to Paris, a classic example of basing one's perception of the enemy's objectives on one's own.[44] He advised Franchet d'Esperey to conduct aggressive raids to ascertain the real situation and to follow up vigorously if the withdrawal proved genuine. Although GQG claimed the enemy were 'retreating', the Third Bureau appreciated that the Germans were accumulating reserves by withdrawing. Nevertheless, they concluded that the offensive should proceed, with appropriate adjustments, to forestall the inevitable German offensive. Nivelle, Micheler and Haig met twice in mid-March to review the evolving situation and decided to proceed as planned. Paul Harris notes that Haig described Nivelle at this point as 'a capable general' and that their relations were 'excellent'.[45]

In reality, the enemy were conserving their forces to meet the next phase of allied offensives. Ludendorff expected the British to continue to attack on the Somme and, after numerous reports, expected the French to assault the Soissons–Reims sector of the front. Concealing their preparations for the expected onslaught was a priority and only with hindsight is it obvious that their intention was to dislocate the Entente's offensive preparations. As the allies moved forward into the territory vacated by the Germans they came across a swath of destruction designed to thwart their pursuit. The brutality and apparent pettiness of the devastation unleashed by 'Operation Alberich' infuriated the advancing French but there was little they could do to harass the perpetrators.[46] Claims that the Entente's forces could have pounced on the retreating Germans utterly ignore the challenge of shifting from static to mobile operations.[47] As the French moved forwards to consolidate on the new front line, d'Alençon grew increasingly concerned by the efficiency of the German withdrawal and the lack of information on their new positions. He wrote to Renouard and Nivelle reminding them of the dangers of conducting an assault against an unknown defensive system.[48]

Circumstances were conspiring against Nivelle's chances of success. Renouard assessed the wider strategic situation in a memorandum dated 24 March. He noted that Italy and Russia were unlikely to conduct major operations during 1917, the British would divert their attention to Flanders if the proposed offensive was postponed, and the Germans were clearly preparing a major strategic operation which could not be allowed to proceed without some attempt at disruption by the Entente during the spring. Despite being responsible for making it work, Renouard had been doubtful of the plan and had even shown an early draft to an incredulous war minister, Lyautey, who apparently compared the concept to an operatic farce.[49] But the operations chief saw few viable alternatives.

On 26 March, Nivelle gathered his senior commanders to discuss options, in particular Mangin's desire for an accelerated timetable and his call for additional reserves for Sixth Army. According to Mangin, the meeting was a wasted opportunity; Micheler was little more than an observer and Pétain's pessimism made progress impossible. Pétain was so paranoid that he complained to Nivelle, in writing, about GQG's Third Bureau's campaign of 'innuendoes' against him.[50]

While the army command struggled with the challenges of an unexpected pursuit, Briand's administration fell. Painlevé, war minister in Alexandre Ribot's new government, disliked Nivelle's plan and was keen to remove him as soon as possible. In his first meeting with Haig, he even revealed his concerns about Nivelle and his own support for Pétain as his potential replacement. Haig was unhappy about being drawn into such a discussion, warily informing the minister that his relations with Nivelle were 'excellent'.[51] Painlevé's enthusiasm for Pétain was based upon the latter's apparent caution about casualties and his genuine concerns about the appropriateness of Nivelle and Mangin's 'grandiose plans' now that Russia's revolution had released additional German reserves. Unfortunately, the war minister's attempts at undermining Nivelle forced the French commander-in-chief to defend his position in Paris, further distracting him from his main responsibility, overseeing the final planning for the offensive.

On 3 April, Nivelle was summoned to meet Painlevé. He assured the war minister that preparations were well in hand and that he would not proceed with the second phase of the assault unless the enemy's first position was secured. Nivelle also agreed that the attack would proceed only under favourable weather conditions. It is worth emphasizing that Nivelle's earlier claim that he could 'rupture' the German front in 48 hours no longer appeared in his reports. As the offensive loomed, Nivelle emphasized that he expected 'a prolonged battle' and highlighted the increased importance of the British attack for diverting German reserves. On 5 April, the former war minister and front-line commander Colonel Adolphe Messimy, acting on behalf of Micheler, visited Painlevé to pass on a note listing the army group commander's concerns about the offensive, and to insist that the minister meet with the army group commanders.[52]

Hoping to obtain a more limited offensive plan than Nivelle's, Painlevé convened the *Comité de guerre* at Compiègne on 6 April so that he could ask all the invited commanders to speak freely and confirm the misgivings that most had already revealed to him in private. Nivelle countered with a memorandum stating that he did not expect the Germans to withdraw units from the Western Front, that they were likely to be preparing for an allied offensive, and that cancellation of his planned offensive would only convince the British to focus their efforts on Flanders instead of coordinating with their allies. In addition, Nivelle stated that he understood his colleagues' concerns but was wary of handing the initiative back to the Germans. Nivelle concluded that he hoped for an 'honourable success' on the Aisne – a marked contrast to his earlier statements.[53]

No notes were taken at the *Comité de guerre*, even though Nivelle wanted the meeting to be recorded. The atmosphere was tense. Painlevé later noted that 'General Nivelle was bitter and haughty…Franchet d'Esperey stayed silent,

Pétain was impassive and cold; Micheler seemed anxious and tormented'. Painlevé began proceedings by reminding the assembled dignitaries that the Russian revolution, America's entry into the war and the German retreat had changed the strategic situation before asking for comments. Nivelle countered by pointing out that the first two factors were unlikely to impact on the Western Front for months and that handing the initiative to the Germans was unwise. He asserted that 'only the offensive can bring victory'. Painlevé suggested that a failed offensive might cause incalculable damage, causing Nivelle to remark that 'one cannot fight half a battle.... We must engage fully or fail to deliver results', and to hint that he might have to resign. Painlevé asked the other army group commanders for their views. De Castelnau reminded the government that the commander-in-chief must have an appropriate level of freedom of action; Franchet d'Esperey noted that cancelling the offensive would disrupt the existing (and fragile) agreement with the British (whose artillery bombardment at Arras had already commenced) but noted that the German withdrawal had made a breakthrough problematic; Micheler stated that the offensive should go ahead but gave the impression to the other attendees that he had 'no confidence in the outcome of the battle' – later claiming that he had been pressured by Nivelle. Pétain apparently shrugged and stated that he thought the plan was feasible but thought that more limited operations were preferable.[54]

Dismayed by the lack of support from his colleagues and undermined by Painlevé's antipathy, Nivelle suggested that he would abandon the offensive if the assault failed to secure its main objectives within twenty-four hours and in that case, he would certainly halt it after forty-eight hours. This statement later proved his undoing. As he had shown at Quennevières, where Nivelle struggled to exploit initial success, a partially successful offensive cannot simply be halted. An incompletely won position must be consolidated and this often requires additional attacks to secure key terrain. After Painlevé summed up the debate, Nivelle handed over what most witnesses assumed was a prepared letter of resignation. This bombshell left Ribot, President Raymond Poincaré and Painlevé with little choice but to support Nivelle as his resignation would almost certainly have provoked an immediate vote of no confidence in the new government. The meeting broke up with no one satisfied by the outcome but without any coherent alternative to Nivelle's plan being offered by his critics.[55] Nivelle, having been distracted by political intrigue, returned to GQG having staked his reputation on a single throw of the dice.

Crucially, the need for secrecy had been undermined by the political debate: deputies expected operational details before making any decision and seemed utterly unaware of the dangers of reviewing such matters in a city riddled with German agents. The French army was also prone to leaks and Pierrefeu was forced to admit that the offensive was unlikely to remain a secret when the instinct to gossip often led French officers to reveal far more than was prudent.[56] Nivelle contributed to this process by giving away key details and making promises of success, that he must have known were exaggerations given his later statements about 'a prolonged battle', to garner the support he believed that he needed to proceed. His habit of sharing his plans with relatively junior subordinates also proved unfortunate as key details of the overall plan for the offensive were captured by the Germans during a trench raid on 4 April.

\* \* \*

The final plan envisaged a direct assault on the Chemin des Dames followed by an attack on the German positions at Moronvilliers to the east. The British attack would precede the former by a week. A test attack on the village of Laffaux on 7 April appeared to show that German machine gunners would survive the bombardment but Mangin, General Olivier Mazel (commanding Fifth Army) and Micheler (having regained his faith in the offensive) remained confident. Mangin noted that he only needed 'four days of good weather…at the moment, I have only two serious enemies: General Micheler and time!'[57] Even at this late date, Nivelle was tormented by his political masters and an outraged d'Alençon finally went to see Albert Thomas, the minister of munitions, to tell him that if the *Comité de guerre* and the war minister continued to pester Nivelle then the commander-in-chief could not be expected to coordinate the offensive.[58]

Once the British operations commenced on 9 April, morale at GQG quickly improved. The rapid capture of Vimy ridge suggested that the methods developed in 1916 might still succeed, although Nivelle and his staff were blissfully unaware that the defences facing the British were incomplete and thus not an indication of what the French might face.[59] They were also not informed that the British commanders were surprised by the ferocity of the German counter attacks and had lobbied Haig for an early end to the offensive.

The weather continued to worsen, often alternating between sleet and snow, making fulfilling Nivelle's promise to Painlevé increasingly implausible. Intelligence reports of new German emplacements on the Chemin des Dames multiplied and it slowly became apparent that the enemy's new defensive system was far more formidable than expected. Micheler reported increased activity, with the number of artillery emplacements identified in Sixth Army's sector alone increasing fivefold and the number of enemy divisions available in GAR's sector increasing to over forty. In that respect, the preliminary British offensive seemed to have failed in its purpose of drawing off enemy reserves. When the battle commenced General Georges Humbert's Third Army was expected to pin the enemy, Mangin and Mazel's Sixth and Fifth Armies would conduct the principal assault with General Denis Duchêne's Tenth Army acting as the reserve. The tanks of the *Artillerie spéciale*, being deployed for the first time, were assigned to Fifth and Fourth Armies (General François Anthoine), in the centre and on the right flank, in the hope of assisting them in breaking through in their supporting attacks and rolling up the shattered German line.

In his final instructions Nivelle noted that 'the spirit of the offensive is not incompatible with caution'[60] and made a number of minor adjustments to account for the poor weather and the reports of increased German reserves. The first phase of the preparatory bombardment of the German defensive system began on 2 April, concealing the process of registration on the main targets until the bombardment intensified on 6 April. From 15 April the heavy artillery (of which 420 out of 2,300 guns were of the most modern types) focused on neutralizing enemy batteries with gas projectiles. Although the quantities of ammunition expended were prodigious, because the French air force proved unable to dominate the skies over the battlefield, the weather impeded spotting and the depth of the enemy position (much of it situated on reverse slopes concealed from French forward observers) absorbed vast amounts of munitions, the barrage had limited effect. These factors compound the error that fire-support was not concentrated as it had been in Nivelle's successful attacks at Verdun. As Pétain had observed when he saw the fire-plan, 'even the waters of Lake Geneva would have little effect if dispersed over the length and breadth of the Sahara'.[61] Postponements of the attack led to artillery ammunition running short and some regiments did not receive their full allocation of shells for the final phase.[62] Ironically, an artillery general's grand scheme would fail primarily because the artillery was not used appropriately.

On the day, GAR's creeping barrage, starting at 06:00 on 16 April, failed to provide adequate cover for the infantry assault. While Nivelle was wrestling with the politicians, many divisional commanders had sent exaggerated estimates of their expected speed of advance:[63] inevitably, the barrage accelerated beyond the advancing infantry and gave the Germans time to emerge from their bunkers and man their machine guns. In places the attack failed. For example, in I and II *corps d'armées coloniales* attacking the ridgeline of the Chemin des Dames (Pinon and the Vauclerc plateau) officer casualties were catastrophic; the freezing infantry soon lost cohesion and their attack faltered under withering fire from all sides. Elsewhere gains were made including at Courcy, Loivre and Berméricourt. V and XXXII CAs seized key positions in the German second line south of Juvincourt. But these localized successes came nowhere near Nivelle's optimistic predictions for the first day and every attempt to flank key positions and roll them up had failed.[64]

Attacks continued on 17 and 18 April and Fifth Army managed to dislodge some of the German units facing Sixth Army, enabling significant advances to be made, but the overall results were still disappointing. GAC commenced its attack on Moronvillers at 04:45 on 17 April, as the weather worsened yet again, and made minor gains but Pétain was disappointed with the failure of the massed tank attacks. He ordered Fourth Army to consolidate and only to proceed 'methodically'. By 20 April, it was apparent that Nivelle's plan had failed; losses had accumulated quickly and the casualty figures for that month were the highest since November 1914. As Foch gloated, 'Well, there's the Somme's revenge': Foch recognized that the Verdun School, led by Nivelle, had failed to appreciate that that the Germans learned from their mistakes.[65] The greatest advance occurred just north of Vailly, in Sixth Army's sector. Micheler and Mangin had continued to bicker during the operation and Nivelle was eventually forced to transfer Sixth Army to GAN on 24 April.

A number of politicians had witnessed the first day's attacks, and after seeing the columns of returning wounded pressure to halt the offensive quickly grew. Staff officers at GQG were stunned by the grim reports from the front, and the drop in their morale was very apparent to visitors, reinforcing the impression that heads would have to roll.[66] Horrified by the news that Nivelle intended further attacks to secure the Chemin des Dames, Painlevé and Poincaré ordered their commander-in-chief to desist, citing the opinions of a number of Nivelle's subordinates. Nivelle was outraged by the suggestion that he would plan ill-considered assaults and insisted that his accusers be disciplined. Painlevé was dismayed by Nivelle's apparent obstinacy and asked Pétain if he would accept command. The latter sensibly refused the initial offer but noted 'if the government orders me to take a position, I am a soldier, I will obey'. In the end, Nivelle's intention to attack Brimont on 27 April left his political masters with no alternative but to intervene in the conduct of operations. Nivelle was confident of success, but the prospect of another failed assault worried the government. Furious, Nivelle suggested that members of the *Comité de guerre* were overreacting instead of recognizing operational realities. To his surprise, Pétain supported him. After hinting that he thought the attack would be too costly, Pétain now supported the idea of a phased operation against Mount Spin before taking Brimont. Painlevé, who found himself being criticized both by the British and his colleagues for not consulting them, backtracked and denied attempting to cancel the attack.[67] In discussion with Nivelle on 24 April, Haig also voiced his concern that cancelling the offensive would impact on the conduct of the next phase of operations on the Western Front – his long-meditated Flanders offensive that Nivelle had agreed to support if his own offensive failed. Haig then saw Painlevé and repeated his argument that a resumption of the offensive was imperative, only to be asked for his opinion of Pétain as a possible commander-in-chief.[68]

Poincaré was still wary of acting against Nivelle, noting that 'we should specify the offences he has committed and be sure that whoever we appoint would have done better'.[69] Painlevé was less cautious and insisted on a decision regarding Nivelle's future before any further attacks could be permitted. The compromise solution, satisfying Ribot's concerns about the impact of dismissing a commander-in-chief so soon after Joffre, was to keep Nivelle and to appoint Pétain as a strategic adviser to the war ministry in Paris with a general oversight of the conduct of operations. The intention was to limit Nivelle's freedom and to undermine his authority.

The British wanted further attacks and Robertson joined Haig and Lloyd George in a delegation that went to Paris on 4 May to meet Nivelle and Pétain. The soldiers agreed a policy of attrition, based upon using a succession of limited attacks supported by artillery, as the only means of maintaining pressure on the Germans.[70] All recognized that there had been some successes during the attacks at Arras and on the Aisne, but Painlevé was reluctant to countenance further assaults unless new methods were utilized to overcome the improved German defences. After the meeting, Haig coldly informed Nivelle of his intention to prepare for a British offensive in Flanders: it was very apparent that the collaborative relationship established at Calais was over.

The new French command arrangement was clearly flawed and on 10 May Painlevé summoned Nivelle to request his resignation. To Painlevé's horror, Nivelle refused, pointing out that a change of command would give the Germans an immediate propaganda victory and would support their contention that they had won a great victory on the Aisne. Nivelle believed that the Second Battle of the Aisne was, at worst, a pyrrhic victory and could not see why he should be removed when the British and his supporters wanted him to remain in command to ensure that pressure on the Germans was maintained.[71] At a second meeting, on 15 May, he again refused to resign. Aware of the bitter events surrounding the dismissal of Foch in 1916, Nivelle stated that he would only countenance an alternative role that enabled him to continue the battle. Wilhelm Balck suggests that this strategy offered his opponents a face-saving solution; that they appoint a new commander-in-chief and offer him an army group command as compensation, thus preserving political primacy while hopefully offering as little advantage to the Germans as possible.[72]

No army group was available and both Nivelle and his enemies breathed a sigh of relief. 'I am finally relieved, the decision is taken, and the fight is over', Nivelle wrote. 'My position was no longer tenable, and all my work was made impossible with continual comings and goings, the idle discussion, underhanded intrigues of others and, with every day, more evidence of the flagrant hostility of the minister of war.'[73] Pétain replaced him. The meal they were forced to have after the official handover of responsibly was, as Pétain's chief of staff Bernard Serrigny recorded, 'exquisite but deadly'.[74]

Nivelle did his best to secure positions for his staff and, contrary to the myth of petulant betrayal of his most loyal lieutenant established by Pierrefeu,[75] subsequently wrote to Georges Clemenceau when he became prime minister to ask him to recognize Mangin's qualities 'even though he has lost the confidence of those under his command'. Nivelle suggested a leave of absence for his protégé instead of an outright dismissal, but Painlevé was determined to have his way. Nivelle's well-meaning efforts appeared muddled or self-serving to almost everyone except Mangin who recognized Nivelle's difficult position and remained his friend. Nivelle's final meeting with Micheler proved to be rather less congenial and they parted bitter enemies: Pierrefeu even suggests that Micheler accused Nivelle of cowardice for attempting to shift blame.[76] Mazel was dismissed without argument: Nivelle had been disappointed with Mazel's self-serving behaviour and poor grasp of fire-planning and may have felt some quiet satisfaction at his removal from command.[77]

Within weeks of Nivelle's dismissal a commission, led by General Joseph Brugère, was set up to investigate the failure of the offensive. Every military aspect was dissected, although the politicians' role was not examined. Nivelle's role in developing or encouraging new technologies and tactics was acknowledged but the commission voiced a number of concerns about his plan. Nivelle and Mangin parried these one by one. Nivelle noted that his choice of the Chemin des Dames was dictated by the importance of the sector as a potential jumping-off point for operations. He suggested that the security leaks were the result of the whole system being insecure, starting with the casual disregard for secrecy shown by deputies who visited the front. Even the documents lost to the enemy were shown to consist only of minor operational details. Nivelle provided evidence on the unpredictable weather during the period and pointed out that it was impossible to be sure how bad conditions would be more than twenty-four hours in advance. Nivelle's contention that a consolidation of positions after the offensive faltered was necessary was accepted immediately by his military colleagues. The artillery plan, in the past Nivelle's forte, clearly failed and the commission heard a range of arguments that suggested that the German defensive system clearly neutralized Nivelle's expanded 'formula', although it did not invalidate a more limited variant.[78] Nivelle pointed out that infantry units needed to be clear about their requirement for artillery support or the GQG planners would not recognize the risks; a point the commission agreed upon.[79]

Mangin vehemently argued that the offensive had been a qualified success, quoting intelligence reports that stated that the German reserves had suffered heavy casualties.[80] Ludendorff's memoirs appear to confirm this assumption:

'Our supply of munitions had diminished to an alarming extent. If the Russian success of July had occurred in April and May I do not see, as I look back, how general Headquarters could have mastered the situation. During these two months of 1917, in spite of our Aisne–Champagne victory, it was the Russian Revolution alone that saved us from serious trouble'.[81] Mangin also argued that the losses were comparable with those in other battles, but this assertion ignored the heavy losses in the first twenty-four hours.[82] Poor preparation for the evacuation of casualties was a key criticism. In fact, the chief medical inspector of the army was dismissed by the government in January 1917 and his responsibilities were absorbed into the ministry of health. Consequently, medical provision was not under the jurisdiction of the commander-in-chief. Nivelle, naturally but unsuccessfully, had challenged this decision as soon as he discovered the new arrangement (from a newspaper).[83] Overall, the enquiry was generally sympathetic to the dismissed commander-in-chief, who was not disgraced. Foch, as military adviser to the commission, was unhappy about the commission's eagerness to stigmatize individuals and treated all attempts to create scapegoats with withering contempt. His conclusion was brutally simple: 'for Mangin an army corps, to begin with, and as soon as possible…. For Nivelle an army, but much later, much later, when he's calmed down.'[84] Brugère was less charitable, although he limited his criticisms to a covering letter that noted that Nivelle was almost certainly not ready for the role of commander-in-chief when he was appointed. Painlevé was bitterly disappointed with the interim report but attempts to change the initial conclusions failed. Clemenceau, who would succeed Painlevé as premier in November, had little interest in a further investigation that might expose the poor relationship between GQG and their political masters.

Painlevé disdainfully described the commission's conclusions as 'rose-water'.[85] In fact, the key flaws in the planning process were identified and the campaign to create politically convenient scapegoats was resisted. It is notable that some units that took part in the offensive assumed that it was a pyrrhic success and, as Nivelle had prophesied, only after the dismissal of the senior commanders did rumours circulate that the offensive had been an unmitigated disaster. Cyril Falls, for example, suggested that 'French politicians in their eagerness to discredit Nivelle circulated fantastically high figures for the losses. The soldier was given the impression that he had been defeated, whereas he had won a success greater than in many battles which had been proclaimed smashing victories.'[86] The politicians, led by Painlevé, shifted all blame onto the military and the Germans made full use of this precious propaganda gift. Painlevé's continuing campaign to assign blame for the failure of the spring offensive entirely to Mangin and Nivelle alone forced Nivelle to write to Clemenceau to demand the right to answer his critics.[87]

The French army's mutinies remain the most famous legacy of the offensive, although their timing and motivation remains contentious. In a valiant effort to exonerate Nivelle, his biographer Rolland contends that trouble began in late April but spiralled out of control in late May, after Nivelle's dismissal, among units in rest areas – although it is worth noting that these were units scheduled to return to the fighting on the Chemin des Dames. Rolland also contends that the concentration of troops in spring 1917 enabled them to exchange information and to encounter *agents provocateurs* eager to radicalize discontented soldiers.[88] Pétain's claim that restoring order was his greatest achievement required him to shift blame for the disturbances on to his predecessor, something he was more than happy to do. The disappointment felt by ordinary soldiers after the perceived failure of the offensive was a major contributory factor in the mutinies, but it is important to remember why they invested so much in Nivelle's promise of decisive victory.[89]

\* \* \*

In December 1917, Nivelle was offered command of the XIX CA in Algeria. Nivelle's new area of responsibility covered France's north African possessions: his remit was the colonial policing of Algeria, Tunisia and the border regions of neighbouring Libya, Sudan, Niger and Senegal. Ever the consummate military administrator, Nivelle threw himself into this new job: he secured aid for wounded veterans, improved the aviation assets available to his command and negotiated with some of the fractious tribal leaders who were taking advantage of France's focus on the Western Front. Once the situation in north and west Africa stabilized, Nivelle concentrated his efforts on mapping France's north African territories: aerial photography and mapping techniques perfected on the Western Front were employed to explore both the desert and the littoral. Nivelle also reviewed the potential of air transportation for opening up the interior and for improving the mail service, creating temporary airfields to support further exploration. When the war ended Nivelle tried to encourage new investment in Algeria, personally sponsoring regional development projects, including the first Trans-Saharan air expedition.

Nivelle monitored events on the Western Front, hoping to receive a further active field command. Pétain's continuing lack of drive clearly irritated him. Clemenceau was aware that several officers and politicians, both French and British, were lobbying for Nivelle's reappointment to command an army group but, conscious that such an appointment would re-open the feud with Pétain, decided to shelve the matter. Unsurprisingly, Nivelle was not invited to the victory celebrations in Paris on 14 July 1919.

After Clemenceau lost office in 1920, Nivelle was invited to join the *Comité de guerre* alongside Joffre, Foch, Pétain and Mangin. In 1921, he served as president of the Inter-Allied Commission in Berlin. The controversy surrounding his role as commander-in-chief continued after the war with Painlevé and Nivelle trading blows through intermediaries (Mangin supporting Nivelle).[90] Nivelle died of influenza complicated by pulmonary congestion in 1924. His ashes were transferred to Les Invalides in 1931.

\* \* \*

Battles in the First World War are often assumed to have been lost by poor generalship and credit is rarely given to the enemy. Pierrefeu used Napoleon's maxim to highlight Nivelle's key failure: 'Do not do what the enemy wants, for the sole reason that he wants it; avoid a battlefield which he has reconnoitred and studied, and still more one that he has fortified and entrenched'; and, more recently, Timothy Lupfer concluded that Nivelle treated the Germans 'as if they were a terrain obstacle instead of an active, intelligent enemy'.[91] In contrast, Hindenburg and Ludendorff recognized the formidable threat posed by the new French commander-in-chief and determined to counter any attempt to repeat his vaunted 'formula'. Those that ignore the influence of their enemies on the outcome of battle rarely succeed. Unsurprisingly, in the English-language historiography, from liaison officer Edward Spears in his inter-war study of the Nivelle offensive, *Prelude to Victory*, through to Cyril Falls in the 1917 volume of the British official history of western front military operations to Elizabeth Greenhalgh and Robert Doughty in more recent volumes, Nivelle is portrayed as 'arrogant' or 'the perfect example of hubris'.[92]

Despite his obvious military talent perhaps, unlike Foch, Nivelle was no match for his adversaries; perhaps, like Joffre, he also fell victim to the intrigues of his supposed friends. Nivelle was a skilled operational planner, a technical innovator and a talented army commander. However, the French military system required commanders to form a network of colleagues capable of supporting them as they ascended through the ranks, and Nivelle's rapid rise to the top and relative inexperience both created enemies and confused subordinates. As Anthony Clayton notes, Nivelle's rise exposed systemic weakness in the French military system that many of his contemporaries were reluctant to acknowledge.[93] Nivelle clearly found interacting with political generals and devious politicians more difficult than he expected and managed to create the lasting impression that he was a schemer obsessed with establishing his reputation. In the end, he proved utterly unable to master domestic and inter-allied political intrigue or the strategic and operational challenges created by his sudden elevation.

Chapter 5

# Marie-Émile Fayolle: The Forgotten Marshal of France

## William Philpott

Six Marshals of France were nominated during and after the First World War.[1] Marshals Joseph Joffre, Ferdinand Foch and Philippe Pétain are the subjects of chapters elsewhere in this collection. Marshal Hubert Lyautey, a colonial soldier and wartime war minister, and Louis Franchet d'Esperey whose successful career had culminated with the command of the allied forces at Salonika in 1918, were promoted to that honour in 1921. In the same year, after some popular clamour and not without some controversy, Marie-Émile Fayolle was also promoted Marshal of France.[2] Between 1914 and 1918 Fayolle had commanded uninterrupted at all levels from division to army group. Indeed, after Nivelle's removal in May 1917, he had been considered for the job of commander-in-chief, but was passed over in favour of Pétain. After the war he was to command France's army of occupation in the Rhineland. It was a fitting reward for a general who, unlike so many other commanders, had managed to avoid *limogéage*[3] for military or political reasons, and had proved himself arguably the best field commander of French forces in the war.

Fayolle's professional persona, which united a soldiers' general's heart with a military thinker's intellect, underpinned his rise and sustained success during a challenging war. On first seeing the carnage of the industrial battlefield Fayolle had wept.[4] Yet he also considered the actual circumstances of war objectively, as befits a military academic fashioned in the same mould as Foch and Pétain. He immediately identified the key lesson for fighting on a firepower-dominated battlefield: against a well-entrenched enemy 'I will attack with the greatest care, with all the artillery and the fewest infantry necessary'.[5] He was to adhere to these principles in future commands: of 70 *division d'infanterie* (DI) from late August 1914 until June 1915 (which thereafter proudly bore the unofficial designation 'division Fayolle') and then of XXXIII *corps d'armée* (CA), which he took over from Pétain; of Sixth Army from February to December 1916, which he led during the Somme offensive; after a period as First Army commander, of France's central army group from May 1917; and, after a break to lead the French forces in Italy and to instruct the reorganizing Italian army over the winter of 1917–18, of the reserve army group from February 1918 until the end of the war. Fayolle proved a popular commander – the men of 70 DI affectionately nicknamed him 'Général Caillebotis' (literally General Duckboard) after his habit of stalking purposefully through the front-line trenches.[6] He was an innovator, with a particular concern for improving artillery methods. Above all, he was successful as a tactical and operational commander in a new style of warfare.

\* \* \*

Fayolle was born on 14 May 1852 into a petty-bourgeois, Catholic family from Le Puy-en-Velay in central France. His father was a lace merchant. Like Foch, he took a batchelor's degree in arts at the Jesuit College in Saint-Étienne before entering the *École polytechnique*, France's leading technical school which prepared students to enter the army's technical branches.[7] Two of his uncles were clergymen and his brother was a Jesuit.[8] Fayolle himself professed a strongly Catholic faith throughout his life. His diary attests to the fact that he put his trust in God or the Virgin Mary on more than one critical occasion;[9] although his own military skill probably counted for more in the outcome of operations. After graduating with honours from the *École polytechique*, Fayolle had joined the artillery. Prominent faith impeded career advancement in the army of the deeply anti-clerical Third Republic. Fayolle's successful but unremarkable forty-one year regimental and academic career had culminated in the rank of *Général de brigade* and command of 19 *brigade d'infanterie* at Vincennes, an appointment which he relinquished in May 1914 in anticipation of a quiet retirement in the provinces growing roses.[10] Fate, and the Kaiser, would soon call him back to his *métier*, and would propel him on an unexpected late-career trajectory that was to take him to the top of his profession. He would joke, his wartime chief of staff Maurice Duval later recollected, that his second career had gone much better than his first.[11]

Fayolle's mobilization appointment was to command a reserve infantry brigade in 70 DI. Immediately he had some good fortune. The divisional commander suffered a nervous breakdown and Fayolle found himself in acting command of the division during its first engagement supporting Foch's XX CA in the reverse at Morhange. Fayolle was by arm of service an artilleryman, had been a professor of artillery tactics before the war, and it was another stroke of luck that assigned the training batteries of the army's artillery school at Mailly as 70 DI's divisional artillery.[12] This combination of a thinking artilleryman with skilled gunners was to prove potent on the battlefield. With his infantry unable to deploy, Fayolle reportedly ordered his guns to deploy forwards and personally supervised the barrage that checked the Germans' advance into a gap that had opened between the two formations, which allowed Foch to disengage his hard-pressed corps.[13]

As a peacetime soldier, Fayolle had pondered on the impact that firepower would have on the battlefield, and now his theories were being put to the test. His career had involved a lengthy period lecturing on artillery tactics at the *École supérieure de guerre* (ESG) from 1898 to 1908 (he was a contemporary of Pétain and Foch who were lecturing on infantry tactics and operations respectively).[14] He took on this appointment at the same time that quick-firing artillery, in the form of the famous French '75', was adopted, and it was his task to assess and explain the impact this would have on battle. With success it would seem. One of his former pupils attested that his course was legendary;[15] another that his lectures were 'brilliant, and irrefutably sensible'.[16] Fayolle was reportedly critical of the way the artillery school chose to employ the 75s, making his point to the school's director during firing demonstrations.[17] His colleague Pétain attested later that as a staff college lecturer he predicted the increasing role of artillery and its employment en masse.[18] A practical rather than an abstract thinker, he remained active in the debates between the advocates of firepower and élan that animated the French army in the years before the war. Fayolle naturally was an advocate of firepower-based tactics (as were Pétain and a later professor of infantry tactics, Marie-Eugène Debeney).[19] This set him at opposites with those who were promoting an offensive doctrine grounded in superior morale rather than technical advantage. His own ideas on the importance of concentrating fire were set out in a volume published in 1913.[20] All this was moot come 1914, since these debates had not yet resulted in an applied operational and tactical doctrine. Although Colonel Louis de Grandmaison's notorious new regulations for the conduct of large formation operations and infantry assaults were issued between October 1913 and April 1914, the army had not had time to adapt before war broke out.[21] Reservists had been trained under the previous regulations, while as Joffre attested, in the higher ranks 'there existed…a too great tendency to take little account of the conditions of modern war'.[22] Fayolle was undoubtedly an exception, Joffre recalling that in his pre-war teaching he had always shown himself to be 'a man of sound common sense, always giving preference to simple solutions'.[23] This doctrinal hiatus left commanders free to respond to the conditions of battle as they judged appropriate. Many of these men had been trained by Fayolle himself, who in his biographer Henry Bordeaux's hyperbolic estimation had 'transmitted to them his method founded in experience, his lucid reasoning and, far from negligible, his acceptance of circumstances and his spirit of self-sacrifice. Such links…fashioned the nation's enduring strength.'[24] Perhaps not, but in the artilleryman's war that would ensue those who understood firepower would prosper and, in great part owing to Fayolle, France had many well-educated gunners.

Fayolle was another who had experienced the indignity of German invasion and occupation at an impressionable age, although not at first hand: his home town was a long way from the fighting and, unlike Joffre and Foch who were a few months older than Fayolle, he did not see military service in the Franco-Prussian War. Nonetheless, the war of 1870–1 reputedly determined his choice of a military career (although that may have been an affectation for many soldiers of his generation).[25] He devoted his career to preparing France for war against Germany – his published study of artillery tactics indicates that he adhered to the principle of 'know your enemy' and studied German artillery practice assiduously[26] – although his retirement in May 1914 might have denied him that opportunity. It would also have prevented him writing a candid diary of his day-to-day tasks and reflections as a senior commander, one of the most insightful records of senior military command produced during the war.[27]

His diary gives an insight into the man. Fayolle was not outgoing or ebullient. From his own pen he comes across as grouchy and misanthropic, constantly complaining about his seniors and his circumstances, judgmental of his subordinates and irritated by visitors. But he also reveals a shrewd, reflective mind, one continually mulling over the theoretical and practical problems that faced a commander adapting to unexpected ways of warfare. His biographer identifies his straightforwardness and rectitude: 'uprightness is the characteristic etched most clearly upon his large and compact face, with clear eyes, ever-youthful Celtic eyes, almost naive, like his unblemished life, free of intrigues and complications'.[28] This is a flattering pen-portrait, one written with flair, full of praise and designed to impress the reader with its subject's human and military virtues. Bordeaux, a moralistic conservative Catholic novelist whose works appealed to a certain type of French person – of whom Fayolle might be judged a typical example – wrote the only brief biography of Fayolle, in 1921, at a time when the events of the war were fresh, and when the public campaign for Fayolle to be made a Marshal of France, in which Bordeaux was a prominent advocate, was at its height.[29] Bordeaux wrote with the advantage of first-hand acquaintance, but his account is tainted by subjectivity: the biography is usefully supplemented by his contemporaneous and detailed diary that was later published.[30] Bordeaux had served on the intelligence staff as a press officer, and in spring 1917 had been appointed to First Army, then commanded by Fayolle. His new general immediately impressed: 'The general is tall, and has a big, pale head, with an air of level-headedness, loyalty and strength. He makes a good impression as a reasonable man of war.'[31] They established a close relationship such that in 1921 Fayolle and Paul Maistre, the other principal 1918 army group commander, would dine with Bordeaux's family and present him personally with the Légion d'honneur. They were, Bordeaux judged, 'the two men I esteemed most during the war'.[32] In the biography, therefore, Fayolle was presented as a man of faith and quiet rectitude, hard-working and principled, the sort of man whom Bordeaux admired. In Fayolle's private diary the inner man is more exposed. Fayolle was devoutly religious: while this may have been a handicap to his pre-war career, his profound Catholic faith was a great comfort to him as the war progressed. At war he was wedded to his profession and committed to his responsibilities. He took only one period of leave during the war, to attend his mother, to whom he was devoted, on her death bed.[33] After dining in April 1916 with his wife and daughter for the first time since the war began he noted laconically, 'they have not changed'.[34] He does not come across as a likeable, easy going or friendly man, although he was certainly a strong-willed and impressive one, who would prove a determined and resourceful commander. 'Profoundly modest, hard-working and conscientious.... He saw things clearly and accurately; he was always calm and methodical' in Joffre's estimation; his achievements in the difficult battles of 1914 marked him out for advancement.[35] That calmness in a crisis was legendary. Only once did he lose his temper, and over a non-military matter: someone cut back the small rose garden that his chief of staff had created at his headquarters on the Somme as a restful place in which he might momentarily escape the burdens of command.[36]

\* \* \*

Fayolle's 70 DI was attached to General Noël de Castelnau's Second Army fighting in Lorraine, and engaged in the defence of the Grand Couronné position around the fortress of Nancy as Joffre marshalled his forces to counterattack on the Marne. Fayolle had passed through his own baptism of fire well – 'I was not afraid,' he noted – although he spent a restless night thereafter, 'haunted by the memory of the wounded'.[37] His division, in contrast, had a brutal induction into modern war: an example of how not to operate when facing concentrated firepower. Under the temporary command of one of its brigadiers – on that day Fayolle was acting commander of the group of reserve divisions – 70 DI mounted a disastrous attack on the village of Hoéville: 'there were too many men in the line…there was no reconnaissance, no artillery preparation'. The division suffered over 4,000 casualties, more than thirty per cent of the division's infantry complement, including three of the division's four infantry regimental colonels killed or wounded. In contrast, the division's artillery halted the enemy's counter attack, without loss.[38] Perhaps Fayolle did not need it, but the lesson was obvious. Advancing again the next day, Fayolle noted, 'We begin, but this time very carefully, very slowly. …I only brought forward...four battalions.... The rest reorganized.... I advanced by stages, under the protection of all the artillery, and after reconnaissance.'[39] The way to operate on the modern battlefield was self-evident. At Hoéville, Fayolle reflected, 'No advanced patrols, no reconnaissance, useless masses of men! No artillery preparation. It was crazy.' The enemy's tactics appeared to be to allow the French to attack, and then to counterattack formations broken by their firepower.[40] Here in essence were the military problems that Fayolle and his peers would wrestle with for the next two years. The solution was also clear: entrenchments would have to be attacked with concentrated artillery and minimal infantry,[41] which required a new type of 'combined-arms' tactics. On 1 September Fayolle was able to record that liaison between the infantry and artillery was finally working.[42] This method served Fayolle's troops well and his division quickly built a reputation as a reliable fighting unit. When it was withdrawn from Second Army, de Castelnau praised it for being as effective as the divisions in the elite army corps it fought alongside.[43] However, under constant bombardment from larger-calibre German guns, to which the 75s with their shorter range could provide no effective response, 70 DI suffered heavy casualties and was forced to give ground like its neighbours: 'it was siege warfare'.[44]

As the 'race to the sea' developed in the autumn 70 DI was redeployed to the open northern flank. A promising command career was almost cut short when, in the confusion of the encounter battle developing around Arras, Fayolle was nearly captured by German patrols. Fleeing in the general's car, his intelligence officer was shot and wounded, and a stray bullet reportedly passed between the two men.[45] A few days later Fayolle had to evacuate his headquarters hastily when a German night attack turned his division's flank. Fayolle had hoped to hold Vimy ridge, the commanding height onto which his division deployed, but this manoeuvre turned his unsupported left flank, the spur of Notre-Dame-de-Lorette fell to the enemy, and he was obliged to retire his troops into the plain behind it. Owing to an oversight, 70 DI was unable to retake the position with a counter attack. Although it was well prepared with an artillery barrage, the infantry advance was checked by barbed wire – the boundaries of French fields rather than entanglements strung by the enemy.[46] That ridge would cost the French and British armies heavily before it was regained in April 1917.

\* \* \*

Fayolle's division enhanced its reputation as a first-class fighting formation in the early battles for that ridge. Fayolle managed the process carefully: his tendency to micro-manage was appropriate as French formations adapted to a new style of fighting.[47] General Duckboard would patrol through his division's trench lines, inspecting and encouraging. On occasion he came close to losing his life. Once, both he and Maistre had to run from enemy shelling when in the forward lines: one accurate shell could have robbed the French army of two future army group commanders.[48] As the battle developed he considered the emerging operational challenges of positional warfare; especially, as befitted a firepower theorist, those of effective artillery control and support.

> German 105mm artillery bombarded Lorette and ours did not reply. Why? Because it is controlled at army level. This is Foch's outrageous conception. ...Also, the heavy artillery fires off the map. It is not ranged on specific objectives by forward observers like the field artillery's fire. Another even more wrong idea. While preparing the attack on Carency all the field artillery was put under the control of the army's artillery commander. One could not move a gun without an order. That's crazy.[49]

Counter-battery fire, a particular obsession, was vexing him: 'One of the characteristics of the current warfare is that the two artilleries cannot destroy each other. The German gunners are always looking for mine and never find them.'[50] Foch at this point was thinking about organizing operations, while Fayolle was responsible for tactics. From their juxtaposed viewpoints an effective synthesis would emerge in time for the offensive they mounted together on the Somme in 1916.

Meanwhile, theories were tested. In the Second Battle of Artois 70 DI, part of Pétain's XXXIII CA was tasked with capturing the villages of Ablain-Saint-Nazaire, Carency and Souchez and intermediate strongpoints beneath the southern slope of Notre-Dame-de-Lorette, covering the left flank of the corps's attack on Vimy ridge and linking it with Maistre's XXI CA's attack on that commanding hill whose tenacious garrison had repulsed numerous attempts to storm it. Fayolle himself abhorred such isolated attacks 'that produced nothing more than a useless loss of men'.[51] He believed in 'the methodical capture of enemy lines successively' rather than rushing them and trying to break through. This would not work unless the enemy's guns had been silenced.[52] Consequently Fayolle did not expect the battle to be a success, dismissing it as an unnecessary and costly political offensive to support allies: France was in for a long war of exhaustion that would run into the next year at least, he judged.[53] Nor did he expect great things from the men he commanded. With the exception of the men in the elite *chasseurs à pied* battalions, his reservists were too old and sluggish, and junior leadership was indifferent.[54] Fayolle was clearly a pessimist, who saw the worst in people and expected difficulties and reverses. However, at that point in the war such an attitude was perhaps more appropriate than the over-optimism he attributed to many of his superiors, which cost men's lives in mismanaged attacks.

Meticulously prepared, 70 DI's attack began well. Fayolle's men broke into an intricate complex of enemy defences, although some of the early gains had to be relinquished as supporting formations failed.[55] Fayolle consolidated his division's gains and prepared the next attack. After five days of sustained fighting, the enemy's tenacious defence collapsed and Ablain and Carency fell into French hands along with 2,300 prisoners. Fayolle's division suffered 2,500 casualties. He judged that his division had performed superbly; which, he was pleased to record, had been noticed by army headquarters. He himself was rewarded with promotion to *Géneral de division*.[56] The principle of short advances well supported by artillery fire as the means to master complex defensive systems, the key tactical lesson from the offensive as a whole, was starting to be appreciated, and 70 DI were instrumental in teaching it.

Fayolle's success brought him to the notice of the commander-in-chief and the war minister,[57] and when Pétain was promoted to command Second Army in June, Fayolle took command of XXXIII CA.[58] Both men had begun their parallel rise through the levels of high command, with Fayolle always one step behind his old ESG colleague. Fayolle, who had an ambitious streak, tempered his own pleasure at advancement with resentment of Pétain's more rapid progress, for example when Pétain received promotion to the rank of *Général de division* and he did not.[59] One of his less endearing traits was a constant grumbling at the perceived deficiencies of his superiors and subordinates. Despite the personal rivalry and griping, he still judged Pétain 'the best general he had come across in the war'[60] – familiarity bred respect as well as contempt.

Fayolle commanded XXXIII CA in the third phase of the Artois offensive, in late September and early October. In the interim he pondered the appropriate methods for fighting in the trenches and breaking the stalemate. He set himself against small-scale, hurried attacks.[61] Both capturing the enemy's defensive system and turning a successful tactical assault into a decisive operational breakthrough would require men and munitions in unprecedented quantities, as well as proper method and preparation. Regarding his own impending attack, he considered Joffre's expectation that Tenth Army could seize the Vimy ridge and advance to Douai in the plain beyond unrealistic. A second German position behind the ridge would have to be taken, and this could not be done until the artillery had been redeployed onto the captured ridge and a new bombardment carried out.[62] This step-by-step tactical approach was out of alignment with operational ambitions. For an operational breakthrough he judged that a large *masse de manoeuvre* would be needed, perhaps nine army corps, over half a million men with appropriate artillery support.[63] Fayolle had not yet abandoned the idea of a single decisive offensive although he was starting to appreciate its nature and complexity; with two or three enemy lines to breach it would be very difficult.[64]

Joffre would essentially put Fayolle's conception into practice in the Battle of Champagne in September 1915, where it would fail largely due to the tactical difficulties of assaulting the second German position that Fayolle had identified. XXXIII CA's attack in Artois would have mixed success in a less ambitious operation: Foch and Tenth Army commander Victor d'Urbal had reverted to more methodical step-by-step advances, attuned to Fayolle's method. However, the enduring problems of close-quarter fighting in strong defensive positions meant that casualties would be heavy. Fayolle, who sympathized with the plight of his soldiers – 'The men must have rare strength to hold on. It is the triumph of discipline…'[65] – could at least take some comfort from the fact that owing to his careful preparation losses in his army corps were considerably lower than in neighbouring corps.[66] Fundamentally, Fayolle recognized, 'It is a major check, because now it is clear that a breakthrough is not possible. What should we do next time? What has occurred confirms the expectations of those who thought it over. It is certain that if one takes the first position one will fail in front of the second if it is far enough behind (around 6,000m).'[67] Tactical principles too were becoming clear:

> We have understood that we cannot run around like madmen in the successive enemy positions. Doctrine is taking shape. For every position there must be a battle, following each other as rapidly as possible. Each one needs a new plan, a new artillery preparation. If one goes too quickly, one risks being checked; too slowly and the enemy has time to make more positions. That is the problem; and it is serious.[68]

Fayolle would apply such understanding to his next major operation.

\* \* \*

Although untried as an army commander, Fayolle found himself managing the French army's main offensive effort on the Somme in summer and autumn 1916. The operation as a whole was under Foch's direction as the responsible army group commander. Conceived as a three-army offensive in February, by June only a single French army, Sixth Army, was engaged to support a British attack further north. Fayolle could be trusted to understand and to employ the more 'scientific' methods that Foch advocated after the battles in Artois (which were essentially those Fayolle had himself used), and also to plan meticulously and to prepare thoroughly. His appointment was welcomed according to the testimony of one divisional staff officer and former student, Commandant Amédé Thierry: better to have a commander who had enjoyed nothing but success since 1914 than the lacklustre General Pierre Dubois who was unpopular and did not inspire confidence.[69] Fayolle immediately set about redressing the climate of fear and removing the petty bureaucracy associated with his predecessor.[70]

Alongside an effective commander there often stands a highly competent chief of staff. In Fayolle's case that was Colonel (later General) Duval, 'the dynamo that drove the French army on so successfully during the battle of the Somme' in the view of their British liaison officer, Captain Edward Spiers.[71] Duval had been one of Fayolle's students at the ESG, although they had had no professional contact since.[72] Duval was 'very sharp, very adaptable mind, with a good understanding of all the complexities of modern warfare'.[73] Fayolle, with his 'clear judgement, ability to grasp details, tenacious and calm, but a little shrunken and aged' meshed with his 'always on the go, lively, cheerful, witty and clear sighted' subordinate despite their contrasting characters.[74] Spiers agreed. Fayolle's 'scholarly, gentle mentality' was well complemented by the energy of his younger chief of staff, 'one of the finest soldiers the war produced'. Fayolle provided 'wisdom', Duval 'the drive'.[75] For Fayolle, the chief of staff should be a sounding board and an effective executor of his commander's wishes, not a distinct voice. But also, as Fayolle would remind Duval, they had different responsibilities: 'Me, I'm concerned with the Germans! My chief of staff is busy with the French!'[76]

If any battle epitomizes Fayolle's style as a commander it is the Somme offensive in which, in contrast to the difficult learning experience of the British forces to the north, Sixth Army conducted a systematic, sustained hammering of the German defence until it reached crisis point in late September.[77] Fayolle took a hands-on approach to planning, studying the ground and intelligence picture carefully and personally drafting the army's plan of operations before fine-tuning it with his staff.[78] Fayolle outlined the methods his army would use in the offensive. It would proceed methodically for objective to objective, without compromising the troops' élan, yet leaving nothing to chance. Each attack would be against a specific objective, limited in width and depth and always preceded by an artillery barrage and careful reconnaissance of the enemy's wire (essentially the same principles he had expounded in August 1914).[79] Although this equated with Foch's scientific battle method, Foch argued for pushing the troops beyond the assigned objective if possible. This difference of opinion would lead to tension between the two men as the offensive progressed.

Initially, Sixth Army scored a stunning success on 1 July, the best by French arms since 1914. Attacking in mid-morning, almost all their objectives astride the river Somme were secured by early afternoon with light casualties. Fayolle might be criticized for not following up this success in the afternoon, although the inter-allied plan only called for his troops to cover the British attack further north. Anticipating the need to storm the German second position before the defence consolidated, Fayolle had made provision for artillery to move up under cover of darkness to support an attack on the second line south of the river the next morning. It was duly stormed, and the French established themselves on the Flaucourt plateau in the Somme bend, from which artillery could support the army's advance north of the river. It was a great tactical coup, a breakthrough in practice as the Germans pulled back to defend the line of the river Somme. But it was not one that the methodical Fayolle had any intention of exploiting. As he had explained to Joffre on the eve of the battle, such a penetration would be too narrow to exploit.[80] It demonstrated what was tactically possible at this point in the war, with good troops and proper preparation. Thereafter, however, the offensive would assume the form that Fayolle had anticipated.

Directing the Somme battle on a day-by-day basis involved constant liaison between Fayolle and his British opposite number, Fourth Army commander Lieutenant-General Sir Henry Rawlinson. When first they met, Fayolle had made a good impression on Rawlinson (not least by providing him with a good lunch): 'He has sound ideas and is very wide awake for a man of sixty-seven.'[81] Spiers suggested that Fayolle and Duval proved 'good comrades' with Rawlinson and his chief of staff Archibald Montgomery. Perhaps the chiefs of staff, 'both very fine men and endowed with the gift of tact and the charm of exquisite manners', held that partnership together.[82] It was not an easy liaison. Although the British attack to the immediate left of the French went better than the rest of their offensive on 1 July 1916, thereafter the point of junction of the two armies was difficult to manage and the advance in this sector lagged behind that of both armies to left and right.[83] As for his allies, Fayolle judged their offensive tactics infantile and costly and felt that their commitment to the battle was wavering.[84]

Fayolle's difficult relations with superiors and subordinates were apparent. He resented Foch meddling in his planning, urging him on too far and too hastily. 'Attack, attack', Foch's brusque, oft-quoted and perhaps misunderstood aphorism, was not well received at Fayolle's calm headquarters.[85] Management of junior army corps commander did not always go smoothly. Spiers recollected that 'the impeccable technician had one fault, he lacked authority when dealing with obstreperous corps commanders. Upon several occasions I had seen General Joffre step in with the weight and force of an 8-inch shell and re-establish instantaneous order amongst General Fayolle's argumentative but now dismayed subordinates.'[86] Duval compensated for his chief's failings. He was in the habit of meeting the chiefs of staff of Sixth Army's corps nightly to review developments and future plans, and Spiers was 'certain that these meetings under Colonel Duval provided the most efficient means of command I saw during the war'. At these conferences heads of sections were present as well as representatives from all the corps. They were told exactly what the Army Commander's intentions were, and exchanges of information took place between them there and then, the duties of all being made to dovetail into each other. There was no secrecy, and each officer was able to get on with his job without having to waste time guessing what the other fellow was at.[87]

Towards the end of September, when Duval was forced to take sick leave owing to eye trouble, the momentum of the offensive slackened. Up to that point Sixth Army had been progressing methodically through the successive defensive positions north of the river Somme. Fayolle's command had expanded to the extent that, at the height of the battle in September, he now had five army corps under his control (at the end of July, operations south of the river had been passed to Tenth Army, the responsibility being considered too much for a single army commander). Fayolle's systematic method of seizing and consolidating enemy positions one-at-a-time had proved its worth, and he strove to improve it further. As a gunner he was concerned with the artillery battle in particular. Counter-battery fire became a preoccupation as the offensive went on, as it was the enemy's artillery that was causing most problems once the troops had taken ground. His own artillery proved effective in breaking up the enemy's counter attacks.

On 12 September Fayolle's forces mounted an attack all along their front against the final German line of defence. It was penetrated at the village of Bouchavesnes on the Bapaume–Péronne road (where Foch's statue now stands): 'Joffre was beaming and embraced me', Fayolle noted.[88] However, the congratulations were premature: as Fayolle had anticipated, the breach was too narrow to be exploited. A follow-up attack on 15 September was mounted too hastily with tired troops in order to coincide with the large-scale British attack at Flers–Courcelette and made only meagre gains for heavy casualties, to Fayolle's anger and regret.[89] It was proof, if that was still needed, that breaking the enemy's line, while tactically possible was operationally worthless.

Although Fayolle's army had come close to a significant victory in mid-September it was not to be. As the weather worsened and the days shortened in late autumn the Somme battle shrank and lost its way. October and early November were spent delivering the sort of small-scale, piecemeal attacks that Fayolle decried to try to penetrate the huge and forbidding wood, Bois St Pierre Vaast, that now blocked Sixth Army's progress.[90] Common sense ultimately prevailed and in mid-November the advance was halted for the winter. After the offensive, Fayolle summed up what he had achieved on the Somme.

> The fact is, the Somme operation was begun without a precise objective. I gave myself one: relieve Verdun, hold [the enemy's] reserves, to be done

> with the maximum of success and the minimum of casualties. I fulfilled this programme. Verdun was relieved. More than 100 divisions passed before us. I had more success than anyone has had in the war and the losses were light.

However, he complained (referring back to 1 July), 'it was necessary to carry off a victory, a decisive victory, with two army corps!'[91] He was more forthright to Bordeaux:

> He favours attacking on a large scale. He condemns the local attacks in 1915 that cost a lot of men for nothing. Even on the Somme we attacked on too narrow a front. We could do nothing at the beginning but help the British. But the British were always behindhand. He admired the British soldiers, good looking and brave men, unafraid of death, quick in *coups de main*, sporting, but they do not know how to make war. The army commanders do not know their corps, there are last minute changes. Liaison is bad. Nonetheless, we might anticipate much of them. And they are very loyal.[92]

Winning such battles appeared, to those who did not understand warfare, not to be contributing to winning the war. Nonetheless, Fayolle acknowledged after the war, the methods and achievements of 1916 underpinned the victories he and the rest of the army would win in 1918.[93]

\* \* \*

In fact, given the punishment inflicted on the German army on the Somme, Fayolle expected that the war could be ended in 1917, and approved of the large-scale offensive battle Joffre was preparing for the spring.[94] It was not to come off, however, as Joffre was moved aside and responsibility for the next offensive passed to General Robert Nivelle. Fayolle did not suffer as badly as some when the senior commands were reorganized at the end of 1916. He retained an army command, being appointed to First Army in the relatively quiet Avre–Oise sector, although he was understandably aggrieved that Nivelle's protégé Charles Mangin had taken over the army that he had brought to a peak of efficiency on the Somme with a view to leading it in Nivelle's offensive. Moreover, General Alfred Micheler, who had commanded Tenth Army alongside him on the Somme, had been promoted to command a reserve army group for the offensive, although 'he did a lot less than me'. Fayolle had achieved a lot on the Somme working closely with Foch, although he suspected that his method was judged too slow and himself too prudent, because he did not seek the elusive and operationally worthless 'breakthrough'.

He objected to the fact that 'colonial asses' – officers who had learned their trade in France's imperial small wars – were in the ascendancy, and rightly judged that the Verdun 'gang' were trying to belittle the success that had been won on the Somme using successive carefully organized, firepower-intensive, limited attacks. In his opinion the tactics that had brought about the recapture of forts Douaumont and Vaux in the autumn were merely 'the methods used on the Somme reconfigured by Mangin'.[95] But such tactics, however effective, did not scale-up to an operational method.[96] Pétain, who showed him round Verdun in early January, 'basically showed me nothing interesting'.[97] Louis Franchet d'Esperey, another 'colonial' who took over Foch's army group, left him flabbergasted: 'He understands nothing,' he carped, perhaps unfairly.[98] Foch, with whom he had always had a volatile working relationship, 'wished to get all I know out of me. Go away, crafty devil!'[99] Such outbursts, even though confined to a private diary, do not present Fayolle as an easy-going man who had cooperative working relationships with his peers.

Essentially, Fayolle appreciated, this was politics at work.[100] He had not been a soldier in the Third Republic for more than forty years without grasping that military sense would on occasion take a back seat to political expediency and personal ambition, even in wartime. Fayolle and his fellow Somme commanders would have to bide their time until the wheel of political fortune turned again, which it would come the spring. Meanwhile, Fayolle set about managing his new army with the care and professionalism he had brought to the previous one. First Army's role in Nivelle's planned offensive was to mount a holding attack between the British to the north and Micheler's strike force to the south. Fayolle himself was doubtful of the plan. He expected a German attack to forestall the allied offensive, just as it had in 1916, and that he was the 'fall guy' whose army would take the blow.[101] In fact, the enemy would disrupt Nivelle's preparations by retiring rather than attacking, and in March Fayolle would find himself organizing a follow-up advance. His fortunes were reviving. In anticipation of breaking the German front Nivelle redeployed First Army to follow-up the offensive. While welcoming this renewed sign of confidence in him – Duval reported that Nivelle judged him deserving of command of an army group – Fayolle remained unconvinced. Micheler, Pétain and others all doubted that success was likely in the changed circumstances, while Fayolle hoped there would be a postponement.[102] In the circumstances, Fayolle reminded his divisional officers of their ultimate responsibility not to send brave men against uncut wire.[103]

Once again politics determined the course of events. When Nivelle threatened to resign a new and weak government backed him despite the collective doubts of his subordinates. The offensive, while not entirely disastrous, fell far short of what Nivelle had promised and his own days were numbered. Fayolle would be a beneficiary. He would be given command of an army group in the next reshuffle of the high command that brought Pétain to *Grand quartier général* and Foch to the war ministry as the government's principal military adviser. The reunited triumvirate of ESG professors would now work closely together until the end of the war. In fact, Fayolle had been mentioned as a possible replacement for Nivelle although, as an experienced, careful commander rather than a political general an important field command was more appropriate. He agreed. Taking on the supreme command was not a role that he coveted, even though he liked to be busy.[104] The day before he had confirmation of his promotion he griped that he was 'bored here doing nothing, because I am unable to do anything'.[105] A fortnight later he was so engrossed in thinking about the strategic and operational challenges that he faced at this critical juncture of the war that he forgot his own sixty-fifth birthday![106]

Replacing Pétain once again, Fayolle inherited *Groupe d'armées du centre* at a time of crisis for the French army, which was gripped by mutinies after the offensive's failure. Fayolle was aware that the strategic complexion of the war was changing, with the decline of Russia and the weakening of France balanced by the intensifying blockade of Germany and the as yet untapped potential of the United States. It had become a war of exhaustion and it was necessary, he identified, that the allies 'endure' – that above all would decide the war that was entering its most difficult phase.[107] His own problems were those of military operations. Since the failed offensive had resulted in 'a regression to the methods of the Somme',[108] their supreme practitioner was needed. Managing his new sector presented 'a difficult job: Reims, Champagne, Verdun. Pray that the Virgin of Victories protects me, protects us. I only have confidence in her, but that confidence is absolute. The situation is made worse by the recent operations.'[109] While the war had aged him like it would any man with such heavy responsibilities, Fayolle was up to the task and Bordeaux was sorry to see him go.

> A fine man, uncomplicated, honest, upright, loyal and inclined to simple solutions. Big, powerfully built yet not elegant, a manly voice, banal utterances that seem to lack conviction. This is a man who is above intrigues, almost naive, but with a genuine conscience. Often lost in thought, a little shrunken with old age, he needs his vivacious chief of staff, Colonel Duval, beside him. Look at his instructions for the Somme; his artillery preparations: they were excellent.[110]

Fayolle was unhappy when Pétain assigned Duval to other duties, for the third time. He passed no comment on his replacement General Joseph Barthélémy, who remained in post until April 1918, suggesting he was a competent substitute.[111]

Fayolle spent the rest of the summer overseeing operations with his customary care and petulance. He monitored the local operations carefully, noting successes and reverses in his diary, and the number of French losses and German prisoners. To some, Fayolle might appear to be a micromanager, but his personal record evidences a determination that the armies he directed should prosper at a difficult time for the army as a whole, and that his subordinates do their jobs well. Several army commanders lost their appointments under his supervision. General Olivier Mazel, who had been one of Nivelle's army commanders in the April offensive, 'made a bad impression. He is unprofessional…panicky. …He constantly changes his mind and cannot make a firm decision.' He lost command of Fifth Army quickly.[112] General François Anthoine of Fourth Army talked too much and struck Fayolle as being over-ambitious. His superior reserved judgement until he demonstrated success.[113] General Henri Gouraud, his successor, also 'made a bad impression. Characterful, but not very intelligent, not very professional and physically diminished.'[114]

His worsening relationship with General Adolphe Guillaumat of Second Army can be assessed from both sides. The two men had taught together for a year at the ESG a decade earlier and, Guillaumat recollected, had enjoyed a good working relationship.[115] In the middle phase of the Somme offensive Guillaumat successfully commanded I CA, and then had praised the level-headed and methodical way of operating that reduced casualties.[116] Yet the relationship soured in the field. Guillaumat complained when his corps was withdrawn from the battle that he received little thanks for their efforts and successes from his army commander.[117] When they resumed their working relationship, it was tense. Fayolle judged Guillaumat to be too pessimistic and grumbling after a local setback at Verdun in late June 1917: he 'had no bottle'.[118] Guillaumat for his part groused frequently to his wife that Fayolle was too old for the job, an 'old fogey' who could not give clear, direct instructions or get a grip on his armies during the anxious period of the mutinies. At the time, he tried to go behind his superior's back to complain to Pétain about Fayolle's attitude.[119] For his part, Guillaumat stood up for himself and tried to stop Fayolle meddling in his operational planning.[120] This may have been a generational clash, an expression of professional jealousy: Guillaumat felt that promoting older generals restricted opportunities for successful younger men, no doubt himself included – he was ten years younger than Fayolle.[121] Fayolle was clearly not an easy man to work under. A hard taskmaster, he kept his subordinates up to the mark. Yet under his management Second Army scored a notable success.

The short and effective Second Battle of Verdun in late August 1917 is a forgotten offensive, but it showcased French military art at that point in the war. The battle combined the principles of 'Pétain tactics' – concentrated and prolonged artillery fire and infantry infiltration – with the meticulous planning Fayolle expected. Guillaumat's army recaptured the western heights of Côte 304 and Mort-Homme in a classic 'bite and hold' operation. 'Yesterday's preparation was excellent. It has lasted seven days, more than two of counter-battery fire, and that night special [gas] shells were employed,'[122] although even the inveterate gunner Fayolle judged the amount of fire-support initially demanded by corps commanders to be ridiculous.[123] Although the battle was a great success, Fayolle had one complaint – Guillaumat had manipulated things so that he received all the credit in the media: 'he's got a nerve!'[124]

The enemy had no real answer to this type of warfare. The Second Battle of Verdun presaged the sort of battles the army would fight in 1918 as it swept the German army from French soil in the late summer and autumn. Then Fayolle would wield the biggest broom. Meanwhile, however, his skills were needed elsewhere.

\* \* \*

The enemy could also mount effective offensives, as they would demonstrate on the Italian front in October when they routed the Italian Second Army at Caporetto. Fayolle was then deputed – not without protest on his part[125] – to the task of stabilizing the Italian front and the Italian army. After Caporetto, French and British divisions were moved south to shore up the crumbling Italian line. By the time they arrived in force, however, the Italians had re-established their defensive front along the Piave river as the Central Powers' offensive inevitably ran out of momentum. The allied divisions that remained in Italy over the winter were a reserve and insurance against a future collapse, but they had to do little hard fighting. Fayolle made sure to deploy them to the critical sectors of the new Piave front, however, as the cement that would hold the Italian defence together while the army rebuilt itself.[126]

As winter set in Fayolle's real role became evident. He was not to command the French troops in the theatre, which were to be led by General Denis Duchêne; 'level-headed' in Fayolle's opinion but with a poor grasp of tactics, who he was pleased to see replaced by his old comrade Maistre.[127] Rather, he was to coordinate the allied forces and to train the Italian army in the latest tactics. There had been some talk of his taking command in the theatre, but since that was judged politically impossible in an allied nation's own territory he was advised to exercise his authority surreptitiously.[128] This would require building good relationships with the Italians and the British forces in Italy led by General Herbert Plumer. Having seconded the British army in its painful baptism of fire on the Somme, it was a role for which Fayolle was well prepared.

However, it was not one that he relished. He saw himself as a soldier rather than a politician and his diary record suggests that frequent visits and dinners with the King of Italy, Italian and British generals and dignitaries were resented because they interfered with his military task of stabilizing the front. While there, however, he was able to indulge his passion for Catholic architecture: the beauty of Italian churches was a regular distraction as he toured the country.[129]

Despite his restlessness in the job, Fayolle's sojourn in Italy should be judged a success. He proved, Bordeaux suggested, a good diplomat, and inspired confidence.[130] He had a new Italian commander-in-chief, General Armando Diaz, to tutor and he found him a willing pupil: 'He made a good impression. He listened', Fayolle noted at their first meeting.[131] But Diaz's battered army needed taking in hand: the Italians needed to learn to organize their defensive positions better and all arms required proper training.[132] The French forces in Italy became an unofficial training school in up-to-date tactics. Impressing Diaz with their military bearing was a way to encourage emulation. Diaz was prepared to take Fayolle's advice on operational and tactical matters – 'you are my experienced senior,' he apparently confided at one point – and under Diaz's leadership, Fayolle noted, the new Italian headquarters settled down.[133] Fayolle returned to France confident that an Italian army under new leadership and French tutelage would now hold.

\* \* \*

Having helped rescue an ally, he would now be given the chance to save his own nation. With a new campaign and a new confrontation with the German army pending he was pleased to be recalled to France in February, potentially to command a general allied reserve which was mooted.[134] He was probably glad to leave Italy having narrowly escaped with his life on two occasions while there: once when the enemy shelled his headquarters and another when his staff car drove into a ravine in the fog (Barthélémy broke his arm in the crash).[135]

Foch and the new French prime minister, Georges Clemenceau, had need of a reliable and experienced senior commander. In the defensive battle as with the offensive, Fayolle would not disappoint. Anticipating a German offensive in the spring, Fayolle was designated to command the newly formed *Groupe d'armées de réserve*, although this seemed to be a command without forces once plans for an allied general reserve under Foch's control had been abandoned, and it would seem without prospects – on the eve of the German spring offensive Fayolle noted in his diary that 'the view is forming more and more that the Boches will not attack'.[136] The allies were caught by surprise, but not without resources. With his reliable chief of staff Duval back at his side until the immediate crisis abated, Fayolle would be assigned the Third and First Armies, the latter under Debeney's command forming and deploying northwards to maintain touch with the retiring British right wing and to cover Amiens. 'It is the final battle', Fayolle noted somewhat prematurely when apprised of the scale and effectiveness of the first German blow.[137] He approached his task with customary calm.[138] Within a few days, the reality of the battle was taking shape. The Germans could be stopped if an effective defence could be organized. This Fayolle did over the last days of March, taking in hand the depleted and retreating British forces as well as fresh French reinforcements which he fed piecemeal into the thickening allied defensive line.[139] On Good Friday, he confidently informed Bordeaux, who was reporting on Third Army's efforts, that the enemy's offensive could be stopped by Easter Sunday, 31 March, which it was.[140] Fayolle's methods were straightforward but tested and effective, echoing his approach in 1914's defensive battles: 'Fayolle... explained the importance of his artillery. He has half as many divisions in line as the Germans, but magnificent artillery with which he makes the lives of the Germans opposite him impossible. At this his warrior's face lit up and he laughed at the thought of the trouble he was giving the enemy.'[141]

It would seem that having the enemy in front of him was less of a trial for Fayolle than having chiefs above him. His diary is rich with complaints about the contradictory instructions he received from his immediate superior Pétain and Foch, recently appointed allied generalissimo. His summation was prosaic but accurate, reflecting both his professional pride as well as less appealing qualities of self-importance and professional jealousy:

> Foch always plays the same role. He is...ready to say if we are successful, 'It is I who have won the battle...'. On the other hand, if the plan fails Pétain will say, 'It is nothing to do with me, Foch's plan was used, not mine'. The truth is that Foch has come up with a plan: close the breach. Pétain has provided the means to do this, but it is I who has directed the battle.[142]

The situation would persist until the end of the campaign, during which Fayolle's love-hate relationship with Foch would dominate his record of events. At heart this was a matter of temperament rather than intellect. At their first wartime encounter Foch had been 'Captain Smasher';[143] ever after the irruptions of this lively, animated man into the calm of Fayolle's headquarters made Fayolle's head spin.[144] Fayolle considered Foch too political and ambitious.[145] He felt that Foch had tried to take credit from him for the achievements of the Somme offensive.[146] He had rubbed up against him again in Italy: 'good riddance' he had scribbled when Foch returned to France.[147] What held the two men together and ensured an effective working partnership was that they saw the war in the same way and were agreed on the way it should be conducted, even if they had different levels of responsibility and hence different perspectives. But Foch had performed the role Fayolle was now entrusted with, and from long acquaintance evidently trusted him to deliver on the battlefield when and where it mattered.[148]

For the rest of the 1918 campaign, in defence and then during the advance to victory, Fayolle managed his subordinate army commanders through successes and the occasional failure with his customary verve and care. At the end of April his sector fell relatively silent as the battle moved to the Chemin de Dames and the Marne, although Third and First Armies kept up an active defence as part of Foch's overall plan to keep the enemy engaged everywhere. Several key positions were won back with carefully prepared but limited local offensives which had become Fayolle's signature style of battle. The first American attack, in First Army's sector at Cantigny on 28 May, came under his scrutiny: 'They attacked with 3 battalions and 83 batteries (!!!). It would be wrong to get the troops used to such an excess of artillery support.'[149]

In June Fayolle's army group gained another army, Mangin's Tenth Army, just before it faced the fourth phase of the German spring offensive, the Battle of the Matz. After the Anglo-French front had collapsed on the Chemin des Dames in May (Duchêne's poor grasp of defensive tactics was largely to blame), Fayolle had prepared carefully. His armies were to implement defence-in-depth tactics. Debeney (who had played a role in drawing up tactical directives when Pétain's chief of staff) seemed to get this idea, although Georges Humbert of Third Army was reluctant to weaken his forward defences in favour of a strong rearward battle zone. 'He will come round', Fayolle anticipated.[150] But there was insufficient time. When the Germans struck on 9 June, therefore, the new defensive system had not been fully implemented and part of Third Army's front was overrun. Still, Fayolle seemed satisfied with his subordinate, if not his soldiers, as he confided to Bordeaux:

> I'm not happy. None of the divisions held their ground as I was expecting. …I was ready for the enemy. The arrangements made with General Humbert were excellent: very few men, if still too many, in the front line; correct deep deployment; the artillery ready and expecting the enemy. I fear lethargy among the troops who could not hold the second position.

Fayolle was unperturbed, having prepared a counter attack with Mangin's fresh army that would stop the German attack in its tracks on 11 June. 'You know, Bordeaux, I have got what I wanted, I am going to counter attack. Then everything will change…. The troops will regain confidence, stop retreating, this is what depresses them.' As Bordeaux observed: 'He is gripped by emotion, a deep love of the motherland, the will to conquer. This simple man is the archetype of both the honourable man and the leader.'[151] Although Mangin did well, he and Fayolle did not see eye-to-eye on operations. In Fayolle's judgement Mangin was a self-centred, boastful and excitable thruster: while other army commanders fought for France, Mangin fought for himself.[152] Reigning Mangin in seemed to be Fayolle's main role as his army group commander.

On the other hand, Debeney warranted closer supervision. Fayolle liked to check his subordinates' plans and often as not Fayolle found Debeney's wanting, being over-cautious and poorly arranged. They would often argue over details.[153] Nonetheless, First Army was the main striking force at Fayolle's disposal in the final advance to victory. This began with the battle of Montdidier, in which Fayolle's armies expanded the blow struck at Amiens on 8 August by the British and First Army (temporarily under British commander-in-chief Field Marshal Sir Douglas Haig's command for the offensive). Thereafter the army group pushed or pursued the increasingly weak and demoralized Germans through the Hindenburg Line to the Franco-Belgian frontier by the time the armistice was signed. Fayolle played his part in this advance to victory, at one point having half the divisions of the French army under his authority.[154] In the closing months of the war Fayolle often griped in private that his contribution to the victory was being ignored, those above him or the army commanders below him receiving all the plaudits in the newspapers.[155] Certainly he was not in the most prominent position of responsibility but, as he rightly appreciated, Foch's grand scheme and Petain's plans could not be brought to fruition without someone who could ensure the field commanders' operations attuned to the wishes of the high command. They provided the ideas, but Fayolle understood and supervised the methods of effective operations: he was 'the artisan of their victories, I stay in the shadows which suits me well'.[156] Perhaps Fayolle's reticence undermined an enduring reputation. As Duval attested in a post-war paean to his late chief that emphasized his modesty: 'How many times have I come across accounts of great events in the press or in books, in which he played a central role, yet in which he is hardly acknowledged, and sometimes not mentioned at all?'[157]

\* \* \*

After the armistice was signed, Fayolle was an obvious choice to command the French forces occupying the Rhineland. Partly this was reward for his service, but also acknowledgment of his abilities to deal with allies who would also provide occupying forces, to impose French authority on German civilians, and perhaps also to control the hot-headed and self-promoting Mangin who would command one of the French armies in Germany.[158] Fayolle judged Germany to be beaten but not broken. The country had not seen war like France had, and the population seemed sullen and unwilling to accept their defeat. They might yet menace France again, especially if the Austrians joined them.[159] From such a perspective the peace treaty when it came was a disappointment: 'the Germans signed without conditions. Peace is made. What a pity! Germany is not crushed and France's future [security] is not guaranteed.'[160] Fayolle had been gearing up for the resumption of hostilities.

After the Bastille Day victory parade in Paris following the armistice Fayolle expressed himself surprised to have been cheered so heartily by the crowd, 'because I believed I was hardly known by the public'.[161] For his own part, Fayolle had no desire to return to his rose garden. The award of a Marshal's baton was mooted and Pétain took up his case, but nothing came of it. He would at least be retained on active duty with full pay, although this took a long time to be confirmed.[162] Eventually he was awarded the Medaille militaire. The citation read: 'Splendid soldier who, since 1914, never stopped fighting the enemy. In 1918, he grabbed them by the throat and played a preponderant part in the victory. He directed his armies with sure judgment, incomparable decisiveness and good sense.'[163] He almost did not live to receive it. Ironically, after so many narrow escapes in wartime, he was nearly killed in a road accident on his own doorstep when returning home to be honoured by his home town.[164]

As encomiums and rewards were handed out after the war, Fayolle seemed to have been overlooked. Joffre, Foch and Pétain were made Marshals of France and the first two were elected to the *Academie française* (Pétain was to be elected in 1931). It took a sustained public campaign before Fayolle was also handed his Marshal's baton in February 1921.[165] He remained on active duty as a member of the *Conseil supérieur de la guerre* and France's military representative at the League of Nations. His final, perhaps surprising, military responsibility was as inspector general of aeronautics.[166] Thereafter he lived quietly in retirement, tending his rose garden back in Clermont-Ferrand. Although he had been defensive of his reputation during the war, unlike many of his contemporaries he had no intention of polishing it in post-war memoirs. He did lend his name to an early series of illustrated popular narratives of the war, but his input was limited to chapters on the Somme and the 1918 campaign.[167] Since he left no memoirs, and his insightful and frank (if not widely read) diary was not published until 1964, after a brief period of fame immediately after the war Fayolle passed like many important First World War figures into relative obscurity. Fayolle died aged seventy-six in 1928 and was laid to rest among France's great military commanders in the vault at Les Invalides.

\* \* \*

Fayolle went to war uncertain of how he would perform. 'I'm afraid of being afraid, of not being up to my job', he confided to his diary on mobilization:

'But I will not be any more frightened than the others and I will do my best.'[168] Still, Bordeaux noted of a later conversation with Duval, 'He hesitated to say so, but he was very happy when war broke out,' because he would get to practice what he had prepared for his whole life.[169] As a gunner about to take command of an infantry brigade he questioned his ability to handle infantry. He was spared this test, entering battle in command of an all-arms formation. Unlike many other senior commanders, his nerve held in the chaos of August 1914.[170] He adapted quickly to an emerging style of warfare that required an intimate understanding of firepower and demanded parsimony in the expenditure of soldiers' lives on an increasingly mechanized battlefield. Within a year of the outbreak of war he was commanding an elite army corps, and within two years directing the French army's most ambitious and sustained offensive to date. Yet he knew his limitations. When the possibility that he would succeed Nivelle was mooted he remarked, 'I do not know if I am capable of this…it is too high for me. In any case, I must consult my conscience.'[171] He certainly enjoyed war – his love for it was almost childlike, Bordeaux observed – even if he shied away from politics: 'He does not see the bigger national picture very clearly, but he knows his army and the harm it can do to the Boches'.[172]

Fayolle, from Bordeaux's and others' testimony, was an impressive if not a very likeable man, whose personality did not endear him to seniors and subordinates. He comes across as self-important and self-absorbed, irascible, morose and critical, although those who entered his inner circle found a different individual, warm, erudite and compassionate. Spiers later remembered him as 'one of the very sweetest and wisest old men I have ever met. …He always made me think of a kind of bird I have never seen or heard of but which I feel must exist somewhere, a kindly, friendly old bird with a short hooked beak and prominent round eyes, whose voice is in keeping with its appearance.'[173] His compassion he saved for his men rather than his colleagues, his charm for his allies – he was probably a better man to meet in a trench or at a dinner table than in a meeting. But Fayolle was also intelligent, determined, methodical and a master of his profession at a demanding and difficult time for his army and nation, 'confident when he believed he had made the right decision after long reflection, without concern for himself'.[174] His confidence was grounded in his deeply held Christian faith – imploring the Virgin Mary for help was a regular refrain when battle loomed[175] – which enabled him to rise to any challenge with dynamism and poise, whether it be to meet a tactical challenge on the battlefield, to direct a sustained offensive, to succour and advise an ally, or to contain and counterattack an enemy offensive. His determination derived from heartfelt patriotism and a deep-seated hatred of the enemy. 'When he says *le Boche* this brave man's voice rises to a pitch of hatred', Bordeaux noted: 'Certainly not from any personal hated of which he is incapable, but hatred of his country's enemies.'[176] From early in the war, Foch and Pétain placed great trust in his martial abilities, and they were never let down. Since he did not rise to the very top, in comparison with his comrades in arms Fayolle is somewhat forgotten. But he was by their side throughout the war and, as possibly the best field commander either side was to produce, well deserved the marshal's baton which belatedly he received. The final word belongs to his loyal chief of staff, Duval: 'He was a true man of war who grew on the battlefield.'[177]

Chapter 6

# Fernand de Langle de Cary: A Pragmatic Survivor

Simon House

Fernand Louis Armand Marie de Langle de Cary was one of the original five army commanders of the French army of August 1914. During the succession of defeats suffered by France in the Battles of the Frontiers, commander-in-chief General Joseph Joffre perforce had to weed out a large number of incompetent generals and replace them with younger and better men. To do this in the heat of battle and yet avoid emasculating the army's command structure, Joffre needed a core of senior officers on whom he could rely to hold the line. General de Langle de Cary ('de Langle') was one of those officers, a soldier of skill and experience, with a firm and resolute character that proved able to stand the stress of modern warfare. Although he lost his first battle, he learned from that experience and became a competent commander. He also proved adept at 'managing upwards', the art of influencing the positive perceptions of one's superiors regarding one's performance. Never was that skill more needed than after his failure in his first battle in August 1914, when he retained his post while many other generals lost theirs. Thereafter de Langle became a key figure in the leadership of France's armies for the two years that followed the Battles of the Frontiers, a formative period in which the French learned the lessons that would build the army that would go on to victory. He led Fourth Army and then the *Groupe d'armées du centre* (GAC) through the Battles of the Ardennes (1914), the Marne (1914), Champagne (1915) and the early stages of Verdun (1916), before falling foul of Joffre for his handling of that last battle and being gracefully nudged into retirement. When he died in February 1927, he was buried at Les Invalides in Paris, in the pantheon of France's most notable military sons.[1]

\* \* \*

Fernand de Langle de Cary was born at Lorient in Brittany on 4 July 1849, into a devout Catholic family. His father was a frigate captain who had taken part in naval operations in the Crimean and Italian Wars; his mother was a wealthy member of the bourgeoisie in her own right, a descendant of the founding mayor of the city of Lorient and generations of sea-faring traders and members of the French East India Company. Fernand, the third child of four, chose the army as his career straight out of school. He was educated at the Jesuit College at Vannes, enrolling in 1867 in the cavalry contingent at St. Cyr – the French army's officer cadets' school. An excellent student, Fernand was almost always first in his class of 274 students, and when he passed out in October 1869 it was as 'major' and 'flag-bearer' (the equivalent of the Sword of Honour winner at Sandhurst). His reward was to have first choice of posting, and he chose the prestigious (and militarily active) *2ᵉ chasseurs d'Afrique* cavalry regiment of the colonial army, based in Oran. Such was his academic excellence and potential, however, that he was immediately given a place at the army's staff college, then called the *École impériale*, which he took up on 1 January 1870.[2]

The onset of the Franco-Prussian War overtook his studies, and *sous-lieutenant* de Langle found himself deployed into the front line of the siege of Paris after the disastrous defeats of summer 1870. His eldest brother, Aldéric, had been killed in battle on the eleventh day of the war. Fernand was more fortunate: attached to the staff of General Louis Trochu, military governor of Paris under the post-imperial Committee for the Defence of Paris, he found a patron who would thereafter sponsor his career. Fernand was wounded during his first taste of combat, the Battle of Buzenval on 19 January 1871. The wound was serious enough – a bullet in the lung from which he nearly died – but 'adopted' by the 'Trochu Set' of surviving senior French officers and nursed by the wife of one whose daughter he subsequently married, Fernand after his recovery was clearly set on a path towards high command. For his services in the war he was promoted to full lieutenant and awarded membership of the Légion d'honneur, before re-entering the staff college in October 1872 to complete his studies. Despite physical frailty as a result of his injury, which inhibited his ability to excel at staff rides and on the exercise field, he nevertheless passed out third in his class.[3]

From 1873 to 1900, Fernand was a member of the elite cadre of French general staff officers, alternating between staff and field postings, gaining experience and promotions as he rose steadily through the peacetime officer corps towards the top. During his twenty-seven years as an officer of the general staff, de Langle settled into a happy domestic life, having married Marie-Françoise-Geneviève de Lemud in 1878. They had three sons, Aldéric, Armand and Pierre, and all three were to join the armed forces. This phase of his career ended in 1900 when, aged fifty-two, he was promoted to *Général de brigade*. With this promotion, de Langle rose in status from officer of the general staff to senior commander.[4]

From 1900 until 1913, General de Langle commanded, successively, a cavalry brigade, an infantry brigade, two different infantry divisions and two different army corps. In December 1912, his seniority and excellent reputation earned him a seat on the *Conseil supérieur de la guerre* (CSG), the body of senior commanders who advised the war minister. With that position went a nomination to command an army in time of war, and de Langle was made army commander designate of Fourth Army. On 31 December 1913, de Langle was made *Grand officier* of the Légion d'honneur in recognition of an unblemished career that duly ended in retirement on his sixty-fifth birthday on 3 July 1914. Exceptionally, however, Joffre ensured that he retained even in retirement the role of commander-in-chief designate of Fourth Army, a measure of Joffre's personal regard for de Langle's qualities as a senior commander in the event of impending war.[5]

\* \* \*

When war broke out in August 1914, de Langle was called out of retirement to take up the army command for which he had been designated. His experience and reliability were qualities that the commander-in-chief, Joffre, required; the two had cemented a good working relationship on the CSG in the years before war. Joffre wrote later of de Langle: 'a firm, upright character, disciplined, full of authority, one could place the greatest confidence in him'.[6]

De Langle's Fourth Army had been designated as Joffre's reserve army under Plan XVII, the counter-offensive strategy to meet a German invasion of France and Belgium.[7] Positioned slightly behind the first line, south-west of Verdun, it could be brought up in support of operations either east or north of the German fortified zone of Metz, depending on circumstances. However, as soon as the war broke out and the Germans attacked the Belgian city of Liège, Joffre decided to bring Fourth Army up into the front line, positioning it along the Meuse river facing north, between General Pierre Ruffey's Third Army and General Charles Lanzerac's Fifth Army. He had effectively committed de Langle to lead a counter attack through the Ardennes, one of two offensives envisaged in the text of Plan XVII.[8]

For many years before the war French intelligence and military analysis had deduced that Germany would choose to violate Belgian neutrality and sweep around the left flank of the French frontier defences. That much proved to be accurate prediction; mistakenly however the French believed that the sweep around their flank would take place east of the river Meuse, not west of the river as actually happened. According to this French pre-war assessment, the Germans would march their main force down the Meuse through the Ardennes towards Sedan,[9] with only a token force – if any – crossing over to the west bank. The counter attack that Joffre envisaged, therefore, was based on that premise, and on the further assumption that a French army gathered secretly in the Ardennes forests might at the right moment burst out, take the enemy by surprise, hit the advancing German forces in the flank and, pinning them with their backs to the Meuse, defeat them in the one annihilating battle that would win the war. This was the mission given to de Langle and his army: to wait while the German sweep through Belgium developed and German intentions were more fully revealed; then to advance secretly into the Ardennes forests and assemble on the northern edge of the woods, awaiting the prefect moment to strike.

Mobilization of the French and German armies was completed by 16 August; and during that period and beyond French intelligence gathering – especially by the primitive French air force – reported numerous German columns marching in a north-westerly direction across the face of Fourth Army and seemingly into the trap that Joffre had planned for. A large German force, named by French staff as the 'Northern Group of German Armies', had been identified gathering around the Belgian fortresses of Liège and Namur. Unfortunately for de Langle's Fourth Army, an additional German army, appropriately also the Fourth (German) Army under General Duke Albrecht von Württemburg, had been gathered, undetected, behind the German frontier with Belgium in the Ardennes. Its mission was to protect the flank of the Northern Group of German Armies from just such a counter attack as Joffre was planning; and when on 19 August it commenced its advance westwards into the Ardennes, it would be perfectly positioned to upset Joffre's plans. Unaware of this potential threat, Joffre deemed on 20 August that enough Germans had passed in front of de Langle's army for the surprise flank attack to begin.[10]

Therefore, on 20 August Joffre issued the order for de Langle to execute the plan starting on 22 August but, significantly, authorizing de Langle meanwhile to send strong mixed-arms advance-guards forward to gain possession of, and guard, the exits from the forests. It was a suggestion that de Langle chose not to accept, for reasons that are unclear. Equally significant was a major skirmish on 20 August between de Langle's cavalry corps (scouting in front of the army north of the forests in the region of Neufchâteau) and elements of two German infantry corps. The significance was that Neufchâteau was on the proposed line of march of the *corps d'armée coloniale* in the very middle of his deployment. Yet de Langle took no special steps in the light of that intelligence. On the contrary, he allowed his corps commanders to lull themselves (and their troops) into a false sense of security when they did march into the forests. It was under these conditions that at 05.30 on 22 August de Langle's five army corps launched themselves into the Ardennes in multiple divisional columns, each allocated a specific road or track through the inhospitable terrain. There was a thick river mist lying over the whole region that day, a product of rain the evening before and summer humidity. The sun burned away the mist only at about 09.00, allowing the French columns on the left to advance undetected for nearly four hours. Thus, de Langle fortuitously achieved the surprise that Joffre had demanded, especially on his left wing where three army corps – XI, XVII and XII *corps d'armée* (CA) – advanced deep into the forests before encountering the enemy. Nothing else on the French side went according to plan. Instead of engaging the left wing of the Northern Group of German Armies, which had actually crossed the Meuse and were on the west bank by this time, de Langle's columns ran into the German screening force – Duke Albrecht's Fourth Army, five army corps spread thinly over 100km of inhospitable terrain. Only three of Duke Albrecht's five corps were engaged in battle on 22 August, the other two being too far away to intervene, so de Langle started the battle with two factors in his favour: surprise and superior numbers. It was not, however, to be a conventional battle as envisaged in French pre-war doctrine: a battle in open terrain carried out in ordered stages and with tight command and control. Instead, it was to become a series of isolated encounter battles as the French divisional columns ran into German columns in the woods and clearings of the central Ardennes; and these encounter battles were to be fought under conditions that favoured German devolved command doctrine and training. Despite being caught by surprise, German divisional and brigade commanders reacted quickly and efficiently and used their superior tactical training and mixed-arms coordination to hold off de Langle's superior numbers all day. Indeed, in two instances, at Bertrix and Rossignol, the local German commander inflicted a heavy defeat on his French opposite number. At Bertrix XVII CA was routed when one of its divisions was caught in column of march in thick forest by a German division arriving unnoticed on its flank. At Rossignol the elite French 3 *division coloniale* allowed itself to be encircled and decimated by the German VI *armeekorps*. In two other instances the local French army corps commander had the opportunity to inflict a similar defeat on the Germans, yet French tactics and training proved unequal to the task. At Maissin XI CA was held off by a single German brigade despite a four-to-one superiority in men and guns. At Nevraumont General Pierre Roques missed an opportunity to break through the centre of the German Fourth Army with his XII CA despite odds in his favour of six-to-one at the decisive point. As the evening of 22 August faded into dusk, de Langle's army found itself thrown back in disarray towards its start-line.[11]

When assessing de Langle de Cary's performance as a commander in his first experience of war, it seems poor by any objective standard; he made many mistakes that contributed to the defeat of his army. His first task, working with his army headquarters staff, was to get five army corps through the dense Ardennes forests without alerting the Germans to this movement. We have already seen, above, that he made two errors of judgement in planning the advance: first, he failed to send out strong advance-guards on 21 August to secure the northern exits from the forests, despite authority from Joffre to do so; and second, he failed to adapt his plans after the cavalry skirmish on 20 August. He compounded those errors by then failing to ensure that on 21 and 22 August his two cavalry divisions fulfilled their orders to track and monitor those German divisions during the crucial march of de Langle's infantry through the forests. His intelligence staff lost track of the two enemy army corps, and then made the incorrect assumption that they had marched away towards the northwest; and de Langle issued no special instructions to his army corps commanders to be particularly vigilant on the march. The consequence was that, despite advancing deep into unreconnoitred territory under cover of the morning fog, each French column was unprepared when it clashed with the enemy within the forests.[12]

De Langle's failures in planning were compounded by his battlefield performance on 22 August. Communication, command and control are the essential requirements for good generalship. Communications within Fourth Army broke down, to the point where de Langle was totally unaware of what was happening to his left-wing columns during most of the day. Remaining all day at his headquarters at Stenay, sixty kilometres behind the heads of the marching columns, de Langle was starved of information. He had not drilled into his subordinate commanders the need to keep him regularly informed of events. For example, General Joseph Eydoux of XI CA sent a message to de Langle at 09.00 that he had occupied his day's objective, the village of Maissin, and was proceeding to assist his neighbouring corps. An hour later he had lost the village to a German counter attack but failed to update de Langle. Eydoux spent the rest of the day trying to retake the village but forgot to report to de Langle until after 17.00.[13] Nor did he set up a proper communications network that would enable units on the march to send and receive reports in a timely manner; there were two forward telegram offices for five corps commanders whose forces were spread along nearly seventy kilometres of front, with couriers, occasionally using a car but more often riding horses, performing the delivery leg. Hours would pass before messages reached their destination.[14] Lacking good communications and therefore knowledge of what was going on, de Langle lost control of his battle, which then fought itself out at corps or divisional command levels without any higher-level intervention. Hence de Langle did not, could not command his army during the 22 August fighting. Only when reports started to trickle in during the night of 22/23 August did he begin to understand what had happened and take steps to regain control and command. Overall, it was a dismal baptism of fire. Where de Langle did redeem himself, however, was in his reaction to defeat. Living up to Joffre's faith in him as a reliable, steady and self-disciplined character, de Langle refused to panic or be overtaken by these disastrous events. He ordered his army corps to retreat, buying time to regroup. By the end of the following day (23 August) he had regained control of his army and was able to stabilize his front and resist further German attacks.

There is one further aspect to de Langle's management style that deserves illumination: his ability to manage upwards. On the night of 22/23 August, the French high command had to decide what orders to give for the next day. Early in the evening de Langle had been made aware of the rout of XVII CA and the consequent large gap in his front. He cancelled his order to renew the offensive in the morning, realizing that he needed time to regroup. At *Grand quartier général* (GQG), however, Joffre insisted that Fourth Army attack in the morning – GQG intelligence bureau reported only three German army corps opposite de Langle's six (the fresh IX CA had arrived at the front) and Joffre expected this French superiority to be converted into success. Rather than confront Joffre with an inconvenient reality, de Langle chose to issue a new order to attack in the morning, an order that he knew could not be executed. His order was word-for-word a copy of that given to him by Joffre. In the early hours of the morning of 23 August, with reports from the front being analysed at all levels, even GQG had come to understand that Fourth Army was incapable of a fresh attack, so Joffre approved de Langle's request to retire behind the Semoy river and regroup.[15] De Langle had managed to retain Joffre's confidence, the measure of which can be seen in Joffre's own recollection of these events: 'I knew de Langle and I was confident in the firmness of his character. If he reported such a condition of affairs I realized that it was an exact statement of the facts.'[16]

\* \* \*

In all the opening battles of the frontiers Joffre's armies were beaten. On 25 August GQG ordered a general retreat to the left bank of the Meuse, behind which Joffre hoped to prepare a counter attack. De Langle marched his men back across that river. They were exhausted, dispirited; and de Langle started to hone his leadership skills in the crucible of war. Once behind the Meuse, he called his corps commanders together to issue a rallying cry: 'Gentlemen, we have retreated far enough. Tell your generals that I am not going any further back. Pass on to them my order to defend the Meuse. Each knows his own role. As for me, I will stand amongst the fighting men.'[17] From 26 to 28 August, de Langle's troops fought hard – and successfully – to hold the line of the Meuse, despite having failed to demolish a bridge at Donchery (near Sedan) over which the Germans crossed and formed a bridgehead on the left bank. When Fourth Army did retreat, it was on the direct orders of Joffre to conform with the backward movement of the whole front to the Aisne river. On 26 August, rather than remaining at his headquarters, de Langle could be seen leading several regiments forward to the front: 'The sight of their chief, upright in the saddle, animated and energetic, gave confidence to both officers and men.'[18] On 28 August, de Langle visited Roques's XII CA, touring the front line 'indifferent to the bombardment' by German artillery.[19] In this defensive fighting de Langle demonstrated strong leadership skills, personal courage and firm command and control, a far cry from his first battle six days earlier. No soldier knows how he will react to actual war; it seems that de Langle reacted well after an initial shock. On 31 August, Joffre paid de Langle a visit, on his way back from having removed Ruffey from command of Third Army. Joffre's observations are instructive. Whereas he found Ruffey 'in a high condition of nervousness' and 'lacking in spirit', he considered that de Langle possessed a demeanour of 'energetic attitude, calm deliberation, in complete mastery of himself'.[20] De Langle's requests to be allowed to counterattack impressed the commander-in-chief, who likened his demonstration of an offensive attitude to that of General Ferdinand Foch, a rising star just appointed to command a new Ninth Army. From 29 to 31 August, de Langle conformed to the French retreat from the Meuse to the Aisne. On 27 August, Joffre had placed the fortified zone at Reims and its garrison under de Langle's command. At 09.00 on 1 September 1914, de Langle set up his Headquarters at Suippes. Although pressed back over subsequent days – de Langle's headquarters would move fifteen times in quick succession before settling down in Châlons-sur-Marne in early October[21] – Fourth Army would turn on its pursuers following Joffre's successful counter attack to the west and restore the French line in front of Reims. That city would become the strong bastion around which Fourth Army would organize and which, in due course, would anchor the major offensives in Champagne. Meanwhile, the centre of activity moved to the left wing while Fourth Army consolidated its defensive positions pending the renewal of a more general offensive in 1915.

\* \* \*

Joffre's operational strategy for 1915 was to attack both flanks of the huge 'Noyon salient' pointing towards Paris that the Germans had driven into the French line before the war of movement settled down into trench warfare during the winter of 1914/15. The northern flank lay in Artois, the southern in Champagne: running tantalizingly close to both was a major lateral railway line that sustained the whole length of the German's Western Front and allowed the enemy to transfer reserves swiftly to threatened points. Coordinated attacks on the flanks would threaten German lines of communication and drive the enemy back to the north-east, towards the Meuse. Joffre outlined his plans in his 'General Instruction Number 8', issued on 8 December 1914.[22] Throughout 1915, therefore, a series of coordinated if not simultaneous attacks took place both in Artois in the north and in Champagne further east against the left (southern) flank of the salient. The early Champagne attacks were to be executed primarily by de Langle's Fourth Army. Eager to take the fight to the enemy, Joffre ordered de Langle on 8 December 1914 to prepare for an early offensive, even though Joffre later acknowledged that 'the reinforcement and re-organization of units were not yet completed and supplies of war material not yet made up'.[23]

Most historians record that the first Battle of Champagne began on 16 February 1915.[24] However a reading of the French Official History shows that French attacks in the Champagne region began on 20 December 1914 and continued more or less constantly until 18 March 1915. There were two distinct phases in the battle, divided by a break of about ten days at the end of January due in part to the weather and in part to the exhaustion and dislocation of the troops. De Langle planned each phase as a separate operation, the second phase being the one generally accorded the historic title of 'First Battle of Champagne'. Despite the post-hoc nomenclature, Joffre had insisted in his orders on 8 December on one continuous battle, so de Langle, managing upwards in his best style, ensured that the break between the two phases was filled by a continuous artillery bombardment and was presented as a necessary part of the preparation phase of the next methodically prepared assault. He also took pains to write to Joffre, assuring him that, in accordance with instructions, 'the offensive will be continued in uninterrupted fashion. But because of the weather, the terrain and the fatigue of the men, the assaults cannot take place for a few days, after which they will be renewed with the greatest tenacity.'[25]

The first phase of the battle had been conducted with little modification to French pre-war tactics, albeit with an increasing emphasis on the weight of artillery used to prepare and support the attack. First choose a principal sector of attack where the breach in the enemy line will be made (in fact de Langle chose two, one in XII CA's sector, one in that of XVII CA); then prepare the attack by using the artillery to destroy the enemy's field fortifications (trenches and, increasingly, wire); then commit the infantry in successive waves, the first wave to take and occupy the enemy's firing trench, the second and succeeding waves to pass through and make the breach. Specific groups of field artillery were designated to move up to the captured firing trench in continued support of the infantry. In practice, the changed conditions of war conspired to offer brief illusions of success without delivering any final concrete result. Wire remained uncut by shell fire, and troops were held up; field artillery had great difficulty getting forward across shell-torn ground; German reserves deployed faster than the French could advance, and dynamic counter attacks retook lost ground, which the French would have to assault again. The action degenerated into a series of uncoordinated local attacks, hence the need for a pause to regroup.

Here was manifest the tactical dilemma of firepower versus shock action in its new form. De Langle's and Joffre's analysis of the first phase of the offensive suggested that a more methodical preparation, more munitions and deep, successive waves of attacking infantry would convert the brief illusions of breakthrough into reality. Anticipating the trend of tactical developments in 1915, de Langle wanted a steadier approach, consolidating gains and preparing subsequent attacks methodically with artillery before launching the infantry forward; Joffre wanted momentum. He also thought that de Langle was employing too few troops at the decisive point and that the frontage of the final assaults needed to be broadened.[26] So the second phase – which we know as the First Battle of Champagne – saw new tactics: an offensive on a broader frontage but a narrowing of divisional fronts, with deeper divisional reserves to sustain forward momentum, and consequently an increase in the number of divisions engaged. More artillery, especially heavy artillery, was employed in longer preparatory bombardments. The need for secondary attacks by the whole army to fix the enemy across his whole front was stressed, but the plan remained for there to be one principal point of concentration through which the army's reserves would pour to widen the breach. Once again, the same external factors conspired to thwart them: the attacks lacked the momentum to exploit a breach before the enemy could reinforce and shore it up; and while the enemy counterattacked, he also dug new lines of field fortifications behind the old. A second line of trenches was excavated behind the firing trench, and soon a third behind that, all connected together with communications trenches to create the sort of interlinked defensive positions that would characterize trench warfare. Villages in the front line were turned into strongpoints, bastions in the organized system of deep, mutually supporting fortifications that was emerging. By 18 March, it was clear that the continuous series of attacks could not be maintained against a deepening defence, and that German resistance had not been significantly weakened. The offensive was called off. Fourth Army's front would settle into relative quietude until the autumn, as Joffre pursued his offensive ambitions in Artois.

\* \* \*

Fourth Army would play a central role when the Champagne offensive resumed in September. Planning for the second Battle of Champagne by Fourth Army staff began on 12 July 1915, with a month dedicated to pure staff work and six weeks to logistical deployment and concentration. It is interesting to note that French President Raymond Poincaré recorded in his memoirs a conversation with de Langle in February 1916, in which de Langle confided that he had never believed that Joffre's objective of a breakthrough (*'percée'*) in Champagne would work; and that he preferred to plan offensives that were conducted by a series of successive blows.[27] Of course this conversation may reflect a good degree of hindsight and belated acceptance of the lessons of 1915. At the time, second Champagne was planned according to Joffre's wishes – de Langle was not one to dispute superiors' instructions. This time General Philippe Pétain's Second Army would attack alongside de Langle's Fourth Army under the general direction of General Nöel de Curières de Castelnau, commanding GAC. It was acknowledged that success depended on huge artillery support.[28]

Fourth Army's initial objective was now more limited if still ambitious: to pierce the German front line and seize the two other lines of trenches in the enemy's defensive system. Defence in depth was becoming increasingly strong compared to even a few months before, and French intelligence had reported that there was now a second defensive system – a further three lines of interlinked trenches – which would have to be tackled after the first objective had been reached.[29] It was also known that certain features of the front line, such as the Butte de Mesnil, the Bois de Souain and the village of Aubérive, had been turned into heavily fortified strongpoints connected by long underground passageways. It was known that in other places there were support trenches situated on reverse slopes that could not be observed which would be difficult to target with artillery fire, even from howitzers with their higher trajectory. To add to the intelligence picture being put together by the French, the complete German order of battle on the front to be attacked had been discovered. So de Langle had received excellent intelligence concerning the defences that he was about to attack. He had also been given more than sufficient time to plan and prepare – two-and-a-half months. De Langle's final plan aimed to break through the centre of the enemy's new defensive system, throwing back the shattered remains (*débris*) onto the flanks. Joffre himself insisted on setting no limit on the advance in terms of specified lines to be reached or terrain features to be seized and held, as he felt that this would inhibit the élan of the best performing troops and hold them back from achieving maximum penetration.[30] Within this overall operational context, de Langle's plan was in accordance with his commander-in-chief's concept, and included a three-day artillery barrage (from 22 to 25 September) by over 500 guns, followed by a general assault by eighteen divisions on a thirty-kilometre front.

The offensive opened on 25 September 1915, and from then until 6 October when the offensive was halted the troops attacked with great courage and with the expected élan. They experienced very heavy losses, and although results were not nearly as good as the senior commanders expected, de Langle nevertheless continued to attack until his immediate superior, de Castelnau, persuaded Joffre to bring the increasingly one-sided battle to an end.[31] De Langle's Fourth Army and Pétain's Second Army between them had taken the whole of the German first defensive system, except the strongpoint at Butte du Mesnil, and on one twelve-kilometre stretch of front had even come up to the second German position. At Perthes-les-Hurlus, the point of their deepest penetration, they had advanced four kilometres, and when they captured the Butte de Tahure they got to within two kilometres of the main lateral railway. On the other hand, there was no breakthrough. As with so many battles in 1915, after the initial well prepared and determined assault on the German front line trenches, order and momentum was lost, and the action degenerated into a series of attritional attacks (although not recognized or intended as such) during which de Langle sought to widen the salient created in the German defensive system by General Ernest Blondlat's elite II *corps d'armée coloniale* on the first day. But the Germans' ability to bring up reserves more swiftly than the French could exploit their gains meant that every new attack was met by fresh defensive forces and by violent artillery and machine-gun fire from both flanks as well as from the front. The attacks eventually just petered out, and de Langle, de Castelnau and Joffre all saw the futility of continuing. At this point in the war, the French had neither the material resources nor the operational understanding to break the stalemate.

\* \* \*

On 12 December 1915, de Langle replaced de Castelnau as commander of GAC when de Castelnau moved to GQG to support Joffre as his chief-of-staff. GAC at that time directed four armies (Second, Fourth, Fifth and Sixth Armies) that were responsible for approximately 250 kilometres of the front between Soissons and Verdun. Undoubtedly the key strategic feature of the section of front that became de Langle's new responsibility (apart from covering Paris) was the *région fortifiée de Verdun* (fortified region of Verdun – RFV), an independent command under General Frédéric Herr, which was subordinated to GAC on 1 February 1916. Three weeks later, Verdun was to be the location of a determined and sustained German offensive that was to threaten the very existence of France. For General de Langle it was to prove a poisoned chalice.

Verdun had been a key French frontier fortress since 1636. In 1914 it was a modern major defensive system consisting of a citadel with nineteen linked outlying forts – the largest of which were Forts Douaumont and Vaux on the heights east of the Meuse – and many minor works (*ouvrages*). However, the doctrine of utilizing a line of impregnable fortresses with field armies manoeuvring behind and between them had been discredited in Joffre's eyes by the fall of the Belgian fortress of Liège in the first ten days of the war. Furthermore, the acute shortage of heavy artillery to support offensive operations in 1915 in Artois and Champagne had led Joffre and his staff to strip Verdun's forts of much of their mobile artillery. Forty-three batteries of heavy artillery had been taken from the forts and distributed in the field; troops had been withdrawn and sent to other fronts, and the infrastructure of the fortifications had been allowed to fall into disrepair. De Langle inherited a fortress that was strong in symbolism but weak in reality, and he was given little time to do anything about it. When the German attack gained significant early success, the French high command from Joffre downwards was engulfed in controversy over whom to blame; and de Langle's name, as commander of GAC, was in the frame.

The German attack on Verdun, launched on 21 February 1916, came as no surprise to the French high command. As early as 2 December 1915, intelligence reports gave indications of an impending major German offensive on the Western Front, with Verdun as the most likely objective.[32] By early February 1916, Joffre had acquired the certain knowledge that Verdun would be the target: on 7 February an intelligence report gave the specific locations of German heavy batteries (380mm and 420mm siege mortars) that had been moved up to Verdun.[33] On 10 February a staff officer at GQG telephoned GAC's staff with the news that a 'grand offensive' by the Germans against Verdun was imminent.[34] From that moment, de Langle had just eleven days in which to prepare to meet the attack. Herr, on the other hand, as commander of the RFV since August 1915, had from the first been mandated to reorganize the RFV as a key defensive position, albeit using manoeuvre rather than static defence as his predominant tactic. Herr's problem was that the offensives in Champagne and Artois had absorbed manpower and occupied the attention of senior commanders. Verdun was of relatively low priority – until it was attacked – and Herr was never given enough men to do the required strengthening works, so progress was slow.

The attack on Verdun was preceded by a very heavy bombardment, and the initial advance of the German infantry met with immediate success. By the morning of the third day, 24 February, Crown Prince William's forces had advanced to within ten kilometres of the centre of Verdun and were threatening Fort Douaumont; its loss would threaten to unhinge the whole French defence on the right bank of the Meuse. What happened over the next forty-eight hours needs to be described in detail, since it led directly to the end of de Langle's military career.

At 19.30 on 23 February, de Langle had telephoned Joffre to inform him that the German advance towards Fort Douaumont (the highest point in the northeast sector of the Verdun defences) might necessitate the abandonment of the French trenches on the Woëvre Plain to the east of the fortress, which would then be vulnerable to enfilade fire. Joffre himself records that he delegated the decision to de Langle while insisting that the rest of the high ground on the right (east) bank of the Meuse be held. Pertinently however, Joffre remembered that, perhaps for the first time, de Langle sounded vague and uncertain on the telephone.[35] De Langle conducted the retirement from the Woëvre up onto the Meuse heights in good order on the night of 24/25 February, and then contemplated whether he would have to withdraw completely behind the Meuse. To do so might easily have been justified on the sound military grounds that he was conducting 'elastic' defence in line with GQG's previous promulgations. However, by that time events had spiralled out of his control.

There were two powerful men who had, separately and for different reasons, come to the conclusion that Verdun would have to be held at all costs; and that since the complete loss of the right bank would cause the city to fall, the right bank had to be held. The first was de Castelnau, at that point Joffre's influential chief-of-staff; the second was prime minister Aristide Briand. De Castelnau had already on the evening of 23 February persuaded Joffre to bring in General Pétain and his Second Army staff (then in reserve overseeing training) to take command of all troops on the left bank of the Meuse. This was logical: it would put the defence of the river Meuse in the hands of one of France's most experienced generals, and free up Herr to conduct the fighting on the right bank under de Langle's supervision. With Pétain in command and with reserves having been ordered forward, de Castelnau instinctively felt that Verdun could and should be held. Following de Langle's request to retire from the Woëvre, however, de Castelnau also seems to have perceived some uncertainty, perhaps lack of resolve, in de Langle's demeanour. That evening de Castelnau sought Joffre's permission to go to de Langle's headquarters and then to Verdun to assess the situation for himself. Joffre apparently told his aides, 'let him do as he pleases',[36] which de Castelnau interpreted as having been granted Joffre's devolved powers. De Castelnau departed shortly after midnight and arrived at de Langle's headquarters at 04.00 on 25 February. During the four-hour time span of that journey, Briand turned up, unplanned and unannounced, at GQG – an unprecedented action and one that turned the defence of Verdun from a purely military issue into a political one.[37] With bad news from Verdun pouring in during the course of 24 February, Briand had come to the conclusion that his government might fall if Verdun were lost. He decided to confront Joffre face-to-face. He found that in the absence of de Castelnau, Joffre's staff officers saw the defence of Verdun in purely military terms and were leaning towards a complete withdrawal onto the left bank of the Meuse, which was more easily defensible. Briand lost his temper and threatened to sack the lot of them, at which point Joffre intervened to promise that Verdun (and the right bank Meuse heights) would be held to the last man.[38]

Neither de Castelnau nor de Langle were aware of this dramatic change in the political climate when they met in the early hours of 25 February, so de Langle felt free to discuss the military rather than political viewpoint. When in private conversation de Langle expressed his doubts whether the right bank could be held, de Castelnau saw further evidence of a lack of firmness and resolve. De Castelnau next visited Herr, and found him 'fatigued to the point of depression' and 'no longer capable of inspiring his command with the energy required by the circumstances facing us'.[39] De Castelnau reported to Joffre who later wrote: 'I was extremely pleased to learn that the real situation at Verdun was not as desperate as it had been represented', another black mark against de Langle.[40] De Castelnau was by now convinced that with reinforcements coming up Verdun could be held, and he used the authority delegated to him by Joffre to take direct command. At 15.30 on 25 February he issued orders giving Pétain sole responsibility for the defence of Verdun, on both banks, leaving a note to be delivered to Pétain when he arrived to take up his post instructing him to hold Verdun 'no matter what the cost'.[41] At this juncture, de Castelnau was unknowingly totally in tune with the unfolding political agenda laid down by Briand, while de Langle was floundering, his usual instinct for managing Joffre's expectations having been blindsided by Briand's intervention and the abrupt turn of events.

It was ironic that during the four hours encompassing Briand's visit to Joffre and de Castelnau's drive to Verdun, de Langle had started to stabilize the situation on the right bank, issuing orders to XXX CA to form a semi-circular defence on a line Bras–Douaumont–Vaux–Eix. It was not enough to convince de Castelnau, however; he was using Joffre's authority to sack generals who were perceived to lack resolution, divisional commanders Generals Étienne Bapst and Léon Deshayes de Bonneval for example.[42] As Joffre was later to write, 'the stability of our front [depended upon] the resolution of the men who commanded [at Verdun]'.[43] De Langle was perceived to be showing signs of lack of resolution: Pétain was now the man who held the confidence of the high command. By 27 February, Pétain's command had been enlarged from Second Army only to absorb the RFV (Herr's command) and General Georges Humbert's Third Army (from de Langle's command) – effectively if not in name creating a new Verdun army group reporting directly to GQG. De Langle was left with the rump of GAC (Fourth and Fifth Armies) and with his standing within the army and more importantly in the eyes of parliament immeasurably weakened.[44]

De Langle might have weathered this particular storm, had it not been for the hurricanes that raged around Joffre and his relations with parliament

# Fernand de Langle de Cary: A Pragmatic Survivor 145

and government. Throughout 1915 Joffre's handling of the war, and the growing casualty lists for little result, had drawn increasing criticism from parliamentarians.[45] By the time of the Verdun crisis, Joffre's enemies were calling also for the heads of his key generals, the 'old guard' that included army group commanders de Langle and Augustin Dubail, the two surviving army commanders from August 1914. The former then took the brunt of criticism for the early failures at Verdun – somewhat unfairly as we have seen. At the same time, he lost the confidence of first de Castelnau and then Joffre. In his memoirs Joffre highlights what was perhaps the key to senior command in the French army of 1915–16: 'The Battle of Verdun offers one more proof that in all the affairs of war nothing is more important than the way the command is exercised'.[46] Until Verdun, de Langle had shown Joffre the behavioural characteristics that met with approval; but on 24/25 February de Langle was wrong-footed by an abrupt change of political direction and paid the price. As early as 4 March, Briand was considering relieving him and replacing him by Pétain, if only to take pressure off the government.[47] Joffre had already realized that to save his own career he would have to throw de Langle and Dubail to the wolves; perhaps he even believed that change was necessary to save Verdun. De Castelnau had taken direct control: at 10.30 on 26 February while still at Verdun he ordered the commander of XX CA to retake Fort Douaumont immediately, before the enemy could settle in. That Joffre's chief-of-staff would issue such an order directly, rather than go via de Langle (still nominally in charge), shows a further weakening of confidence in the GAC commander. Also on 26 February, de Castelnau reported on the situation at Verdun to Joffre. Tellingly, this report included the sentence: 'The situation on the Verdun front would not have been so clearly understood at all levels of command if it had not been for your very clear and very firm order of 24 February.'[48] De Castelnau was taking over in managing upwards. He then turned the screw on de Langle, calling for a formal report on his handling of the Verdun defence. De Langle's response would not have made any difference; calling for such a senior commander to justify himself in writing was signal enough of what the inevitable outcome would be. Nevertheless on 3 March, de Langle sent a ten-page report to de Calstelnau, detailing a day-by-day record of the actions he had taken to improve the defence of Verdun between 1 February when he took over command of RFV and 24 February on the eve of the German offensive.[49] De Langle was too experienced in the ways of French military politics, having been close to Joffre for so long, not to see the writing on the wall. His report nevertheless was penned to support his honour and his reputation, whatever the outcome:

The RFV was attached to GAC on 1 February. The general commanding GAC went immediately to inspect the terrain and the defences on the northern and south-eastern fronts. He found that the front-line trenches were incomplete (especially lacking overhead protection) and that the successive lines of supporting trenches were insufficient.[50]

De Langle showed that he would go down fighting for his reputation. It made no difference. On 23 March 1916, Joffre received a letter from Roques, who was now war minister, demanding that four generals – de Langle, Dubail, and army commanders Étienne de Villaret and Victor d'Urbal – be removed from their commands.[51] To save himself, Joffre had no option but to comply. These bureaucratic manoeuvres take time: on 2 May, after a decent interval to save face and with sufficient time for Pétain to settle in to his new role, de Langle handed over command of GAC (which absorbed Pétain's detachment once more) to Pétain. Placed at the disposal of the war minister, de Langle's last mission was an inspection trip to North Africa, and in December 1917 he was retired from active service.

\* \* \*

In retirement de Langle wrote posthumously published memoirs that were both dull and, perhaps unsurprisingly, particularly hostile to Joffre.[52] It is clear that he was, first and foremost, concerned for his reputation and wished to leave behind the best interpretation of his wartime performance. It is equally clear that he felt aggrieved that the commander whom he had supported so faithfully had in the end deserted him. After his death in 1927 he was interred alongside other honoured wartime commanders in the crypt at Les Invalides.

General de Langle de Cary was not an outstanding commander, but he was a 'safe pair of hands' during the first two years of the war, at a time of considerable turn-over within the cadre of French generals. He was a stalwart, learning from experience and in the main executing his missions with competence. He showed leadership skills, personal courage and, especially, calm resilience in the face of adversity. At the same time, he conducted his later battles, particularly in Champagne, according to Joffre's wishes and against his better judgment. Until his final fall from grace over Verdun, de Langle exhibited particular skill in what is known today as 'managing upwards'; that is to say, ensuring that Joffre's perception of his performance never fell to the point where he lost the confidence of the commander-in-chief, as did two of his fellow army commanders of July 1914, Ruffey and Charles Lanrezac. On balance, Fernand de Langle de Cary served France well. If nothing else, his term of command helped buy time for the talented generals who would win the war such as Pétain to come to the fore.

Chapter 7

# Paul Maistre: Missing in Action

## William Philpott

General Paul Maistre's statue stands on a promontory of the infamous hill of Notre-Dame-de-Lorette in Artois, scene of intensive close-quarter fighting over the winter of 1914–15. The army corps commander whose troops fought on and finally took that commanding height from which the Germans – and nowadays his effigy – overlooked the French army's positions in the plain below went on to greater things. He was an effective army commander: the late October 1917 Battle of Malmaison in which the Chemin des Dames was finally taken was his set-piece masterpiece. In the final campaign Maistre led the *Groupe d'armées du centre* (GAC), directing operations against the German forces between Reims and Verdun, including the Franco-American Meuse–Argonne offensive and many now forgotten but successful battles fought by the armies in his group. The subject of a short adulatory biography written shortly after the war by Henry Bordeaux, the general staff publicist charged with reporting on his operations at Verdun and in the Battle of Malmaison, Maistre fell thereafter into obscurity.[1] His post-war career was short, and he died in 1922 aged 64, before the biography was published. Indeed, his biographer begins by noting that he was already falling from public awareness, hardly featuring in the newspapers' arguments about which wartime commanders deserved a Marshal's baton. This, Bordeaux speculated, was down to his own self-effacing personality: 'on account of his modesty, his shunning of popularity, his nobility of spirit and heart that refused to take credit for victories won due to his sagacious leadership'.[2] He did not live long enough to write a memoir (and probably would not have wished to) and left no private papers. He does not feature in Paul Gaujac's collective study of French wartime commanders although more obscure figures are included.[3] Although the man himself remains a shadowy figure, his military record is distinguished. One of the group of scholar-generals who rose to the most senior command positions by 1918, Maistre ranks among the best fighting generals produced on either side during the war.

\* \* \*

Maistre was born in Joinville, in the Haut-Marne *département*, on 20 June 1858, the son of a tax collector originally from the Auvergne. He was educated at the catholic seminary at Langres before attending the French military academy St Cyr, graduating top of his class. By his own attestation he had no particular military vocation but signed up in order to relieve his family of the burden of supporting him.[4] He was later an instructor at that school as well as passing through a series of regimental postings in the infantry, his branch of service, and serving on the French army's intelligence staff. He passed out third in his class from the *École supérieure de guerre* (ESG) in 1889: his later superiors Alfred Micheler and Robert Nivelle were in the same class, passing eleventh and thirteenth respectively. He would lecture at the ESG from 1899 to 1902. He was an assistant professor on the course in strategy and grand tactics while Ferdinand Foch was professor (1899–1901).[5] Future leaders Philippe Pétain and Marie-Émile Fayolle were also contemporaries on the teaching staff.[6] Since, unlike Foch, he did not publish his staff college lecture course, his intellectual position is difficult to gauge. In 1908 he published a detailed study of the Franco-Prussian War Battle of Spicheren (6 August 1870), on the basis of which his biographer concluded that he accepted Foch's precepts and should be numbered among those pre-war advocates of the offensive.[7] But, like Foch whose views underwent considerable revision in the decade after he ceased to lecture at the staff college, it would be fair to assume that Maistre also followed the active doctrinal debates in the French army and would have modified ideas originally formulated in 1904 over subsequent years in response to operational developments and technological advances: how, precisely, it is impossible to say. What is clear is that Maistre believed in intellectual capacity and appropriate military education grounded in doctrine rather than innate ability as the foundation of effective command, as he would himself go on to demonstrate. Also, that proper intelligence, effective staff work, initiative and flexibly were the roots of success on the battlefield, not moral forces or firepower alone about which his colleagues had been arguing in the run-up to hostilities.[8]

After the staff college, from which he was reportedly dismissed for political reasons – this was the time of the *affaire des fiches* and intensive republican suspicion of conservative Catholic officers that delayed the career progression of talented men who would rise to the top in the coming war – Maistre returned to regimental duties. First, he commanded 79ᵉ *régiment d'infanterie* (RI) in the elite XX *corps d'armée* (CA) based at Nancy.[9] As a regiment of the covering force that protected the Franco-German border, it was maintained near full strength in peacetime, and gave Maistre an excellent opportunity to develop his own command style. A highly experienced educator, he devoted himself to training active and reserve officers, and to learning more about his profession. This included a year's attachment to a field artillery regiment (including a short period in command), where he would have reflected on the combined-arms methods that would become the mainstay of wartime tactics. He published his opinions in service journals, for example a detailed critique of a mixed brigade map exercise which evidenced his interest in combined-arms tactics.[10] This experience carried on in his next appointment, command of 109ᵉ RI which he turned from a mediocre to an excellent regiment, and brought him briefly to a temporary brigade command before he was called to serve on the staff at the ministry of war from August 1912. As a staff brigadier-general he assisted members of the *Conseil superièure de la guerre*, composed of France's putative senior leaders in wartime. He was appointed to the personal staff of General Fernand de Langle de Cary, who had been one of Maistre's staff college teachers, in March 1914.[11]

* * *

On mobilization Maistre took up his designated wartime role as chief of staff of de Langle de Cary's Fourth Army, which was destined to spearhead commander-in-chief Joseph Joffre's counter offensive into the Ardennes in late August and to withdraw rapidly thereafter.[12] This early setback did not seem to harm either man's career: both would go on to lead army groups. De Langle redeemed himself in the retreat by successfully disengaging the enemy's pursuit in the Battle of the Meuse on 27 and 28 August – a challenging feat of arms approached, Major Maurice Gamelin reported to GQG, with 'perfect confidence' by de Langle and his chief of staff[13] – and tenaciously holding the hard-pressed French centre in the Battle of the Marne. Maistre's role in these events is hard to discern. As a quiet but effective chief of staff he served as a conduit between his chief and GQG, and drafted operational orders for the units under command, a task for which his pre-war teaching career no doubt prepared him well.[14] Joffre certainly noticed. Seeking competent replacements for the many senior commanders who had performed so badly in the opening weeks of the war, he promoted Maistre to command XXI CA after the Battle of the Marne: he served briefly under Foch's command in Ninth Army as the French advance came to a halt in the Champagne region east of Reims in mid-September. De Langle, who had had no forewarning of the change, was sorry to lose him: his assistance had been invaluable since the outbreak of war.[15] He would note later that Maistre was 'an officer of great character and rare ability…in whom I had complete confidence'.[16] While he would never return to staff duties, Maistre's understanding of how to run a military formation would have underpinned his success in the years that followed. But his first efforts, trying to hold the village of Souain after it had been seized from the enemy on 15 September, proved costly in the face of powerful enemy artillery fire and aggressive counter attacks. The dynamics of the new warfare were becoming apparent. French forces could seize enemy positions; holding on to them was a very different challenge.[17]

Maistre's accelerated promotion, passing over a period of divisional command, contrasts with that of his fellows. Both securing divisional commands during the chaos of the opening campaign, Pétain did not receive a corps command until late October 1914 and Fayolle not until June 1915. But Pétain was to be promoted to army command in June 1915 (a reward for his army corps' success alongside Maistre's in the Second Battle of Artois) and Fayolle in February 1916, while Maistre would wait thirty-two months, until May 1917, before he got the step up to army command. Pétain was an army group commander from May 1916 (he replaced de Langle de Cary), Fayolle from May 1917; but Maistre would have to wait until June 1918 for his most senior command.[18] One can only speculate as to why he was leapfrogged by his staff college peers. He was a few years younger but certainly as experienced. Perhaps there was a wealth of senior command talent emerging and not enough higher commands to go round. Perhaps he fell foul of his superiors. Adolphe Guillaumat, another army commander, makes a cryptic reference to his being the 'bête noir of the marshal', but provides no details.[19] But given some of the mediocre men who passed through army and army group command before Maistre (such as Micheler, under whose command he served from September 1916 to May 1917),[20] perhaps it was simply bad luck. Maybe his reluctance to push himself forward and take credit for his successes, his overriding sense of duty and God-willed destiny emphasized by Bordeaux, held him back in an echelon where politics and the ability to self-promote counted as much for preferment as professional competence.[21] Fayolle, whose ancestors also hailed from the Auvergne, used to refer to Maistre as his 'cousin', and their characters had much in common: reliable, calm, sensible, noble and of strong Catholic faith.[22] These traits were to produce an effective field commander whose intellectual preparation made him equally adaptable to the challenges of trench warfare.

\* \* \*

Maistre's XXI CA (13 and 43 DIs) was redeployed to the open northern flank of the French armies as the outflanking 'race to the sea' developed during late September and early October. The army corps joined General Louis de Maud'huy's newly formed Tenth Army and was committed to the battle north of Arras, to check the German advance along the Notre-Dame-de-Lorette spur at the northern end of Vimy ridge. Second only to the heights around Verdun, this hill was destined to become the French army's hallowed ground, owing to the tooth-and-nail fighting for its crest that ensued over the winter of

Joseph Joffre led the French army and directed allied strategy from 1914 to 1916, before falling into political disfavour.

General Joffre (centre) confers with Second Army commander General Noël de Curières de Castelnau (left), who would become his chief of staff and right-hand-man in 1916.

Ferdinand Foch, a soldier–scholar who would rise to the topmost position of generalissimo of the allied armies in 1918.

Philippe Pétain commanded the French army from May 1917, restoring its morale and fighting effectiveness after a period of crisis.

Robert Nivelle commanded the French army from December 1916 until May 1917, but the failure of his eponymous offensive brought his promising career to a premature end.

Marie-Émile Fayolle, who led Sixth Army successfully in the Battle of the Somme and was the principal French army group commander in 1918, was among the best field commanders the war produced.

Joffre (left) and de Langle De Cary (centre) confer with an unidentified colleague during pre-war manoeuvres.

Fernand De Langle de Cary (centre) learned his profession the hard way in 1914, remaining a mainstay of the army's higher command until a lacklustre performance in the Battle of Verdun obliged him to retire in 1916.

Paul Maistre's statue stands on the spur of Notre-Dame-de-Lorette, captured by his XXI CA in spring 1915.

Pierre Roques, war minister in 1916, was a political general who proved out of his depth as a field commander.

Marie-Eugène Debeney was both an effective staff officer and field commander, rising to command First Army by 1918.

General Debeney (centre) is decorated in the field by generals Fayolle (left) and Pétain (right).

Charles Mangin was a very effective but often difficult army commander whose stop–start career was notable for its controversies.

Maurice Gamelin, future commander-in-chief in the next war, would start the war as Joffre's aide-de-camp, ending it as a highly competent and decorated divisional commander.

Jean Estienne was an innovator in gunnery and aviation who earned the epithet 'father of the tanks' for his work in developing and leading the new French armoured forces, the *artillerie spéciale*.

Paul Maistre rose slowly but surely to command an army group by summer 1918, having served as a chief of staff and commanded a corps and an army with distinction.

1914–15. Topped with a basilica and lantern tower erected between the wars, it is the site of France's largest First World War necropolis (and nowadays of a twenty-first century Ring of Remembrance commemorating those of all nationalities who died in the Nord–Pas de Calais region during the war).[23] The effigy of the commander whose troops struggled on and eventually secured the hill sits slightly apart and itself tells a story. Initially sited within the national memorial, being deemed inappropriate for a cemetery Maistre's statue was later moved to overlook the village of Ablain-St-Nazaire and the spur's southern flank, the ground on which the men of XXI CA fought: it stands at the location of Maistre's wartime command post. The stone general does not stand alone: beneath him, staring up at his beloved commander, holding his gaze, stands a rock-solid *poilu*. Sculptor Max Blondat's memorial – that bears the inscription 'to the glory of General Maistre and the XXI CA' – is one not merely to a commander but to the men of the elite unit that he led and moulded.[24] It is stone testimony too to Maistre's style of command. Like his comrades Pétain and Fayolle he was a soldiers' general, solicitous of his men's welfare and conscious that he held their fate in his hands and that therefore painstaking care was necessary in his operational planning. He was also willing to play down his own role and acclaim that of his soldiers: 'Don't mention me. Nothing of significance is achieved in this war except through the French soldier's admirable spirit' he told the assembled journalists following his most famous victory at Malmaison.[25] He also had good subordinates. His first corps chief of staff, General Antoine Baucheron de Boissoudy, who would later lead 43 DI in 1916, would get an army command himself in due course; ironically on exactly the same day Maistre would get his.

Piecing together the actions of Maistre's units over the eight months XXI CA fought for the hilltop would be well-nigh impossible – near daily short-range fights connected the regular larger-scale thrusts that pushed the Germans back metre-by-metre along the spur.[26] (Preserved trenches in the small museum on the northern edge of the promontory suggest the reality of fighting in improvised trenches only a few metres apart.) When the fighting died down in October 1914 French troops had a tenuous hold on the western end of the ridge, with the Germans holding the crest some 800 metres away. By the time Masitre's men secured the feature in May 1915 nearly 100,000 casualties had been incurred by the two sides – the majority by the French who were obliged to attack. Such fighting over small but dominating areas of high ground, a recurring feature of battles from 1915 to 1917, epitomizes the cruel and manpower-intensive style of the new warfare to which Maistre and other commanders would have to adapt. Notre-Dame-de-Lorette, being the first of these fights, was among the worst. But his troops acquitted themselves well. Of one success in the early phase of the battle, Foch recollected, 'Only infantry as good as that of the XXI Corps could have retained possession of the position it had captured.'[27]

Like Pétain and Fayolle, whose XXXIII CA he fought alongside, Maistre would approach the task professionally, reflecting on and applying the theories he taught before the war to the challenges that he faced on the battlefield. Jonathan Krause has studied these for the Second Battle of Artois in spring 1915, the French army's first set-piece offensive using new tactics distilled from the lessons of the fighting over the winter of 1914–15. Maistre came to appreciate the importance of intensive artillery support for any attack[28] – not always easy in such close-range fighting – no doubt drawing on his time as both an infantry and artillery regimental commander before the war.[29] It ensured his corps would do better than others in the first well-prepared assault (excepting Pétain's XXXIII CA that gained a temporary foothold on Vimy ridge). On 9 May the crest of Notre-Dame-de-Lorette was finally seized and consolidated. Now Maistre's troops overlooked the enemy's positions. Progress thereafter was steady but inconsistent, as was always the case in a localized offensive against an alert and reinforced enemy. By the time the battle wound down in mid-June, XXI CA had pushed on to the western edge of the village of Souchez, one kilometre beyond the crest of the ridge. (It would require another major offensive, in September, before Souchez was fully occupied by XXI CA.) Throughout the developing operation Maistre had promoted the new tactical paradigms and suggested areas for innovation and improvement to his subordinates. Krause identifies proper training in the use of grenades and the deployment of artillery observers to the front line alongside the infantry as significant developments in XXI CA's battle techniques. 43 DI even tried a night attack on 9 May to achieve an element of surprise.[30] Maistre was proving to be a commander with a grasp of detail and prudent in his use of his soldiers, like Pétain one of the 'intelligent commanders [who] would no doubt have taken the best ideas, merged them with their own and created a viable system'.[31] Nonetheless, responsibility for Notre-Dame-de-Lorette would identify him with the early war commanders who gained a reputation for being careless with soldiers' lives.[32] His tough sector precluded any great successes, and that may explain why, when the commander-in-chief next came calling for an army commander, Pétain was chosen from the corps commanders of the Second Battle of Artois.

It meant that Maistre would lead his army corps through the Third Battle of Artois in September and the attritional battles of 1916. When the offensive towards the Vimy ridge was renewed by Tenth Army in the autumn, XXI CA pushed its line two kilometres eastwards into Givenchy, at the northern end of the ridge. Methods by this point had become more scientific and systematic: there would be no attempt to repeat the dynamic thrust onto the ridge that had promised much but delivered little in the second battle. The German defence was determined and inflicted heavy casualties on the French assault troops, although it could not break their spirit. On one occasion, Maistre called for volunteers from the exhausted men of 109ᵉ RI that had held the recently captured 'Givechy work' against repeated counter attacks to drive off yet another. Several hundred men marched back to the French trenches to ensure that the position they had defended at heavy cost would not be lost by their replacements.'[33]

After a period of rest and training over the winter of 1915–16, XXI CA, now comprising four infantry divisions, found itself thrown into the defence of Verdun, under Pétain's direction. It relieved XX CA in the hard-pressed sector around Fort Vaux at the beginning of March and for a fortnight Maistre's men resisted all that the enemy would throw at them. Here Bordeaux, attached to corps headquarters to report on the defence, encountered Maistre for the first time: 'he was welcoming, but obviously preoccupied; an intelligent face, slightly sad, upright, conscientious, clear sighted'.[34] Maistre was anxious about the position in his sector; so much so that the more unflappable Joffre, who dined at his headquarters, remarked sarcastically on his obvious edginess.[35] Maistre was prepared to delay an attack ordered by his superior Pétain to save lives and ensure success: 'here the chiefs dare to speak the truth: there is no sycophancy or desire to please, merely collaboration for the common good'.[36] From witnessing such rational acts of command, Bordeaux would come to venerate Maistre as the epitome of the noble, conscientious general, the true spirt of France at a time of national emergency: 'A conscientious man, a concerned, anguished leader, yet who knows how to arrange things once he has made his mind up. With a precise, clear mind, for whom matters of life and death are simplified by faith and love of his country.'[37]

Pétain's *noria* system, which cycled units into and out of the battle before they were fought out, ensured that XXI CA's tenure of the critical point in the Verdun sector was brief. Afterwards the corps gained a long period of rest and training in quiet sectors before their next fight. It did not see the hell of Verdun again: by the time Maistre's formations were redeployed to attack the Somme offensive was entering its third month and its most intensive phase. When XXI CA went into battle in mid-September Maistre had three divisions under command: 120 DI joined the corps' 13 and 43 DIs, to be replaced by 62 DI in late October.

To coincide with Romania's entry into the war, in September Joffre and Foch, the responsible army group commander, chose to extend and intensify the pressure on the enemy on either side of the Somme river. XXI CA joined the forgotten army of the Somme offensive, Micheler's Tenth Army, fighting south of the river in the Santerre plain. On 4 September Tenth Army launched its first large-scale offensive, three army corps attacking between Barleux and Chilly in a south-easterly direction. By the time XXI CA relieved the central corps in the Ablaincourt sector on 19 September the battle was in full swing and Maistre was obliged to fight an intensive, gruelling contest against a determined enemy. In addition, the final stage of the offensive was a battle against the elements as much as the Germans: the ground around Ablaincourt was by mid-October 'a vast lake of mud'.[38] Such fighting required methodical preparation and careful management to ensure progress with acceptable casualties. Maistre's 14 October operation against Ablaincourt village was so singular that it was acknowledged by the commander-in-chief in his memoirs: 'in [a] well-prepared [attack the] XXI Corps, commanded by General Maistre, captured Ablaincourt with astonishing ease, the battalion which took the village having had only two men wounded, while the enemy left in our hands 1,200 prisoners'.[39] It was the sort of dynamic and effective action that well-prepared and trained French troops were capable of by this point in the war. But still such an effective first strike could not be exploited. Maistre's troops fought to maintain control of the village – more accurately the mud-filled shell holes where the village had once stood – for the next four weeks. It would not be firmly held until 7 November, and German counter attacks continued for some days afterwards. Since battle was now material-intensive, although the type of fighting was similar, unlike on the hills of Artois infantry losses were relatively low.

\* \* \*

Although his immediate superior, Micheler, was promoted to lead an army group, Maistre's success at the unfashionable end of the Somme front was not enough to earn him promotion in the reshuffling of senior commands that followed Joffre's replacement by Nivelle in December 1916 (although his former chief of staff and 43 DI's commander, de Boissoudy, had received a corps command from Joffre immediately following the successful attack on Ablaincourt, suggesting Maistre might have been rewarded had Joffre remained in post.) Micheler's army went to General Denis Duchêne, whose II CA had fought as part of Tenth Army since the opening of the offensive: he was an authoritarian and unpopular commander whose career would end ignominiously on the Chemin des Dames in 1918. Although his command was wracked with mutinies in May and June, he did survive the first debacle on the Chemin des Dames the next spring, into which Tenth Army was deployed for its second, attritional phase.[40] Maistre's corps was held in reserve for the exploitation phase of Nivelle's offensive which never came. He ensured that it was well trained and ready, but by the time it was committed to the second phase of the battle Maistre had been moved upwards. Perhaps appropriately, he replaced Nivelle's disgraced protégé General Charles Mangin in command of Sixth Army on 4 May. Maistre was surprised, and not entirely happy with his promotion. He would be leaving his experienced and devoted staff and would have to build relationships with a group of less agreeable officers: 'Do not congratulate me, but hope that I am up to the task and pray for me...' he suggested to his subordinates on taking their leave.[41] It would seem that he was successful. His GQG liaison officer, Lieutenant-Colonel Godfroy, remembered a convivial mess, and a talented and effective army staff managed by a personable and skilled commander: 'I hold the memory of this estimable man in the highest esteem; modest, profoundly decent, with qualities of a great leader: character, tenacity, sang-froid, military erudition.'[42] Happily, his old army corps would be one of those under his command. He would soon demonstrate aptitude in the new appointment.

Having done so well on the Somme, French troops had been badly let down in the next phase of the war, and the summer and autumn would be spent rebuilding morale and fighting spirit after widespread mutinies that particularly affected troops in the Chemin des Dames sector that Maistre took responsibility for. Maistre himself was in favour of extreme measures against agitators who tried to exploit the mutinies for political ends. He issued an order for two left-wing parliamentary deputies who had reportedly been distributing anti-war propaganda among the troops to be arrested. They eluded their hunters; but Maistre attested that if they had been caught, he would have had them shot.[43] Such an extreme action would no doubt have brought a premature end to a burgeoning career. But Maistre was right that the mutinies were a military act and required a military solution. The new commander-in-chief, Pétain, set about rebuilding morale with judicious concessions to the rank and file, a material-intensive rather than manpower-intensive operational method, and a series of limited, morale-boosting offensives. In this renaissance Maistre would play a prominent part.

Maistre's Sixth Army would contest the western end of the Chemin des Dames ridge over the summer. Here the final operation of Nivelle' offensive, the Battle of Laffaux (5–7 May) fought immediately after Maistre took command of Sixth Army – which would partly redeem the fortunes of the fledgling French tank arm, the *artillerie spéciale*, after its lacklustre performance in the first phase of the Nivelle offensive[44] – had established the French front lines just below the forward edge of the ridge, which expanded into a wide, flat plateau at its western end. To seize that plateau would require scaling-up the successful methods used at Ablaincourt: as Godfroy later summarized, 'Maistre used his painstaking and precise approach and the experience acquired in Artois and on the Somme' to mount 'an immense mopping-up operation'.[45] The unsteady morale of the troops under his command meant that Maistre would have to wait five months before he could complete the task. The Battle of Malmaison (named after an obsolescent nineteenth-century fort that sat atop the ridge), like the commander who directed it, is largely forgotten, perhaps because it did not conform to the stereotype of a Western Front offensive. Short, dynamic, decisive, the 'perfect offensive' in the view of one of the few English authors who acknowledges it, Malmaison demonstrated the sophisticated combined-arms methods of the French army by this point in the war and the new operational principles of 'bite and hold'.[46]

Three French army corps, including XXI CA, seized the plateau on a cold, rainy day in late October. 'Confident, but constantly worrying', Maistre prepared meticulously as always.[47] Maistre conceived an artillery-centric battle: indeed, his demand for heavy guns to support the operation was considered excessive even by Pétain who had been one of the architects of the new tactics. He would 'use all available resources to render the ground untenable for the enemy…[yet] it would be necessary for the infantry to dislodge them step by step which required developing their offensive sprit and capacity to manoeuvre.'[48] The fire-plan was based on intimate intelligence of the enemy's positions on the plateau, gathered by aerial observation and interviews with German prisoners and even former inhabitants of the area.[49] French medium tanks would support the infantry advance against the forward German positions on the plateau. By the time the attack went in, as intended most of the hard work had been done by the artillery during six days of intensive bombardment. The bombardment had been lengthened by two days owing to poor weather; the commander would leave nothing to chance. And in the final hours beforehand, being apprised that the Germans had learned of the time of attack and planned a disrupting counter bombardment, Maistre advanced the jumping off time by thirty minutes.[50] This meant that the infantry would have to go over the top in darkness, but such eleventh-hour improvisation meant the enemy would be taken by surprise and infantry lives might be saved. In the first phase of the attack the assaulting waves of infantry had to do little more than round up the dazed German garrison who had been trapped underground for days by the shelling. Pressing onwards beyond the barrage, those few tanks which had been able to get forward across waterlogged and shell-smashed ground supported the infantry onto their second and final objectives at the rear of the ridge, which was in French hands by nightfall.[51] Outflanked and too 'shell-shocked' to counterattack, the Germans were obliged to surrender the rest of the Chemin des Dames ridge without a fight over the following days. In all the enemy lost 50,000 killed, missing and captured and 200 guns, while the French suffered only 14,000 casualties: the balance of attrition has shifted decisively in France's favour. Maistre's tour de force demonstrated the way forwards for an army that had become thrifty with human lives but profligate with shells and bullets.[52] The success monetarily went to Maistre's head, however, and he had to be persuaded by Pétain not to try to follow up in the direction of Laon which would negate the primary purpose of the attack, to restore confidence and morale with a cost-effective operation limited in time, space and objective.[53] The method confirmed how the better French commanders had adapted to the realities of warfare. Bordeaux, who observed the battle, suggested later that it should have served as a lesson in command at the staff college, written up by its architect, like Spicheren.[54] But Maistre died before he could do so, and instead General Marie-Eugène Debeney's August 1918 Battle of Amiens–Montdidier, developed along the same lines as Malmaison, became the principal model.

'What a soldier!' commented Guillaumat: but it was unfortunate that Maistre's striking success at Malmaison was overshadowed by the smashing blow inflicted by the enemy on the Italians at the same time.[55] Yet Maistre's star was finally rising. A few days after the battle he was elevated to *Grand officier* of the Légion d'honneur. Bordeaux painted a pen-portrait of his hero shortly afterwards:

> He has the air of a gentleman. Medium build, ordinary face, craggy, Frankish, fair with striking brown eyes, a little agitated, worried over his work but with an inner calm. His straightforward welcome, his clear, young-man's laugh. He said to me: 'If I had failed I would have nobody to blame but myself. I was given what I asked for; nobody changed my plan; the troops were good.' His fine success did not excite him; always so unaffected.[56]

In December, when a reliable general was needed to command the French forces that had been sent to Italy following the collapse of the Italian Second Army in the Battle of Caporetto, he was selected: Pétain confirmed that it was on account of his achievements at Malmaison that he was chosen. Reluctantly, Maistre swapped places with Duchêne of Tenth Army.[57] Fayolle, who was overseeing allied support to the Italian army, was certainly unhappy with the unimaginative and potentially dangerous Duchêne,[58] and no doubt pleased to be working with his old comrade again.

Maistre's role in Italy was less to command than to teach; to demonstrate to the Italians how to conduct the sort of material-intensive operations that were producing results in the French sector of the Western Front. The shaky Italians needed morale-boosting victories like Malmaison. Maistre would give them one, and at the same time he would demonstrate to the less experienced Italians French methods for a simple, limited operation.[59] The capture of Monte Tomba at the end of December was, he wrote to Godfroy, 'a Malmaison in miniature, and the Austrians were a second-tier enemy'.[60]

Monte Tomba, an 870m forward bastion of the Monte Grappa massif, flanked and dominated the new Italian line established on the river Piave to the south. Seizing it would terminate another attritional struggle in the foothills of the Alps that the Austrians had forced on the weary Italians since their precipitate retreat at the end of October. It was to be a relatively small-scale but dynamic and decisive operation, in which artillery would do the main work. Three battalions of *chasseurs alpins*, elite French mountain troops, from 47 DI would spearhead the final infantry assault, seizing the promontory with an assault from the flank. After nearly three days of heavy bombardment by French and Italian batteries they overwhelmed the surviving Austrian defenders, killing more than 500 and taking over 1,500 prisoners and 8 guns, effectively putting the 50th Austrian division out of action. Techniques for capturing dominating positions had come a long way since 1915 and Notre-Dame-de-Lorette. There XXI CA had lost many thousands over months. French casualties were less than 250 on Monte Tomba and the ground was secured in just a few hours. The Italians were inspired and sought to emulate such methods in future attacks.[61] Maistre was learning too. Fayolle endorsed his recommendation that such *coups de main* against inferior opposition would need less artillery support in future; neutralizing fire could be privileged over destruction and therefore increase the element of surprise.[62]

After Fayolle returned to France in anticipation of an enemy spring offensive, Maistre was left in charge of French forces in the Italian theatre. This was a political as much as a military role, and he would spend much of his time visiting Italian and British commanders and regulating relationships between the three allied armies in the field.[63] It was good preparation for his return to France with Tenth Army at the end of March 1918. Deployed initially in the north to support British troops, thereafter Maistre's commands would always require close liaison with allied formations.

* * *

When Erich Ludendorff struck the first blow of his spring offensive against the British front south of the river Somme France moved to her ally's aid – somewhat ponderously it appeared during the immediate and nerve-shredding crisis in the last days of March 1918, but quickly enough given the tempo of offensive warfare at that moment in the war. Some French divisions were redeployed back from Italy to the Western Front, and Maistre came with them, in early April reconstituting Tenth Army west of Amiens as Foch's reserve army to support the British. (Foch had just been appointed allied generalissimo in response to the German offensive). By the time it was ready French and British forces had contained the immediate danger and so Maistre's army remained in reserve. The next emergency on the French front came in late May, when the German army smashed through Duchêne's positions on the Chemin des Dames and advanced rapidly towards the river Marne. A skeleton formation during the spring, Tenth Army was activated, added to Fayolle's *Group d'armées de réserve* and filled up with divisions to meet the German threat. Maistre would find that he had little more than a fortnight in charge before his army was ceded to Mangin. Maistre was chosen to lead the *Group d'armées du nord* (redesignated *Group d'armées du centre* (GAC) on 6 July), alongside his old colleague Fayolle. Maistre was the final army group commander appointed in the war; and he might never have got an army group command. He was not elevated owing to someone else's failure, but selected when General Louis Franchet d'Esperey was moved to take command of the Salonika Front (although he was second choice: General Debeney declined the promotion).[64] He would find an old subordinate and comrade, General René Mollandin, as his chief of staff: he had been a sub-chief of staff in Fourth Army in August 1914 and had replaced Baucheron de Boissoudy in command of 43 DI during the Somme offensive.

Including allied and inter-allied formations, five army groups were operating along the front in summer and autumn 1918 (two US armies formed a sixth in late September 1918 with integrated French formations). Engaging such a large and diverse force into a vast encounter battle at the time of greatest national crisis since the first Battle of the Marne was a very different challenge to seizing high ground through a managed and limited set-piece operation. Maistre rose to it. An army group commander's role (equivalent to Joffre's in 1914) was operational; that is, to control a sequence of battles on an extended sector of the front, 'preparing and coordinating the separate operations of his armies, managing reserves to commit them to the critical point or to exploit success'.[65] As his counterpart Fayolle noted of the responsibility: 'Foch says "attack", Pétain provides the wherewithal, sparingly as always, and I carry things out.'[66] There were initially four armies in GAC, Fourth, Fifth, Sixth and Ninth (a small 'reserve' army constituted for the Marne defence and counter offensive and dissolved in August). Fourth Army was commanded by General Henri Gouraud, Maistre's former superior when he commanded XXI CA, who apparently responded to Maistre's self-effacing expression of regret that he now found himself commanding his former chief, that no subordination would be more acceptable to him.[67] Maistre clearly inspired confidence in his subordinates. Sixth Army would redeploy to Flanders in September, when Maistre also became responsible for coordinating operations with the American army as the Franco-American Meuse–Argonne offensive developed from late September until the armistice.

Maistre's first task was to reconstruct the allied line and halt the most rapid German advance since 1914. Tenth Army was committed to the western flank of the developing salient south of the Aisne, to contain the German penetration. Maistre fed his divisions into the battle as they arrived, consolidating a defensive front before Mangin relieved him in mid-June. The army group he took over held the line eastwards from Tenth Amy's line, south-eastwards along the western flank of the Marne salient (Sixth Army) across the base of the salient at Château-Thierry (Ninth Army) around the city or Reims that had become a forward bastion of the new French line (Fifth Army) and into the Champagne, where Maistre had first fought as a corps commander in September 1914 (Fourth Army).

The first challenge he faced as army group commander was meeting Ludendorff's optimistically titled 'Peace Offensive', the final German attack that was designed to force the French lines either side of Reims in a two-pronged attack, Marneschutz–Reims. Making full use of a developing intelligence picture of German intentions (even down to learning the exact time of the German assault from a raid on the eve of battle), Maistre was able to deploy his defensive forces and reserves to absorb and then counterattack the German assault as Foch, with a wider scheme in preparation, wished.[68] When the enemy's blows fell on 15 July they were contained. The defensive lesson so disastrously taught by Duchêne's army's collapse only a few weeks earlier, the need for elastic defence-in-depth, had been quickly learned. As Bordeaux suggested:

> General Maistre adopted these principles as his own with the fervour with which he had taught at the war college. Personally, both in meetings and through written directives, he acted to make sure all understood the need to follow them completely and to overcome the reservations that many lower echelons expressed against abandoning ground, that had been won and held with great sacrifice, to the enemy, and whose possession… ensured observation and was extremely important for the defensive security of our positions.[69]

Gouraud was receptive; Fifth Army commander General Henri Berthelot less so.[70] To the east of Reims, Fourth Army had prepared to absorb the German blow by thinning manpower in its front lines, drawing the enemy into open space on the parched and dusty Champagne heights and then destroying the attackers' forces with artillery and machine-gun fire. The plan worked admirably when the enemy attacked on 15 July. This overwhelming success left Maistre's reserves in hand for reinforcing Fifth Army, whose positions west of Reims were under pressure from German forces that had broken through their front lines. To their left General Anthoine de Mitry's Ninth Army, that had resisted the development of defence-in-depth having a strong forward position resting on the river Marne, was caught by the full weight of the German bombardment. The enemy forced a bridgehead across the river, but made limited forward progress thereafter: Franco-American forces drew in then halted the Germans on the heights south of the Marne. Overall, the initial German effort produced disappointing results and within a couple of days Ludendorff called off the offensive.

The Germans in the Marne salient, tiring after three days of frustrated progress, were counterattacked with great energy in the first stage of Foch's counter offensive, the Second Battle of the Marne, which commenced on 18 July.[71] Mangin's Tenth Army stove in the western flank of the German salient in the Battle of the Soissonais, supported by Sixth Army to the south (which was transferred to Fayolle's army group on 21 July). Extending the battle around the Marne salient, Maistre's Ninth and Fifth Armies smashed in the front west of Reims and followed up the enemy, forcing him from the salient in two separate phases of operations, the Battle of the Ourcq (18–28 July) and the Battle of the Tardenois (29 July–2 August). The latter forced a German retreat to the line of the Vesle river as their positions in the salient, attacked from both sides, had been rendered untenable. 'We were lucky to have at GAC a real soldier, General Maistre, whose outlook is not limited…he loves everything about war', commented Guillaumat.[72] Yet in that phase of the counter offensive Maistre's role seemed largely to be to enforce the demands of his superiors for pressing the attack upon his fractious subordinates, anxious about the fatigue of their troops and clamouring for fresh reserves. While clearly finding his intermediary role frustrating, he did his best to reconcile the two.[73]

In the advance to victory French operations are generally played down in English-language studies that privilege British or American achievements in the final campaign.[74] France's armies also advanced steadily, effectively and carefully to link Franco-allied operations on the wings – storming fixed defensive lines where they encountered them, following up retreating German rearguards betweentimes – demonstrating strong operational control within the parameters of generalissimo Foch's overall strategic conception for destroying the German army. These were not flashy or costly operations – the veteran French army, unlike its new American allies, was too canny by 1918 to rush and hope – but cumulatively they pushed back and wore out the enemy forces in front of them as Foch had envisaged. Maistre was in effective control of one-quarter of the allied front as the advance commenced, but it being the sector that connected the Anglo-French attack on the Hindenburg Line to the north and the Franco-American advance in the Meuse–Argonne to the east, his role was more one of supporting than leading the charge. As his offensive front shrank as the allied armies advanced during the autumn, his command reduced with it. His four armies of July were down to two by the end of the Marne counter offensive.

Maistre directed Fifth Army on his left, supporting Tenth Army as is retook the Chemin des Dames and thereafter keeping pace as it advanced to the Franco-Belgian frontier. Fourth Army on the right would advance in the Champagne before engaging in the second phase of the Meuse–Argonne offensive with the Americans. Maistre's role in managing this series of large battles has passed into obscurity – perhaps, obliquely, evidence that they were well run and effective operations and caused no controversies, unlike those of the Americans who Maistre was called upon to sort out.[75]

Cooperating with thrusting and somewhat headstrong US commanders was a final challenge, which Maistre managed with common sense and discretion. Ever sensitive to the tendency of Frenchmen to try to 'give orders' to their inexperienced ally, American commander-in-chief John Pershing had to be handled tactfully. As an allied contingent commander, Pershing expected direct lines of communication to the generalissimo and his immediate subordinate, Pétain (and used them to complain if he was unhappy with how things were shaping up). This complex chain-of-command left the GAC commander marginalized.[76] When it came to coordinating field operations in the Meuse–Argonne offensive, Maistre had to ensure Fourth Army and the First US Army, initially under Pershing's command, worked to the same plan. It would not be easy, as the methodical and cost-effective methods practised by the French after years of experience did not mesh easily with the Americans' dynamic but shambolic 'open warfare' concepts that Pershing felt would rush his troops to Mezières and victory.[77] Foch's constant urging for more rapid progress to intensify pressure on the enemy did not improve things.[78] On one occasion at least Pershing ignored Maistre's intervention on behalf of Foch, having already made his own plan.[79] Yet the old fable, that the tortoise can beat the hare, proved prophetic.

The first phase of the offensive was disappointing. Gouraud's army made steady progress, with Fifth Army supporting it on its left and disengaging Reims, while the Americans' initially rapid advance collapsed into logistical chaos and stalled. The battle would be paused and reorganized, with Fourth Army's reliance on American coordination reduced as their front extended westwards, with US forces being closely 'shouldered' by French formations on both sides for the later stages of the offensive.[80] As the armistice approached the Franco-American forces were approaching the line Mezières–Sedan. Owing to the symbolic importance of the site of France's 1870 defeat by the Prussians, it had been agreed that Sedan should be retaken by French forces, with lines of advanced being assigned accordingly. But as American forces approached the city Pershing tried to claim the prize, wishing to ignore agreed boundaries and proposing, rather tactlessly, to take Sedan and present it as a trophy of war to France. Maistre, magnanimously according to Pershing, consented. Perhaps, however, Maistre was merely trying to mollify Pershing's complaint that the Frenchman had tried to give him orders when urging that First US Army press its attack. If anything, Pershing was complicating pre-agreed arrangements in pursuit of American glory, demonstrating 'vanity and selfishness' in Donald Smythe's opinion. It proved moot. As US formations marched across each other's lines of communication in pursuit of Pershing's ambitions, logistical chaos ensued once again. The local French commander had to warn the Americans that their troops had crossed into the French sector and were likely to come under French bombardment. By the time this was sorted out the war was effectively over: French troops would reach Sedan on 10 November, the day before the armistice was signed.[81]

\* \* \*

When the war came abruptly to an end in November 1918 there was no obvious future career path for a recently appointed yet successful army group commander. Fayolle was appointed to command the French army of occupation in Germany while Maistre was left to demobilize the formations under his command. Although Maistre himself seemed unconcerned about his future, Guillaumat was displeased that his 'brave and honest' friend was treated so indifferently.[82] In June 1919, Maistre was made an inspector general of the forces, responsible for the infantry. He was appointed to the *Conseil supérieur de la guerre*, at whose meetings he would forcibly argue the case for sustaining the fighting spirit of his beloved infantry; for keeping it up to strength and arming and training it for modern war rather than lapsing into peacetime indifference. Maistre appreciated that the post-war world would be far from peaceful, and that France needed to maintain the military superiority that she had developed during the war.[83] He also appreciated that warfare had changed fundamentally since 1914. As president of the court of enquiry into the fall of the fortress of Maubeuge in September 1914, he acquitted the governor, General Henri Fournier, and his subordinates of negligence. Subsequent experience excused the mistakes of that time: he and the wartime generals learned and prospered from their own. As Bordeaux stated: 'He himself understood that the art of war can be taught at staff college, but it must adapt to circumstances, to manpower, material, logistics, and in a four-year struggle one had constantly to modify one's ideas, improve, correct mistakes.'[84]

Maistre died unexpectedly from the complications of appendicitis in July 1922, while still on active duty, aged 64.[85] His statue was inaugurated at Notre-Dame-de-Lorette in 1927: he had been chairman of the committee established to build a monument to France's sacrifices there.[86] In 1931 his remains would be among those of seventeen wartime generals reinterred in the crypt at

Les Invalides, including his former chief de Langle de Cary and his 'cousin' Fayolle.[87]

\* \* \*

Maistre, Bordeaux suggested, was a 'loyal servant' of his nation, lacking in the ambition of some of his better known contemporaries; one who trained officers to fight the war that was to come and led them effectively in it.[88] He accepted pre-war the basic operational and tactical principle that success in war comes from the offensive, but one properly resourced and prepared, and was guided by such straightforward logic in his actions at all levels of command.[89] When in command he never lost a battle: XXI CA supposedly never had to give up ground won while under his leadership.[90] As an army commander he was trusted to deliver, whether it be restoring morale (to both French troops and Italian allies) or taking ground. His army group command was brief but effective; his post-war career also brief but still promoting the principles that had informed his teaching and command careers. His premature death meant that unlike several of his contemporaries he left no memoir. However, since he did not court publicity – even if in Guillaumat's estimation he deserved it[91] – he probably would have remained silent on his war, unless perhaps he wished to teach the lessons he had learned about warfare to the next generation.

'Men are the opposite of monuments', Maistre once wrote to Bordeaux: 'When one approaches them they appear smaller.'[92] Maistre's effigy depicts two larger-than-life men, the French soldier who fought willingly and died bravely *pour la patrie* and a commander who rose to the challenges of leading him through adversity to victory at increasing levels of responsibility. Bordeaux attests that the trials of Notre-Dame-de-Lorette hung heavily on his subject ever after – whatever his responsibilities he remained an infantryman at heart. Yet, as Maistre rose higher fretfulness over the fate of his soldiers diminished as he learned better how to employ them, became more confident in his preparations and more certain that the effort and sacrifice he demanded of them was appropriate and proportionate. His humanity never left him, but his ability and experience made his tasks more bearable; his lessons from the war were well learned and well taught to those he led.[93] A modest and self-effacing man, Maistre would not have liked any fuss made over his achievements, and may have resisted the erection of a statue after his death. But he would have been pleased to see the men he led honoured alongside him.

Chapter 8

# Pierre Roques: A Political General

Simon House

General Pierre Roques is something of an enigma in the English-speaking world. Virtually unknown outside his own country, he was nevertheless a very important figure in the immediate pre-war period as well as during the first two years of the war. During a forty-year career in the army, Pierre Roques achieved lasting fame in France as the 'father of the French air force' and scaled the heights of his profession, becoming minister of war in 1916. His career, it would seem, was measured by incremental levels of success, his legacy an unblighted pedigree of military excellence. He was the very essence of a political general, well versed in the ways of the labyrinthine and byzantine bureaucracy of the Third Republic's war ministry, within which he spent long periods of his career. It is scarcely surprising therefore that when recent research uncovered the facts of his first exercise of command in battle in August 1914 – in which he threw away France's best opportunity to win a victory in the opening phase of the war – it also became clear how he used his political skills to escape censure at a time when incompetent commanders were being weeded out wholesale and sent to await their fate at the military base at Limoges.[1] Indeed he not only escaped censure but was soon rewarded with promotion to command an army, before becoming minister of war. Much of his career was tied to that of General Joseph Joffre, commander-in-chief from 1914 to 1916, whose career path he followed in the early days. Joffre's patronage was undoubtedly a significant factor in Roques's survival as a senior commander and his comparative success.

In many ways Roques epitomizes what was wrong with the French military system of promotion, a system that was largely responsible for the many French defeats during the early Battle of the Frontiers. An engineer by branch of service, he lacked wide experience of mixed-arms command; he lacked staff training; he lacked experience in command of large bodies of troops. Yet in August 1914 he commanded an army corps. On the positive side, he was extremely intelligent, personable and a good administrator. He was well connected, politically reliable, and a proven operator within the engineering directorate of the war ministry. None of these positive qualities fitted him for command of a field unit against well-trained German opposition.

\* \* \*

Pierre Auguste Roques was born on 28 December 1856 into an ordinary middle-class family in the small village of Marseillan, situated some fifty kilometres south-west of Montpellier on the Mediterranean coast. Roques enrolled in the *École polytechnique* in 1875 and on completion of his studies in 1877 joined the engineering branch of the French metropolitan army. His unit, 2ᵉ *régiment du génie* went abroad when it was attached to the 1882 South-Oranian expedition to suppress a tribal revolt in southern Algeria.[2] It was the start of a twenty-year phase in his career as an engineer attached to France's colonial army. Roques's colonial career followed closely that of his senior colleague and friend, Joffre.[3] Pierre Rocolle wrote that Roques had never attended the *École supèrieure de guerre* but 'was linked to Joffre by their engineering backgrounds and by a friendship born of their time together in the Far-East'.[4] In fact, Joffre and Roques seem to have worked together on only one occasion before the war; they both served in Tonkin from 1886 to 1888, both ranked as captains, with Joffre being of the 1st class and Roques the 2nd class.[5] By 1889, both Roques and Joffre were back in Paris serving in the war ministry. Joffre was attached to the office of the director of engineering; Roques occupied a supernumerary post, which he held for over two years. In 1892, Roques took another two-year posting overseas, this time to build infrastructure in the newly acquired colony of Dahomey (now Benin) in West Africa. Roques was now in command of a battalion of engineers. Afterwards Roques returned, supernumerary once more, to the war ministry. In 1897, Roques returned to the colonies, this time building railways in Madagascar. During his eight years there he progressed from battalion commander to the more grandiose role of director of engineering (*Directeur du génie à Madagascar*); he was promoted to lieutenant-colonel and then full colonel. When he returned to Paris in 1906, he was fifth on the seniority list of engineers, and yet became director of the engineering department at the war ministry ahead of three others, succeeding Joffre. Roques was promoted on 25 March 1906 to the rank of *général de brigade* to go with his new job.

Roques's tenure, from 1906–11, coincided with the birth of French military aviation. The Wright brothers' first powered flight on 17 November 1903 had shown the potential of heavier-than-air machines; Louis Blériot's cross-Channel flight on 25 July 1909 had signalled the viability of the aeroplane as an immediately effective military asset. Roques took full advantage of the opportunity granted him by this significant technological development. The engineering directorate of the French army had always been the home for scientific and technological innovations: new inventions such as railways, the telegraph, the telephone, fixed observation balloons and dirigibles had all come under the jurisdiction of the engineers.[6] In that tradition the newly appointed director Roques met the Wright Brothers' representatives in 1906 with a view to buying one of their flying machines.[7] The purchase never happened because the negotiators failed to agree on price, but Roques's interest was piqued, and (perceiving the military potential of aeroplanes) he thereafter maintained a strong personal interest in developments in aeronautics.

If this period of Roques's military service was marked by his increasing interest in aviation, it also saw him promoted to the then highest rank in the army, *général de division*, in 1909. Roques became one of the youngest generals in the army, without ever having commanded a field unit larger than a battalion of engineers building railways in the colonies. He had only briefly seen active service in Dahomey, where he had been wounded in battle at Koto in October 1892.[8] Overnight he became eligible to command an infantry or cavalry division, which he would go on to do in 1912, when he took command of 7 *division d'infanterie* (DI).

For the moment, however, he was fully occupied with the fledgling French air force, using it as a vehicle to enhance his career. Blériot's cross-Channel flight suggested the military potential of the aeroplane as a mobile observation platform. The artillery directorate of the war ministry, recognizing this potential, wanted aircraft for artillery spotting, and they wanted them under their own control. On 10 November 1909, the war minister, Jean Brun, authorized the director of artillery to create a section of military aviation at Vincennes, commanded by Commandant Jean-Baptiste Estienne.[9] Roques, however, had already made his move. In September 1909 he had bought five aeroplanes – two Wright biplanes, two Henri Farman biplanes and one Blériot monoplane – with which to begin experiments into military aviation.[10] Throughout the winter of 1909–10, arguments raged as to whether there should be a unified command structure for the air service and if so, which service should own it. In this bureaucratic contretemps Roques showed his political skills. He won the power struggle on behalf of the engineers, persuading the minister to sign an order on 7 June 1910 giving the engineers total control over all military aviation.[11] It had been a hard fought contest, with Estienne attempting but failing at the last minute to snatch the prize for the artillery by stepping beyond his remit and organizing the world's first air raid by his aircraft on the training camp at Châlons.[12] Having beaten off Estienne's challenge, Roques demonstrated another aspect of his political skill by allowing Estienne to retain a considerable degree of independence when his artillery flying service was absorbed into Roques's department. Nevertheless, in the long term, Roques's political success had significant adverse consequences: Estienne eventually abandoned aviation for another innovation (the French 'tank' or *artillerie spéciale*); Roques's engineers concentrated upon technological improvement rather than military requirements, driving development towards faster aircraft of longer range and higher ceiling rather than short-range, stout observation platforms; and hence

France entered the First World War without any organization or capability to use aircraft to direct artillery fire on the battlefield.[13]

Military aviation was the technical theme of the 1910 French army manoeuvres. Roques used the occasion to make his air service the centre piece of the event. Success in front of the president, prime minister, war minister and all the senior officers, not to mention foreign observers and the world's press, gave the ambitious Roques the fame that he undoubtedly sought. He subsequently lobbied hard for the creation of a military aviation section within the engineering directorate, succeeding when on 22 October 1910 the war minister created the 'Permanent Inspectorate of Military Aeronautics'. Roques by now had ambitions to make military aviation a separate directorate, with himself as its first director reporting directly to the war minister. To that end in October 1910, he published plans for an air show at Reims in the following year. The event was sponsored, paid for and organized by Roques specifically to test aircraft against his own wider military requirements. Potential suppliers (only French companies could apply) competed not just for prizes but for military contracts.[14] Technological development would henceforth be driven by the engineers of the military aviation section. Thanks to Roques's innovative and ground-breaking work, the French army had by the end of 1911 achieved a two-year technological and organizational lead in military aviation over all other major powers. Roques's success was rewarded when, on 29 March 1912, a new law was passed that established *L'Aéronautique militaire* as a separate arm independent of the engineers.[15] Power is consolidated by money, and Roques was careful to acquire his own budget; indeed he managed to get that portion which he carved out of the overall engineering budget supplemented by an extra sixteen million francs.[16] With this, Roques had achieved what he set out to do: establish a permanent French air service as an independent branch of the metropolitan army with its own healthy budget. He had also established his own reputation, and it was time to move on and up.[17]

\* \* \*

Roques's reward for his success in the engineers and in aeronautics was to be given his first field command, despite his evident lack of relevant experience. After a scant sixteen months in charge of 7 DI, on 18 August 1913 Roques was promoted to command an army corps. This is rapid promotion indeed, especially for one so inexperienced in general military command, and who lacked both staff college training and experience commanding a combined force of infantry, artillery and cavalry. He had yet to prove that he had the skills to lead an army corps into battle.[18]

So it was that when war broke out Roques was commander of XII *corps d'armée* (CA) within General de Langle de Cary's Fourth Army. His army corps mobilized and concentrated in the region south-east of Sedan on the Franco-Belgian border. On 21 August, Roques received orders to advance the next morning northwards across the river Semoy and to occupy the small town of Libramont, an important railway junction in the central Ardennes on open ground just north of the great band of forests that characterised the region. Roques's corps was in the centre of a general advance by Fourth Army (five army corps, each of two divisions) intended to trap and annihilate the German forces known to be marching across its front towards the river Meuse between Dinant and Namur.[19]

Between Roques and his objective lay the German *21 Reserve Infanterie Division* (RID), one of four German divisions of the German Fourth Army that had entered the central Ardennes on 18 August and had also targeted Libramont and its railway junction; rapid lateral communications across the front were strategically and operationally important to both sides.[20] The Germans got to Libramont first and had been discovered by reconnaissance units of Fourth Army's cavalry corps on 20 August, and a four-hour skirmish had taken place.[21] However, intelligence gathered from the event was not properly disseminated; communication and command failures within Fourth Army headquarters led to Roques's columns being completely unprepared for a possible (probable) clash with the enemy south of Libramont on 22 August.[22] It therefore came as a complete surprise when, after a four-hour approach march, Roques's reconnaissance cavalry reported enemy infantry columns directly in his path, marching from east to west towards Dinant. Fortunately, the enemy were just as surprised to meet the French, for the German high command had gained no inkling of the start of the French offensive and XII CA's march north had been concealed by thick early morning mist that had prevented air reconnaissance on both sides.[23] This accounted for the fact that 21 RID was spread out in marching columns moving westwards when cavalry scouts encountered each other. Both sides hastily deployed for battle.

The advantage lay wholly with Roques. Not only had his advance caught the enemy by surprise, but his forces considerably outnumbered them. Less than half of 21 RID managed to deploy to confront Roques's force; the other half was caught in the nearby town of Neufchâteau by the rapid advance of a brigade from the corps on Roques's right. Roques had at his disposal five brigades of infantry (four of regular troops and one of reserve troops) against one brigade of German reserve troops; he massed over one-hundred-and-twenty field guns against eighteen; he had a complete regiment of regular cavalry against one reserve cavalry squadron; and his forces possessed forty-eight machine guns whereas the German reserve formations had not yet been issued with any. An opportunity presented itself to crush this opposition and to march on to the objective (Libramont) fourteen kilometres away.[24]

Roques was also in an excellent flanking position; his corps was marching in two powerful columns at right-angles to a very weak enemy on its line of march. The French left-hand column, which consisted of the whole of 24 DI with XII CA's artillery regiment, cavalry regiment and brigade of reserve infantry in support, would encounter the German advance guard, a single regiment with six guns. The odds in favour of the French on this three-kilometre stretch of battlefield were more than six-to-one. Furthermore, the French advance had caused the German advance guard to divert their westward march southwards to meet the enemy. The German commander deployed two battalions of infantry with one in reserve in a thin firing line, with its right flank hanging in the air, open to envelopment if the French so chose. Beyond the open German flank lay ten kilometres of undefended, if difficult, forested ground, with the nearest German unit over fourteen kilometres away at Libramont.[25] Only the terrain stood in the way of a French movement around the German flank: thick woods lined the last range of hills between Roques's troops and their objective, with small forest tracks bisecting the trees. But such terrain was not impassable, as the Germans were to prove on other parts of the Ardennes battlefield that day. Roques and his staff simply lacked the skill and experience to implement anything other than a straightforward frontal attack.

For more than eight hours, from the moment that the cavalry scouts reported the presence of the enemy to the moment when, with dusk approaching, the firing died away, Roques's two divisional commanders battered away at the thin line of German riflemen. By nightfall, Roques had only succeeded in advancing his left wing (24 DI) two kilometres from where the initial encounter took place. His right wing (23 DI) had actually retreated one kilometre during the day, having at one stage early on nearly broken the fragile German line. Some of 23 DI's gunners had run away in panic under the well-directed fire of the few German guns opposing them. The panic was infectious, and several infantry battalions had to be rallied by their brigade commander before they could be persuaded to re-enter the firing line.[26] In short, XII CA threw away a golden opportunity to drive through the centre of the whole German line, jeopardizing the implementation of the German offensive plan; and, for lack of battlefield reconnaissance, its commanding general, Roques, did not even know it.

The reasons for Roques's failure to capitalize on the opportunity presented to him are complex. An underlying condition of endemic lack of practice and training across the whole French pre-war army meant that the officers and troops that Roques had to work with were arguably even less well prepared than their German reservist opponents.[27] Roques himself had had no opportunity to lead his whole army corps in even one large-scale field exercise since taking command in 1913.[28] Without a staff college education and without experience, training or practice, he was forced to learn his craft on the battlefield. This explains why he allowed his two divisional commanders to engage in frontal attacks which failed to gain ground despite their superiority in numbers and firepower. He gave no orders throughout the day to his cavalry regiment (which was under his personal command) when it could, indeed should have been used on the flanks and rear of the enemy to discover and report battlefield intelligence. He responded to unnecessary calls for help from his right-hand division (whose commander panicked) and moved his powerful corps artillery from his left to his right wing, with the result that it spent all day moving rather than firing. He allowed his two reserve infantry regiments to be committed to a defensive battle on his right (where in fact they were not needed) rather than to support an enveloping move on his left where the decisive point of the battle lay. In short, he was hardly more than a passive observer of the fighting.

Despite this obviously lacklustre performance, Roques's career was saved by a number of extraneous factors. The risk of his career ending was very real.[29] During the Battle of the Frontiers from 3 August to 3 September 1914, fifty generals commanding armies, army corps and divisions were removed from their posts for failure.[30] But Joffre and de Langle were distracted from examining Roques's performance because it was one of relative success compared to what was going on either side of him. On his left, XVII CA was caught in the flank by a German division while traversing a forest, and was routed; on his right, the elite 3 *division d'infanterie colonial* encountered the German VI *Armeekorps*, was enveloped on both flanks and decimated where it stood.[31] Roques's achievement was simply not to have been defeated; and at the time his lost opportunity and the weakness of his opponents were unknown. Indeed, as his wartime career prospered, so he was able to 'spin' his indifferent performance to good effect, to make himself one of the heroes of 1914. He spoke to the journalist Henry Bordeaux in early 1915 'with a certain pride of his old corps, the 12th, one of the few that did not retreat without orders'.[32]

But Roques knew that his corps could and should have done more; during the night of 22–23 August he removed both his divisional commanders, replacing them with brigade commanders who had demonstrated more competence and drive during the day.[33] Roques also took care to draft his report to de Langle and to Joffre in suitably self-exculpatory terms: his corps had been attacked (sic) by 'major German forces' (not the case!)[34] and had resisted manfully. Its casualties were heavy (they were not!),[35] yet the corps had managed to hold its ground. Roques may have lacked field experience, but he understood the byzantine workings of the military bureaucracy, and he knew how to draft a report.[36]

* * *

Roques escaped censure for his conduct on 22 August 1914. On 23 August, the Fourth Army retreated, and continued to retreat until the first week in September, when Joffre ordered his armies to turn and fight on the Marne. During this withdrawal, Roques's corps manoeuvred as directed by de Langle: fighting rear-guard actions then disengaging, followed by a fighting retreat to the next natural barrier, where the cycle would start again. Roques's force had to conform to the movements of the army corps on the left and right (and they to its movements), so that as far as possible, Fourth Army retreated in one long line and as a coherent, controlled, unit. Roques was given little scope for initiative, merely invited to obey orders and conform to detailed direction.

Nevertheless, Roques's leadership and direction of his corps during the period of the retreat to the Marne (23 August–3 September) was marked by a series of unforced errors that lead to the conclusion that he continued to be a poor manager of troops. On 23 August he was ordered to hold the Florenville clearing, a bridgehead for a potential counter attack on the north bank of the Semoy river. He mishandled his two divisions, allowing one to retreat too far because its troops were (he claimed) too tired and seeing the other retire 'briskly' of its own volition, having perceived that its left flank was in danger of being turned by a German mixed-arms column.[37] When ordered to turn and resume the offensive Roques sent a note to de Langle stating that his whole corps needed a full day to prepare any new attack. While this exchange of commanders' views was taking place, Florenville, the last French foothold on the right bank of the Semoy, was abandoned, more by accident than design.

On 25 August, Roques figured in another incident of inept confusion in command. Roques's troops retreated behind the river Meuse despite orders to stand and hold the north bank, leaving a gap in the line.[38] He was ordered to make a hasty about-turn and march his troops back to their previous positions. He was slow in executing this recovery manoeuvre, however, and his advance had to be covered by the two army corps either side of his.[39] Roques was ordered to counterattack to restore the line but (according to the official historian) this did not take place because the troops were not in a position to intervene.[40] Nevertheless, de Langle's report to *Grand quartier général* (GQG) on the events of the morning of 25 August refer to 'the energetic counter attacks directed by General Roques in person'.[41] One can only conclude that either the official historian got it wrong when examining all the evidence with hindsight in 1923, or that at the time Roques was still performing an excellent job 'managing upwards' if not in the field. A flurry of messages between Roques and de Langle show how Roques managed to justify his actions and blame confusion of orders.[42] On 29/30 August, de Langle issued orders to General Roques to attack an enemy column identified by French aerial reconnaissance. However, it took so long for Roques to prepare the attack (again reporting that he would be unable to comply until the following day), that the attack was called off. On all these occasions, Roques continued to demonstrate that he lacked the dynamic leadership skills required to drive a French army corps into effective action.[43] Nevertheless, during the retreat to the Marne Roques had again managed to keep his reputation intact.

In December 1914, with the German invasion of France contained, Joffre decided to promote First Army commander General Augustin Dubail to command a group of armies on the French right flank, and Roques was given command of First Army. Pierre Rocolle sees this appointment as one of Joffre's *'grandes indulgences'* – patronage.[44] He cites the opinion of Commandant Pichot-Duclos, who was working at GQG at the time, who did not believe that Roques merited the promotion because '[commanding] an army is too much for him. He directs it like a *chefferie*;[45] he calls for a plan of attack and approves it; he has no idea how to prepare an attack by an army, nor how to command it.'[46]

Roques took command of First Army on 5 January 1915. The army held about 100 kilometres of front from the fortress town of Nancy on the river Moselle to Saint-Mihiel on the river Meuse. It was a quiet sector of the front, although the term 'quiet' is relative, and Roques found himself involved in continuous planning for local attacks, some quite extensive, in support of or as diversions from the main events. His mission was to pin down German reserves and, if possible, regain territory in the Woëvre region.[47]

On 8 April 1915, Joffre ordered Dubail to use Roques's First Army to mount an attack, 'methodical and yet powerful enough to allow us to gain ground wherever possible', to draw the enemy's attention away from offensive operations that were being prepared in Artois and Champagne. Roques submitted a plan to launch three separate attacks in succession, from right to left along his whole front. Joffre was sceptical about Roques's plan, observing (but not insisting) that to make a serious and permanent gain of territory it needed a focussed effort on a judiciously chosen single objective.[48] Roques, however, persisted with his three smaller attacks which ended up as a series of simultaneous but uncoordinated attacks and counter attacks. Nor did he meet his prime directive, for despite committing 204 regular and 32 territorial battalions, he only managed to pin down 173 German battalions.[49]

Thereafter, First Army was ordered to remain on the defensive and dig and strengthen its defences, mounting only small local attacks if the circumstances were right. Roques's first attempt, a divisional-strength attack from 20–25 June, was not a success and provoked more criticism from Joffre, who wrote that the attack had been improperly prepared and very poorly executed, 'which explained the mediocre results'.[50] Despite this criticism, Roques continued with his local attacks throughout July, to little purpose.

Planning for the major offensive in Champagne, which would take place in late September 1915, began in July. GQG once again wanted diversionary attacks and asked all army commanders not involved in the main offensive to submit plans. Roques put forward several ideas which his staff worked on throughout August and September, but these were finally abandoned owing to a lack of resources.[51] In this manner, Roques's tenure of command of First Army passed with him cast in a minor role, achieving nothing of significance.

* * *

Unexpectedly, in March 1916 Roques was invited by Prime Minister Aristide Briand to become minister of war after General Joseph Gallieni resigned on the grounds of ill health. This sudden elevation begs the question: what qualities did Roques possess to offset his mediocre military prowess and fit him for ministerial office? Two French historians who have written of the August encounter battles in the Ardennes have referred briefly to Roques's personality. Henry Contamine wrote: 'This engineer with little presence, short, with a goatee beard and strawberry birthmark, was a friend of his old comrade in arms, Joffre, as well as a man of valour who would rise to great heights'.[52] Rocolle, quoting Pichot-Duclos, wrote: 'his ability to command fell far short of his unfettered intelligence'.[53]

We have one further key source regarding Roques's personality. Henry Bordeaux, writer, diarist and information officer at GQG, got to know Roques very well during his time commanding First Army. He worked for a time as one of Roques's liaison officers. From Bordeaux we gain valuable insight:

> Invited to dinner with General Roques who commands First Army. He lives in a modest billet with a pharmacist whose house is pleasantly laid out. He prefers that to the neighbouring chateau. …The general, short, disfigured by a strawberry birthmark on his left cheek (the soldiers called him the 'disk'), the other side of his face being normal and unblemished, his eyes clear, probing and a little sad. Simple, friendly, without any affectation: one quickly finds him to be a reflective soul, grave, of wise judgement, very calm, cautious, with a clear and penetrating outlook and a kind solicitude for people. He is overall *très sympathique*.[54]

By 15 March 1915, Bordeaux was Roques's liaison officer. He had noted Roques's courteous and calm behaviour, his lucid analysis of Joffre's manoeuvre on the Marne. He further noted how Roques complimented him on his books and talked of France after the war – the need to preserve the union in order to increase prosperity: '"There is a need to establish moral discipline in the nation".'[55] Also in March 1915, Bordeaux witnessed a stormy exchange between

Roques and his superior, Dubail, who wanted Roques to attack and eliminate the Saint-Mihiel salient. Roques did not like the idea and wanted to retreat: he cited the season, a sea of mud on the ground, a shortage of artillery. Dubail got angry, called Roques a coward and finally took away from him responsibility for half his sector of front line, giving it to II CA commander General Augustin Gérard. Bordeaux writes that from that moment he worried about the chances of success of Dubail's offensive, for he (Bordeaux) respected Roques's wisdom.[56] In August Bordeaux wrote of another occasion that demonstrates Roques's lack of arrogance, his consideration for others. In this case his host, the owner of the house he was lodging in insisted on retaining his wife's private room between the two rooms allocated to the general. "'[We must] think of him", the general told me with a smile, "every time we cross this space."' Bordeaux went on to comment: 'General Roques, his benevolent manner, his sad blue eyes, soft, calm. He reminded me of our day at *Les Éparges*, of the false reports that were received, the capture of Marchéville, etc. I was astonished by his scepticism. He must know that such things must be corrected.' On this occasion Roques turned the conversation to the subject of Bordeaux's books, even suggesting a new subject – the history of a French village at war. Surprisingly Bordeaux notes that he later actually wrote that book.[57] On 4 November 1915, after dining yet again with Roques, Bordeaux accompanied him and the other guests on a visit to the trenches. Roques did not flinch at the occasional bullet or shell, remaining upright and shaming others to do the same, although one tall officer joked that Roques's diminutive stature ensured his head was safely below the parapet.[58]

From Bordeaux's observations we may form an idea of Roques's personality. He seems intelligent and charming enough to progress through the lower echelons of power within the ministry, yet perhaps not forceful enough to make his mark at higher level. Principled, he was not afraid to stand his ground against Dubail despite the adverse effect on his career. He did not lack physical courage but was by nature cautious and reflective rather than thrusting and aggressive. This is the man who stood on the crest at Nevraumont, unwilling to take a risk and launch his troops, unprepared, against an unknown enemy. Yet this is also the man who, the very evening after the battle, had already reflected upon and judged the weaknesses of his subordinates and was willing to dispense with their services, replacing them with better men. Clearly a complex character, unsuited to command in the field yet able to avoid major catastrophes if not create major victories. Overall, a clever, intellectual, refined character who might be better suited to an administrative or policy job within the ministry.

* * *

On 25 March 1916, after more than a year of mediocre performance as an army commander, Roques was suddenly asked to become minister of war. His predecessor, the renowned colonial officer Gallieni, was unwell – he would die of prostate cancer some months later – and he was both weary and angry that his vocal criticisms of Joffre's handling of the war had been ignored. He and Joffre had first clashed in 1914 over the defence of Paris and the Marne campaign when Gallieni had been commander of the Paris garrison;[59] the clashes continued, from October 1915 onwards between minister and commander-in-chief.[60] Finally in early March 1916 Gallieni penned a formal letter to the French cabinet that was highly critical of Joffre and his conduct of the war over the previous eighteen months. When the cabinet refused to accept the letter, Gallieni resigned and Roques was appointed in his place. Officially, Briand chose the minister and put the name to the president of the republic for endorsement, merely consulting the commander-in-chief before doing so. However, at least two reputable sources have written that Roques was Joffre's choice. General Adolphe Guillaumat, who as former minister of war Adolphe Messimy's chief of military cabinet was in the running for selection, wrote that 'Joffre insisted on Roques', continuing enigmatically with the phrase 'that explains many things'.[61] Jere Clemens King wrote that 'Briand acceded to Joffre's suggestion that a suitable war minister could be found in General Pierre Auguste Roques'.[62] King wrote about the friendship between Joffre and Roques, that they had been classmates at the *École polytechnique* and colleagues in Indo-China; he also confirmed the poor opinion of Roques's performance as a field officer, going on to comment that '[in] political circles Roques passed for a military man able to play the game according to accepted rules'. There was only one big question about his suitability for the job of minister of war: could he play the game well enough at that higher level? Indeed, King went on to comment that 'Joffre related that he had only one misgiving about General Roques: "I feared, somewhat, his lack of character vis-à-vis the parliamentarians".' And King also quoted a contemporary source (Charles Bugnet, who worked in the war ministry and at GQG) who characterized Roques as '[c]onciliatory, gentle, affable, with no more obstinacy than authority, he could frighten no-one'.[63] Joffre would later write in his memoires that 'Roques's weakness – which he mistook for cleverness – brought about a confusion of powers whose climax was reached when the session in Secret committee began in December 1916'.[64] However, Joffre was writing with hindsight, after Roques's lacklustre support had contributed to Joffre's dismissal. At the time of Roques's appointment, the question of his ability to perform at ministerial level was moot. His experience, indeed success, before the war as director of engineering and then aviation spoke in his favour and he was well-known by the politicians and comfortable in the corridors of power within the war ministry; on the other hand, as the comments above suggest, there were doubts about his strength of character. On balance, it would appear that Joffre chose someone he thought (hoped) would be an ally, a buffer between him and parliament, in direct contrast to the combative rivalry of Gallieni.[65]

Roques took up his post at a time of heightened political and military turmoil in France. The German attack at Verdun in February 1916 had gained significant early success, including the capture of the central and symbolic Fort Douamont. French attempts to recapture lost ground (and the fort) and re-establish their position sucked division after division into what was increasingly seen as a slaughterhouse.[66] Criticisms of Joffre's command were increasing in number and in volume, and not only among military men such as Gallieni. After the initial period of patriotic fervour of the *Union sacrée* in 1914, when people and parliament stood in uncritical solidarity behind the military leadership, parliamentary criticism of Joffre's handling of the war began in earnest following the bloody repulses of the great French offensives of 1915. Joffre's dictatorial control over the *zone des armées* (a designated buffer zone behind the front line that was under military control) – he forbade journalists and members of parliament from visiting and reporting on any activity, imposing strict censorship and secrecy – was increasingly seen as a challenge to democracy. Indeed, in many ways Joffre's approach to civil–military relations bore some of the very features that French politicians had feared since 1870 and that had been exemplified by the 'Boulanger Affair' of 1889: a single powerful general ignoring parliament, potentially posing an existential threat to the republic and capable of mounting a coup d'état.[67] Such fears were groundless but were present deep in the psyche of many left-wing republicans and could be manipulated by factional leaders seeking political advantage.

Verdun was grist to the parliamentary mill; it was also a cause of deep dissatisfaction and resentment within the ranks of the high command, pitting generals more strongly against politicians. Bordeaux recorded a conversation between President Raymond Poincaré and General Philippe Pétain (then commanding at Verdun) on 13 May 1916. Poincaré asked whether Verdun could be held; Pétain replied in the negative, adding that he was preparing plans to evacuate the whole of the right bank of the Meuse. Poincaré then stated that to lose Verdun would be a 'parliamentary catastrophe'.[68] Soon afterwards General Nöel de Castelnau, Joffre's chief of staff, went to Verdun and on his own initiative cancelled all orders to retreat. Although military tactics might require giving up ground, political strategy required Verdun to be held to the last drop of French blood. Joffre's plan for 1916 had put everything behind the great allied offensive that would take place on the Somme;[69] the Germans had pre-empted him at Verdun.[70] Every division committed to the 'slaughterhouse' was a division less for Joffre's drive for victory and he sought to commit just sufficient of his reserves to hold Verdun but no more.[71] It was a balancing act that played into the hands of his political enemies. By March 1916 he needed an ally as minister of war, a buffer between him and parliament.

Roques's first official event was a baptism by fire: he attended the interallied conference in Paris from 26–28 March, three days after his appointment. Surrounded by such luminaries as British Prime Minister Herbert Asquith and French premier Briand, not to mention General Sir Douglas Haig and Joffre himself, Roques (according to the minutes) sat through the whole event without feeling able to contribute to the discussion. He did, however, attempt to assert his authority in other ways. One example, recorded by Bordeaux from a story recounted to him by GQG officer Colonel Pénelon, perfectly illustrates the point: '[Roques] had to make a short car journey [shortly after he took up post] with the president and with Joffre. He firmly placed Joffre in the front beside the chauffeur, on the folding seat, thus affirming his superiority'.[72] This somewhat petty behaviour, at a time when great things were afoot, has been noticed and recorded several times. Bordeaux cites another instance when Roques wrote to Pétain asking him to explain why a Catholic mass had been held in a Verdun barracks. Ardent anti-clerical republicans insisted on the separation of religion from the state, so perhaps Roques sought to curry favour with that faction on this occasion. Pétain's carefully styled reply – that he had more important matters to attend to, begging the minister not to worry about such trifles (*vétilles*), 'for anything that raised soldiers' morale was good' – hints at disdain and puts a perspective upon the way Roques chose to 'play the game'.[73] Roques's colleague General Guillaumat wrote: 'Nothing could be more stupid than Roques's first pronouncement, prescribing that officers and NCOs pay their rent. As if there were not more urgent things to tackle.' Yet Guillaumat was not an enemy of Roques; he would dine with him frequently and on one such occasion described him as 'a friendly and brave man'.[74] It was just that Roques's management style as minister attracted attention in that he tended to pick on trifling matters – those *vétilles* – to assert his authority. This is not just the subjective opinion of two diarists; one can find evidence of it in the archives and the documentary annexes to the French official history of the war, correspondence that demonstrates that interfering in the minutiae of running the war was part of Roques's *modus operandi*. A couple of examples may suffice. On 21 March 1916 Joffre wrote to the minister requesting that more cavalrymen be assigned to the trenches, rather than waiting behind the lines for a breakthrough to occur. On 6 April Roques replied with three pages of detailed argument against Joffre's proposition, only to give in to Joffre's pressure some weeks later when on 12 May he conceded that Joffre might suppress two cavalry divisions and create eight regiments of *Chasseurs à pied* (light infantry) in their place.[75] Then there was an issue on 22 May when

Roques decided that he wanted to reduce each cavalry squadron in Paris to 100 sabres (men) and reallocate the excess manpower to the artillery. Joffre's reply on 2 June suggested a smaller reduction to 140 sabres. On 8 June, Roques conceded that the reduction should be to only 140 sabres. He then asked to be kept informed of how and when the reductions would be made.[76] This is petty stuff, suggesting a man struggling to find his place at the higher level; a man arguing with his former superior officer now his subordinate in order to impose his will.

This is not to say that Roques abrogated his ministerial responsibility. Standing between prime minister Briand and the cabinet on the one hand and commander-in-chief Joffre and the high command on the other, as well as representing the military in parliament, Roques had no option but to become engaged, especially as the political row over the conduct of the war intensified. Roques's first major criticism of Joffre's handling of the war came just two weeks into his ministerial career. He informed Joffre that 'certain points in the vicinity of Verdun did not seem to be fortified strongly enough'.[77] It sounds like yet another point of detail, and indeed Joffre saw it as interference and was indignant, but the criticism did at least emanate from the strategic necessity to hold Verdun. But it did reflect a charge raised by parliamentary deputies rather than the minister of war himself that Gallieni had already been investigating on their behalf, so it was perhaps merely unfinished business.[78] But it indicated Roques would be no pliant mouthpiece for GQG. Next, Roques took back from Joffre the ministerial power to appoint and to remove key generals – a power that a previous war minister Alexandre Millerand had delegated to Joffre after the *Union sacrée*. This was a political move that had teeth. Roques relieved army group commanders de Langle de Cary and Dubail and army commander Victor d'Urbal of their posts as they had reached the compulsory age of retirement, and also recalled Gérard (who had once been Gallieni's chief of staff in the colonies) to an army command.[79]

If Roques in his time as a departmental director at the ministry had convinced the politicians that he was a military man who knew how to 'play the game', then on at least one occasion in May 1916 he demonstrated that skill. Two or three articles critical of Joffre's handling of the February 1916 crisis at Verdun appeared in the press. Given the tight censorship of the first two years of the war, these leaks were surprising. So too were the rumours that Roques had at the very least allowed information to be leaked.[80] Without being overtly implicated, Roques (if the rumours were true) had been actively working to increase his power at the expense of the commander-in-chief. A kinder interpretation might be that, in contrast to Joffre's obdurate and uncompromising stonewalling, Roques was seeking to defuse tensions by feeding the critics some scraps. If so, Roques was playing a dangerous game, for he risked giving the parliamentarians the opening they sought to get at Joffre. In relating this incident King describes both Briand and Roques as 'devious politicians', although events would show that Briand had the greater skill. As prime minister, Briand was, as much as Joffre, subject to increasingly vociferous parliamentary criticism which he sought to deflect wherever possible onto both his war minister and his commander-in-chief. At the same time, he was ultimately responsible for both and therefore was constrained to defend them when to do otherwise would destabilize his government.[81] Briand enlisted Roques into the working of this balancing act and Roques willingly engaged, hoping thereby to deflect criticism onto Joffre. Like Janus, Roques ended up facing both ways; at times he defended Joffre against parliamentary criticism, at others he joined those attacking Joffre. During May and June 1916, Roques joined with Briand and other critics to force Joffre to dismiss key members of his staff who were lesser targets of parliamentary wrath, deemed complicit in the 'bloody strategy at Verdun'.[82] The outcome of these political manoeuvrings, however, was the setting up of a 'secret' session of the Chamber of Deputies to investigate the responsibility for the 'sickening casualties' at Verdun.[83] The session began on 16 June 1916 and lasted six days. A barrage of criticism was directed at Joffre and his staff, but the arguments lacked teeth so the 'devious' Roques felt emboldened to defend the commander-in-chief. Bordeaux had been recalled to GQG on 15 May and watched these events unfold. He wrote on 12 June that General Maurice Pellé, sub-chief of staff at GQG, had asked him to prepare a brief for Briand to use in Joffre's defence before the Chamber of Deputies.[84] On 3 July Bordeaux recorded that he had received feedback from Pellé; that Briand had saved himself (and Joffre) using Bordeaux's brief, helped by a slice of luck in the form of disastrous news of a crisis on the Italian Front where that ally's army appeared to be in full retreat – suddenly it was not the moment to change commander-in-chief. Roques did not acquit himself so well, his speech being considered too long and boring.[85] This is not the only reference to Roques's poor oratory: Bordeaux noted that at Gallieni's funeral on 1 June 1916 Roques's speech was so long that the six horses harnessed to the hearse became decidedly skittish. Rather cattily, Bordeaux then made reference to Roques's birthmark: 'At least I saw the good profile, but I pity those who could only see the damaged cheek.'[86]

The secret session ended with a parliamentary success for Briand and a reprieve for Joffre, with his supporters winning a vote of confidence by 440 votes to 97.[87] Briand's oratory – and the crisis in Italy – carried the day; several of his loyal staff officers were thrown to the wolves, but Joffre was given three months to gain success at Verdun or go.[88] Joffre had weathered his biggest political storm so far but emerged weakened. Roques, however, who might have felt that he had increased his stature at Joffre's expense in the lesser game of blame for Verdun, had in fact been perceived to have nailed his colours to Joffre's mast because of his advocacy before the secret session. Roques had in effect won a minor point or two but had failed to score in the greater game that was in play, over parliamentary control. Despite the vote of confidence, Joffre's opponents continued their attacks, calling for parliamentary commissioners to be appointed to supervise the high command's future conduct of the war. This political oversight, or 'interference' as Joffre would call it, was no more to Roques's liking than to Joffre's since Roques's ministry would come under equal scrutiny. In attempting to play on both sides and in conceding minor points, Roques was inadvertently opening a breach in Joffre's 'stonewall' that his opponents were widening and exploiting. Roques was failing to show the strong leadership that the situation and his position required, just as Joffre had feared.

During early July, the opening of the Somme offensive broadened the scope of potential parliamentary scrutiny and opened fresh possibilities for success or failure for the high command. Then Roques overreached himself. Visiting Pétain at Verdun, he made comments regarding the disposition of artillery units that was a purely military issue. Once again Joffre made objections with a view to putting the minister in his place. To assert his authority over the *zone des armées* Joffre cancelled a presidential visit, claiming he could not attend, thereby drawing both the president and prime minister into the ensuing petty quarrel.[89] This time Joffre had overreached himself; but neither Roques nor Joffre came out of it well, their political capital further diminished. Earlier in August when Poincaré had visited the Somme with Roques and Joffre, Bordeaux had written: 'Poincaré said nothing but looked intimidating. Joffre seemed deep in thought, ruminating like the bull in a Leconte de Lisle story. Roques was unable to mask his strawberry birthmark.'[90] Bordeaux's caricature of Roques as no more than a blemish, when once he had been so sympathetic to the man, highlights Roques's diminished status and political weakness.

In late August a fresh crisis threatened to engulf both Joffre and Roques. This time the issue stemmed from Romania's potential entry into the war on the allied side. One of the conditions set by the Romanian government for joining the war was an allied offensive against Bulgaria by the Army of the Orient commanded by General Maurice Sarrail.[91] Therein lay the seed of another devastating rift between Roques, Joffre and Briand.[92] The background, in brief, was this. Sarrail had long been the darling of the left-wing factions in parliament, the 'republican' general whose political affiliations made him unassailable. He had commanded VI CA during the disastrous and costly opening battles on the frontiers and had been promoted to command Third Army on 30 August when General Pierre Ruffey was dismissed.[93] In June 1915, however, Sarrail was 'already being touted as a successor to Joffre' by republican politicians; when Sarrail's performance against the Germans in the Argonne in July was questioned, Joffre took it as excuse to remove him from his post.[94] Unlike others, however, Sarrail's republican credentials meant that he could not be dismissed or retired to Limoges. Instead, after a parliamentary outcry, he was found a new 'army' command in the Mediterranean which ended up becoming that of the inter-allied Salonika expedition after Bulgaria entered the war on the side of the Central Powers.[95] His Army of the Orient had grown with time and Salonika had become a second front, an alternative theatre of war that included the Balkans, which had been brought under GQG's direction at the end of 1915. Throughout 1915 and early 1916 Sarrail had continued to play politics, such that the embers of 1915's *Affaire Sarrail* continued to smoulder in Paris and at GQG.

The underlying tensions between Joffre and Sarrail would erupt to the surface in August 1916 over Romania and Roques would once again find himself in the middle of a political maelstrom.[96] Throughout August and September, the Romanian question and the second *Affaire Sarrail* rumbled on alongside ongoing criticisms of inactivity at Verdun and the perceived slow progress on the Somme.[97] Sarrail was accused by Joffre of dragging his heels in launching the required offensive against Bulgaria; he in turn complained vociferously about his subordinate, General Émilien Cordonnier. Joffre, both frustrated and sensing an opportunity to finally get rid of Sarrail, submitted a list of Sarrail's faults and mistakes, and called on the government to reprimand him. This had two important consequences: it prompted a vigorous parliamentary backlash by the republican left that yet again put Briand on the spot; it also precipitated a chain of events which placed Roques squarely in the eye of the storm. Joffre requested that de Castelnau be sent to Salonika to report on Sarrail's performance. Joffre wanted a report that had been written by his loyal subordinate on another army subordinate which he as commander-in-chief could influence and use against Sarrail in discussions with Briand. Instead, Briand chose to send Roques out to investigate, taking the matter out of Joffre's hands, out of army control: the war minister would present an 'unbiased' judgement both on Joffre's list of Sarrail's faults and on Sarrail's defence and own complaints. The outcome expected by Briand was a report that he could use to rebuff the republicans. Roques was to surprise and disappoint him, for he wrote a genuinely impartial report that largely let Sarrail off Joffre's hook and failed to provide Briand with ammunition to use against the parliamentary republicans.[98] Roques had made a fundamental mistake at a crucial moment in the 'game' – one that would lead directly to his demise: 'Briand was angry with Roques for having embarrassed him with his unexpected defence of Sarrail, which had been one of the causes of the harassing second secret committee.' So Briand sacked Roques and replaced him with General Lyautey, 'the royalist proconsul of Morocco'.[99] King's commentary condenses events that started in early August and concluded in early December in order to link Roques's visit to Salonika directly to his removal by Briand. Bordeaux in his diary takes a more nuanced day-by-day view that brings in the complex interaction of various other factors – the progress of the fighting on all fronts, the political in-fighting, the human relationships, and so on. On Monday 28 August 'Romania comes into the picture. ...It is the event that might at last break the stalemate of this long war.'[100] A few days later Bordeaux met Roques, 'who recounted his speech at the latest secret committee. He had "pulverized" his opponents and saved the General Staff. At least that is what he claimed.'[101] On 9 September Bordeaux noted 'Disquiet over the Army of the East. Sarrail more the politician than the soldier is perceived as doing nothing, and the Bulgarians have profited from his inaction [over Romania].'[102] And yet Roques had publicly backed Sarrail, as we have seen, and in doing so had weakened his position, a point that Bordeaux had picked up on. On 20 September Bordeaux dined with Pétain at Verdun, who 'complained that the government had sent the minister of war to ask me if I was on top of the situation (*si j'avais tenu ce propos*)'.[103] To write of 'sending' the minister with a 'message' reinforces the impression of Roques's lack of individual authority. On 18 October, Bordeaux recorded that the *Affaire Sarrail* had become venomous.[104] The wily Briand prepared to make both Joffre and Roques his scapegoats. At that day's cabinet meeting, when Joffre's list of complaints about Sarrail was discussed, Briand left Roques to handle the difficult situation on his own. Bordeaux commented that Roques had managed to defuse and dismiss the affair ('*escamote l'affaire*') – at least for the time being.[105] Briand continued to put pressure on Joffre, underlining the generalissimo's weakened position. When the allies met in mid-November to agree on the plan for 1917, Briand took a hard line with his commander-in-chief: Joffre was instructed to 'persuade the English to send more troops to Salonika and to take over more frontage on the Western Front'.[106] The implied 'or else' reminds us that the three-month moratorium set by the first secret session (and endorsed by parliamentary vote) in July 1916 had expired. By 23 November the pressure had risen to the point that Bordeaux wrote that 'the menace of the secret committee hangs over GQG, senior people are anxious'.[107]

By the end of November, the military situation in Romania was getting much worse, culminating in the fall of Bucharest on 7 December. On 8 December the government was defeated in a vote on the Romanian debacle in the Chamber of Deputies, for which Roques and Joffre were held responsible by Briand. The premier decided to sacrifice the pair to buy his government time to weather the crisis, and Roques was the first to go. On 12 December Lyautey, who had been summoned from his post as Resident-General of Morocco, arrived in Paris. Lyautey was a senior and experienced colonial soldier with a reputation untarnished by the failures on the Western Front. Roques was immediately dismissed and Lyautey was announced as the new minister of war.[108] Joffre survived in post for only another twelve days, being replaced by General Robert Nivelle as commander of the army, now hopefully fully back under political control.[109]

\* \* \*

Although the termination of his tenure as war minister signalled that Roques's career had peaked, it was not at an end. As was often the case within the French army, when removed from a post a general simply reverted to his permanent rank of *général de division* and was given a new job – in Roques's case, a return to army command at Fourth Army. This posting lasted only three months, until 25 March 1917, when Roques was again reassigned on the fall of Briand's government, this time to oversee inspection of the rear areas. With no political cover, his army group commander Pétain acted quickly to replace him as an offensive was pending and he judged Roques incapable of conducting offensive operations.[110] Roques was a spent force, and nobody quite knew what to do with him. At least this last wartime job matched his skill set. When the war ended he briefly served as chair of the engineering technical committee of the army, suggesting his career had come full circle,[111] before retiring on 24 February 1919. He did not live to enjoy any new life in retirement. He died, at Saint-Cloud only a year later, on 26 February 1920. Although initially buried in his hometown of Marseillan, his mortal remains were later moved to Les Invalides in Paris, where he now lies at rest among the great military commanders of France.

It is difficult to reconcile the facts of Pierre Roques's military career with the prestige and status that he was afforded in life and in death. His achievement in founding the French air force was undoubtedly worthy. His failure in the Battle of the Ardennes, which perhaps denied France a stunning early victory, remained hidden from view until very recently. His periods as army commander and as minister of war were unremarkable; but he was well-connected, and he had the political skills to preserve his reputation throughout his career. That, perhaps, marks him out as a product and relict of the French pre-war military system: not a brilliant commander but a very political general.

Chapter 9

# Marie-Eugène Debeney: A Fighting Professor

## William Philpott

In the 1920s Marie-Eugène Debeney rose to the top of the French army, serving as chief of the general staff from 1924 to 1930. In wartime he commanded an army after serving as Philippe Pétain's chief of staff at *Grand quartier general* (GQG). Yet he remains a shadowy historical figure, who has never attracted a biographer. Perhaps Debeney himself should be held responsible for this invisibility. He left no private papers, and his former chief of operations, General Léon Godfroy, noted in his unpublished memoirs that 'a contempt for politicians and a horror of publicity held [Debeney] back from the public, in a state of relative isolation of which he was proud'.[1] In the brief account of his war service that he did write, the preface to an inter-war military treatise, he excused himself from having kept a full record: 'to write memoirs one had to take notes day by day; I had neither the time nor the inclination for this; when one is doing a demanding job, one is reluctant to retreat into oneself, one is absorbed by worrying about others and the country'. Unfortunately for future historians, he did not think his own activities would be of interest, nor did he feel the need to justify his wartime actions.[2] A very successful army commander in 1918, Debeney is overdue for recognition as one of France's foremost First World War generals.

To his fellow soldiers Debeney was a man with many virtues, who inspired devotion in his subordinates. Godfroy's memoir was partly written as testimony of his old chief's affection and patronage: 'it was the honour of my life'. The pen-portrait he painted suggests a skilled soldier of great character:

> Tall and thin, with a fine bearing and a noble, dashing countenance, [Debeney] could disconcert on occasion with a glacial or ironic welcome. But when it came to military matters, on operations he could make an objective judgment of a situation with singular clarity. Endowed with offensive spirit, indomitable, a careful manager of the soldiers he commanded with fondness yet able to engage them wholeheartedly when necessary, he was in the top rank of our wartime leaders.

Godfroy noted Debeney's positive traits of character: 'sensitivity, kindness, loyalty and chivalrousness'.[3] An appraisal of Debeney's wartime career suggests that Godfroy's judgement reflects a deep knowledge and understanding of the commander he served in 1918.

\* \* \*

As both a senior staff officer and a general officer in field command, roles in which he alternated during the war, Debeney demonstrated skills of military leadership and organization appropriate to the process of adapting to modern industrialized warfare. In consequence he rose through the ranks and responsibilities of higher command. A lieutenant-colonel in 1914, he began the war on the staff of General Augustin Dubail's First Army, fighting in Alsace. Chief of operations to begin with, in mid-September he became the army's chief of staff and was promoted colonel when his predecessor was sent to command a division. By 1918, he was in command of that army himself. He is best remembered in Britain as the man whose army attacked alongside General Sir Henry Rawlinson's Fourth Army in the Battle of Amiens–Montdidier (8–11 August 1918), and subsequently supported the right wing of Rawlinson's 'Hundred Days' advance through the Hindenburg Line and beyond.

Field Marshal Sir Douglas Haig left a slight, unfair, yet long-lasting impression of Debeney, who was subordinated to British command for the Amiens offensive. When visited by Haig late in the afternoon of 8 August, Debeney was apparently 'much distressed and almost in tears because three battalions of his Colonial infantry had bolted before a German machine gun'.[4] Haig was prone to emphasizing French failure in his personal record, and British authors have subsequently taken Haig's self-serving jottings as historical fact.[5] Such a narrative allowed Haig to accentuate his own army's achievements and to believe he was directing operations, a situation that did not exist in practice.[6] 'I told Debeney that the British advance would automatically clear his front… his cavalry should be sent forward as soon as possible to co-operate on the right of the British who had already pierced the German line of defence', the diary entry continued. Thus, Debeney has only a bit-part in the British narrative of victory. Debeney's own responsibilities were more extensive than supporting the British (which the French archive record suggests he did rather more effectively than English-language accounts allow). As well as managing XXXI *corps d'armée* (CA) that attacked on the morning of 8 August alongside the Canadian Corps, Debeney had four other front-line army corps under his control that he fed into the battle during 8 and 9 August, extending the operation southwards to pinch out Montdidier in collaboration with General Georges Humbert's Third Army. As for the chain of command, General Marie-Émile Fayolle, Debeney's army group commander (with equivalent level of responsibility to Haig), recorded testily: 'Debeney is under Haig's orders…but nonetheless it was me who organized the attack east of Montdidier' with Debeney's XXXV CA on 9 August.[7] This uncertain experiment in subordinating one nation's army to the command of another proved short-lived.

Despite his practice of downplaying the French army's efforts, Haig's view of Debeney himself was more positive. Haig had met him on 2 June 1917 when, as Pétain's recently appointed chief of staff, he had visited British General Headquarters to brief Haig on the crisis of morale then gripping the French army, and the limited support that could be given to Haig's planned Flanders offensive in consequence. Despite the difficult circumstances, Debeney made a good impression: 'I thought him straightforward and businesslike', noted the British commander-in-chief, a man not given to flattering estimations of Frenchmen.[8] While Haig's record gives some insight into his talents, assessing Debeney only through British eyes gives too limited a perspective on a senior officer who had an intellectual understanding of modern war, talent in command and the ability to train his troops to a high level of efficiency.

Debeney had risen to the very important role of army chief of staff on the strength of a distinguished record as a fighting general. The formations Debeney commanded in battle, 25 *division d'infanterie* (DI) at Verdun and XXXII CA on the Somme, were among France's most effective fighting units in the difficult attritional battles of 1916. Army command followed in December 1916, initially in a quiet sector. After becoming chief of staff in May 1917 he assisted Pétain in retraining and rehabilitating the army following its 1917 mutinies, returning to army command in December. After the German spring offensive, he redeployed to the vital Avre sector, where in extremely challenging circumstances he reformed his army, blunted the German penetration of the British Fifth Army's front and secured the point of junction between the British and French armies. Debeney certainly had a good war: in him France possessed a first-class soldier, fitted to senior responsibilities in both war and peace.

\* \* \*

Debeney came from Bourg-en-Bresse in the Ain *département* (between Lyon and the Swiss frontier). Born on 5 May 1864, after attending the French military academy St Cyr he joined France's elite infantry, the *chasseurs à pied*, in 1886, serving for a time with Lieutenant Pétain, eight years his senior. Their careers would overlap thereafter. A staff college course in the early 1890s – he passed out twelfth in his promotion, in 1893[9] – set the pattern of his peacetime career, in which he rose through the commissioned ranks in an alternating series of staff and command appointments. Then in 1909, when Ferdinand Foch was commandant, he joined the teaching staff at the *École supérieure* de *guerre* (ESG), as assistant professor of infantry tactics, working with Pétain who was then course director. In 1911, he replaced Pétain as professor of infantry tactics when the latter returned to regimental command. Pétain, Debeney and another chasseur officer, Louis de Maud'huy (who would also command an army early in the war), bright stars of the teaching establishment nicknamed the Pleiades, supposedly sought to inculcate a 'chasseur culture' into the ESG, stimulating rather than stifling intellectual debate by critiquing earlier theoretical perspectives. In particular, Debeney's ideas set him against Colonel Louis de Grandmaison, who preached a different approach to warfare. Debeney prepared a new infantry tactical manual stressing the dominance of firepower and the importance of the machine gun on the modern battlefield. In the doctrinal debates between advocates of firepower or offensive shock action that divided the French military establishment in pre-war years such ideas were contentious, and his redrafted training manual was not issued.[10] Yet as director of the ESG's applied infantry tactics course before 1914 his ideas would have reached many of those officers destined for command and staff roles in the coming conflict. It proved to be a conflict that needed the adaptive intellectual approach of the military academic to understand and overcome its unprecedented challenges. Debeney was one of a number of pre-war military thinkers and educators whose sharp minds enabled them to respond dynamically when faced with static positional warfare.

Before then, however, the war of manoeuvre which confounded so many pre-war French military theorists had to be fought. The newly promoted Lieutenant-Colonel Debeney found himself appointed sub-chief of staff in General Dubail's First Army, which launched France's first probing attack into Alsace with VII CA on 7 August. The mismanaged attack revealed failings in command at the top of the army. The town of Mulhouse was occupied then rapidly relinquished in the face of a strong German counter attack. For his mishandling of the operation the corps commander General Louis Bonneau was *limogé*, the first of the extensive sackings by which commander-in-chief General Joseph Joffre cleared out the peacetime deadwood at the top of the army in the early weeks of the war. Debeney was charged with investigating the reasons for VII CA's defeat: the troops were exhausted and had not had a hot meal for three days.[11] Command was at fault, but also logistics. Tactics clearly needed rethinking, and the former staff college lecturer was not averse to giving catch-up classes in the field.[12]

Debeney acquitted himself well in preparing subsequent offensive and defensive operations as First Army resumed the attack into Alsace in strength in mid-August then retired once again in the face of strong German opposition. Joffre was particularly impressed that Dubail and his staff had anticipated GQG's demand to redeploy troops westwards for the Marne counter attack and had prepared appropriate movement orders.[13] There is evidence that the army was adapting to the type of slogging, positional warfare that was emerging as the two sides came to a standstill in September. A First Army instruction of 11 September, drafted by its chief of operations, identified from experience that tactics would need to be modified. Infantry would need to be economized and the artillery deployed to give it effective support. Infantry should seek to gain ground under cover of darkness and 'afterwards profiting from the undoubted superiority of our material...the two arms should together obtain decisive results'. The infantry should advance in small columns using ground cover where possible; once a position was taken it should be immediately fortified with deep, concealed trenches, supporting defences and clear fields of fire.[14] Debeney had quickly discerned the war's tactical essence, although it would be some time before such insights would be shaped into a definitive combined-arms doctrine for trench warfare. Indeed, the methods suggested at this early point were rather naïve – artillery fire in the afternoon, infantry attacking at night, digging in on the objective – but the principles were correct. The instruction suggests a primitive conception of infiltration tactics: perhaps it reflects the *chasseur* light-infantry ethos of its author. But, as Debeney reflected after the war, this early recognition of the need for predominant firepower would impose an indeterminate delay before the army could get on with the job.[15] The war had rapidly become one of entrenchments and artillery duels. Debeney's first job as army chief of staff was to draw up a plan for creating and deploying a heavy artillery group to support the First Army that was now digging in.[16]

Debeney remained Dubail's chief of staff until May 1915. Although Dubail's war memoir is anodyne, rarely passing comment on an individual, he was clearly satisfied with Debeney's performance. When his first chief of staff General Marie-Georges Demange was redeployed to command a division Dubail chose Debeney as his replacement and secured his immediate promotion to the rank of colonel.[17] Dubail was happy to have him accompany him to the newly formed *Groupe d'armées de l'est* (GAE) which Dubail took command of in January 1915. Dubail would use Debeney as his agent, sending him to subordinate formations to ensure that army orders were properly executed.[18] This would have given Debeney insight into how the affairs of higher formations were run in wartime. The patronage and support of a rising senior commander would no doubt have eased Debeney's advancement in the testing early phase of the war during which many of his fellows revealed their unsuitability for wartime soldiering.

Moving, at his own request, to command a division in May 1915 would give him a new set of skills. Initially Debeney took over 57 DI in First Army on 8 May, with the acting rank of *Général de brigade*, but he was quickly moved – his replacement was his old superior Demange – as he was considered too junior to have authority over all the divisions defending the Belfort region.[19] On 18 May he took command of 25 DI that he was to lead for a little under eleven months. This was a direct swap with Demange and Godfroy, then on the divisional staff, was pleased: his fussy, micro-managing commander was replaced by a man who was 'alert, smart, with a serious but friendly face' and contemptuous of unnecessary paperwork.[20] The division was in XIII CA, located from July in the relatively quiet Sixth Army sector in Picardy between the Somme and Oise rivers. It comprised a mixture of metropolitan regiments from the Auvergne and wartime-raised Zouave and tirailleur battalions of the so-called *Armée d'Afrique*, actually filled up largely with Parisians. Debeney himself retained a 'particularly fond' memory of commanding these solid, reliable troops, even if their day-to-day experience of the trenches was routine.[21] It was at least a relatively tranquil situation in which a general who had never commanded a fighting formation before could learn his trade. He devoted effort to training his troops, and allowed his staff to visit the front line rather than tying them to their desks to process paper. 'The general was rigorous but calm and benevolent; he grasped things quickly and clearly and made rapid decisions', Godfroy recollected: the headquarters' mess became a place of rest rather than tension.[22]

Debeney's regime would prepare the division well for what was to come. For a fortnight 25 DI took its turn in the cauldron of Verdun after the enemy switched operations to the left bank of the Meuse in mid-March. Debeney's regiments received the whole weight of the Germans' follow-up attack on the Mort-Homme heights, defending them with bravery and tenacity under the hellish bombardment that characterized the early phase of an offensive at this point in the war. The details of the division's local actions would be impossible to piece together and unnecessary for this study; it was typical Verdun fighting, in which the defences 'were for the most part clusters of shell-holes, where isolated groups of men lived and slept and died defending their "position" with grenade and pick-helve'.[23] Debeney recollected joking with General Paul Maistre as they waited for their troops to deploy, after receiving Joffre's warning that any commander who gave orders to retreat would be relieved of his command, 'At least he has made his mind up; that's good!'[24] Joffre's order to stand firm galvanized officers and men.[25] Debeney's men performed well enough, and their leader rose to the challenge effectively enough, for his career to prosper. The division's citation at the end of the tour identified its commander as a

> general officer of the top order, notable in the leadership of his division for his tirelessness, bravery, sang-froid, great energy and high-order military knowledge, demonstrated…in a series of vigorous counter attacks and in the defence of the important position which he was responsible for.[26]

Debeney was promoted to command XXXVIII CA on 4 April 1916, shortly after his division was withdrawn from Verdun. Debeney was sad to leave the regiments he had formed a personal attachment to: he reflected later that command of higher formations, army corps and armies, did not promote such an identification with and attachment to subordinate units as divisional command.[27] The XXXVIII CA's sector was relatively quiet: it defended Reims while bigger battles raged elsewhere along the front. This command would again give Debeney several months to acclimatize to his wider responsibilities as he conducted a 'petty war' of localized small-scale attacks and counter attacks.

Debeney had the good fortune to shift his command again, taking over XXXII CA on 19 September, on the eve of its deployment to the Somme battlefield. (He replaced General Henri Berthelot, another rising star, who had been selected to command the French military mission to the Romanian army.) XXXII CA was a much more suitable command for a fighting soldier. The corps had seen action in the September 1915 Champagne offensive and at Verdun, and its component divisions, 40 and 42 DIs, were battle-hardened. Moreover, XXXII CA was about to enter the epicentre of the raging Somme offensive. For that fight Debeney's command was reinforced with some of the best troops in the army – the 66 DI of *chasseurs à pied* reinforced with an additional independent *chasseur* brigade – bringing Debeney back to working with units from his own branch of service.

XXXII CA deployed to relieve formations in Fayolle's Sixth Army that had made significant forward progress during early September. Fayolle's forces had finally broken through the German third position into open country at Bouchavesnes on the Bapaume–Péronne road on 12 September: the breach had however been too narrow to exploit, and it had become clear that the formations sustaining the advance since the end of July were fought-out and would have to be replaced before the offensive was renewed. After playing a part in repelling the largest German counter attack made during the Somme offensive between Allaines and Rancourt – this massacre of largely inexperienced troops under concentrated French artillery and machine-gun fire is largely forgotten[28] – Sixth Army's offensive resumed against the remnants of those shattered formations. On 25 September, XXXII CA's objective was Rancourt village (today the site of the *Souvenir français*'s Battle of the Somme memorial chapel), which was stormed by 42 DI advancing 'as if on exercise', although the attack was contained by machine-guns positioned along the edge of the huge wood beyond the village, Bois St Pierre Vaast.[29] One participant remembered an attack supported by an intensive rolling barrage sweeping away defenders stupefied by the weight of French artillery fire.[30] Less visible was the gas-shell barrage that neutralized the enemy's artillery.[31] In contrast to their recent experience at

Verdun suffering under the German guns, the French troops' morale was high now that their own artillery was overwhelming.[32] Debeney's pre-war emphasis on firepower as the mainstay of effective infantry tactics had been realized in his first major set-piece attack: by this point in the war, it had become standard operational practice. But there is evidence that commanders were trying to inject more dynamism into offensive tactics by this point, to better exploit such easy successes. Fayolle had instructed on the eve of the operation that field guns should be brought up quickly following an attack.[33] On the day, the troops were surprised to see artillery batteries galloping up behind them and unlimbering to shell the routes along which German reinforcements would come.[34]

It was not known at the time, but this would be the French army's last dynamic thrust in a battle that was about to atrophy into localized, muddy and bloody trench fighting as autumn rains set in and turned the battlefield into a quagmire. The troops would be denied the 'breakthrough' that they were eagerly anticipating at this point in the offensive.[35] Debeney's army corps would remain in the sector throughout October, contesting the edges of Bois St Pierre Vaast and the trench-scored village of Sailly-Saillisel to its north, which the French were trying to occupy to outflank the wood. It would take Debeney's troops more than a month to fight their way into and through the village, trench-by-trench, one ruined building at a time, and when the offensive petered out in mid-November Bois St Pierre Vaast would remain in enemy hands.[36] Relative to that of other formations bogged down to either side, Debeney's success was notable: 'This XXXII CA is really very good', Fayolle noted after one successful French counter attack.[37] The official artillery staff report indicates the sort of firepower-intensive operations that Debeney was conducting. His corps was operating on a single-division front backed by three or four 75mm divisional artillery regiments (effectively the divisional artillery of the whole corps); two corps' medium artilleries; four or five groups of long-barrelled heavy artillery; between three and seven groups of short-barrelled 155mm howitzers; one or two groups of 280mm mortars; one group of 270 mm mortars; and one or two 370mm mortars (plus each division's complement of trench artillery when in line).[38] The inevitable consequence was a battlefield churned into a clinging morass through which the infantry had to crawl slowly forwards.[39] Debeney did what was required of him, but by that point he had, like his superior, come to question the wisdom of continuing to press forward in such conditions.[40] By the end of XXXII CA's tour his units were understrength and he was pleading with his army commander for fresh reinforcements.[41] He had advanced the front line one-and-a-half kilometres, but it had been costly, attritional fighting and this achieved little in a dying offensive.[42] Debeney was not without his critics. General Antoine Baucheron de Boissoudy, a fellow *chasseur* who would succeed him in command of Seventh Army and who had commanded V CA on XXXII CA's right during the difficult operations against Bois St Pierre Vaast in late October and November, attested that Debeney was 'too keen on useless attacks, careless in managing manpower, a little narrow in outlook'.[43]

Debeney later acknowledged that on the Somme the French army had 'the necessary material for mounting offensive actions along extended fronts, and soon, one anticipated, along the whole front, in a word, the pace of operations had finally changed'. Compared with the defence of Verdun, this was better for troop morale as the French held the initiative and were on the offensive: 'It is as hard as Verdun, but all the same it is better', was, Debeney remembered, the troops' axiom.[44] But to deploy and employ this material effectively, his artillery commander recommended, 'it is desirable that commercial and industrial attitudes and methods penetrate every branch of the service and the administration', especially in appointment of commanders by aptitude not rank.[45]

\* \* \*

That principle seemed already to be operating. Another short period of success earned Debeney a further promotion. In the reshuffle of commands that followed Joffre's replacement by Robert Nivelle, Debeney was rewarded with promotion to army command (one of several successful Battle of the Somme corps commanders promoted at this point, suggested by Joffre himself).[46] General Adolphe Guillaumat, who also benefitted, taking over Nivelle's Second Army after having commanded I CA on the Somme on XXXII CA's left, was pleased for Debeney: 'I hold him in high esteem'.[47] Guillaumat expected him to improve further: 'he may be a professor, but he can change because he is young'.[48] But Debeney's first tour as an army commander was to be uneventful. He took over Seventh Army in the always quiet sector of the line extending northwards from the Swiss frontier. His army was essentially used for resting and training formations that were to form the reserve for Nivelle's coming offensive. Briefly he came under Foch's command, when the future generalissimo acted as GAE commander when General Nöel de Castelnau was sent on a mission to Russia in the spring, which reacquaintance would have been to his advantage when he was back in command of an active army in summer 1918. Moreover, his deployment to the end of the line meant he would not be associated with the disaster that befell the army in the spring. Debeney himself later expressed disquiet at the change of command: Joffre had had the confidence of the army after the victories at Verdun and on the Somme, and his plan for a decisive offensive in early 1917 was promising.[49] Foch's advance on the Somme had 'reawakened the spirit of the offensive in our army and given it the confidence that success would follow from careful preparation and bold execution',[50] a moral advantage which Nivelle's period of command wasted.

\* \* \*

In the search for a replacement army chief of staff after Nivelle's offensive failed, Debeney was an obvious candidate: it might be speculated because he was known to and appreciated by those who had run both the Verdun and Somme battles. He replaced General Ferdinand Pont at GQG on 2 May. (Pont had not been informed of his dismissal and was livid when Debeney turned up unexpectedly in his office to replace him.)[51] Guillaumat again welcomed his comrade's appointment: 'of undeniable merit…in whom I have confidence, worthy and honest'.[52] Debeney himself was ambivalent: he did not know Nivelle and, having commanded in the field, he did not relish the prosect of a return to staff work. But he accepted his duty, and he would perform effectively in the role, although not without difficulties in the highly charged political environment of GQG. Although he had advised Nivelle not to offer his resignation, he no doubt shared the relief throughout the army when his old ESG colleague Pétain replaced Nivelle on 17 May.[53] He was to serve as his chief of staff until the end of the year, but reluctantly. Immediately he asked Pétain to return to army command – it was customary for the commander-in-chief and chief of staff to come from different arms of service and Pétain and Debeney were both infantrymen – but Pétain demurred for the time being. General François Anthoine, a gunner, was currently preparing his army for the Battle of Flanders and Pétain insisted that he should remain in command for that offensive (which it turned out would last until November).[54] General Edmond Buat felt that Pétain would have wanted his old ESG assistant by his side and had engineered his appointment in anticipation of his succeeding Nivelle.[55] Godfroy tells a rather different story: that war minister Paul Painlevé tried early on to remove Debeney from GQG because he did not show suitable deference to politicians, and thereafter he was on borrowed time. Certainly, he was not one to be browbeaten by politicians. On one occasion armaments minister Albert Thomas took him to task for addressing him as if he were giving orders to a subordinate. Debeney shot back to the heavily-bearded minister, 'Certainly not! If you were under my orders, I would have made you cut your hair a long time ago.' That witty riposte cleared the air and the two men became firm friends thereafter.[56]

Although General Pierre des Vallières for one regretted that the new command team deprived the field army of 'two tactical experts of the first order', the new GQG regime was generally welcomed.[57] In fact, tactical improvements were central to reinvigorating a weary army. Debeney would have had a hand in drawing up the series of GQG directives that codified operational doctrine and set realistic goals for an army that was recovering from a major crisis in morale occasioned by Nivelle's failure and a reversion to attritional warfare. He oversaw the establishment of a 'training section' (*Section d'instruction*) to collate lessons from the front to inform tactical and operational learning and training and a 'commission of overhaul' (*Commission de refonte*) to address operational doctrine for higher formations.[58] In truth, this was more a codification of practice that had been developing over two years than the introduction of a new tactical–operational system, but it would disseminate best practice throughout an army whose units' performances had been mixed up to this point. In the immediate morale crisis, he even drafted the speeches that Pétain and other GQG officers delivered to placate mutinous regiments.[59]

Debeney brought experience, stability and good sense to GQG, but he found his responsibilities taxing. 'Calm and serious, but showing the impatience of a man who is ill', he supposedly subsisted on a diet of plain pasta and toast rather than give in to his malady.[60] The stress probably derived from the fact that he clashed with other GQG staff officers; in particular the head of the operations section, General Maurice de Barescut, over the role of artillery.[61] (De Barescut had been director of the artillery course at the ESG when Debeney was teaching the infantry course and this may have been a resurgence of pre-war doctrinal disagreements.) Not all colleagues were disagreeable: the job gave Debeney the chance to advance talented men he had worked with and whom he trusted. Debeney chose his old divisional operations officer, Godfroy, to become liaison officer with the Sixth Army in the mutiny-ravaged Chemin de Dames sector, and his Seventh Army chief of staff, Lieutenant-Colonel Léon Zeller, also came to work with him at GQG in the operations bureau.[62]

The new system would demonstrate its merits in the army's successful limited offensives in late summer and autumn 1917; supporting the British offensive in Flanders from July to November; the Second Battle of Verdun in August; and the *pièce de resistance*, Sixth Army's Battle of Malmaison which seized back the Chemin des Dames at the end of October. While operationally effective, restorative, and appropriate to the moment and the state of the French army in autumn 1917, Debeney acknowledged that such battles were not a strategic solution, merely a holding pattern until the allies were in a position to attack in sufficient strength to destroy the enemy's reserves.[63]

\* \* \*

In December 1917, Debeney asked to return to army command. The heavy burden of administrative staff work was tiring and, he later attested, he found commanding troops more satisfying.[64] GQG information officer Henry

Bordeaux noted at the time that 'Debeney, rigorously correct and honest, lacking breadth, hostile to innovation, would be better as an army commander'.[65] Debeney did a direct swap with Anthoine of First Army,[66] which after the Flanders offensive was now holding a quiet sector in Lorraine – the same sector Debeney had known when First Army chief of staff in 1914.[67] On 22 March, the day after the German spring offensive opened, this calm was to end abruptly. New orders were received: 'without stopping for one minute we jumped in the car; we left for the Battle of France'.[68] Debeney had been called to Picardy to construct and lead the army that Pétain was forming to go to the aid of the hard-pressed British and plug a widening gap between the British army's right and the French army's left wings. Maxime Weygand, Foch's chief of staff, suggested he was chosen as the crisis demanded leaders 'of the highest quality and widest experience'.[69] Debeney had been one of Foch's army commanders when he ran GAE in spring 1917, and Foch was now the government's military adviser in Paris.[70] Pétain briefed him on his way to battle that his was a 'sacred mission' and that the honour of the army was at stake.[71] He was to remain in the thick of the action until the Armistice was signed.

Debeney's account of the final campaign gives an insightful glimpse into the perspective and role of an army commander on the more dynamic battlefields of 1918. 'Army command is fascinating: one sees directly the whole scope of operations and one guides a powerful instrument of war; one strikes the blow, and one knows the impact.'[72] He took with him a skilled staff team, who he had got used to working with in the quieter period in Lorraine, which included his trusted head of operations Godfroy, who he had taken with him from GQG. He approached his task with the calm, level-headed demeanour of a true leader.[73]

First Army would conduct three phases of operations in the war's final year. The first, 'short, but terribly stressful', involved improvising a defensive line between Amiens and Montdidier to close the gap in the allied front. The second, 'preparatory' period, from mid-April to August, saw First Army consolidating its defences then mounting a series of localized attacks along the valley of the Avre river to improve its jumping-off line for the anticipated allied counter offensive. From 8 August until the armistice, First Army was in the vanguard for the 'victorious offensive, which rolled out in fits and starts as was dictated by modern tactics and the intensive use of material'. It fought three set-piece battles, Montdidier, St Quentin and Guise, conducting pursuit operations in between.[74]

Years later, Debeney remembered the civilian refugees intermixed with British stragglers fleeing from the advancing Germans who, on seeing his staff car flying his general's fanion exclaimed: '"Come quickly! Take courage! It will all go well now." They counted on the French doing better than the

British. Although my army at the time was only six officers!'[75] Debeney and his staff would rise to the challenge. In Amiens cathedral a wall-plaque bears the inscription:

> We pay tribute to General Debeney, victor of the Battle of Picardy who, in realizing the plan conceived by Marshal Foch, formed in the heat of battle between 26 March and 5 April in liaison with the allies the army which achieved the victory on 8 August that liberated Montdidier and the territory of the Somme.

As he approached the battle, however, Debeney was not confident that Amiens could be secured, although he expected a great victory over the enemy to the west of the city.[76]

Debeney's First Army was to reform alongside Humbert's Third Army to try to maintain contact with the British army's right wing that was pulling back towards Amiens. Initially it was an army headquarters without troops, bombarded with a slew of conflicting and hard-to-execute orders from senior commanders,[77] so Debeney developed a simple scheme that conformed with his primary objective 'to maintain at all costs liaison between the British and the French': he would attach those troops that were in the sector – both British stragglers and newly-arriving formed French units – either to Humbert's left or to the British right, thereby shrinking the gap a bit at a time. But a gap persisted between the two French armies, which the enemy might exploit. Enemy intelligence learned of the arrival of fresh French reinforcements and turned southwards expecting to meet them, temporarily relieving pressure on the British front.[78] Montdidier fell to the Germans on the evening of 27 March – Debeney and his staff reportedly slept with loaded rifles by their beds that night, there being no formed body of troops between the enemy and First Army headquarters until the early hours of the next morning. However, in a January 1919 assessment, Debeney identified Ludendorff's switch of his troops' line of advance southwards to exploit a tactical opportunity rather than pursuing his strategic purpose as the reason for German failure: it gained him a window of opportunity in which to gather his forces while reliving pressure on the hard-pressed junction between the allied armies.[79] Debeney as yet had only a handful of divisions under command, and wished to wait until these were fully deployed with supporting artillery units before engaging them. Foch objected, and so on 28 March he improvised with Humbert an immediate counter attack with only partial artillery support. This slowed the Germans' momentum but did not halt their advance.[80] It gained time to deploy more French units, and Debeney and Humbert's hard-pressed forces successfully held the German advance over subsequent days allowing other divisions to deploy northwards and to close the gap with the British left. By early April the immediate crisis was over, although a final powerful enemy thrust towards Amiens, at Villers-Bretonneux on 4 April, had to be contained and counterattacked the next day before the battle subsided. Debeney and his staff toasted the end of 'the great battle for France' with champagne that evening.[81] He had achieved the most difficult of tasks in demanding circumstances and, French President Raymond Poincaré noted, had the bearing of a leader and radiated confidence.[82] However, his achievement went unrecognized and unrewarded owing, Godfroy speculated, to Pétain being jealous of his former chief of staff's triumph: the former apprentice was outdoing the master.[83]

Debeney's army thereafter held the front in the Avre sector, adjacent to the British army. First Army mounted a series of well-resourced but localized operations to advance the French front line,[84] an element of Foch's strategy to keep pressure on the enemy all along the front to contest the initiative and divert him from his offensive scheme. One of these was the Battle of Cantigny on 28 May; an insignificant operation in the wider scheme of things and essentially a political battle, but notable because American troops mounted their first successful attack. The French army's material-intensive methods were demonstrated: as well as French light tanks and flamethrower teams to strengthen the assault force, Debeney found the three attacking American battalions eighty-three supporting artillery batteries, much to Fayolle's consternation.[85]

Debeney was a strong advocate of General Charles Mangin's surprise counter attack in the battle of the Matz that checked the fourth German offensive.[86] Around this time there was a proposal that Mangin, who had been attached to Debeney's headquarters as a supernumerary army corps commander, should replace Debeney in command of the First Army and that Debeney would succeed General Louis Franchet d'Esperey, who was taking up the command at Salonika, at *Groupe d'armées du centre*. Prime minister Georges Clemenceau held off from making any command changes while battle was engaged, and in the event Debeney, who remonstrated that he wished to keep his army command, lost out to Maistre of Tenth Army, who received Pétain's endorsement over his former right-hand man.[87] His own army group commander Fayolle, although customarily grumpy and quicker to record subordinates' faults than to praise them in his private diary, was generally happy with the aggressive and successful series of operations that pushed First Army's line forwards during June and July – especially when Debeney did so within his means rather than demanding three divisions to take a village.[88]

In his new command Debeney collaborated closely with the British army for the first time. It took time to establish a good relationship with Rawlinson who commanded British Fourth Army on First Army's left: their bond had to be forged in April 1918's challenging circumstances. In the tense days of early

April, Debeney was not confident that Rawlinson's troops would hold their positions in front of Amiens.[89] When a counter attack was organized against Villers-Bretonneux that had fallen to the enemy in late April, Rawlinson found it difficult to pin down French support, and Haig felt obliged to intercede with generalissimo Foch to get Debeney to offer more active assistance.[90] In fact, Debeney and Rawlinson had arranged on 13 April that the British would be responsible for defending Villers-Bretonneux, and the French Hangard village to the south, an agreement which Rawlinson wished to tear up at the moment of crisis. Debeney's forces were fighting hard to hold Hangard which had also fallen temporarily into enemy hands on 24 April and, ever prudent, he delayed his counter attack until early in the morning of 26 April when the situation was clearer and his troops were properly ready. Despite, in French estimation, only weak British support the counter attack was a success.[91] Coordinating operations between allied forces at short notice had always been problematic. Things settled down when the battle subsided, and reportedly by July, having conducted successful local operations in tandem in the interim, when preparing the first stage of Foch's counter offensive the two allied generals' relations were cordial.[92] However, solidarity in defence did not carry on into the final advance, during which Rawlinson complained frequently about Debeney's failure to carry out agreements. To 'deb' became a term of derision at Fourth Army headquarters, Basil Liddell Hart reporting waspishly: 'the practice of so timing your own push that your neighbour pushed first, and thus loosened the resistance that faced you'. This was the sign of an army and commanders that had become 'weary and wary', Liddell Hart asserted.[93] This sentiment was shared by Haig, who felt that Debeney's army was only making progress because the Germans gave ground voluntarily.[94] In fact, First Army remained heavily engaged from August to November 1918.[95] Debeney's penchant for carefully prepared and steady attacks and for lateral exploitation rather than frontal assault – 'progressively dislocating the various sectors of the front', a principle he later attributed to Foch[96] – learned from four years' experience, was perhaps not properly appreciated in the British army.

Although formally subordinated to Haig for the Battle of Amiens, the first operation of Foch's counter offensive, the chain of command seems in practice to have been confused: Debeney still received instructions from his army group commander Fayolle, and also generalissimo Foch, who insisted on expanding the offensive southwards as it made progress, such that between 8 and 11 August the battle of Amiens expanded laterally into the battle of Montdidier that Debeney and Humbert were fighting alongside the British. On 8 August Haig had told Debeney to join hands with the British at Roye and to move his cavalry up to operate on the British right as soon as possible, suggesting he saw the French forces as playing a supporting role. (In fact, Debeney brought his cavalry forward to operate with his own right-wing corps on 10 August, but in the face of strengthening enemy opposition chose to stand them down rather than risk a massacre.)[97] Although Debeney's two left-flank army corps were operating in a south-westerly direction to extend the British front of attack, his two right-flank corps joined the battle on 9 August, moving north-eastwards to pinch out the Moreuil salient and facilitate the advance of Humbert's forces to the south as the battle expanded.[98] In the confusion, Debeney adhered to the guiding principle of command that he had assimilated in the spring: stick to the key idea and improvise the detail of operations according to circumstances.[99] His method worked. His army had a twenty-five-kilometre advance and ten-thousand prisoners to show for it: sixteen German divisions were engaged and defeated.[100] In victory Haig could at least be magnanimous, sending Debeney warm congratulations and praise on his army's reversion to French command.[101] In contrast, once again there was no official acknowledgment of Debeney's achievement from GQG.[102]

After Montdidier, Debeney's troops pushed forwards in a series of operations that entailed 'heavy fighting' until they came up against the defences of the Hindenburg Line.[103] This deep defensive system was to be stormed in cooperation with Rawlinson's army in late September and early October 1918. The British like to take a lot of credit for breaking the Hindenburg Line. In fact, the enemy chose to base their principal resistance around the small city of St Quentin in the French sector, which Debeney's forces invested in their hardest fight of the counter offensive.[104] The primary task of First Army was to 'support at all costs the right of the British Army', which involved them in very intensive fighting. Operations that began with an attack south of St Quentin extended northwards to keep touch with the advancing British and envelop the city from both flanks, a manoeuvre that 'encountered the strongest sort of resistance'.[105] It took twelve days, and the efforts of four army corps, to reduce the position, before the enemy finally withdrew in First Army's sector leaving behind 5,000 prisoners, many casualties and much materiel.[106] As First Army's soldiers were giving their all to sustain the joint advance, Haig of course complained that Debeney was dragging his feet and asked Foch to urge him onwards.[107]

First Army would advance as far as any allied formation in the last months of the war. Debeney would subsequently pay tribute to the high state of training of his soldiers and the skill of the commanders and staff officers who directed them in their final operations.[108] Weary certainly, wary understandably, but determined and competent until their task was accomplished. The final advance, the pursuit, culminating in the Second Battle of Guise (4–6 November) in which the enemy's final, desperate attempt to establish a solid defensive line was brushed aside, was a different style of warfare, which used firepower to facilitate manoeuvre. 'The army's mentality had changed completely; offensive warfare was working and created an atmosphere of confidence and initiative; trench warfare was finally forgotten and in its place manoeuvre warfare was paramount... "the firing line that marches forwards" as I would call it later.' Deservedly and proudly, the honour would fall to Debeney to grant the German armistice plenipotentiaries safe passage across his front as the war drew to a close – well worth being woken in the middle of the night for![109]

In September, Debeney's contribution to the impending victory was recognized with promotion to the grade of *Grand officier* of the Légion d'honneur, which came with a glowing citation and Foch's personal congratulations.[110] Making war was good for him, Bordeaux judged. He had lost the pallor of the previous year, his brown eyes lit up and he was in a great mood: the trials of 1917 were behind him, he was rightly proud of his recent success at Montdidier, and his country and army were now well-led and on the verge of liberation.[111] Fayolle, his immediate superior, was often critical of his principal subordinate (as he was of most subordinates and superiors). He complained that Debeney 'did not have enough grasp of detail'; was 'too small minded'; 'a quibbler and giver of [unwanted] advice'; 'crotchety and intolerable'. He felt Debeney requested relief of his units too often, although that might be expected of a commander who was sensitive to the morale and staying power of his men as Debeney always had been.[112] Such comments might say more about Fayolle than Debeney. Those who served under him painted a more intimate and laudatory picture. 'He showed his true worth during the crises, remaining affable and smiling, but taking counsel from nobody', Godfroy remembered. 'As a witness to his decisions, as well as a frequent confidant of his thoughts, I can certify that he intended the great things that he achieved – an uncommon occurrence – and that far from being controlled by unfolding events, he bent them to his own will.'[113]

Godfroy summarized Debeney's supreme achievement in the allied cause in 1918:

> The battle of the Avre in March and April 1918 when he re-established a position compromised by the disaster to the British Fifth Army, the magnificent operations crowned by the victories at Montdidier, St Quentin and Guise, which brought First Army from the banks of the Avre to la Capelle where the German parliamentary [peace] delegation presented itself, remain models. They set the seal on a talent of the first order, flexible, bold and methodical.[114]

When commanding a division in 1915, Debeney had asserted that the war would end with the French army winning a great victory against the German army on the Western Front.[115] He did not know then that he would be instrumental in that process: probably no other allied army commander did better in 1918.

* * *

After the war Debeney was appointed the first commander of the reopened ESG, and head of the *Centre des hautes études militaires* (CHEM), holding the posts until January 1924. His first task was to rewrite the curriculum based on wartime experience.[116] He also joined the *Conseil supérieur de la guerre* and became inspector general of military schools.[117] In that post he developed and inculcated new infantry regulations and operational precepts grounded in wartime lessons. He drew upon his former subordinates to reconstruct the teaching staff. Godfroy would join Debeney's staff at CHEM in 1920, after an earlier recommendation had been refused.[118] Debeney's own operations would inform the army's post-war curriculum.[119] Ninety-fourth RI's defensive actions at Sailly-Saillisel in October 1916 and successful attack on 8 August 1918 alongside the Canadian Corps were offered as examples of appropriate infantry tactics.[120] Louis Émile Mangin, XXXII CA's chief of staff on the Somme who also taught at CHEM, wrote a study of 47 DI's chasseurs that he commanded in the battle of Montdidier and afterwards.[121] Most significantly, Marius Daille published a study of the Montididier offensive and Lieutenant-Colonel Alphonse Grasset published a study of 42 DI's successful attack on 8 August 1918.[122] Daille had been a divisional chief of staff during the offensive and taught military history at the ESG. He was allowed to see, and quoted at length, Debeney's own post-war memorandum of the battle.[123] These texts would have formed the reading material of ambitious junior officers preparing for the next war.

After four years at the ESG, Debeney would be chosen to replace Buat (who in 1918 had been the final GQG chief of staff, and who died suddenly in post at the age of 55) as army chief of staff. As it was, he was reluctant to take on the responsibility, resisting the call from war minister André Maginot for a week. Yet, dutifully, he would continue in the role for six years, the longest incumbent during the Third Republic up to that point, serving eight war ministers in the volatile politics of the inter-war state.[124] In that post he would manage France's military occupation of the Ruhr, the last ripple of the recent conflict with Germany, as well as suppress colonial insurgencies in Morocco and Syria.

His main focus, however, was on France's future security in Europe. Debeney is generally remembered, and with hindsight criticized, for instigating France's inter-war defensive posture and supporting the construction of the extensive system of frontier fortifications that bore war minister Maginot's name. Debeney's reversion to a faith in massive defensive fortifications made some sense. Fieldworks alone were inadequate: even though they had been designed after two years' experience of defensive warfare, Debeney was well aware that, come 1918, both German and French defensive systems were easily overwhelmed owing to the rapid pace of change in material-intensive warfare.

After retiring from active service, Debeney published a military treatise which included a brief biographical sketch, but he left no memoirs or private papers.[125] Indeed he began this treatise with a strong critique of memoirs as a genre. Quickly-published memoirs were simply the pleas of 'losers' keen to save their reputations. Later memoirs – he suggested thirty years should elapse before writing memoirs – while more 'serene' might be mistaken for 'truth'. Memoirs were most useful, he suggested, for examining the character of the memoirist: this came across in Joffre's memoirs, he judged, but sadly not in Foch's who he had watched closely in his interactions with the British during 1918. He felt his own actions were of little interest and, having no case to plead or hindsight judgments to proffer, preferred to write on the nature of war from personal experience.[126] This would suggest a man of integrity, but rather dry and wedded to his profession: he did not court publicity like some of his peers. Little is known of his private life. He was Catholic and conservative, as were many senior officers of this era, but unostentatiously so. He had been married, but had suffered the personal tragedy of losing his wife and being left alone to bring up six children.[127]

Debeney's treatise, *La Guerre et les hommes* (*Men and War*), was, intentionally, the distillation of a lifetime's experience of military education, management and command in the most intensive war France had fought.[128] The book was dedicated to his old comrades from 25 DI, XXXII CA and First Army; and to his two sons, both wounded in action. The work followed on from earlier writings about the value of a professional versus a conscript army, a debate that was animating French military thinkers in the 1930s.[129] While Debeney supported the mechanization of French forces – he had himself coined the adage, 'the old army smelled of dung; the new army smells of petrol' – he felt that the switch to a professional army was unrealistic and would compromise French defensive security.[130] Published in 1937 as war clouds were again gathering, *La Guerre et les hommes* appeared too late to have any appreciable impact on the way the French army would prepare for and make war. As in 1914, the Germans were to catch the French army in doctrinal turmoil and, second time around in summer 1940, were to achieve the decisive victory that Debeney and his colleagues had previously denied them. Debeney might take a share of the blame; but the reality was that the senior officers of 1918 were still very much in harness in France between the wars; in Germany the next generation came to the fore.

\* \* \*

Debeney's wartime career progression shows how a skilled and intelligent general could rise rapidly to positions of responsibility. Debeney certainly had a good war: in him France possessed a first-class soldier, fitted to senior responsibilities in both war and peace and, unlike many general officers who found their careers truncated once war ended, Debeney would continue his rise to the very top of the army. One might speculate whether as a professor Debeney would have risen to be the head of the army in peacetime; his wartime field service and success probably counted for more. But he certainly embodied the qualities, emphasized in the introduction, of both the 'soldier' and the 'professor' that underpinned effective wartime leadership. He alternated staff work experience with command as the war progressed, holding senior staff appointments in an army, an army group and at GQG, and commanding a division and an army corps effectively in the 'learning' battles of 1916. Debeney thought about as well as conducted war. He had been a pre-war instructor at the ESG, so he brought an understanding of theory and a commitment to learning from experience to his practice.[131] Not without justification did he remember long afterwards that one of his staff college instructors, General Négrier, had predicted that the next war would be won by the more intelligent army.[132] In the judgment of Weygand, who succeeded him as chief of staff in 1930, Debeney 'combined the personal qualities and military skills of a leader… [he was] a high-quality soldier, a man with heart and character.'[133] His 'farsightedness, profound insight and steadfast character place him in the same lineage as Joffre and Foch', Godfroy reflected in 1945, when he wrote his memoirs: 'He exceeded them in his tactical understanding, and even possibly in his understanding of the troops.'[134] Such an assessment stands as a fitting epitaph to one of France's all-but forgotten heroes. A soldier whom Pétain knew intimately and could trust, Debeney was the right man to call upon when the crisis of the war on the Western Front occurred. However, Godfroy's testimony indicates that his talents and success came to be resented by his mentor and prevented him rising even higher in wartime.

Perhaps he was a hero from an earlier age however, of a sort that modern France has little use for. The choices of the next war cost Debeney his reputation, and his life. Forced like so many to choose in the difficult circumstances of a divided France, as might be expected from a senior military figure, he supported the Vichy regime and his old comrade Pétain. (Debeney's eldest son Victor, who had lost an arm in the Great War, was Pétain's private secretary.) This led to an ignominious and tragic end for one of France's great soldiers. Debeney died at the age of 79 in his home town, Bourg-en-Bresse, on 8 November 1943, of complications from wounds sustained in an August assassination attempt by the resistance. Pétain did not attend the funeral.[135]

Discredited by his association with the disastrous inter-war 'Maginot mentality' and loyalty to his old chief Pétain during the Vichy years, Debeney became a marginal figure in the history of the war, the butt of British jokes and a fall-guy for apparent French laggardness in the final advance to victory. It was his misfortune to serve his final command in support of a largely unappreciative British army.[136] What Debeney had achieved for the French army at all levels of command and management was remarkable; the support he gave to the British in 1918 was highly effective, if unshowy, as French methods had become by that year. The people of Amiens knew who their saviour had been, and the rest of France owed a debt of gratitude to Debeney and his like, the successful commanders who defended then liberated national soil, and who tried – but ultimately failed – to protect that sacred earth from a future German invasion.

Chapter 10

# Charles Mangin: 'This Devil of a Man'

Tim Gale

Charles Marie Emmanuel Mangin was one of the most controversial French generals of the First World War. Known by many in France as 'the butcher' for his alleged carelessness with his soldiers' lives, he served in most of the large-scale French operations on the Western Front from 1914 to 1918, with the exception of the Battle of the Somme. He was deeply unpopular with his peers, General Marie-Émile Fayolle calling him 'this devil of a man',[1] and he courted considerable controversy after the war with his support for an independent Rhineland. He was dismissed from command on two occasions during the war, once for insubordination, but he was simply too efficient as a senior commander to remain unused. Even a brief examination of his wartime career demonstrates that Mangin, notwithstanding his reputation in some quarters, was a very effective commander by any standards and certainly one of the best army commanders on the Western Front.

\* \* \*

Mangin was born on 6 July 1866, at Sarrebourg in Lorraine. His father was arrested during the Franco-Prussian War for communicating with the French authorities and the family was detained in Nancy for the duration of the war.[2] This inculcated a life-long hatred of the Germans in Mangin and a desire to join the army from an early age. He followed his brothers into St Cyr on his third attempt and, after graduating in the lower order of passes, he became a *sous-lieutenant* in 1[er] *régiment de marine*, which had a bad reputation for indiscipline at this time.[3] He fought in numerous colonial actions over the next twenty-five years from Morocco to Tonkin (including participating in General Jean-Baptiste Marchand's Fashoda expedition) and was wounded many times. Colonial service was a double-edged sword. On the one hand, it taught officers to think on their feet and to read terrain accurately and quickly. It was also about leading from the front, a habit Mangin would never lose, and meant that colonial officers saw considerable combat, unlike their metropolitan colleagues. However, there was a strong streak of indiscipline in the colonial army that led to most officers in the metropolitan army viewing colonial soldiers with some disdain, although their dashing exploits were popular with the French public.[4]

It is worth considering some events in Mangin's time in the colonial army as they demonstrate certain traits that would prove useful in the Great War, along with others that would get him in some considerable trouble. There were four actions during Mangin's very busy colonial career which perhaps best illustrate the strengths and weaknesses he would bring to the Western Front, these being the action at Diéna, 24 February 1891, the battle of Sidi Bou Othmann in 1912 and the actions at Casba Tadla and Casba Kisba in 1913. The first demonstrates his considerable personal bravery and leadership; the second showed his abilities as a commander; the third manifested the perennial difficulties he had with following orders; and the fourth was an example of him underestimating the enemy, something that he would learn hard lessons about in 1914 and 1915.

In February 1891, Lieutenant Mangin, as a section commander, participated in an attack on a rebel position at Diéna, in modern-day Mali.[5] Diéna was a collection of fortified villages, one of which was holding a rebel force, this village having a redoubt in the north. At daybreak, French troops commanded by Colonel Louis Archinard encircled the village. Archinard had five companies of infantry and four pieces of light artillery, facing 1200 rebels armed with rifles.[6] Mangin's section of thirty men took position at the north side of the village, with his friend Captain Jean-Baptiste Marchand's company on his right, Marchand having sixty men. Archinard moved two of his guns to the north of the village and they made breaches in each of the two salients that flanked the entrance to the village. Marchand's section attacked the right-hand breach, but Marchand was wounded and his unit was forced to fall back. Archinard then ordered Mangin and his section to attack the left-hand breach. 'At a gymnastic pace' the section advanced, Mangin at its head with a revolver in his hand. He was the first man through the breach, 'naturally' he told his parents, and he entered the village only to be immediately wounded in the hand.[7] As he fought his way through a series of courtyards in the village, he was wounded again, this time a large wound on his thigh; 'I was furious', he later wrote to his parents. He carried on, however, until a bullet went through his jaw, a wound that would leave him permanently scarred. This was too serious for him to ignore and he had to pass command, very reluctantly, to another lieutenant. Although he was badly wounded, he refused to be evacuated and continued to send updates to Archinard until the French were in full control of the village. His section lost four killed and eleven wounded, with the overall French losses being 14 dead and 110 wounded.[8] However, the rebels defending the village had lost nearly 690 men. Archinard's official report concerning

Mangin's bravery was published in the *Petit journal* in Paris to much public acclaim.[9]

Thus, the action at Diéna established Mangin's reputation in France for considerable personal bravery and for small-unit leadership. Further fame came due to his participation in the Expedition to the Nile, led by his friend Marchand. However, it was to be in Morocco that his colonial reputation reached its zenith; but it was also there that his career very nearly came to a premature end.

Initially it seemed that his actions in Morocco would establish Mangin as the pre-eminent colonial soldier in France, at least in the eyes of the public. In September 1912, Colonel Mangin led a relief force to free Marrakech and six French hostages held there from the hands of the rebel leader El Hiba and his Saharan irregulars. Mangin had 5,000 men under command, supported by a large baggage train of camels and mules, and twelve 75mm artillery pieces and eight machine-guns.[10] The column ran into El Hiba's main force on the rather desolate plain of Sidi Bou Othmann early in the morning of 6 September. While the Moroccans significantly outnumbered Mangin's force, having roughly 15,000 men in the *harka*, they could not match French firepower, many of the irregulars being only rudimentarily armed. As the French advanced slowly in two squares across the plain, they were attacked by the entire *harka* but Mangin did not allow the French troops to fire until the Moroccans were within half-a-mile. At this range French fire was deadly and, despite the Moroccans bravely rallying numerous times and returning to attack Mangin's column, it was so effective that Moroccan resistance was broken by 09.00.[11] El Hiba's forces fled back to Marrakech in disorder, having lost some 2,000 men, with French casualties only being two dead and twenty-three wounded.[12] Mangin had to rest his troops, having marched them forty-seven miles through the difficult terrain and then fighting off El Hiba's *harka*, all in only thirty hours. In order to maintain pressure on the rebels, he sent a flying column to relieve Marrakech and rescue the hostages, both of which were achieved. By the time Mangin arrived in the city, El Hiba's revolt was over.[13] Mangin's organizational skills and leadership in combat were very evident at Sidi Bou Othmann, the battle itself becoming seen as one of the greatest French victories in Morocco. However, his success at Sidi Bou Othmann seemed to remove any inhibitions that Mangin had about insubordination and this would lead him into serious trouble.

The French premier in 1917, Georges Clemenceau said of Mangin: 'Mangin was a great soldier and a great commander, but he did not think that obedience was made for him.'[14] This trait was quite in evidence during 1913 in Morocco. Hubert Lyautey, French *Résident général* in Morocco, sent Mangin to organize the friendly tribes along the Oum er Rbia river, as a counterweight to the powerful Zain tribes. Mangin was given specific orders not to cross the river under any circumstances, but he believed that the provincial capital of Casba Tadla on the other side of the river was a major strategic prize. Disregarding Lyautey's clear instructions, Mangin launched an assault on the town, which proved to be a great success. However, Lyautey was furious and ordered him back across the river, a tricky manoeuvre that cost the French column more casualties than the attack on the town had. There followed a long argument between the two men about French strategy in Morocco, Lyautey wanting to use the tried and trusted methods that he used so successfully in Tonkin and Madagascar.[15] Mangin, by contrast, wanted to take a more direct military route to the subjugation of the Moroccans and, as was his way, he refused to stop demanding that Lyautey allow him to take military action against the various Moroccan rebel factions. Mangin had quite clearly disobeyed his orders at Casba Tadla and was aware that he had to avoid this in the future, so he simply bombarded Lyautey with demands that he be allowed to launch an attack on another rebel stronghold at Casba Kisba.[16] While Lyautey had grave doubts about the wisdom of this operation, he appears to have got to the stage of exhaustion with Mangin and reluctantly agreed to his plans. Not for the last time, Mangin seriously underestimated the opposition, failing to take into account that the enemy were much better armed and motivated than those that had opposed him during the Marrakech campaign. In addition, the terrain was mountainous and difficult, offering none of the long fields of fire found on the plain of Sidi Bou Othmann. Mangin's column failed to establish French control of Casba Kisba and lost significantly more men that had been the case at Casba Tadla. Mangin was humiliatingly forced to retreat. Lyautey sent General Louis Franchet d'Esperey, commander of French troops in Morocco, to see Mangin and haul him over the coals. Both men felt that Mangin had now become too much trouble to want to retain him in Morocco. It was made clear to Mangin that it would be better if he returned to France without causing a scene; but, in exchange, Lyautey had to agree to put a permanent French garrison in Casba Tadla, something that he had been very reluctant to do. This at least meant for Mangin that he had got his own way in this aspect of French policy in Morocco. He was also promoted to *Général de brigade*, based at the *État-major général des troupes coloniales*, on his return to France, making him the youngest general in the French army.[17]

Mangin's time in Africa had convinced him that the French army should utilize the enormous source of manpower available in the colonies, particularly in West Africa. He wrote a book, *La Force noire* (1910), to argue the case for recruiting more colonial manpower to redress the shortfall relative to Germany.[18] The racial prejudices of the time mean that his suggestion caused great public controversy and there was little action from the authorities.[19]

Opponents of the *force noire* included even senior colonial officers such as Lyautey, who was against using West African troops as he believed them to be 'an enormous bluff'.[20] However, Mangin was to be shown to be correct by events and, by 1918, the French army contained large numbers of troops from the colonies, many of whom were used as elite shock-troops.[21] There is no doubt that Mangin's consistent advocacy of West African troops prior to and during the war was a significant factor in their eventual wide-scale use in the French army.[22]

In addition to his very busy military career, Mangin's personal life was not without incident. In 1900, he married Madeleine Henriette Jagerschmidt who tragically died in childbirth only a year later. Mangin would subsequently marry Antoinette Charlotte Cavaignac, daughter of a French minister and granddaughter of a general, in 1905. They had a very successful and close relationship, which would produce eight children, with Mangin writing to Antoinette almost every day while he was on campaign, his letters to her rather undermining the idea of Mangin as a hard-hearted butcher of men.

\* \* \*

Upon mobilization in 1914, General Mangin arrived at Laon and took command of *8e brigade d'infanterie*, which was covering the Meuse river. The brigade was attached to General André Sordet's cavalry corps, but the cavalry was unable to advance and was ordered to retreat almost as soon as Mangin's brigade arrived to join it. Mangin and his brigade then saw first-hand the disorganized French retreat from Belgium. During the retreat, there was a telling meeting between Mangin and his future commander-in-chief, Philippe Pétain. Stopping for a midday meal, Pétain produced some cold meat, bread and a piece of cheese and proceeded to eat these off his lap. By contrast, Mangin's staff served him a steak, with fried potatoes and a salad, and a bottle of wine, all on an improvised table. Pétain was most put out; 'How did you get all that?' he said, 'don't you know we are at war?' 'That is precisely why I need to be well-fed', replied Mangin, 'I've been at war all my life and I've never felt better than now. You've been at war for fifteen days and you're nearly dead!'[23] Typically, Mangin was correct in his analysis but very undiplomatic, particularly in reminding Pétain of his greater combat experience – although Pétain learned from the example and acquired himself a good cook![24] It is perhaps unsurprising that he was unpopular with his peers and those commanding him, although he usually attributed this to being a colonial officer rather than from any fault in himself.[25]

In late August, Mangin's brigade was rushed in to shore-up the very badly-led 5 *division d'infanterie* (DI) – part of the equally inept III *corps d'armée* (CA) in Fifth Army – and was almost immediately engaged in fighting-off a strong

German attack on the village of Onhaye.[26] This was one of Mangin's finest hours. His soon-to-be army commander, Franchet d'Espèrey, met him as the battle was almost over and wrote:

> I arrived just as our foes were fleeing under cover of nightfall. The flames from the burning village lit up the dark and I saw Mangin waiting for me, smiling, victorious, impassive beneath the hail of bullets fired by the retreating enemy. I can see him still; the fiery glare of those deep-set eyes, that determined jaw struck by an iron bullet at Diéna.[27]

On 31 August, 5 DI's commander General Elie Verrier was dismissed in disgrace and Mangin replaced him.[28] One young officer in the division's staff, Henri Dutheil, was delighted at Mangin taking command. He wrote to his parents that 'having had at our head a walking ruin, we now possess one of the best generals in the French army'.[29] Dutheil was particularly surprised by the number of motor vehicles that Mangin brought to the division: 'It certainly passed the number assigned to a corps by GQG in this period' and included an Opel sports-car that Mangin's staff had captured from the Germans during the fighting on the Franco-Belgian frontier.[30]

In the early mobile fighting Mangin never hesitated to take direct control of situations when necessity required it. Indeed, he wrote to his wife that it was in his opinion a heresy for higher commanders and their staffs to remain confined to the rear.[31] There are many examples of Mangin directly intervening in the thick of the action, a typical one being in September 1914. During an attack on the village of Courgivaux, the advance battalions of 5 DI were hit by an effective German counter attack, which seriously disorganized the village's defenders. Mangin arrived and restored order, personally directing his riflemen's fire against the advancing German infantry.[32] The German fire was so close to the general that one of his staff kept ducking. An annoyed Mangin pointed out to him that 'It is completely futile, by the time you've lowered your head the bullet has passed'.[33] The fighting was particularly fierce, the division suffering 1,624 casualties over two days of fighting.[34]

After this action, Mangin's division joined the general advance across the Marne, meeting only sporadic German resistance until, just west of Reimsat at the villages of Brimont and Courcy, Mangin learnt a hard lesson about overextending both himself and his men. He was also to learn that his colonial tactical experience would not translate to the Western Front. Initially the attack on Brimont, on 13 September 1914, went well, with the French infantry occupying all their objectives, but by the following day they were pinned down by German artillery fire and unable to advance. Mangin audaciously pushed two battalions at night into the chateau near Brimont, confident that he would be able to reinforce them in due course. However, daylight showed that the

German positions were too strong to allow either an advance or a relief. In fact, Mangin had let too many forward parts of his line become isolated, a very serious error. This resulted in his troops being pushed out of their forward positions in some considerable panic when subsequently attacked by the Germans, leaving the two battalions in the Chateau surrounded and with little choice but to surrender.[35] Mangin was humiliatingly forced to retire his division, having lost 4,855 officers and men between 13 and 18 September, with only one regiment in the division avoiding significant casualties. Typically blaming his peers rather than himself or his troops, Mangin wrote to his wife that the failure at Brimont had been the result of the adjacent divisions (one of which was commanded by Pétain) not advancing and therefore leaving him exposed, further arguing that the French front line could have been stabilized further north of Reims if his attack had been successful.[36] However, he was honest enough to admit that he had put the division into position at night before the tactical situation was clear to him. His failure at Brimont is probably better explained as the result of trying to apply colonial methods against a modern European army. His isolated forward positions, quickly reinforced, might have worked in colonial action actions against irregular troops, who would not have had the firepower or the training of the Germans. Fayolle later complained that one of Mangin's primary faults was that he underestimated the enemy and Brimont was probably the most egregious example of this.[37]

The division was not to be engaged in another major action until the spring of 1915 and Mangin had the opportunity to consider the course of the war so far. The army had performed poorly for a number of reasons; the troops and their officers were badly instructed and 'the high command remains confined to the rear'.[38] The army corps had tended to operate without liaising with each other and many of their commanders were 'deplorable'. Mangin was particularly critical of French material preparations for the war, complaining of a lack of heavy artillery, machine guns and aircraft: 'I lead a sort of war of siege', which would require a systematic delay of the Germans until 'time and the Russians work for us'.[39]

Mangin's division's most significant operation in 1915 was the Battle of Artois in May and June. Tenth Army launched an offensive against Vimy ridge on 9 May, after a powerful (for the time) artillery preparation by 782 field guns and 293 heavy artillery pieces, lasting several days.[40] Although initially highly successful, with advances of several kilometres in places along the twenty-kilometre front, the offensive quickly got bogged down over the following days, with heavy French casualties. At Neuville-Saint-Vaast, south-east of Vimy ridge, 39 DI had, at great cost, fought to the outskirts of the village, but by 26 May it could go no further and was relieved by Mangin's division.[41] The division's initial attack on 1 June was unsuccessful and Mangin was obliged to improvise another approach; he decided to shell the rear of the village heavily, thereby isolating the garrison from reinforcements, and to attack the village itself head-on. This was largely due to the impossibility of effectively silencing German machine guns on the village's flanks because of their proximity to the French lines.[42] With direct artillery support, both French and German, only available outside the village, the infantry fought it out in Neuville with small arms. This played to Mangin's colonial-army strengths, in that it was a close-quarters infantry fight like that at Diéna, which was a battle of wills as much as anything else. Although 5 DI captured a great deal of German material along with the village, casualties were high: 72 officers and 2,530 men, of whom 624 were killed.[43] However, Leonard Smith's research shows that, although high, Mangin's casualties were actually lower than those of other Tenth Army divisions in Artois and he had rather more to show for it.[44]

General Robert Nivelle took command of III CA on 23 December 1915 and in March the following year the corps was moved into the Verdun area as reinforcements for the defensive battle raging there. Mangin immediately struck up a rapport with Nivelle, writing to his wife that Nivelle 'understood the war' and that their military ideas were in close accord.[45] Once at Verdun, Mangin was almost immediately in action, III CA and his division taking up an aggressive posture on the right bank of the Meuse river from 28 March 1916. Commander-in-chief Joseph Joffre found Nivelle's approach much more to his liking than the more cautious methods of Second Army commander Pétain and, in due course, the latter was removed from control of the Verdun front by being promoted to command the *Groupe d'armées du centre* (GAC), with Nivelle taking command of Second Army on 1 May 1916.

Under Nivelle's close direction (an integral part of his command-style), Mangin became famous throughout France for his operations against Fort Douaumont. German machine guns and artillery observers in the fort, captured at the end of February, were able to observe virtually the entire Verdun front and from there dominate the battlefield. An initial attack on the fort on 22 April saw Mangin's infantry repelled relatively easily. On 8 May, a catastrophic ammunition explosion occurred within the fort, killing hundreds of Germans inside and sending a huge plume of smoke into the air. Although Mangin immediately made plans to attack the fort, he required approval from Nivelle, Pétain and even Joffre. Typically for the French army at this point in the war, this lengthy chain of command slowed planning significantly and there was a serious lack of security, with the Germans soon becoming aware of the impending operation. To Mangin's annoyance, the forces initially available to him were gradually whittled down by General Léonce Lebrun (Nivelle's replacement as III CA's commander) and Nivelle, as was the artillery support. However, he was able to use over 300 guns against the fort, including four huge 370mm mortars. The artillery preparation took place over five days, and was directed by one of the French army's finest artillery-commanders, Jean-Baptiste Estienne (shortly to become the commander of the French tank force), giving Mangin reasonable grounds for confidence in its effectiveness.

The superstructure of the fort was indeed badly damaged by the artillery preparation but, unknown to the French, the main part of the fort was not. The assaulting French infantry were hit almost immediately they left their trenches by a heavy German barrage but within eleven minutes the survivors were on the fort.[46] A stalemate ensued as the French were unable to penetrate the fort beyond the outer tunnels and the Germans were equally unable to get the French off the top of the fort. Despite getting reinforcements to the fort, the French situation deteriorated and a strong German counter attack eventually forced them to retire from the fort. The casualties in 5 DI had again been high: over two days it had lost over 5,000 officers and men, a particular shock being the surrender of an entire French battalion.[47] Mangin blamed his failure, as at Brimont, on the adjoining divisions failing to protect his flanks and the fact that he had not been given all the men and material he had asked for, the latter an implicit criticism of Nivelle.[48] With hindsight, it is probable that more artillery would not have produced success but it was reasonable at the time for Mangin to expect that his artillery preparation would cause havoc to the defence and his planning was not at fault here. However, he now knew that further operations against the fort would be futile without substantial artillery reinforcements.

On 24 May, Lebrun telephoned Mangin and ordered a new attack, which Mangin told him was 'impossible', adding that it was 'an attack for the gallery'.[49] Lebrun immediately relieved him of command.[50] Mangin had been plagued by accusations from the interior that he was careless with his troops, leading him to write in May 1916 to his wife that 'whatever one does, one loses a lot of men'.[51] This reputation meant that there was going to be little political pressure to reinstate him and so he demanded a formal military enquiry, which was refused. Although Pétain was reluctant to reinstate Mangin, Nivelle pressed Joffre and agreed to take personal responsibility for this 'pig-headed' officer.[52] His reputation as a 'man-killer' was to have serious repercussions for Mangin in 1917 but, for the moment, he was under the patronage of the French army's rising star and, in the middle of June, he was promoted to command XI CA. Nivelle and Mangin's forces were in a defensive posture until September, as Verdun became subordinate to the needs of the Battle of the Somme. When the Somme was in its dying stages, Joffre turned his attention back to Verdun, desperate for a successful operation to silence disquiet in Paris.

Fort Douaumont, now as much a potent symbol as a military objective, remained in German hands. In September, Mangin suggested an operation pushing up to the fort, which was gradually extended to include seizing the fort itself. Both Nivelle and Pétain were careful to impose restraints on Mangin, since they knew he wanted to absolve his previous failure, and they were involved in the planning to a very detailed level.[53] In addition to three infantry divisions, Nivelle was able to muster for Mangin a formidable amount of heavy and super-heavy artillery; five *groupements* of heavy guns, mainly modern 155mm pieces, and a super-heavy artillery *groupement*, which included batteries of both heavy guns and mortars, as well as a pair of 400mm railway guns.[54] Of course, prior to the attack on 24 October, Mangin argued that he did not have enough support, but in the event the operation was more successful than anyone had expected. The French infantry managed to recapture Fort Douaumont and advance up to Fort Vaux, which the Germans evacuated a few days later. As the balance had now shifted decisively to the French, a second operation took place in December to disengage the recaptured forts. This essentially replicated the methodology of 24 October but produced even greater results. A heavier preparation than in October enabled Mangin's infantry to sweep across the battlefield, capturing over 11,000 Germans and a large haul of materiel.[55]

The operations at Verdun were to have far-reaching consequences. Nivelle and Mangin were seriously misled by their success and thought that they could apply the methods of Verdun on a much larger front, which was to produce one of the most dangerous crises for the French army in the war. For the moment though, it appeared to the politicians that Nivelle could win the war and he became commander-in-chief and in turn promoted Mangin to command Sixth Army on 19 December 1916.

The Nivelle offensive is covered in another chapter of this volume and therefore only Mangin's part in the offensive will be considered here.[56] Mangin's role was one of the most controversial episodes in a controversial career, particularly with regards to his alleged influence on Nivelle and his conduct of Sixth Army's operations. His defenders point to the fact that the overall plan was devised by Nivelle, his main manoeuvre force being the *Groupe d'armées de reserve* (GAR) commanded by General Alfred Micheler, who was to plan the operation on his front. GAR consisted of three armies. Tenth Army was in reserve to exploit success, while Fifth and Sixth Armies were expected to 'completely rupture' the enemy front.[57] As Sixth Army commander, Mangin was responsible for planning the action on his front under the direction of his immediate superior, Micheler. Thus, it was argued that Mangin was under the supervision of two senior officers and should be absolved of responsibility for the failure of the offensive. This is not entirely in keeping with the facts as Mangin's tendency to be a difficult subordinate was at its worst during this period.

Despite a cordial start to their relationship, Mangin soon began to have a series of increasingly vehement disagreements about his army's plans with Micheler, who believed that Mangin's outburts were encouraged by Nivelle.[58] The situation deteriorated quickly, culminating in a furious row between Mangin and Micheler at a planning meeting at Sixth Army headquarters in February, in front of Nivelle. Mangin spent half-an-hour detailing what he saw as the deficiencies in Micheler's orders, to which Micheler responded by pointing out that his orders were directly in line with those he had received from Nivelle.[59] In particular, Mangin was demanding control of Tenth Army's forward divisions and their entry into the offensive. This was in order to allow Mangin to reinforce quickly any success on his front but Micheler, not unreasonably, felt that this should be his prerogative as army group commander.[60] However, Nivelle failed to support Micheler and the latter stormed out of the meeting, stating that he could not be responsible for Sixth Army. Nivelle subsequently wrote to Micheler saying that he had 'seriously remonstrated with Mangin' about his behaviour but, in an astonishing departure from normal command protocol, Micheler was instructed that any further disagreements between them should be brought to Nivelle to resolve.[61] When Micheler quite improperly told Georges Clemenceau about his difficulties with Mangin, Clemenceau sharply told him that 'when a subordinate disobeys you, you break him or you are not a leader'.[62]

Micheler was now in an impossible position; Mangin was difficult to command at the best of times and Nivelle had completely undermined Micheler's authority. The situation was actually worse than Micheler knew. Nivelle had simultaneously written to Mangin severely criticizing Micheler, stating that it was only Micheler's political support that prevented his dismissal.[63] Micheler was left with little choice but to leave Mangin to organize Sixth Army's operation, although in the event the bad feeling between them had little effect on the unfolding of the offensive. Thus, Micheler holds little responsibility for Mangin's conduct of Sixth Army, although Mangin's orders reflected exactly those he received from Nivelle. There is no evidence that Mangin influenced Nivelle's overall plan and, indeed, he constantly warned Nivelle and Micheler about the necessity of good weather for the success of the operation, urging them to delay the offensive until the summer. The crucial problem was that the overall conception of the offensive was flawed, rather than any part of its execution by Fifth and Sixth Armies, and this was Nivelle's responsibility alone, as the official enquiry would find.

Indeed, Mangin had warned both Nivelle and Micheler that the offensive should be delayed until the weather got better and that he needed air superiority since unhindered air observation was crucial for success.[64] By early April, Mangin was alerted by General Antoine de Mitry, commander of VI CA, to there being major problems on the latter's front with air observation, as the French had not attained air superiority and their spotter aircraft were met with German fighters whenever they took to the air.[65] Further problems were created by the very bad weather during the last stages of the preparatory bombardment, which prevented the French planes from making effective observations. Conversely, the Germans had excellent observation of the French positions.

Sixth Army's British liaison officer Edward Spiers visited Mangin on 15 April, the eve of the attack, and later wrote 'I think of him that day as the embodiment of the soul of war: iron, unflinching resolution, confidence that knows no doubt'.[66] However, the next day Sixth Army's infantry quickly discovered that their chief's confidence was misplaced; the too diffuse artillery preparation had not damaged the German defences along the Aisne as at Verdun. Instead of a sweeping advance through destroyed German positions, in most places the fighting quickly became heavier and the advance much slower than had been planned for. The German artillery observers were largely untouched by the bombardment and were able to rain down heavy and accurate artillery fire on Mangin's infantry, causing significant casualties. Another unpleasant surprise was the large number of German machine guns that only unveiled themselves as the French infantry advanced, many of which had not been in prepared positions but hidden outside of the trenches and casemates.[67] However, over the following days, gains were made, the French eventually capturing over 28,000 prisoners and a significant amount of materiel.[68] This came at the cost of 36,000 casualties in Sixth Army and 43,000 in Fifth Army, not enormous compared to previous offensives but concentrated in a two-week period, exacerbating their impact.

Within days of the offensive starting, Paris was filled with rumours about catastrophic casualties and the government subsequently forced Nivelle to suspend offensive operations.[69] At this point, Mangin's reputation came to work against him; despite the fact that Sixth Army had fewer casualties than Fifth Army and, indeed, had done rather better, Mangin became the focus of public anger about the failure of the offensive. In a vain attempt to protect his own position, Nivelle decided to sacrifice Mangin; he asked Micheler to report that Mangin had mishandled Sixth Army during the offensive. Despite their previous differences, Micheler refused to do so, saying Mangin was a very competent officer.[70] Nivelle then told Mangin that he had lost the confidence of his subordinates (although he gave a completely different reason to the government for the dismissal) and he was to be relieved of his command.[71] A furious Mangin returned to Paris, starting a public feud with the minister of war, Paul Painlevé, that was to continue long after the war. At one point, Mangin had to be forcibly removed from Painlevé's outer office as he was refusing to leave without seeing the minister. To make matters worse, Micheler wrote a highly critical letter about Nivelle and Mangin to the government and asked to retire.[72] Mangin, however, refused to go quietly and made what was undoubtably a real threat to resign his commission and then rejoin the French army as a private soldier. This caused significant alarm in the government as it would have been unthinkable to allow Mangin to serve in the ranks. The government then quite disgracefully ordered him to live outside Paris while it was decided what to do with him. President Raymond Poincaré was told by premier Alexandre Ribot that Mangin was 'roaming' Paris making complaints and Poincaré was asked by senators Paul Doumer and Georges Clemenceau to stop Mangin's 'unjust' treatment.[73]

The official inquiry into the Battle of the Aisne, conducted by generals Joseph Brugère, Ferdinand Foch, and Henri Gouraud, thoroughly investigated the actions of all the major military participants in the offensive. (It should be noted, however, that it only took testimony from Nivelle, Micheler, Mangin and Olivier Mazel, commander of Fifth Army). The commission looked at all the allegations against Mangin in respect of how he had handled his command of Sixth Army and his relationships with Nivelle and Micheler. The Brugère Report found that he had followed Micheler's orders, which had in turn been set by Nivelle. (As discussed above, in relation to Micheler, this was not entirely true.) The enquiry was not uncritical of Mangin; it recommended that this 'brilliant commander' needed to moderate rather than stimulate further his 'excessive zeal'.[74] However, this did not change the government's attitude – particularly that of Painlevé who would soon become its head – and Mangin remained without a command until December 1917, when Georges Clemenceau, who had become premier, offered him an army corps command.

Mangin accepted command of IX CA, engaging in little combat until the German 1918 spring offensives. After some hard defensive fighting when deployed to help contain the first German spring offensive in Picardy the corps moved to a quiet sector in late April and Mangin was marked for promotion to an army command. However, an emergency arose that required all Mangin's organizational and fighting talents. In commander-in-chief Pétain's assessment, Mangin was 'a dangerous man, who needed to be contained, but if reigned in, could render great service'.[75] These conflicting sides of his character were on display as he went back into battle in earnest.

On 9 June, the German Eighteenth Army launched the 'Gneisenau' offensive against French Third Army near Montdidier, the intention being to drive through the French positions, take Compiègne and open the road to Paris. Third Army commander General Georges Humbert had pulled back his forces to partially absorb the anticipated attack but fifteen German divisions in the first line swept through his army, capturing 8,000 French troops and advancing more than eight kilometres on the first day. The second day saw further French reverses but Humbert's superior, Fayolle (now commanding GAR), had anticipated this. He had intended to allow the Germans to form a pocket, which he would then attack from two sides, but his plan was wrecked when a crucial section of the French front line collapsed, triggering a more general withdrawal. He was left with little option but to strike the German advance on only one flank. Mangin had been promoted to command Tenth Army on 7 June but, when he met with Fayolle to confirm his command, Fayolle asked him to organize a counter attack, which had to be carried out 'as soon as possible'.[76] Generalissimo Foch arrived and put further pressure on Mangin by saying the attack should take place the following morning, although Fayolle advised Foch that this was 'impossible' and that the operation would take at least two days to organize.[77] Mangin agreed with Foch and told Fayolle that the attack would take place the following day. Fayolle's order for the counter attack, issued at 16.00 on 10 June, gave Mangin discretion as to the exact details of the attack; saying only that it should take place on 11 June and be oriented according to the German positions at the time of the operation, the latter condition at Mangin's insistence.[78] Thus Mangin was given the shortest possible time in which to organize this operation, although at least he was given some discretion over its timing.

His *groupement* (an extemporized and reinforced army corps) was formed out of five infantry divisions, along with two additional field-artillery regiments, four French tank battalions and a brigade of British armoured cars.[79] It had just over twenty heavy-artillery batteries in action with some artillery support from adjacent First Army, as well as a few super-heavy guns from GAR.[80] Two squadrons of aircraft were attached to the four attacking infantry divisions for liaison and directing artillery fire, with another two squadrons operating in air superiority and bombardment roles.[81] Just two hours before the attack was to begin, commander-in-chief Pétain tried to withdraw one of the *groupement's* divisions but Mangin created such a fuss that this order was rescinded, with even Fayolle admitting that Mangin was right to protest.[82]

The attack on 11 June was largely a success, the French being greatly aided by a heavy morning mist which prevented the German artillery coming into action until the afternoon. The operation was declared over the following night when it became clear that the German offensive had been stopped in its tracks. Mangin's counter attack had pushed the Germans back three kilometres, across an eight-kilometre front, the enemy losing large numbers of machine guns and taking heavy infantry casualties. However, the cost for the French of what became known as the Battle of the Matz was also high; the tanks had been particularly badly hit, with 69 out of 159 tanks deployed being destroyed.[83] This lesson was learned quickly by Mangin; in all his subsequent operations, his tank units were amply covered by dedicated artillery. With the battle over, Mangin's *groupement* was dissolved and Mangin took over Tenth Army.

\* \* \*

As the pressure of the final German offensives was being absorbed and dissipated, French thoughts turned to an offensive of their own. In June 1918, Foch had drawn Pétain's attention to the key importance to the Germans of the major rail junction at Soissons; by mid-July, this was supplying the troops of German Ninth and Seventh Armies all the way down to Chateau-Thierry at the apex of the recently formed Marne salient.[84] Foch waited until the last German offensive finally petered out in mid-July before launching the starting moves of his counter offensive, the first of which was to be at Soissons, with Tenth Army making the primary effort, supported by Sixth and Ninth Armies. While German attention was focused east of the Marne salient, around Reims and the mountains of Champagne where their most recent and final attack had focused its energy, its western flank was left vulnerable. Previous experience of poor French security had led the Germans to assume they would be alerted to any allied build-up in plenty of time to shift forces to that sector of the front, complacency that was to cost them dear.

Mangin submitted his initial plan to Fayolle on 20 June.[85] This was approved and the long process of assembling Tenth Army clandestinely in the Forêt de Retz (south-west of Soissons) began. It was reinforced with fresh French divisions and with the relatively newly formed 1st and 2nd Divisions of the American army (each the size of a French army corps). These divisions were very inexperienced, but their large size made them a potent force on the battlefield. The French put some of their best divisions in the front line, including a number with North-African troops: for example, 38 DI had in its ranks the most decorated regiment in the French army, the *régiment d'infanterie coloniale du Maroc*. Mangin's call in *La Force noire* had by now been heeded, due to necessity, and it is indicative of French manpower shortages that this colonial regiment, recruited from troops based in Morocco, now had one battalion of troops from Madagascar, while a third of the troops in the other two battalions were from Somalia.[86] Mangin carefully organized his reserve and made sure it was mobile; II *corps de cavalerie* (CC) was to act as the main army reserve and a motorized reserve was created to support it. Two mobile infantry *groupements* carried by lorries were formed, one a mix of French and American battalions.[87] Five mobile 75mm field-gun groups were also attached, although they were to begin the battle firing in the opening barrage, then limber-up and join the reserve.[88] II CC was to be supported by a dedicated fighter squadron.[89]

The terrain in front of Tenth Army was in most places good going, not being broken up by shell holes and having comparatively gentle slopes onto the numerous plateaus. However, there was a series of large ravines with steep, heavily vegetated slopes cutting across the battlefield. These were impassable to French tanks and provided covered positions for the defenders. Mangin said 'avoid the ravines' in his orders but this was simply not possible. In addition, the small hamlets and villages in the area were all built of stone and thus easily turned into very strong defensive positions. Facing Mangin was the German Ninth Army, comprising a mixed batch of ten infantry divisions, some rated first-class by French intelligence but most of mediocre quality.[90] The German troops on the Soissons front had not had enough time to fortify their positions in more than a rudimentary fashion and the trench lines were quite weak in comparison with the heavily fortified positions of previous years. Most of the German heavy artillery was in the process of being moved north for the planned 'Hagen' offensive and was therefore in short supply. However, the Germans were amply provided with machine guns and were expert at positioning them.

For the first time, the French were to launch a large-scale attack without an artillery preparation, using their tanks to make the initial penetration through the German lines. This approach had been under consideration since 1916 but caution had prevented its implementation.[91] However, the success of the British tank attack at Cambrai and experimental small-scale operations during the first half of 1918 increased confidence that a large-scale engagement using this methodology could be successful.[92] While clearing the Forêt de Retz, Mangin and Tenth Army had the opportunity to practise this combined-arms approach and launched a number of highly successful small-scale surprise attacks with tanks, without any artillery preparation.

The main thrust of Mangin's attack was to be made by XX and XXX CAs, the former with five divisions, the latter with four. The two corps were genuine combined-arms units; they had between them nearly 500 field-guns, 280 heavy artillery pieces and 100 aircraft.[93] As there would be no artillery preparation, each corps had a strong tank element attached, which was ordered to advance ahead of the infantry, to neutralize machine guns and any strong points not destroyed by artillery fire which would begin only at the moment of attack. The assault was scheduled for 04.35 so that the tanks could get into action in semi-darkness. In addition to the normal counter-battery fire and attempts to blind the known German artillery observation posts, it was decided to add smoke shells to the barrage, a lesson Mangin learned from 11 June.[94]

For the first time in a major offensive, the French maintained tight security, although that was a double-edged sword, as it meant that commanders at all levels were only given their orders at the last minute. Although the Germans were completely surprised by the attack, the security measures taken had serious ramifications for the organization of the offensive. Most divisional commanders only received their final orders to move into line less than ten hours before the attack. Units were forced to deploy at night with all the subsequent disorder that entailed: 1st Division arrived in XX CA's zone during the evening of 17 July to be told that they would be attacking at 04.35 the next morning, leaving next to no time for reconnaissance and preparation.[95]

When the attack began, visibility was limited to only 'a few yards' due to the morning mist and the smoke barrage.[96] This helped the French infantry and tanks overwhelm the forward German positions and it may well have been a major factor in the weakness and slow response of the German artillery to the attack. The German defensive barrage largely missed the forward allied battalions, although it did hit the supporting battalions in the forward divisions, in some cases causing significant casualties. The initial attack was a great success: for example, Foreign Legion battalions overran all the German positions in front of them in less than two hours, although at the cost of 420 casualties.[97] These losses have to be balanced against the success of the operation; the allied armies' 'tactical surprise was complete' according to one German war diary.[98] However, as the day wore on, allied units got separated from each other and the fighting became localized and smaller in scale. For example, shortly after leaving their front line, a company from 16th US infantry regiment got separated from the rest of its battalion because of the smoke and mist. As the mist lifted, the company was pinned down behind a small hill by heavy machine-gun fire, which required their rescue by a battery of French tanks.[99]

Despite Mangin's best efforts, the reserve that had been so carefully assembled barely got into action. At 07.15, Mangin ordered II CC to advance and prepare to support the infantry.[100] It took two hours for the cavalry to get moving and there was some confusion among the divisional columns moving in the forest, making progress very slow.[101] Around 11.00, Mangin ordered II CC's commander General Felix Robillot, who was at Mangin's forward command post, to advance the cavalry to the front line but Robillot raised a number of objections to these orders.[102] This meant that the cavalry was still nowhere near the front line by the early afternoon. The motorized infantry battalions had left their waiting position around 13.00, heading towards the front.[103] However, because of the congested roads they had made little progress by 17.00 and Mangin stood them down; it was clear that the cavalry would not get into action, except on foot.[104] The dismounted cavalry finally got into action an hour later, along with the divisional armoured cars.[105] The light-tank reserve contributed little to that day's fighting; at 07.25, the three light-tank battalions were released to XX and XXX CAs but no tanks got into action until early evening.[106] For example, one battalion, *3e bataillon de chars légers*, had considerable difficulty moving forward through the heavy traffic in the forest, competing as it was with XXX CA's rear elements. It was not until the early evening that its first company arrived at the front line, although it did not get into action.

Thus, the initial attack was very successful, but momentum waned as the day progressed. Pétain and Fayolle arrived at Tenth Army headquarters at around

18.00, with the former declaring that the operation had been a 'great success' but suggesting that 'it was necessary to stop the operation and consolidate the captured positions'.[107] Mangin was furious and argued that they were on the verge of 'decisive results', which would be jeopardized if the attack did not continue at the same pace. Pétain repeatedly told Mangin that he had no reinforcements to give him. The argument got so heated that Pétain walked out, without promising any reinforcements but not having made his orders for Tenth Army clear either. Mangin typically took advantage of Pétain's failure to issue him a firm order and told his chief of staff that as he had not been told to stop the operation he was going to continue the offensive, ordering a new attack to start the next morning. Although there were now fewer tanks and infantry to engage positions that had not been taken with more of both the previous day, Mangin believed that maintaining pressure on the retreating Germans was essential. Mangin slyly informed Foch, via his liaison officer, that he was continuing the offensive in line with what he understood to be Foch's orders, in a move intended to prevent Pétain from intervening.[108] This incident is a good example of Pétain's excessive caution, even Fayolle feeling that Pétain was 'very restrictive' on this occasion.[109] To his considerable annoyance, Mangin was forced to carry on the battle with troops of waning effectiveness and few reinforcements, which resulted in disorganized and uncoordinated attacks with diminishing results over the following days. However, the French threat to Soissons meant that the German army had to retreat from the Marne salient and thus the operation had been a significant success, although in Mangin's view not as successful as it might have been if he had been given more resources.

By 23 July, Tenth Army had come up against German defences that were well-prepared and equipped and from then on it would be a hard and slow fight. Mangin continued to push the Germans back slowly for the next two months, with the only notable action taking place on 20 August against German Ninth Army.[110] Mangin's characteristically well-organized assault penetrated the German line up to four kilometres in depth, Tenth Army capturing over 8,000 prisoners.[111] During the following three days, Mangin chased German Ninth Army up to the line of the Oise and Ailette rivers (from where their offensive had begun in May), which left the adjacent German armies in an exposed position and forced them to retreat.[112] As the Germans were being pushed back, French thoughts turned to the liberation of Lorraine. Mangin was chosen to lead this highly significant operation. However, the armistice was signed before this attack was needed.

\* \* \*

Mangin was a highly controversial figure in France after the war, largely because of his activities in the Rhineland, where he commanded an army of occupation. Foch and Mangin, among many other senior French officers, believed an independent Rhineland was essential for post-war French security but this was not acceptable to Clemenceau and the French government, nor to the other allied governments. However, Mangin quite inappropriately established close links with leading separatists in the Rhineland, offering support and encouragement to declare independence. A cabinet minister, Jules Jeanneney, was sent by Clemenceau to investigate the situation and his report was damning. Jeanneney suggested that Mangin's meetings with the separatists were 'more frequent than was advisable' and that this was to all intents and purposes 'a kind of collaboration'.[113] With no allied or French government support, the separatist movement was doomed from the outset and all that Mangin's support for it did was tarnish his reputation in French political circles.

Mangin's interference in the politics of the Rhineland not only infuriated the French government but also German nationalists across the country. The latter were further outraged that Mangin's occupation force included West Africans, calling it a 'black shame' on the motherland.[114] The German nationalists' deep enmity towards Mangin and his African troops was long lasting. Corporal Adolf Hitler, for one, would not forget this supposed outrage: when Paris was occupied in 1940, Hitler ordered German troops to blow up Mangin's statue in the Place Denis Cochin.[115]

These controversies were perhaps the main reason that Mangin was overlooked for honours and promotion after the war, a cause of considerable bitterness to his family. Just after Mangin's sudden premature death from a ruptured appendix at the age of 59 in 1925, Pétain arrived to offer sympathy to Madame Mangin, telling her that the government was to award her late husband the highly prestigious *Médaille militaire*. This was coldly refused, Antoinette Mangin telling Pétain that there had been plenty of time to award this to her husband while he was alive.[116]

Although much was written about Mangin during the inter-war period, little has been written about him since, other than a biography by one of his sons, and he is largely forgotten in modern France.[117] This is unjust as, from this brief survey of Mangin's wartime career, it can be seen that he was a highly intelligent and capable officer, who contributed a great deal to France's victory. Although it was never in doubt that Mangin was a fighter, it took time for his organizational talents to develop in a war where the latter was just as important a quality for a commander as the former. Leonard Smith criticizes Mangin's operations with 5 DI, but these took place in the early phase of the war when Mangin and the French army were learning how to fight modern warfare. It took time to find the right balance between the various combat arms, a problem that all Mangin's contemporaries also had to grapple with. Mangin had found this balance by 1918, perhaps even before, and the Battles of the Matz and the Soissonais are testaments to Mangin's talent as a combined-arms commander. His greatest triumph was commanding Tenth Army during the Second Battle of the Marne, where his skill ensured that the Germans were struck one of the hardest blows in the war. Although he had few friends in the higher echelons of the army, senior commanders simply could not ignore his technical abilities. Pétain said at Mangin's funeral that the 11 June 1918 operation was one of the 'greatest feats of arms in the war' and that Mangin may have been the only man capable of achieving it.[118] Perhaps his old colonial commander, Lyautey, summed-up Mangin best: 'There is no man more capable of getting you into a mess…and there's no one more capable of getting you out of it.'[119]

Chapter 11

# Maurice Gamelin: A Successful Apprenticeship

Martin Alexander

Maurice Gamelin is seldom name-checked in books or documentary films, except to exemplify failure when he commanded French land forces in 1940. Yet he was 'a good soldier' in the words of France's minister of national defence from 1936–40, Edouard Daladier (an infantry captain on the Somme in 1916 where Gamelin commanded a brigade of light infantry, the *chasseurs à pied*).[1] During the First World War Gamelin was a high-achiever both in staff roles and commanding a brigade and division in combat. Serving in staff appointments Gamelin displayed talent as an imaginative yet also pragmatic planner. He also became a respected and courageous leader, commanding from infantry battalion level up to acting corps command.[2] His career is an example of how relatively junior officers who demonstrated effective tactical and operational leadership could rise rapidly in wartime, while the reputations of more prominent generals of the early- and mid-war periods were plummeting.

\* \* \*

Born in Paris on 20 September 1872, of a family originating in Lorraine, Gamelin attended the *École Stanislas* on the Rue du Montparnasse, a few streets from the French war ministry where his father was a senior official. In 1891 Gamelin entered St Cyr, the French army's officer academy, passing out two years later at the top of his class of 449 cadets. Newly-commissioned, Lieutenant Gamelin joined France's colonial army and went first to French North Africa with the 3rd Algerian *tirailleur* regiment. Attached to the army's mapping department, he proved a talented military cartographer. Eager to enliven his charts of the sand sea, the djebels, wadis and ergs, Gamelin introduced coloured and three-dimensional designs. These were quickly adopted to replace previously 'austere and dismal' monochrome maps. In Algeria he developed an observer's eye for ground. His 'syntheses of the terrain became so remarkable that solutions to tactical problems often spoke for themselves.'[3] Back in Paris from 1899 to 1901,

Gamelin shone at the *École supérieur de guerre* (ESG), graduating second in his class. With an agile intellect, he was keen and quick to broaden his experiences and opted for his required secondment to a higher staff to join fifteenth military region based in Marseilles. There he examined the problems of defending the Alps and the coastline of Provence. On promotion to captain, Gamelin spent an obligatory two years from spring 1904 in the Vosges commanding part of 15$^e$ *bataillon de chasseurs alpins* (BCA) at Remiremont. The *chasseurs* or 'Blue Devils' (designated by their baggy blue berets) were elite light infantry, that specialized in tactical reconnaissance, raiding and surprise attack.

When in March 1906 General Joseph Joffre was appointed to command 6 DI he sought the view of General Ferdinand Foch on who might make a good adjutant. 'Gamelin', replied Foch, who had taught him at the ESG, unhesitatingly; 'he's one of the very best'.[4] The patronage of these future leaders would no doubt have accelerated Gamelin's career. Ange Pierre Cornu de la Fontaine, who had pipped him for first place at the ESG, was still a colonel in 1918, becoming an army chief of staff only in the last month of the war. So Gamelin was summoned to 6 DI staff (whose chief, and Joffre's future wartime chief of staff, Colonel Maurice Pellé, had also recommended him to Joffre).[5] Within the French higher command, Joffre himself was rapidly rising. 'Warrior, diplomat and administrator' as he was, Joffre saw similar qualities in Gamelin. Now a major, Gamelin remained with his new patron – in the dual sense of boss and supporter – when the latter in 1908 assumed command of the second military region based at Amiens and when, late in 1909, Joffre joined the *Conseil supérieur de la guerre* (CSG), the army's governing board, as inspector-general of rear areas.[6] Gamelin's skill was in interpreting Joffre's views to other senior generals and to the political milieu at the war ministry. Promotion above the rank of major would, however, require him to have commanded a battalion. He therefore left Joffre in September 1911 for two professionally fulfilling years at Annecy, leading 11$^e$ BCA. Returning to Paris in December 1913, Gamelin spent six months in the operations branch (3$^e$ Bureau) of the general staff. This brought him 'well up-to-date with the big issues'. In March 1914 he became chief of staff to Joffre in the latter's role as vice-president of the CSG, with Major (later General) Georges-René Alexandre fulfilling the same function for Joffre in the latter's capacity as chief of the general staff.[7]

Despite their difference in rank, Gamelin and Joffre constituted a true partnership with Gamelin a trusted confidant and counsellor. In 1911 Foch, now commanding the ESG, had already told Gamelin that 'Joffre listens to you and you'll be involved with the big questions'.[8] Joffre described Gamelin, Alexandre and four other trusted aides – none yet more senior than major – as 'my immediate collaborators'. These were officers of whom Joffre said, 'I kept a long time at my side and who left me only for the period necessary to accomplish their service with troops. All of them performed…magnificently.'[9] In wartime Gamelin would serve as Joffre's conduit to the operations bureau at *Grand quartier général* (GQG), and support him during the difficult days of the retreat from the frontiers and Marne counter attack.[10]

\* \* \*

As the war intensified, Gamelin's career flourished. In the field he would command a brigade and later a division and, briefly in 1918, lead an ad hoc corps. These important levels in the army's command hierarchy – army corps, divisions, brigades and battalions – remain comparatively unstudied by historians. Yet operational command has its own significance and singularities, and its challenges merit attention. So do the officers who, especially in 1918, succeeded in directing the operational war not from chateaus behind the lines but from quite close – often dangerously close – to the fighting's sharp end.[11] Gamelin was not safely in the rear. His leadership in the field demanded that he repeatedly risk his life and show courage and steadiness to his subordinates. Three of Joffre's six staff officers of September 1914 would be killed by the summer of 1918. Gamelin and his colleagues had to lead from where they could, often under fire, assess situations fast, issue orders clearly, and act with purpose.

Gamelin also needed, and rapidly acquired, skills in civil–military politics. It was his blending of frontline command with military politics that assured Gamelin his high reputation after 1918. As another wartime officer, Lieutenant-Colonel François de La Rocque, wrote in 1934:

> beyond a certain level, aptitude for command, a function of personal responsibility, and aptitude for General Staff duties, a function of technical capacity without personal responsibility, correspond to temperaments that are absolutely distinct. Only men possessing both […] can be great leaders.[12]

Gamelin exemplifies the many officers who rose rapidly after the September 1914 clear-out by Joffre of over 100 generals who failed in the Battle of the Frontiers.[13] Officers escaping dismissal, death or severe injury were promoted in an army fast revising its tactics, rejuvenating its leadership and expanding its firepower, especially its heavy artillery.[14]

At GQG Gamelin was permitted wide authority by delegation. As Lieutenant Colonel de La Rocque explained it: 'Whatever the readiness to comply and goodwill among his executive officers, no matter how distinguished the chief he can only command, through the good days and bad, if he possesses a "right arm".'[15] After the stalemating of the German invasion in late 1914, directives from Joffre as French commander-in-chief appeared with Gamelin's signature on them. This happened with such regularity that Gamelin effectively became Joffre's guide, critic and conscience – in the words of R.G. Nobécourt, his 'helmeted philosopher'.[16] Gamelin was credited with the strategic masterstroke of switching fresh divisions by rail and road in early September 1914 from the Vosges and Lorraine to the Marne.[17] There the German advance was halted and France remained in the war.[18]

On 1 November 1914 Gamelin was promoted lieutenant colonel and went to the front to command 2ᵉ *brigade de chasseurs* (BC), which in January 1915 became part of the newly-formed 47 *division d'infanterie* (DI). Among its units were his old battalion, 11ᵉ BCA, which had acquitted itself well on the frontiers and been commended by General Ernest Jacques Barbot, commander of the parent 77 DI, and Colonel Germain Passaga (2 BC's previous commander). Now, Gamelin benefited from an additional patron, 47 DI's commander from March 1915, General Gaston d'Armau de Pouydraguin.[19] This phase of the war saw Gamelin's *chasseurs* fight on the hartmannswillerkopf and Lingekopf in the Vosges, engaged in bitter battles among dense hillside forests for control of these commanding peaks.[20]

By early autumn 1915 Gamelin had re-joined Joffre's staff at GQG, helping to prepare the Artois and Champagne offensives that September.[21] He also took a hand in developing prototype French armoured fighting vehicles. The idea for these, the 'land battleships' or *cuirassées terrestres*, was brought to Joffre in 1915 by an artillery officer, Colonel (later General) Jean-Baptiste Estienne. Now the head of the operations bureau at *Groupe d'armées de l'est*, Gamelin had to assess Estienne's proposals. By January 1916 he was 'satisfied' that land battleships represented 'a viable project.'[22] Gamelin would much later, between 1936 and 1940, be a strong supporter of developing tank divisions in the French army.

Gamelin was at Joffre's side at GQG in early 1916 when the Germans on 21 February began their assault on Verdun. Despite the importuning of the local commander, General Philippe Pétain, Joffre remained parsimonious in reinforcing the sector's defenders. He decided some French divisions would not be chewed up in the Verdun meat grinder. With a French counter offensive anticipated, assault divisions such as 47 DI, which was attached to XX *corps d'armée* (CA) – nicknamed the 'Iron' Corps – for the first stage of the Somme offensive, were kept back. In Allain Bernède's words, the supreme headquarters, with Gamelin on its operations staff, 'refused to let itself be hypnotized by Verdun'.[23]

Indeed, while at GQG at this time Gamelin drafted the tactical instructions that the French would apply in their sector on the Somme where Sixth Army under General Marie-Émile Fayolle was deployed astride the river. Jonathan Krause has suggested that the French army had fairly rapidly (if unofficially) reverted to the 1897 regulations in autumn 1914 and begun issuing new regulations for trench warfare in early 1915. French combat doctrine now formally discarded the misguided principles of the 1913 regulations.[24] Husbanding the infantry was now prioritized. On 8 January 1916 a new 'Instruction on Offensive Fighting by Small Units' had been issued. That built on the French army's 27 December 1915 'Note on the Lessons from the Battles of September [1915]'. These pamphlets altered how infantry combat was conceived: 'The struggle is not with men against matériel... The infantry rapidly suffers attrition... avoid, therefore, as much at the outset as during the course of an offensive action, giving the fighting line too much density.' Expressions such as 'capture at all costs' were axed from the revised French instructions. Combined-arms warfare was emphasized. The other arms were assigned clear infantry support roles: an 'attack must therefore never be launched without it being preceded and accompanied by effective action from the artillery'.[25] This document was followed by the 'Instruction of 26 January 1916 on the Offensive by Large Units' that superseded a note from 16 April 1915. In Michel Goya's words, the goal 'remained...to drive a breach through the adversary's organized defences, but henceforth by...a lengthy operation made up of a series of methodical attacks against the enemy's successive positions'.[26] Updating and innovating however, was not a once-and-for-all event; rather, it was a process of continual improvements and the creation of a virtuous, repetitive cycle of ideas, practice, reflection and doctrinal codification.

Using these newly refined methods, the French assaults in July and August 1916 in the Somme valley achieved significant successes. These contrasted with British setbacks further north. Success can be ascribed in part to improved French company and platoon tactics, but also partly to increased and more efficient artillery support, and closer all-arms cooperation.[27] New weapons had entered French service. Mobile light-machine guns (*Fusils-mitrailleurs* – FMs), rifle-grenade launchers, and portable Hotchkiss 37mm cannon sufficiently light to be worked forward into no man's land to maintain close fire-support even if the infantry advanced rapidly beyond the range of artillery support would be available to Gamelin's *chasseurs*. Thanks to such resources, Gamelin's brigade, and others, could take on and conquer unsilenced enemy strongpoints on their sector with their own firepower. French formations had most evidently improved their methods for offensive war.[28]

Newly promoted colonel, Gamelin returned to command his brigade in 47 DI on the Somme. This was an important resumption of frontline command for Gamelin. His battalions deployed in the marshy Somme valley just south of the British forces (153 DI immediately adjacent the British, and then 47 DI on 153 DI's right). Once more Gamelin demonstrated his talents as a planner and organizer while also leading his soldiers under fire. This combining of staff and frontline roles stood him in good stead.

On the Somme Gamelin's brigade went into action in the second or attritional phase of the offensive.[29] On 20 July 1916, in the vanguard of General Maurice Balfourier's XX CA, 47 DI assaulted the German intermediate position. Initially 'stopped short by machine-gun fire', the attack resumed with success thanks to the infantry's tactical agility, air support and combined-arms work.[30] Gamelin's brigade assaulted the Hem Plateau on the right. The attack was effective now that heavier artillery support had modified the attack–defence equation. General de Pouydraguin insisted that the assaulting French infantry benefit from the strongest available barrages, with heavy 155mm guns supplementing the vast numbers of 75mm field guns. A relentless storm of shellfire struck the German lines.[31]

By this point in the war Gamelin was showing himself to be a dynamic field commander. He was also a comparatively young one – he was 44 years old on 20 September 1916. He was always smartly uniformed, cutting a dapper look in contemporary photographs.[32] He insisted his men be impeccably turned out, convinced that smart appearance generated pride in one's unit, aiding efficiency and morale. In this he was somewhat unusual. Many French commanders showed little concern for what the British army calls 'spit and polish'. One American Red Cross volunteer, Maud Sutton-Pickard, remarked that 'French generals seldom look smart' and appeared 'awfully old; probably relics of 1870'.[33] Yet she would have exempted Gamelin and his troops. So did his army commander, Fayolle, who 'had not seen "a better spectacle since the start of the war"'.[34] Gamelin, in short, led by good example. In late July 1916 his men supported attacks on German entrenchments south of the ruined village of Maurepas. The 47 DI was then rotated back from the front, its casualties unremarkable in relation to its success and with no compromise to the formation's fighting effectiveness. With replacements incorporated, 47 DI returned to the front on 10 August. The next day the stirring conduct of the *chasseurs* pleased Fayolle, who recorded in his diary 'the taking of Wood No. 2 North by Gamelin…success all along the front; 165 prisoners taken'.[35]

Other contemporaries commented on the qualities of successful leadership at Gamelin's operational level in the chain of command. Major-General John Seely, who commanded the Canadian cavalry brigade in 1916, wrote, 'Foolish people think… that in modern war a commander cannot impress himself upon his men by personal contact. This is a complete delusion. …Indeed, not only is it easier, but it is more essential…because the ordeal is more prolonged.'[36] The *chasseurs*' Captain Belmont had put it thus: 'An army officer, a leader of men, must above all be a character: his men must feel, almost instinctively, that he is someone to be respected.'[37] With operations still mired in stalemate in late 1916, it was being understood that successes depended on good methods, training and coordination of all available weapons systems.[38] Gamelin clearly appreciated this. His direct superior, General de Pouydraguin, described him as a 'methodical organizer' with a 'lucid mind and sound judgement... a noteworthy tactician, the perfect leader of infantry'.[39]

By the end of his tour on the Somme, Gamelin was an experienced front-line commander adept at planning, drafting instructions and staff work according to the most up-to-date doctrinal principles. Gamelin and his brigade epitomized the revival of the French army's reputation secured by Fayolle on the Somme.[40] Even so, learning remained a step-by-step process – and a costly one. But lessons were identified and quickly incorporated into practice. A new instruction published on 27 September 1916 altered French infantry platoon organization and tactics. This was translated within three months by British General Headquarters, whose own changes in platoon structure and training followed in early 1917 (British adaptations were probably encouraged after some key and talented British officers visited the French at Verdun in January 1917).[41] Nor was it just their British allies who paid respects to the improved French tactics. The enemy also took notice, one German writing that:

> Just like us, the French deploy in combat with the smallest possible sub-units. The British attack in masses, and are willing to accept the severe losses among their inexperienced new regiments.... The French soldiers are better trained and more skilful than the British. When their leaders are lost the troops show more independence, for they have a better grasp of the tactical situation.[42]

After his star shone on the Somme, Gamelin was promoted on 11 December 1916 to command of the newly-raised 168 DI in XX CA as an acting brigadier-general. But the elevation was short-lived. After a week he was instructed to return to GQG, a move stillborn when Joffre was moved on 17 December. After a short period assisting Joffre during his relocation to Paris, from January to April 1917 Gamelin became chief of staff to the *Groupe d'armées de réserve* under General Alfred Micheler, mustered to exploit the expected success of the Nivelle offensive. In the general rearrangement of commands following Nivelle's failure Gamelin escaped censure and was given command of 9 DI holding the Juvincourt-et-Damary sector on the Aisne on 7 May 1917 after Micheler's army group was dissolved.[43] Comprising the 4$^e$, 82$^e$ and 313$^e$ *régiments d'infanterie* (RI) and refitted in the late winter of 1916–17, 9 DI had prepared under command of General Joseph Gadel for its part in the Nivelle offensive on the Chemin des Dames. As that operation began, it successfully assaulted Juvincourt and the German second line defended by 9$^{th}$ Bavarian Reserve Division on 16 April. But the following day 9 DI failed – though acting in concert with 10 DI – to capture the hamlets of Musette and Ville-au-Bois and the division was withdrawn to Ventelay on 19 April for rest and to integrate replacements.

The 9 DI's troops now became downcast. The official history of the 66ᵉ *bataillon de chasseurs à pied* (BCP) records drily that it had to organize new positions 'in difficult conditions without shelter, under intensive shelling and harassing fire from machine guns'.[44] Morale and discipline were everywhere fragile as the failure under Nivelle sparked French army 'mutinies' in spring 1917 from which 9 DI, now under Gamelin, was not immune. Between 28 May and 3 June incidents occurred in 82ᵉ RI, 313ᵉ RI and 66ᵉ BCP (in the last of these cases triggered by the trauma, five days before the 16 April assault, of the commanding officer, the adjutant and all three company commanders being wounded while conducting a reconnaissance).[45] A protest by infantry of 313ᵉ RI at Brouillet on 28 May 1917 took the form of raucous cries of 'à *bas la guerre*' ('down with the war'). At Arcis-le-Ponsart a soldier struck Colonel Albert Sohier, 9 DI's divisional infantry commander. Behind the front at a concert party, a female artiste singing the *Marseillaise* 'was drowned out by soldiers breaking into the Internationale.[46]

Gamelin restored order by deploying a firm fist in a velvet glove. A small number of courts-martial were convened. One man was executed on 13 June, with three others sentenced to hard labour. More soldiers were shaken than insubordinate.[47] As a whole, wrote Captain René Arnaud, French troops by 1917 saw through pomposity and were 'almost infallible' when passing judgements about their officers.[48] This worked to Gamelin's advantage because he had commanded men under fire and run great personal risks. Gamelin's pragmatic and humane acts of clemency mitigated the necessity for field punishments. This was good man-management, restoring order and fighting effectiveness. Nobody ever accused Gamelin of acting the martinet. Through experience and courage he had earned his men's respect. He also subscribed to instructions from General Philippe Pétain, who had now succeeded Nivelle as commander-in-chief. In the words of Robert Doughty: 'Knowing the importance of having soldiers see and trust their commanders…[Pétain] prescribed weekly meetings on the grounds that "by explaining, one achieves understanding and…cohesion." He also directed general officers and members of their staffs to "show themselves frequently in the trenches".[49]

From 16 June, and during July and August 1917, 9 DI remained to the rear, resting and refitting at Bourgogne camp. One occasion of welcome relief from the horrors of the front-line was a ceremony in November 1917 to confer a divisional commendation on 66ᵉ BCP.[50] 'The initiative for this citation was due to Gamelin – a former *chasseur* – who, after having commanded with glory a battalion sub-group in the Vosges at Hilsenfirst, and on the Somme before Bouchavesnes, had since June 1917 assumed command of 9th Division.'[51] From mid-January 1918 Gamelin's men were ordered to Concevreux where they formed working parties for the engineers, before reforming as a fighting formation at Estrées-St-Denis in early February.[52] As regards the coming spring fighting, Gamelin's stalwartness was evident in his telling British officers who came to ask about his dispositions on 16 March: 'I'll give up no trench before 10 o'clock at night. I'll then counter attack both enemy flanks simultaneously while we re-establish more solidly to the rear. From there, I'll not shift.'[53]

On 21 March 1918 the allied lines were struck by 'Operation Michael', the first phase of Ludendorff's spring offensive. The Battle of Noyon in late-March 1918 is a case study of the skills, sangfroid and authority now possessed by Gamelin in directing successful defensive actions. As British lines south of the Somme gave way, 9 DI was deployed to General Georges Humbert's Third Army to meet the German onrush – its infantry boarded lorries on 22 March ready to travel to the Guiscard sector south of Ham, squarely in the path of the onrushing German right wing. Horsed elements of 9 DI set out forthwith via Conchy-les-Pots, Gamelin reporting at 22.00 to Pellé's V CA headquarters in Noyon town hall. His orders were to relieve a crumbling British division during the night of 23–24 March (perhaps the British whom the French author and war chronicler Henry Bordeaux would later see 'huddled round little camp-fires before Clermont, their part-lit faces singing sad songs at half-throttle'); and if that were impossible, to secure high ground rising up from Senlis Wood.[54]

When Gamelin's cavalry squadron and horse-drawn field artillery reached Conchy they were stopped by army traffic marshals who had orders to clear the roads for motor transport. This forced the mobile elements to halt until dawn on 23 March and prevented 9 DI's gun-teams deploying before nightfall.[55] Despite lacking artillery support, a battalion of 82e RI from Gamelin's division combined with another from 329e RI to repel a German assault at twilight.

The next day, 24 March, the pressure mounted when a *cuirassier* regiment, on foot and out of ammunition, fell back into Gamelin's positions. Immediately advancing 82e RI into the breach, Gamelin warned its colonel that 'any rearward movement might be read as a signal for a general withdrawal'.[56] When the reinforcing 89e RI from 10 DI arrived at dusk on 24 March, Gamelin ordered its leading battalion to act aggressively in the spirit of Pétain's principles of 'active' or 'energetic' defence established between November 1917 and February 1918 – holding outpost and front lines lightly with a defence in depth, with troops dispersed to reduce casualties to artillery preparations but always seeking to disrupt and deflect the force of intended enemy blows by frequent raiding to capture German prisoners and gather situational and enemy order-of-battle intelligence. The troops should be 'maintained in a posture of suspense', ordered Pétain, 'conducting rewarding localized attacks that would improve the alignment of our frontline, hit the enemy at sensitive points (taking prisoners) or worsen his topographical situation, and assist subsequent operations.' The key principle in Pétain's instruction was that 'prepared well, these attacks are liable to retain us the operational initiative without excessive losses...whereas the enemy, the moment he senses we are merely passive, will strike comparable blows at us. *Taking blows will ultimately cost us dearer than dealing them out.*'[57]

Harnessing these principles, Gamelin's infantry put up a remarkable defence even though on 25 March 1918 fog cloaked the battlefield till noon and silenced the divisional artillery which could neither see nor range any targets. Aircraft could not take off and communications at ground level were hampered because the telephone network remained in the hands of British operators till midday. As night fell 9 DI's artillery and infantry had almost exhausted their ammunition; but Gamelin managed to replenish them several times 'via a tireless shuttle of the horsed transport, some caissons going right up onto the firing line to resupply the soldiers'.[58]

In desperate fighting the regiments of 10 DI and 9 DI banded together as the battle ebbed and flowed around Drisolles. When German pressure on 10 DI forced it back onto Sermaize – placing enemy spearheads at Beaurains, 2km north-west of Noyon – Gamelin was assigned to lead an *ad hoc* army corps comprising 9 DI, 35 DI and two attached infantry regiments along with unusually large quantities of artillery.[59] In many military careers there comes a 'make or break' moment: this was Gamelin's. Learning of the situation at Beaurains, Gamelin realized time was pressing and that he must 'try to take control of the direction of events' in what was, as he said with almost English understatement, 'a tricky situation'.[60] Gamelin ordered 9's DI artillery to execute a night movement and bring their guns back into action at daybreak to support the frontline from Porquéricourt to Noyon. With General Henri Mareschal, commanding 35 DI, Gamelin established a joint headquarters south-west of Noyon. As Pierre Le Goyet relates, 'From 26 March, having been reinforced and with his frontage back to a normal length (6 kilometres), Gamelin accepted battle and managed to seal the breach.'[61] Uncompromising in a crisis, Gamelin reprimanded an artillery colonel for withdrawing his guns as the French position wobbled instead of supporting the hard-pressed infantry to the last.[62] From 26 to 31 March, Gamelin demonstrated a potent but controlled energy that gave his *ad hoc* corps the firm leadership that ensured it fought unflinchingly along a 16-kilometre front though attacked by four German divisions.

Gamelin acknowledged 'the magnificent conduct of the three regiments of 9 DI' in the Battle of Noyon, one being the last unit permitted to fall back onto better positions and fresh troops. Not merely careful with his men's lives, Gamelin displayed tactical deftness in these operations. His 9 DI's intervention as the British Fifth Army's right wing disintegrated helped stabilize a situation near to breaking-point. Consequently the German advance in the Oise valley was slowed, gaining time for a new army under General Marie-Eugène Debeney to be deployed to link the left of the French front anchored by Gamelin's defensive efforts with the receding British right wing in front of Amiens.[63] In summing up Gamelin's role at Noyon, in what he called a 'delicate mission', Pierre Le Goyet writes: 'With reduced resources, on a frontage of 10km to 18km, without prepared defensive positions, faced by a numerically very superior enemy, Gamelin could do no more than conduct a fighting withdrawal but, thanks to the dispositions he made, he slowed the advance of the enemy and through his artillery inflicted severe losses.'[64] This fighting withdrawal had entailed 'a hasty deployment on a chaotic battlefield' as British troops slipped past to the rear in headlong retreat. Throughout the crisis Gamelin remained master of the hour and the situation. He had staged 'an organized withdrawal' and then directed successful resistance.[65] One eyewitness on 30 March 1918 wrote 'that in my mind's eye I'll always see Gamelin that day, returning from the fight still smoking with satisfied ardour, with the right to show some pride after these eight days of struggle'.[66] Indeed his actions at Noyon had cemented his reputation. Bordeaux, who encountered him briefly on the same day, noted Gamelin 'is the youngest general in the army, forty-five or forty-six years old, very ambitious, very conceited, but plays the game well. In a helmet he is manly, but he seems rather common. Justly, he sings the praises of his division…which has defended step by step the ground in front of Noyon.'[67] For his part, Gamelin credited success to the commanders of the infantry of 9 DI and 35 DI, Colonels Albert Sohier and Fernand Moreigne: a 'major part of our results' were, he declared, owed 'to their initiative and energy'.[68] Otherwise put, faced by the testing points of spring 1918, Gamelin appears to exemplify Lieutenant Colonel de La Roque's later emphasis on command requiring that 'a consistent and reciprocal relationship' be fashioned 'between leaders and executives'. Command to be successful was 'a business of intelligence, feel and drive [élan], but also a business of organization and experience'.[69]

As June turned into July 1918, the French forces rallied all along the front. The last German assault was repelled and counter-attacked in the Second Battle of the Marne, in which, once again, Gamelin and 9 DI played a full part. In the Champagne sector east of Reims attacking German forces were drawn into a prepared defence in depth and, advancing beyond the range of their own field guns, 'came up against the bulk of the French forces entrenched in the main battle zone' and were pulverized by the 'dreadfully accurate French artillery'.[70] Gamelin's division was committed west of Reims to the follow-up counter offensive by General Henri Berthelot's Fifth Army. Gamelin, once again directing an ad hoc corps, was gratified that his own 9 DI had a leading role as it attacked alongside the British 51ˢᵗ (Highland) Division on the left bank of the River Ardre.[71] Gamelin's division used the improved tactics and technologies introduced since 1917 to devastating effect. Coordinated layered and creeping artillery barrages were now directed by airborne observers linked by wireless to the gun lines.[72] Herbert Sulzbach, with the German artillery on the receiving end, noted that from August 1918 the French *division aérienne* or 'aerial division' with 600 massed aircraft gave close air-to-ground support to every French assault.[73] The French army had evolved into a formidable instrument of attack, capable of tactically sophisticated and dynamic operations at short notice.

Gamelin's 9 DI took a full part in pushing the Germans back in the 'Hundred Days' offensive of 8 August to 11 November 1918. The division's 4ᵉ RI was re-organized in mid-September under Lieutenant-Colonel Lachèvre, and spearheaded the assault across the river Vesle. Two battalions approached the water's edge after dark, then attacked at 05.30 on 30 September. Many men reached the enemy' side of the river across a narrow gangway constructed by French army engineers. Some crossed on a rickety ladder purloined from a nearby farm; others simply swam over to join the fight. An NCO, Sergeant Fays, won the Medaille Militaire for single-handedly taking 54 Germans prisoner, and by nightfall all the regiment's objectives had been secured. On 1 October Bouvancourt village was taken and two days later the reconnaissance elements of 4ᵉ RI jumped the Aisne canal, repulsing counter attacks as they went. In just four days 4ᵉ RI progressed 14 miles, in places 'crossing completely open ground at a run'. They liberated two villages and captured 254 German troops with three officers and 25 NCOs, seizing 20 machine guns, two 74mm mortars and an intact wireless station.[74]

The successful actions of 9 DI in the war's latter stages – in defence around Noyon as well as on the attack during the Hundred Days – showed that Gamelin had forged a resilient and capable instrument of war.[75] His soldiers had regained their confidence and enjoyed support from the lavish amount of new technologies available to allied formations.[76] Improved battlefield methods paid dividends. Impregnable signals security preserved surprise; creeping artillery barrages let the infantry move with a curtain of steel before them; near-continuous aerial observation and air-to-ground attacks directed by wireless pulverized German strongpoints.[77] Nor were Gamelin and his colleagues now averse to employing their enemy's methods. 'The French have imitated us in everything', noted Sulzbach on 19 July 1918, 'a short surprise barrage on a broad front, and attacking in massive numbers …a thing we can't compete with any more.'[78]

Like other formations, Gamelin's 9 DI alternated during the Hundred Days between violent action at the sharp end of the French advance to victory and periods to the rear to regroup and integrate replacements for their losses. In August 1918 82e RI, out of the front line, helped to repair war damaged buildings in the villages behind the front and tackled agricultural tasks, 'in particular harvesting a lot of the summer wheat'.[79] On 25 August it was soldiers from 82e RI who marched past French premier Georges Clemenceau when he visited the armies. Nicknamed 'the Tiger', Clemenceau blended Republican patriotism and earthiness. His manner was much appreciated by French troops. As the parade swung past the saluting dais, the men let rip a thunderous cheer. Grinning broadly, Clemenceau turned to Gamelin and asked if the show of enthusiasm was authentic. 'Oh, it's for real', replied Gamelin; 'You were the first to shout *"merde"* at the Boches!' 'That's true', quipped Clemenceau: 'I've always liked shitting on people. I started with my wet-nurse!'[80]

Battlefield success always carried a price in lives; but that was the 'fatal law of this man-eating war', for the Western Front was always about attrition.[81] Yet the field generals of France were, by the summer and autumn of 1918, competent and experienced, and had gained the tools and given their men the techniques to succeed.[82] The war diary of 82e RI notes that in the first ten days of August 'training and trials to practise infantry action in combination with assault tanks was carried out, the army commander Berthelot being present for one of the exercises'.[83] The achievements in 1918 were fashioned by adaptable and tactically innovative commanders. They were also the fruits of the courage and resilience shown by the French poilus, ably led by men with similar experience and know-how to Gamelin's. A balanced assessment of the performance by French field commanders must weigh the progress and improved battlefield success of the latter part of the conflict against the errors and bloodbaths of its earlier years.

\* \* \*

Gamelin's post-war career, in which he rose to the very top of the army, can only be summarized briefly here. After November 1918, Gamelin's career took off thanks to his successful wartime commands. From 1919–24 he led the French military mission in Brazil and in 1925–6 he served as high commissioner in Syria, a territory administered by France after the collapse of the Ottoman Empire. Between 1931 and 1935 Gamelin was chief of the French army general staff and then the first chief of defence staff from 1938 to 1940.[84] This stellar career would end ignominiously. He would command French land forces in their disastrous encounter with the Germany army in May 1940, and be removed halfway through the battle as politicians sought a scapegoat for wider failings in France's inter-war military preparations. That is an oft told story which cannot be reprised here.

Emerging field commanders such as Gamelin were crucial to the 'strong resurgence' of the French land forces during 1918 under the senior direction of Foch, Pétain and Fayolle. These combat generals, let us call them, possessed 'extraordinary powers of persuasion' as Captain Charles Delvert of 101ᵉ RI put it after an inspirational briefing from Gouraud (another wartime star who rose from brigade to army command). These officers energetically enacted Foch's instruction of 27 October 1918 for the final plan of operations: 'From now on, there must be no more setting of objectives. Throw the troops in a direction… and get going!'[85] They managed to ensure that 'the fatigues of the campaign were forgotten'.[86] The revived confidence in the French army's ranks ensured that its soldiers motivated by combative generals such as Gamelin succeeded in 'turning the tide once and for all'.[87] Gamelin surely echoed General Edmond Buat's sentiment that 'victory is like luck; it only deserts those who have stopped believing in it.'[88]

## Chapter 12

# Jean-Baptiste Estienne: Father of the Tanks

## Tim Gale

General Jean-Baptiste Estienne was known in France as the 'father of the tanks' for his work in setting-up and running the French armoured force, the *Artillerie spéciale* (the AS), during the First World War. Today he is largely a forgotten figure, which is surprising considering that his contribution to the development of the tank in general was rather more significant than many better-known figures of the period connected with armour, for example J. F. C. Fuller in Great Britain. No single man made such a major contribution to the armoured forces of his country as did Estienne, a contribution that required both political as well as military acuity. Maxime Weygand, chief of staff to allied generalissimo Ferdinand Foch, said that Estienne 'was a scholar combined with a leader of exemplary military virtues; he loved his men, was careful with their lives and was inspired by the highest [military] ideals'.[1] He would need all these qualities to see his vision of a French tank force become reality. There are two major strands in Estienne's wartime career: his development of tank tactics and his struggle with the political and military bureaucracy over tank design, manufacture and the organization of the AS.

\* \* \*

Estienne entered the French army in 1884 as an artillery lieutenant, following a year at the artillery school at Fontainebleau. By 1891, he was a captain and was supervising the military factory at Bourges, giving him direct experience of military–industrial liaison and production processes. He invented numerous pieces of military equipment, including a rifle-harness to enable soldiers to fire while advancing, although this was not adopted for service. His reputation as an innovator led to him being appointed to organize the French army's aviation in 1909, which involved setting up from scratch a laboratory studying aerodynamics, a construction centre and a pilot school at Maison Blanche, part of the artillery service park at Vincennes. Estienne found it difficult to interest the war ministry in his innovative plans for artillery observation from the air and he was moved in 1911 to the air squadron at Lyon. He was subsequently attached to the engineer service and then appointed to command the artillery park at Nice, being promoted to colonel in 1913. He was recalled to Vincennes in 1914 to take charge of military aviation where he constructed two observation aircraft with detachable wings. This innovation meant that they could accompany an artillery regiment's road column, being carried on a trailer pulled by a lorry.[2] At the artillery base at Chalons extensive experimentation in air observation for artillery was made with these two aircraft and their pilots, which would prove useful only months later after the war had begun.[3] Thus, his pre-war service had given him direct experience of both technical and organizational innovation as well as service with all the major branches of the army. His experience organizing French military aviation also alerted him to the changing fortunes involved in the development of new ways of war.

Estienne had also been a keen student of recent wars. A close friend from the military aviation service, Lieutenant Bellenger, served as a French observer during the Balkans Wars, reporting to Estienne on the effectiveness of field fortifications and machine-gun fire.[4] This led Estienne to believe that field-craft and long-range infantry weapons were making direct artillery fire increasingly less effective. In February 1912, he wrote that although the technology of cannons had considerably improved, this had not been matched by their killing power on the battlefield.[5] He believed this to have been the lesson of the Russo-Japanese War, and the wars in the Balkans further confirmed this opinion. He believed the solution to increasing the artillery's effectiveness was indirect artillery fire based on observation from the air: 'the aeroplane is the eye of the artillery', he said before the war.[6] He subsequently published a report explaining how a section of observation aircraft could be organized within each artillery regiment and the advantages that this would bring to the artillery, although this was largely ignored by the military authorities.[7] Another aspect of the Balkan Wars that had intrigued Estienne was the defensive strength of field fortifications, and how to overcome them without entering into full-scale siege warfare. He told one of his officers in August 1914 that he thought an agricultural tractor could be modified to carry a 120mm gun across broken terrain, his thinking at this point being along the lines of what would now be called a self-propelled gun rather than a tank.[8] Further development of this idea was forced to wait, as Estienne was mobilized days after this discussion.

Estienne arrived to command 22ᵉ *régiment d'artillerie de campagne* on 3 August 1914; this was a field-artillery regiment that acted as the divisional artillery for 6 *division d'infanterie* (DI), soon to be commanded by General Phillipe Pétain, part of III *corps d'armée* (CA). He was accompanied by the two Blériot aircraft and three pilots that he had worked with at Chalons, something which he had organized on his own initiative.[9] Two aspects of the

August fighting demonstrate Estienne's capabilities in both leadership and organization. Estienne, having written on the power of leadership before the war, was 'an inspiration' to his regiment during the difficult retreat of 1914.[10] When adjacent 5 DI's command structure collapsed completely on 23 August as the division's commander and his staff had fled, Estienne intervened to help its regimental commanders organize themselves.[11]

Always an innovator, Estienne quickly saw that the challenges of the industrialized, firepower dominated battlefield would need radical solutions. He told several officers of his artillery regiment on 25 August that 'victory will go in this war to that of the two belligerents that is the first to place a 75 cannon on a vehicle that can move on all terrain'.[12] On 6 and 7 September 1914, the fire of the divisional artillery was successfully concentrated by Estienne on a German fortified artillery position, identified by air reconnaissance, on the edge of Montceau-les-Provins, allowing the infantry to occupy the area.[13]

Estienne's experience on the Western Front during 1915 could only accentuate his belief in the need for a means to push infantry quickly through heavily defended areas, as he had concluded from his studies of the Balkan Wars. His solution was the idea of an armoured vehicle (*cuirassé terrestre* – land battleship, a term also used for early British tank concepts) and he wrote to the commander-in-chief General Joseph Joffre suggesting this idea.[14] Estienne's first two letters disappeared into the bureaucratic labyrinth at *Grand quartier général* (GQG) and he only elicited a response after writing to Joffre directly.[15] Unlike his staff, Joffre immediately recognized this was an idea worth pursuing and Estienne was summoned to GQG eleven days later.[16]

Estienne's initial proposals were to use massed armoured vehicles in a surprise attack without a preparatory artillery barrage, a very radical idea at a point in the war where lengthy artillery preparations were seen as essential. The land battleships were to advance in front of the infantry, clearing trenches as they advanced.[17] These vehicles would be able to traverse obstacles on the battlefield, cross trenches up to two metres wide and survive enemy fire. Thus at the beginning the tanks were conceived primarily as mobile-gun platforms to assist the infantry. He also made a claim that was bound to attract attention in the always cost-conscious French army; would not 30,000 tonnes of tanks be more useful than 30,000 tonnes of shells, he asked?[18] Presciently, he warned Joffre against setting up a committee to look at his proposal, as this would be incompatible, he said, with producing the first vehicle both quickly and in total secrecy.[19] GQG quickly came to the conclusion that Estienne's proposal was viable and valuable but the project soon ran into difficulties with other elements of the French military–political bureaucracy.[20]

There was opposition in particular from the influential General Léon Mourret, commander of technical services in the *Direction de service automobile*

(DSA), which was responsible for all motor transport in the French army. There was certainly a degree of inter-agency rivalry in both the DSA and Mourret's attitude to Estienne and the AS. (Being initially organized as a part of the French artillery arm, the tanks were designated as 'special artillery' and organized in line with French artillery practice.) Mourret's reservations should also be seen in the context of the finite resources that were available to the DSA. With hindsight, it is clear that the tanks were a useful addition to the French army's arsenal, but this was by no means self-evident in 1916 and Mourret was hard-pressed to provide the level of service from the DSA that the army was demanding. In relation to engines, the tank project had to compete with not only the demands of motor transport but also of aero-engines. A continuing shortage of vehicles and engines meant that there was a constant debate about prioritization, a factor that had a considerable impact on the manufacture of tanks, as engines for the former would have to be diverted to the latter. It is also worth noting that Estienne's project would not be insignificant in terms of costs; the estimate in early 1916 was that the 400 tanks ordered, with their associated armament, would cost more than 24 million francs.[21]

While discussions were taking place within the military and with the government, Estienne had been making initial approaches to industrialists he hoped might take on this complex engineering project. He met an equally mixed reception, the major issue being French industry's lack of experience and interest in tractors. For example, Estienne first approached the great French industrialist and automobile engineer Louis Renault, but Renault simply had too many military projects already underway and his factories were working to their full capacity.[22]

Fortunately, Estienne then met with representatives from the Schneider factory, which had been experimenting with American-made Holt tractors, one of its engineers having already begun work on an armoured vehicle.[23] This information persuaded Joffre to order 400 tanks, subject to satisfactory trials, that should all be delivered by the spring of 1917.[24] After final experiments with a Holt tractor in February 1916, the armaments minister, Albert Thomas, informed Joffre that he was placing an order for 400 tanks from the Schneider factory, to be delivered by 25 November 1916. The factory was contracted to deliver 100 tanks per month after a five-month start-up period.[25] Thus it took less than three months from Estienne's initial approach to Joffre for this ambitious project to be taken up by the army. This usefully illustrates how quickly the French army and government had changed from their glacial pace of adaptation and innovation seen before the war to a significantly faster turn-around, provoked by the national emergency they were facing. Considering the lack of experience with tractors in general and armoured vehicles in particular, it is perhaps unsurprising that the tank designed by Schneider was very primitive, being essentially a rectangular armoured box on tracks with a short-barrelled 75mm gun mounted on the front right side, giving a rather restricted field of fire, and one machine gun on each side. The armour-plating was proof against machine-gun and small-arms fire although the tanks could not be made impervious to direct artillery fire and armour-piercing shells. The major flaw lay with the engine, which struggled to move the thirteen-and-a-half-tonne tank faster than walking speed, a reflection of the primitive state of automobile technology of the time.

As the French tank programme was a military and industrial project, control and responsibilities were split between the army and the government.[26] Thus Estienne was caught in a complicated web of civil–military bureaucracy right from the start. The AS was initially attached to the *Sous-secrétariat de l'artillerie* (under-secretariat for artillery), part of the *Ministère de la guerre*, with Albert Thomas in charge as under-secretary. When Thomas became armaments minister in November 1916, the *Sous-secrétariat de l'artillerie* was placed under his ministry's control and so too was the AS. The ministry also controlled the DSA, which supplied all the technical staff for the AS, including Estienne's chief technical advisor Major Aimé Doumenc (who had conceived and run the famous *voie sacrée* road train that was to sustain the Battle of Verdun). As commander of the AS, Estienne was instructed to report to both Albert Thomas and the chief of the DSA.[27] In addition, the DSA ran the AS camps outside of the zone controlled by the military and was responsible for the initial training of AS personnel.[28] Two other parts of the ministry were closely involved with the tank programme. The *Sous-secrétariat d'etat des inventions* (under-secretariat for inventions) was responsible for military inventions and the *Sous-secrétariat d'etat des fabrications de guerre* (under-secretariat for war manufacture) was responsible for military manufacturing. As the department with ultimate responsibility for the army, the *Ministère de la guerre* was also involved. Thus Estienne was required, to some degree or another, to negotiate with two ministers, the DSA, two under-secretaries and, of course, GQG over all tank matters.

Perhaps nothing illustrates the bureaucratic in-fighting within the French tank project as much as the story of the St Chamond tank (although also see the discussion on the Renault light tank below). After production had commenced on the Schneider, Joffre and Estienne were astonished to be informed by Albert Thomas that he had placed an order with the St Chamond factory for 400 tanks, these being of a new design from the successful artillery designer Colonel Émile Rimailho.[29] Within the AS it was widely believed that its proponents' primary specifications for this design were for it to be bigger (over twenty tonnes), more sophisticated (with an electric transmission) and better armed (with a 120mm gun, four machine guns and a crew of nine) than the Schneider design.[30] This is not an unreasonable criticism, as much is made in Thomas's note to Joffre of the large size of the St Chamond and the beneficial effects on morale this would have.[31] Given the limits of French industrial production, the pursuit of these two tank designs simultaneously was hardly prudent and it was to place great strain on the factories involved.

The deficiencies of the St Chamond design were all too obvious from the first prototype; the tank was soon nicknamed the 'elephant on the legs of a gazelle'.[32] The primary issue was that the tracks were far too short and narrow for a body that was substantially larger than that of the Schneider design. In addition, the St Chamond used a petrol engine to drive two electric motors, one for each track, via an overly ambitious electric transmission that was beyond the capabilities of the factory's engineers to make reliable. Estienne immediately identified the problems with the tank's engines and tracks during his initial examination of the tank. He pointed out that the ground pressure of the St Chamond was twice the recommended maximum for tracked vehicles and that the engine was underpowered for such a large vehicle, although at least this inspection gave him the chance to quash the DSA's desire to put a flame-thrower into the tank.[33] However, the tank was now on the production line and had to be used, despite its numerous deficiencies, creating further difficulties for Estienne and the AS.

Estienne returned to his artillery duties while the initial technical developments were being undertaken. In March 1916, Estienne returned to III CA as commander of its artillery and subsequently served with it at Verdun under command of the future commander-in-chief General Robert Nivelle, giving him further first-hand experience of the way that the war was developing.[34] He asked Joffre for three months' secondment to organize the 'tracked vehicles' on his return from a mission to see the British tank programme in June and it was agreed he would command the AS as a *général de division*.[35] However, it was only in August 1916 that the first AS personnel arrived at Fort Trou d'Enfer, just outside Paris. By October 1916, Estienne had a small but highly proficient staff. Colonel Jean Monhoven, an acknowledged tactical expert from one of France's elite regiments (2$^e$ *régiment d'infanterie coloniale*), was to supervise and advise on tactics, while Doumenc, one of the most competent officers in the DSA and the primary organizer of the successful French supply effort at Verdun, gave advice on technical matters.[36] A major camp was subsequently set up at Champlieu, near Compiègne, and this remained the location of the primary AS headquarters until it was forced to move by the German advance during the spring 1918 offensives.[37] As well the camps at Champlieu and Marly, there was an AS camp at Cercottes, north of Orléans, which took delivery of the tanks from the factories and prepared them for their units.

As the AS was slowly forming, a new disruptive element became apparent as Estienne encountered the full force of the obstructive French military and civilian bureaucracy. Despite Estienne warning Joffre against forming a committee to guide the tank project, a committee was duly formed in December 1916 – the *Comité consultatif de l'artillerie d'assaut* (hereafter referred to as the *Comité*). The *Comité* was led by Jules-Louis Breton, head of the *Sous-secrétariat d'etat des inventions,* and had over twenty members, including representatives from the AS, the DSA, the artillery, the ministries of war and armaments, as well as the three factories producing tanks.[38] Unsurprisingly, this resulted in an argumentative and unwieldy body, with its members often pursuing very different agendas. In particular, Mourret's initial lack of enthusiasm for the tank project was shared by a significant number of other members of the *Comité*. However, initially the *Comité* was not entirely unhelpful, and a number of design faults were rectified as they became apparent during testing. Concerns immediately arose over the Schneider's armour, particularly in relation to it being proof against the German SmK armour-piercing round. It was agreed that additional armour (an extra 5mm) would be fitted, although this modification was to take place after the tanks were delivered. The initial St Chamond engines needed immediate retooling by the factory because they were simply not powerful enough for the tank.[39]

\* \* \*

Having secured the tank programme, Estienne set about devising how the tanks would be used in combat. The first instructions on tank tactics were issued by GQG in August 1916 and were essentially just a refined version of the initial ideas Estienne had presented to Joffre. The tanks were to enable an offensive to take possession of the battlefield over several hours, on a large front, all the way to the enemy's artillery line. This would be done in such a way as to make the ensuing infantry attack merely a matter of occupying the taken positions, with cavalry following-up to exploit this success. To maximize surprise and shock, the tanks were to advance simultaneously on their objectives, which would both ensure a quick advance and conserve ammunition. Therefore, the initial tank tactics were predicated on the tanks being a complete surprise to the Germans.

There was thus considerable dismay in France when GQG heard on 1 August 1916 from General Pierre des Vallières, head of the French military mission to British general headquarters, that the British intended to use their own tanks on the Somme.[40] Joffre had warned Thomas that if the Germans found out about the tanks they could widen their trenches 'in a night', which would mean the French tank designs would not be able to cross the trenches without infantry assistance.[41] When Estienne had visited Lincoln in June 1916 to examine the British tank programme he had tried to persuade the British of the importance of delaying the initial use of tanks until they could be used in large numbers simultaneously by both armies.[42] Director of the Mechanical Supply Department, Albert Stern, was asked by the French to intercede with Britain's Minister of Munitions, Edwin Montagu, to stop the tanks being used until the spring of 1917, when French tanks would be ready. Montagu saw British commander-in-chief General Sir Douglas Haig in early September 1916 to discuss this but the latter, although sympathetic, was not prepared to change his plans at this late stage.[43] The most disastrous result of the tanks' appearance on the Somme for the French was exactly the one that Joffre had predicted. Almost immediately, the Germans had begun to widen their trenches significantly, which instantly compromised the ability of the French tanks to operate independently of the infantry.

Nonetheless, the Somme certainly offered an opportunity for the French to learn from the experience of the British tanks: but, unfortunately, it was difficult to discern what parts of this experience were generally applicable and which were particular to that engagement. For example, the French military mission's report on the British tanks' suggestion that direct artillery fire would not be a problem for tanks was highly misleading, as the French were to find out.[44] On the other hand, GQG abandoned thoughts of mounting a 120mm gun on the St Chamond largely due to British reports on tank gunfire in action.[45]

A new tactical approach had to be developed and Estienne set out new parameters for the tanks in October 1916. The role of the AS was now to precede the infantry and be 'their guide and light'.[46] Although the tanks were armed with cannons and machine guns, their main strength was considered to be the ability to keep advancing under enemy fire: Estienne summed up the purpose of tank guns as 'only fire when you cannot march'.[47] A tank attack was to have three distinct phases. In the first, the tanks would help the infantry take the successive trenches of the first enemy position. Each enemy artillery battery would then be attacked by specific tanks, in conjunction with an infantry attack. The last tactical phase would be a tank attack on the second enemy position, where previous French attacks had usually been halted due to the fact it was beyond the range of most of the French artillery. This process, theoretically, would be completed in less than three hours, achieving a penetration of up to six kilometres. It is important to note that Estienne mentioned that the tanks should attack only when under the cover of fog or dim early morning light. One very effective but simple measure that the Germans had taken after the British tank attack was to widen their trenches, which immediately removed the French tanks' ability to operate independently of the infantry. There was no possibility of modifying the existing French tank designs to enable them to cross wider trenches and making a way over these for the tanks became a vital task for the supporting infantry.

The first French tank combat operation was undertaken using this methodological framework and was far from a success. Two AS battalions participated in Fifth Army's attack at Juvincourt on 16 April 1917, as part of the Nivelle Offensive. Having been promised that the enemy artillery would be totally suppressed, the tanks made their approach march in long single-file columns, in broad daylight and in full view of the German artillery observers, who were nearly all on commanding heights above the battlefield. One tank battalion was shot to pieces by indirect German heavy-artillery fire without even getting past the first German trenches. The other battalion's commander was killed when his tank was hit by a shell before his units could deploy. His battalion carried on and some isolated tanks penetrated more than three kilometres further into the German lines than did the infantry. However, these modest successes had been bought at a considerable human and material cost; 76 tanks out of the 132 engaged that day were put out of action, with 57 being destroyed by German artillery, and a considerable number of officers were killed.[48]

Estienne took the opportunity to analyse the 16 April attacks in detail and make sure that mistakes were not repeated when the tanks next went into action two weeks later at Laffaux at the western end of the Chemin de Dames ridge.[49] The lengthy approach march on 16 April had been identified as a serious mistake; this time, three batteries of each company were placed close to the French front lines before the operation so that they could advance at the same time as the infantry.[50] The tanks were more closely integrated with the infantry than they had been on 16 April, primarily through placing the tank companies' command posts with those of the infantry divisions. Each battery of tanks had specific tasks and objectives (unlike on 16 April where objectives had been given to the companies), with one battery held in reserve, giving the company commanders some tactical flexibility. This thinking was also applied to the battalions. It was agreed that the in-line formation used on 16 April had been impossible to control, and so this time the battalions were echeloned in depth, giving the company commanders more tactical options. Particular attention was paid to protecting the tanks from enemy artillery fire, as this had proved to be the tanks' greatest threat on 16 April.[51] There was also to be an aircraft dedicated to keeping the commander informed of his tanks' movements and to signal artillery fire onto enemy anti-tank batteries, with fighters dedicated to chasing off any enemy fighters or artillery-observation aeroplanes.[52] This resulted in a very successful operation, the tanks' participation only marred by mechanical difficulties, with few casualties and all objectives taken. The twelve St Chamonds had considerable difficulty operating on the damaged and uneven terrain, six breaking down, with one being destroyed by German artillery fire.[53] Thus the results were considerably better than those of 16 April, particularly as only one tank had been destroyed.

After Nivelle was dismissed and Pétain took charge of the French army, the latter decided to refine the army's tactical approach through a series of battles with strictly limited objectives. One of these, the Battle of Malmaison in October 1917, was to re-establish trust within the army that the tanks were an effective weapon. At Malmaison Sixth Army had thirty-eight Schneider and thirty St Chamond tanks to support three attacking infantry corps, as well as copious amounts of artillery. There was no attempt at surprise; over five days, French artillery fired just over one-and-a-half-million shells at the German positions.[54] When the operation was over, the French had advanced in some places nearly six kilometres and had captured over 11,000 prisoners and significant amounts of material. The battle demonstrated that the tanks would suffer comparatively light casualties provided that the enemy artillery was efficiently suppressed; only two tanks were destroyed and there were eighty-two AS casualties, light compared with later engagements. The experience gained in 1917 was considered sufficient to enable provisional tank regulations, written by Estienne in conjunction with his officers, to be issued at the end of the year.[55] This doctrine was so well thought-out that it only required one subsequent set of major modifications, due to the introduction of Renault light tanks, in July 1918.[56]

As well as refining tactics, Estienne had been involved in a bureaucratic struggle over what was to be the most successful tank design of the war, the Renault light tank. It would take all of Estienne's considerable energy and patience to nurse this revolutionary tank into production. The idea for a light tank appears to have germinated in Estienne's mind during his visit to the British tank factory at Lincoln in 1916, when he saw that the British tanks were going to be heavier than the French designs.[57] As an artilleryman, he was used to the concept of different classes of artillery and realized that the combination of the heavy British tanks and the French mediums would potentially give a tank force more flexibility in combat.[58] Estienne had a fortuitous meeting the following month with Louis Renault and the latter agreed to make a preliminary study of a light tank. Estienne's initial specifications were for a six-tonne tank with a machine gun in a revolving turret and a two-man crew.[59] Estienne approached Mourret at the DSA in order to formalize an arrangement with Renault but Mourret refused to do so and Estienne was once again forced to appeal directly to Joffre. He pointed out that the production of light tanks would be easier for French industry than for the medium tanks and that production could be implemented quickly, suggesting that 1,000 be ordered.[60] Joffre wrote to

Thomas asking for an order to be made for this number, but Thomas refused unless a working prototype could be demonstrated satisfactorily.[61]

A prototype was duly shown to the *Comité* in December 1916 and there was a heated debate about its merits. There were numerous objections from members of the committee, largely centred on reservations about its small size; Mourret started the discussion by stating that the Renault was far too small to be of any use and that it was too lightly armed.[62] Estienne responded that this could be a decisive method of bringing machine guns to the front line and reminded the *Comité* that the decision to develop a light tank had already been made by the commander-in-chief. After further argument, the *Comité* agreed to a small initial order.[63]

However, during January and February 1917 the ministry continued to delay moving the project forward. Exasperated by this, Estienne arranged for the Renault prototype to be tested at Champlieu, which led to a huge argument with Thomas, who accused Estienne of over-stepping his authority and colluding with Renault, the implication being Estienne had a financial interest in the light tank.[64] Estienne responded that he was simply trying to make progress with the design and that he had no intention of bypassing the *Comité*. Indeed, he had informed the DSA prior to the proposed test and the test itself had been very useful on a technical level.[65] Further tests on the Renault by the *Comité* and its subsequent positive reports persuaded Nivelle to give priority to tank production, in particular recommending concentrating resources on the light tanks.[66] There were further delays, including one caused by Thomas unilaterally suspending production, but it was soon apparent that the Renaults were clearly technically superior to the existing medium tanks. As Estienne had foreseen, the battlefield mobility of the light tanks was a major advantage, as they could go where the French medium and British heavy tanks could not, and even Mourret came to support the light tank design.[67]

Pétain's accession put someone in charge who was convinced of the tanks' utility. He had ordered 2,000 Renaults upon becoming chief of the general staff, with a further 2,500 subsequently ordered when he became commander-in-chief.[68] The size of these orders presented the ministry with a new and difficult manufacturing problem, as there had already been a considerable delay in delivering the medium tanks. Although Thomas had promised to deliver all the Schneiders in 1916, the majority of them were delivered during 1917, with the final deliveries only taking place in 1918. There were even greater delays with the St Chamonds; in fact the delivery of the initial order for four hundred tanks was never completed, with only 294 being delivered to the army during the war, the last three of these arriving as late as September 1918.[69] The ministry also began to count tank deliveries in terms of tanks that had left the factories and had arrived at Cercottes depot, rather than tanks actually delivered to the army in a usable condition. This made the delivery schedule look better but was obviously of no use to the army.[70] Given the ministry's failure to keep to the medium tank delivery schedules, it is perhaps not surprising that manufacturing the light tanks was likewise subject to lengthy delays. It should also be noted that these issues meant that Estienne was just as often fighting French bureaucracy as he was the German army.

In addition, it quickly became clear that the Renault factory would not be able to deal with the increasing scale of its orders. Estienne had to suggest in July 1917 that the United States should be asked to manufacture light tanks to alleviate the burden on French industry, a good example of his foresight.[71] Other French factories were brought in to help with manufacture but by October 1917 only 114 light tanks had been manufactured and the majority of these were not delivered to the army until the following year; by December 1917 the army had thirty-one unarmoured Renaults available, for training only.[72]

Although Thomas was replaced by Louis Loucheur after a change of government, the latter was to prove just as resistant to prioritizing light tank manufacture as his predecessor. Loucheur decided that heavy tank designs should take priority over the light tanks, despite continual opposition to this from Pétain and Estienne. Pétain had to write several sharp letters to Loucheur to speed up manufacture. Two-hundred-and-twenty-five light tanks were finally delivered in March 1918 but all needed 'complete revision' by the factory due to poor manufacture.[73] Loucheur refused to accept that the tanks were defective: he told President Raymond Poincaré that the light tanks were ready but that Estienne was 'hesitant' to use them, 'under a variety of pretexts'.[74] Only by July 1918 were there over a thousand light tanks in service with combat units.

While the arguments over light tanks raged on, there were also serious problems with the medium tanks that needed addressing. The Schneiders' alarming propensity to catch fire was partially addressed, after much argument in the *Comité*, by moving the main petrol tank to the rear of the vehicle. The St Chamonds' tracks were widened, something Estienne had been asking for since he saw the prototype. Although Estienne had emphasized in November 1916 the importance of keeping good stocks of spare parts, as the tanks were in effect being tested in the field there was a continual problem caused by the shortage of spares.[75] For example, in May 1917 thirty out of the sixty-one St Chamonds in the army were unusable due to a lack of spares.[76] Indeed, this situation deteriorated to the extent that St Chamond deliveries to the army had to be halted altogether until the spares situation could be resolved. Notably, in mid-November 1917 only nine Schneider companies, out of sixteen, were immediately ready for action and not one of the St Chamond companies was ready.[77]

Estienne was not just in conflict with the ministry over technical issues; there was also much acrimonious debate over the organization of the AS. This came to a head in June 1917, when Estienne wrote to Pétain asking to rationalize the organization of the AS. In anticipation of the arrival of large numbers of light tanks, Estienne wanted to create a base for the AS in each army group. Each base would largely be self-contained, with sufficient material, spares and mechanics to maintain operations in its sector. Estienne argued that the tank arm would be equal in size to the French air service by the end of 1917 and thus should be largely autonomous as the air service was.[78] GQG largely supported Estienne's proposals, as did the *Ministère de la guerre*, but Thomas refused to cede any of his ministry's powers over the AS. His replacement Loucheur took up a similar position and arguments about the reorganization continued throughout the autumn. These were only resolved when Georges Clemenceau became premier in late 1917. Clemenceau came to power determined to stamp his authority across the government and he was well aware of the army's displeasure with Loucheur. However, Loucheur was too talented to be disposed of and a compromise was agreed. The AS was moved to the control of the *Ministère de la guerre* (Clemenceau was war minister as well as prime minister) and only tank manufacture was left under the armaments ministry.

Thus, only by the beginning of 1918 was Estienne solely reporting to, and under the direct control of, Pétain. For the first time since its inception, the AS and Estienne were free of interference from the political bureaucracy and had the full support of the government. This was highly significant as it meant that the development of the AS was now entirely under the control of Estienne and the army and that, for the most part, the issues connecting technology, organization and doctrine were finally brought together. The titanic struggle in 1918 would severely test the newly organized AS.

The heavy defensive fighting during the German offensives of 1918 meant that AS units were often thrown into action in desperate counter attacks that were not in line with the tank regulations but required by necessity. There was thus little scope to test many of the ideas contained in the tank regulations until the allies went on the offensive. Estienne was particularly interested in using the tanks in a surprise tank attack without a preliminary artillery preparation, something he had first proposed in 1915. The generally mediocre results from the French tank actions of 1917 had meant this idea was not given any credence within the army until the stunning success of the British attack at Cambrai in November 1917, which demonstrated how massed tanks could be used to gain surprise and help break into the enemy's trench lines.[79] Estienne and his staff undertook a series of small-scale actions during the first half of 1918 to test whether the AS could use this methodology, one example being a small-scale *coup de main* attack on Third Army's front, without an artillery preparation.[80]

The action was a great success, giving confidence that this methodology could be used successfully in a large-scale engagement.

The opportunity to put this to the test arose during the allies' counter offensive to the final German offensive in July 1918. The major rail junction at Soissons had become of key importance; by mid-July this was supplying two German armies in the Marne salient. German attention had moved to the east of the Marne salient where an offensive either side of the city of Reims was being planned and its western flank near Soissons had been left vulnerable. This was largely due to a German assumption that there would be plenty of notice if the French decided to mount an operation in the area. It was an ideal place to try a large-scale surprise attack; to make the surprise complete, the French would have no preparatory artillery bombardment, the tanks providing the infantry with the firepower to tackle defences usually destroyed by the preparation. In line with the regulations, the jump-off time, 04.35, was chosen so that the tanks could get into action in semi-darkness; and it was also decided to add a large number of smoke shells to the barrage.[81] As at Cambrai, the tanks would go forward with the first wave of infantry, just as an intensive artillery barrage was unleashed. Following the tank regulations, the initial intention had been for the light tanks to accompany each division attacking in the first wave, but there were simply too few for this and instead they became the army reserve. General Charles Mangin's Tenth Army was given 2$^e$ AS brigade, comprising two tank regiments. This was assembled on the army's front from 14 July, although even the battalion and company commanders were not informed about the coming offensive in other than the most general terms until 17 July, the eve of the attack.[82]

French security was tight, and the Germans were caught by surprise when the French infantry and tanks advanced on 18 July, against German defenders stunned by the enormous artillery barrage. The forward German positions were quickly overrun by the tanks and within hours it was clear that the operation was an unqualified success. However, as the day went on the tanks and the infantry began to be involved in small-scale actions that negated the advantages that they had initially gained. This pattern continued for the following days during which uncoordinated actions continued to push the Germans back, although at a slower rate than on the first day. Estienne had warned in the regulations that the AS 'is used-up quickly on the battlefield' and this is starkly shown by the Battle of the Soissonais. On 18 July 1918, Tenth Army had 226 tanks engaged, the following day only 105 tanks went into action. By 20 July Tenth Army's AS had only thirty-two operational tanks, although, through great overnight efforts by the maintenance crews, 100 were available for combat the next day. The following morning, there were only three usable tanks and the AS was retired from the battle into the army reserve that evening.

The Battle of the Soissonais raised a number of issues connected with the tank regulations, although these were more to do with their implementation than any problems in their prescriptions. Indeed, such was their dissatisfaction at the way the tanks had been used in operations during July and August, Pétain and Estienne collaborated on instructions for the infantry and artillery commanders that reiterated important points from the tank regulations.[83] A reminder was issued on 9 September 1918 stating that the important prescriptions of the *Instruction* of 14 July 1918 were 'often forgotten in the last battles' and that this failure gave 'poor results'. The note summarized the essential lessons for tank employment as laid down by the regulations issued since December 1917. The primary lesson had been that tanks were only to be used en masse, as per the regulations. It stated that using weak tank units gave 'no results', as did using weakened infantry units with the tanks. To avoid using depleted tank units, it reminded infantry commanders that it was necessary for tank reserves to be held at army, divisional and regimental levels, in order to maintain a continuous tank presence during the battle. However, infantry commanders, at every level, were determined to keep infantry casualties to a minimum and sending in the tanks instead offered an obvious alternative, even if using them in small-scale attacks was contrary to the regulations. Although the note clearly stated that the conditions contained in the regulations 'must be accepted' by the infantry officers, this was to remain a problem.[84]

Despite the continuing struggle with infantry commanders over implementation of the tank regulations, the remaining AS engagements were for the most part successful. As the war ended, Estienne was planning a large-scale tank attack for a planned offensive into Lorraine, only abandoned when the armistice was signed. Almost immediately the war finished, the AS was integrated into the infantry arm, against Estienne's advice as he thought it should remain a separate branch of the army like the artillery and air services.[85] Estienne realized that the limitations shown by the tanks in the war would soon be overcome as technology improved and continued to argue that this would enable them to play a much wider role than just infantry support. However, the tanks' infantry support role was now firmly imbedded in French military thought and, eventually realizing that his arguments were being largely ignored by the government and army, Estienne retired from the army in 1922. He threw his energies over the following years into various innovative civilian projects, including promoting a trans-Saharan expedition by tracked vehicles. He died in 1936, a respected but largely marginalized figure in the French military.

Although Estienne had demonstrated throughout the war a better understanding of the limitations of the tanks than many of his army contemporaries and, after the war, a better conception of their future potential, he is largely unknown today. This is most unjust as he was indeed the 'father of the French tanks' and without his considerable energy it seems unlikely that the French tank force would have contributed so much to the allied victory. As Pétain said in 1936, 'General Estienne led by example, his activity exceeding all that could be expected', a fitting tribute to one of France's most innovative officers of the First World War.[86]

# Bibliographical Note

Studies of the wartime French army in the English language are limited, but their number is growing all the time. This short survey indicates key works and suggestions for further reading.

**Introductory**
The best recent introduction to the French army as a wartime institution is Elizabeth Greenhalgh, *The French Army and the First World War* (Cambridge University Press, 2014). Its coverage of military operations is necessarily limited, and these are reviewed from the perspective of strategy and higher command in Robert Doughty, *Pyrrhic Victory: French Strategy and Operations in the Great War* (The Belknap Press, 2005). Douglas Porch's chapter on the French army in *Military Effectiveness*, vol. 1, *The First World War*, ed. Allan Millett and Williamson Murray (London: Unwin Hyman, 1988) is important but out-of-date. Jere Clemens King, *Generals and Politicians: Conflict Between France's High Command, Parliament and Government, 1914–18* (Berkeley: University of California Press, 1951 & Westport, Conn.: Greenwood Press, 1971) is a masterful survey of the army's place in wartime French politics that has stood the test of time.

**Operations**
In recent years several monographs have engaged with aspects of the French military effort in the war or specific military operations, notably those by contributors to this book: Michael Neiberg, *The Second Battle the Marne* (Indiana University Press, 2008); Jonathan Krause, *Early Trench Tactics in the French Army: The Second Battle of Artois, May–June 1915* (Routledge, 2013); Tim Gale, *The French Army's Tank Force and Armoured Warfare in the Great War: The* Artillerie spéciale (Ashgate, 2013); Simon House, *Lost Opportunity: The Battle of the Ardennes 22 August 1914* (Helion & Co., 2017). The Battle of Verdun has attracted considerable attention, although largely viewed as an industrialized slaughterhouse rather than a managed military operation. Alex Axelrod, *The Battle of Verdun* (The Lyons Press, 2016) is the latest of this genre. Perhaps the best are Ian Ousby, *The Road to Verdun* (Jonathan Cape, 2002) and Paul Jankowski, *Verdun: The Longest Battle of the Great War* (Oxford University

Press, 2014). The important French contribution to the Somme offensive has belatedly been explained in William Philpott, *Bloody Victory: The Sacrifice on the Somme and the Making of the Twentieth Century* (Little, Brown, July 2009). The Nivelle offensive has also been considered by David Murphy in *Breaking Point of the French Army: The Nivelle Offensive of 1917* (Barnsley: Pen & Sword, 2015), but a wider evaluation of the achievements of the French army in that year is needed. Several studies have been made of the French army's mutinies in that year, John Williams' *Mutiny 1917* (London: Heinemann, 1962) being the standard but now dated English-language account. Important context is provided by Len Smith's longitudinal case-study of changing French military morale and discipline, *Between Mutiny and Obedience: The Case of the French 5th Infantry Division during World War 1* (Princeton: Princeton University Press, 1994). France's 1918 battles await their historian. Until then William Philpott's chapter, 'France Leads the Way to Victory', in Peter Liddle's edited volume *Britain and Victory in the Great War* (Pen & Sword, 2018) challenges the prevailing Anglo-Saxon judgement that the French army was a spent force in 1917 and 1918. The huge and detailed, but dry, French official history, *Les Armées françaises dans la grande guerre* (Paris: Imprimerie Nationale, 11 tomes in 105 vols, 1922–1937), with its extensive documentary appendices, is a mine of information and essential for any study of the French army in the war, although it does not offer much in the way of criticism, either of individuals or particular operations. It is now available and searchable online through the *Bibliothèque nationale*'s digital platform Gallica at https://www.memoiredeshommes.sga.defense.gouv.fr/fr/arkotheque/inventaires/ead_ir_consult.php?fam=11&ref=FRSHD_AFGG_ead

## Doctrine

The recent translation of Michel Goya's important 2004 work on French doctrinal development, *Flesh and Steel: The French Army's Transformation During the First World War and the Invention of Modern Warfare* (Pen & Sword, 2018) supplements Douglas Porch's influential but now rather dated work on the problems of the pre-war army, *The March to the Marne: The French Army, 1871–1914* (Cambridge University Press, 1981).

## Command and Commanders

There is no dedicated study of French command and commanders during the war. Certain themes or periods have been looked at, with a focus on the end of the war. Coalition command is considered in Roy Prete, *Strategy and Command: The Anglo-French Coalition on the Western Front, 1914* (Montreal & Kingston: McGill-Queen's University Press, 2009) and Elizabeth Greenhalgh, *Foch in Command: The Forging of a First World War General* (Cambridge: Cambridge

University Press, 2011). David Zabecki has offered a comparative assessment of senior commanders in the final year of the war in *The General's War: Operational Level Command on the Western Front in 1918* (Bloomington, Ind.: Indiana University Press, 2018). In French, Claude Franc's *Le Haut commandement français sur le front occidental, 1914–1918* (Paris: SOTECA, Éditions 14–18, 2012) offers an introductory survey of the war's commaders in the context of how the war developed. Biographies of individual commanders in English and French are indicated in the notes to this volume's chapters. Glenn Torrey's *Henri Mathias Berthelot: Soldier of France, Defender of Romania* (Iași and Oxford: The Centre for Romanian Studies, 2001) and Jan Tanenbaum, *General Maurice Sarrail, 1856–1929: The French Army and Left-Wing Politics* (Chapel Hill, NC: University of North Carolina Press, 1974) are valuable biographies of generals not included in this collection.

# Notes

**Preface**
1. André Bourachot, *Marshal Joffre: The Triumphs, Failures and Controversies of France's Commander-in-Chief in the Great War*, trans. Andrew Uffindell (Barnsley: Pen & Sword, 2013), p. xii.

**Introduction**
1. Henry Bordeaux, *Le Général Maistre* (Paris: Les Éditions G. Crès & Cie, 1923), pp. 126–7.
2. The literature is vast and still growing. For a brief introduction see the companion volume to this collection, *Haig's Generals*, ed. Ian Beckett and Steven Corvi (Barnsley: Pen & Sword, 2006).
3. The thesis that between 1914 and 1918 France created 'the first modern army' has been proposed in Michel Goya, *La Chair et l'acier: L'Armée française et l'invention de la guerre moderne (1914–1918)* (Paris: Tallandier, 2004). The work is available in translation: *Flesh and Steel: The French Army's Transformation During the First World War and the Invention of Modern Warfare*, trans. Andrew Uffindell (Barnsley, Pen & Sword, 2018).
4. There have been some recent survey studies such as Robert Doughty, *Pyrrhic Victory: French Strategy and Operations in the Great War* (Cambridge Mass.: The Belknap Press, 2005) and Elizabeth Greenhalgh, *The French Army and the First World War* (Cambridge: Cambridge University Press, 2014). Other studies integrate a broad chronology of the development of the Western Front campaign with the front-line soldier's experience: for example Anthony Clayton, *Paths of Glory: The French Army 1914–18* (London: Cassell, 2003) and Ian Sumner, *They Shall Not Pass: The French Army on the Western Front 1914–1918* (Barnsley: Pen & Sword, 2012). For a survey of the literature see William Philpott, 'Review Article: France's Forgotten Victory', *The Journal of Strategic Studies*, 34 (2011), pp. 901–18.
5. For example, Roger Fraenkel's polemical, *Joffre: L'Âne qui commandait des lions* (Triel-sue-Seine, Éditions Italiques, 2004) and *Joffre, l'imposteur: Les Mensonges de la grande guerre* (Paris: Éditions Jourdan, 2014).
6. Pierre Miquel's *Le Gâchis des généraux: Les Erreurs de commandement pendant la guerre de 14–18* (Paris: Plon, 2001) is an extreme case, dwelling on the mistakes in each year of the war while making no attempt to balance the narrative with successes, which increasingly outnumbered such errors.
7. A 'cult' has grown up around Foch for example. See the essays in the volume published to mark the ninetieth anniversary of the end of the war, *Ferdinand Foch: Apprenez à penser*, ed. Rémy Porte and François Cochet (Paris: SOTECA, Éditions 14–18, 2010) which was accompanied by the publication of his collected writings: *Maréchal Foch: Œuvres complètes*, ed. André Martel (Paris: Economica, 3 vols, 2008).
8. Michael Neiberg, *Foch: Supreme Allied Commander in the Great War* (Dulles, Va.: Brassey's Inc., 2003); Sir James Marshall-Cornwall, *Foch as Military Commander* (London: Batsford, 1972); Basil Liddell Hart, *Foch: The Man of Orleans* (London: Eyre & Spottiswoode, 1931); Sir George Aston, *The Biography of the Late Marshal Foch* (London: Hutchinson & Co., 1929). Roy Prete, *Strategy and Command: The Anglo-French Coalition on the Western*

*Front, 1914* (Montreal & Kingston: McGill-Queen's University Press, 2009), the first volume of a planned trilogy, focuses on Joffre's role as a coalition commander but is not a full biography. André Bourachot, *Marshal Joffre: The Triumphs, Failures and Controversies of France's Commander-in-Chief in the Great War*, trans. Andrew Uffindell (Barnsley: Pen & Sword, 2013) is the only English-language study of Joffre, itself a translation from the original French.

9. Richard Griffiths, *Marshal Pétain* (London: Constable, 1970); Nicholas Atkin, *Pétain* (Harlow: Longman, 1997). Assessments of Pétain's military career depend heavily on Guy Pedroncini, *Pétain: Général en chef, 1917–18* (Paris: Presses Universitaires de France, 1974).
10. Prete, op. cit.; Elizabeth Greenhalgh, *Foch in Command: The Forging of a First World War General* (Cambridge: Cambridge University Press, 2011).
11. See for example, William Philpott, 'France Leads the Way to Victory', in *Britain and Victory in the Great War*, ed. Peter Liddle (Barnsley: Pen & Sword, 2018), pp. 185–203.
12. 23 August 1914, *The Memoirs of Raymond Poincaré, 1914*, trans. George Arthur (London: William Heineman Ltd, 1929), p. 86.
13. Douglas Porch, 'The French Army in the First World War', in *Military Effectiveness*, vol. 1, *The First World War*, ed. Allan Millett and Williamson Murray (London: Unwin Hyman, 1988), pp. 190–228: 225.
14. Douglas Porch, *The March to the Marne: The French Army, 1871–1914* (Cambridge: Cambridge University Press, 1981).
15. Goya, op. cit., pp. 89–112.
16. Max Hastings, *Catastrophe: Europe Goes to War, 1914* (London: William Collins, 2013), pp. 159–60 and 169–70, is the latest in a long line of derivative accounts whose lineage can be traced back to Winston Churchill's and Basil Liddell Hart's superficial yet influential inter-war histories.
17. Porch, op. cit., p. 219.
18. Quoted in John Seely, *Adventure* (London: William Heinemann Ltd, 1930), p. 150, remembering a conversation with Foch at the 1912 British army manoeuvres.
19. Jules Maurin, 'Sous le drapeau', in *Histoire militaire de la France*, vol. 3, *1871–1940*, ed. André Corvisier (Paris: Quadrige, 1997), pp. 99–118: 105.
20. Porch, op. cit., pp. 213–28 passim.
21. Simon House, *Lost Opportunity: The Battle of the Ardennes 22 August 1914* (Solihull: Helion & Co., 2017), pp. 187–202 passim.
22. As evident from the diaries of artilleryman and later marshal of France Marie-Émile Fayolle: 'Bataille en avant de Nancy (19 août–11 septembre 1914)', Maréchal Fayolle, *Cahiers secrets de la grande guerre*, ed. Henry Contamine (Paris: Plon, 1964), pp. 21–34 passim.
23. House, op. cit., passim.
24. Pierre Rocolle, *L'Hécatombe des généraux* (Paris: Éditions Lavauzelle, 1980).
25. 'Written Statement of the Conference Held at Chantilly, December 6th 1915', The National Archives, Kew, WO 106/1454.
26. Jonathan Krause, *Early Trench Tactics in the French Army: The Second Battle of Artois, May–June 1915* (Farnham: Ashgate, 2013).
27. For a detailed analysis of early-war artillery developments see Jonathan Krause, 'From Balletics to Ballistics: French Artillery, 1897–1916', *British Journal for Military History* [www.bjmh.org.uk], 5 (2019), pp. 58–80.
28. Goya, op. cit., pp. 294–301 and 333–9. For early air warfare See Simon House 'Three-dimensional Warfare – The Invention of Aerial Combat', *British Journal for Military History* [www.bjmh.org.uk], 5 (2019), pp. 40–57: 50–7. For the development and use of French tanks see Tim Gale, *The French Army's Tank Force and Armoured Warfare in the Great War: The* Artillerie spéciale (Farnham: Ashgate, 2013).

29. Jonathan Boff, *Winning and Losing on the Western Front: The British Third Army and the Defeat of Germany in 1918* (Cambridge: Cambridge University Press, 2012), pp. 248–50.
30. This aspect of Joffre's role has been well covered by historians: Prete, op. cit.; William Philpott, *Anglo-French Relations and Strategy on the Western Front, 1914–1918* (Basingstoke: Macmillan, 1996).
31. For the most detailed case study see Krause, *Early Trench Tactics*.
32. Ibid., pp. 66–73.
33. 'Enseignements à tirer de nos dernières attaques', by Foch, 6 December 1915, in *Les Armées françaises dans la grande guerre* [AFGG], tome III, *Les Offensives de 1915: L'Hiver de 1915–16* (Paris: Imprimerie Nationale, 1923), annexes vol. 4, annexe 3122, pp. 383–90.
34. Ibid. and 'La bataille offensive', 20 April 1916, *Groupe d'armées du nord*, Service historique de la défense, Vincennes [SHD], 18N148.
35. 23 March 1916, Contamine, op. cit., p. 155.
36. 21 January 1916, ibid, p. 142.
37. 'Instruction personelle et secrète pour M. le général Sir Douglas Haig et le général Foch', by Joffre, 21 June, AFGG, tome IV, *Verdun et la Somme*, vol. 2, *La Bataille de Verdun et les offensives des alliées (1 mai 1916–3 septembre 1916)* (Paris: Imprimerie Nationale, 1933), annexes vol. 2, annexe 1385, pp. 316–8: 317–8.
38. William Philpott, *Bloody Victory: The Sacrifice on the Somme and the Making of the Twentieth Century* (London: Little, Brown, 2009), pp. 98–130 passim.
39. Ibid., pp. 344 and 354–7.
40. 'Speech on the unveiling of the statue of General Foch', by Debeney, 1926, fonds Foch (don Fournier-Foch), SHD, 1K129/3.
41. Philpott, op. cit., pp. 382–4.
42. Ibid., pp. 389–90.
43. Ibid., p. 99.
44. Ibid., p. 267.
45. 8 January 1917, Contamine, op, cit., p. 197.
46. Ibid.
47. See Jere Clemens King, *Generals and Politicians: Conflict Between France's High Command, Parliament and Government, 1914–18* (Berkeley: University of California Press, 1951 & Westport, Conn.: Greenwood Press, 1971).
48. Doughty, op. cit., pp. 341–2.
49. Philpott, 'France Leads the Way to Victory', pp. 188–91.
50. Note by Foch, 3 November 1916, fonds Weygand, SHD, 1K130/9/6.
51. Untitled and undated memorandum [c. January 1917], in 'Après la Somme: Études', idem, 1K130/3/J.
52. Note by Foch, 24 November 1916 and 'Repercussions de l'offensive de la Somme sur l'emploi des disponibilités, l'usure et la fixation des effectifs des allemands', 1 December 1916, idem, 1K130/3/J.
53. 'The Memorandum of July 24th [1918]', by Foch, in Marshal Ferdinand Foch, *The Memoirs of Marshal Foch*, trans. Col. T. Bentley Mott (London: William Heinemann, 1931), pp. 425–9.
54. William Philpott: *Attrition: Fighting the First World War* (London: Little, Brown, 2014), pp. 327–34.
55. 8 January 1917, Contamine, op. cit., pp. 197–9.
56. Paul-Marie de la Gorce, *The French Army: A Military–Political History*, trans. Kenneth Douglas (London: Weidenfeld and Nicholson, 1963), pp. 51–4.
57. Bourachot, op. cit., pp. 1–2.
58. Claude Franc, *Le Haut commandement français sur le front occidental, 1914–1918* (Paris: SOTECA, Éditions 14–18, 2012), pp. 284–9.

59. William Philpott, 'Marshal Ferdinand Foch and Allied Victory', in *Leadership in Conflict, 1914–1918*, ed. Matthew Seligmann and Matthew Hughes (London: Leo Cooper, 2000), pp. 38–53.
60. Marie-Eugène Debeney, *La Guerre et les hommes: Réflexions d'après-guerre* (Paris: Librairie Plon, 1937), pp. 10–12.
61. Quoted in 'Translator's introductory note', in Foch, op. cit., p. xvii.
62. Bordeaux, op. cit., p. 127.
63. Debeney, op. cit., p. 9.

## Chapter 1

1. Winston Churchill, *The World Crisis* (new edition, London: Odhams Press, 2 vols, 1938), i, pp. 950–73. See the discussion in William Philpott, *Bloody Victory: The Sacrifice on the Somme and the Making of the Twentieth Century* (London: Little, Brown, 2009), pp. 598–603.
2. 'Le Maréchal Joseph Joffre', in Paul Gaujac, *Les Généraux de la victoire* (Paris: Histoire & Collections, 2 vols, 2007), ii, pp. 12–15.
3. Marshal Joseph Joffre, *The Memoirs of Marshal Joffre*, trans. T. Bentley Mott (London: Geoffrey Bles, 2 vols, 1932), i, pp. 55–8. The text of the Franco-Russian convention is included here.
4. Ibid., i, pp. 58–61.
5. Quoted in Glenn Torrey, *Henri Mathias Berthelot: Soldier of France, Defender of Romania* (Iaşi and Oxford: The Centre for Romanian Studies, 2001), pp. 45–6.
6. William Philpott, 'Managing the British Way in Warfare: France and Britain's Continental Commitment, 1904–1918', in *The British Way in Warfare: Power and the International System, 1856–1956*, ed. Keith Neilson and Greg Kennedy (Farnham: Ashgate, 2010), pp. 83–100.
7. William Philpott, 'The Making of the Military Entente, 1904–1914: France, the British Army, and the Prospect of War', *The English Historical Review*, 127 (2013), pp. 1155–85.
8. William Philpott, 'The Strategic Ideas of Sir John French', *The Journal of Strategic Studies*, 12 (1989), pp. 458–78.
9. Discussed in Simon House, *Lost Opportunity: The Battle of the Ardennes, 22 August 1914* (Solihull: Helion & Co., 2016), pp. 141–210 passim. Marshal Joseph Joffre, *Mémoires du Maréchal Joffre, 1910–1917* (Paris: Plon, 2 vols, 1932), i, pp. 41–101, relates at length his pre-war skirmishes with the French government in chapters summarised in an appendix of the English-language translation of his memoirs: Joffre, *Memoirs*, ii, pp. 583–95.
10. William Philpott, *Anglo-French Relations and Strategy on the Western Front* (Basingstoke: Macmillan, 1996), pp. 19–20. GQG had a haphazard approach to gathering and using intelligence at the start of the war. Apparently, an indiscreet captured German officer revealed over dinner at General Charles Lanrezac's Fifth Army headquarters the strength of the enveloping German right-wing armies, which intelligence was dismissed by Joffre's director of operations and intelligence, Colonel Henri Berthelot: Général Léon Godfroy, 'Souvenirs militaires, 1894–1945', Papiers Léon Godfroy, *Service historique de la défense*, Vincennes [SHD], 1K534, p. 276. See the discussion in Torrey, op. cit., pp. 56–61.
11. House, op. cit., passim.
12. Joffre did not usually take such decisions personally but would act decisively on reports of failure from subordinate army commanders. The process of dismissal is discussed in André Bourachot, *Marshal Joffre: The Triumphs, Failures and Controversies of France's Commander-in-Chief in the Great War*, trans. Andrew Uffindell (Barnsley: Pen & Sword, 2013), pp. 180–7.
13. 25 and 26 August 1914, Raymond Poincaré, *Au Service de la France: Neuf années de souvenirs*, vol. 5, *L'Invasion* (Paris: Libraire Plon, 1928), pp. 176 and 180–1.
14. Cited in Godfroy, op. cit., p. 361.
15. Staff work at GQG is discussed in Torrey, op. cit., pp. 46–68 passim.

16. Godfroy, op. cit., p. 361.
17. Joffre, *Memoirs*, i, p. 254; Richard Holmes, *The Little Field Marshal: A Life of Sir John French* (London: Weidenfeld & Nicholson, 1981), pp. 238–9.
18. Joffre, op. cit., i, p. 321.
19. Ibid., i, pp. 294–5.
20. William Philpott, 'Kitchener and the 29th Division: A Study in Anglo-French Strategic Relations, 1914–1915', *The Journal of Strategic Studies*, 16 (1993), pp. 375–407: 379.
21. William Philpott, 'Britain and France go to War: Anglo-French Relations on the Western Front', *War in History*, 2 (1995), pp. 43–64: 50.
22. General Amédé Thierry, 'Souvenirs de la Somme', SHD, 1K1698, pp. 15–16.
23. Quoted in Roger Lloyd-Jones and M. J. Lewis, *Arming the Western Front: War, Business and the State in Britain, 1900–1920* (Routledge: London, 2016), p. 126.
24. Joffre, op. cit., i, p. 14.
25. Ibid., i, pp. 321–2.
26. *The Times*, 15 August 1914.
27. 1 April 1915, in Maréchal Fayolle, *Cahiers secrets de la grande guerre*, ed. Henry Contamine (Paris: Plon, 1964), p. 96.
28. Joffre, op. cit., i, p. 317.
29. The title of part III of ibid., ii, p. 325.
30. The relationship is explored in Philpott, 'Kitchener and the 29th Division', pp. 385–99 passim.
31. Joffre, op. cit., ii, p. 370.
32. Ibid., ii, p. 327.
33. For an analysis see Jere Clemens King, *Generals and Politicians: Conflict between France's High Command, Parliament and Government, 1914–1918* (Berkeley: University of California Press, 1951).
34. Joffre, op. cit., ii, pp. 331–3 and appendix to part III, ii, pp. 596–607.
35. King, op. cit., pp. 36–66 passim.
36. Bourachot, op. cit., p. 125.
37. Joffre, op. cit., ii, pp. 372–6.
38. William Philpott, 'Squaring the Circle: The Higher Co-ordination of the Entente in the Winter of 1915–16', *English Historical Review*, 114 (1999), pp. 875–98: 890–2.
39. Joffre, op. cit., ii, pp. 385–6.
40. Ibid, ii, p. 426.
41. Yves Gras, *Castelnau: Ou l'art de commander, 1851–1944* (Paris: Éditions Denoël, 1990), pp. 263–7.
42. Général Marie-Eugène Debeney, *La Guerre et les hommes: Réflexions d'après-guerre* (Paris: Librairie Plon, 1937), p. 49.
43. Joffre, op. cit., ii, p. 329.
44. 'Written Statement of the Conference Held at Chantilly, December 6th 1915', The National Archives, Kew, WO 106/1454.
45. 25 December 1915, John Charteris, *At G.H.Q.* (London: Cassell & Co., 1931), pp. 125–6.
46. 14 and 28 February and 2 May 1916, in *The Private Papers of Douglas Haig, 1914–1919*, ed. Robert Blake (London: Eyre & Spottiswoode, 1952), pp. 129, 134 and 141. Joffre was then 64 years old, Haig ten years younger.
47. Haig diary, 7 April 1916, Field Marshal Earl Haig of Bemersyde papers, National Library of Scotland, Edinburgh, Acc. 3155-105 fol. 67b.
48. Philpott, *Anglo-French Relations*, pp. 112–26 and *Bloody Victory*, pp. 56–100 passim.
49. Joffre, op. cit., ii, p. 617.
50. Ibid., ii, p. 618.
51. 14 and 28 June 1916, *Journal de marche de Joffre (1916–1919)*, ed. Guy Pédroncini (Vincennes: Service Historique de l'Armée de Terre, 1990), pp. 14 and 28.

52. 20 June 1916, ibid., p. 19.
53. Bourachot, op. cit., pp. 158–69 gives a balanced evaluation of the two sides of the argument.
54. 14 March 1916, Henry Bordeaux, *Histoire d'une vie* (Paris: Libraire Plon, 13 vols, 1951–73), vol. 5: *Douleur et gloire de Verdun, 21 février 1916–2 janvier 1917* (1959), p. 40.
55. King, op. cit., pp. 115–22.
56. 3 July 1916, Bordeaux, op. cit., pp. 155–6.
57. King, op. cit., p. 123.
58. Philpott, *Bloody Victory*, pp. 82–6.
59. 31 May 1916, Blake, op. cit., p. 146.
60. 28 June 1916, ibid., p. 150.
61. 'Instruction personelle et secrète pour M. le général Sir Douglas Haig et le général Foch', by Joffre, 21 June 1916, AFGG, tome IV, *Verdun et la Somme*, vol. 2, *La Bataille de Verdun et les offensives des alliées (1 mai 1916–3 septembre 1916)* (Paris: Imprimerie Nationale, 1933), annexes vol. 2, annexe 1385, pp. 316–8: 317–8.
62. 2 July 1916, Pedroncini, op. cit., p. 32.
63. Philpott, op. cit., pp. 215–6.
64. 'L'Offensive de la Somme', Fonds Foch, SHD, 1K129/1.
65. Joffre, op. cit., ii, p. 478.
66. 11 August 1916, Pedroncini, op. cit., pp. 82–4.
67. 12 August, ibid., pp. 85–6; 12 August 1916, Blake, op. cit., pp. 160.
68. 27 August 1916, Blake, op. cit., pp. 162–3; 27 August and 9 September 1916, Pedroncini, op. cit., pp. 100–1 and 113.
69. 7 September 1916, Pedroncini, op. cit., pp. 110–11.
70. 13, 14 and 18 September, ibid., pp. 116–17 and 120.
71. Philpott, op. cit., pp. 344–77 passim.
72. 11, 29 and 30 September and 4, 6 and 18 October 1916, Pedroncini, op. cit., pp. 115, 130–1, 132–3 and 140–1.
73. 10, 16, 19 and 20 September 1916, ibid., pp. 114, 119 and 122.
74. 26 September 1916, ibid., pp. 127–8.
75. 15 November 1916, ibid., p. 160–1.
76. David Lloyd George, *War Memoirs of David Lloyd George* (London: Odhams Press Ltd, 2 vols, 1938), i, pp. 544–75 passim.
77. 27–30 November and 1, 3, 4 and 7 December 1916, Pedroncini, op. cit., pp. 169–71 and 173–8.
78. 13 and 27 December 1916 and 'Note particulière', ibid., pp. 181–7 and 194–6.
79. See William Philpott, *Attrition: Fighting the First World War* (London: Little, Brown, 2014), esp. pp. 231–53.
80. 7 November 1916, Pedroncini, op. cit., p. 155.
81. 18 April 1923, Bordeaux, op. cit., vol. 8, *L'Enchantement de la victoire, 1 août 1919–31 décembre 1923* (1962), pp. 291–2.
82. The documents are collated in Fonds Joffre, SHD, series 14N.
83. 2 February 1918, Bordeaux, op. cit., vol. 6, *L'Année ténébreuse, 3 janvier 1917–21 mars 1918* (1959), p. 261.
84. 'Conversation du 6 Octobre 1917 avec le général Foch', quoting Foch, Pedroncini, op. cit., pp. 228–9.
85. Ibid.
86. 11 June 1917 and 'Organisation du commandement américain en France', [September 1917], ibid., pp. 219–20 and 225–6.
87. 'Note sur l'unité de commandement', 12 December 1917, ibid., pp. 243–5.
88. 24 March 1918, in Poincaré, op. cit., vol. 10: *Victoire et armistice* (Paris: Libraire Plon, 1933), p. 85.

89. 28 March 1918, ibid., p. 94.
90. 29 June 1918 and 'Conversation avec le commandant François-Marsal du cabinet du ministre', 2 August 1918, Perdoncini, op. cit., pp. 272–3 and 282.
91. 26 and 29 Janaury 1920, ibid., p. 322.
92. There was some opposition among the academy's membership, but in the end only one abstention. 14 and October 1917 and 14 February 1918, Bordeaux, op. cit., pp. 206, 232 and 270.
93. 2 February 1918, ibid., pp. 261–2.
94. 19 December 1918, Pedroncini, op. cit., p. 297. His words are quoted in Général Debeney, 'Nos grandes écoles: viii: L'École supérieure de guerre', *Revue des deux mondes*, 37 (1927), pp. 84–103: 86–7. He had decided on the theme some months earlier, advised by Bordeaux and his staff officers: 2 and 27 February 1918, Bordeaux, op. cit., pp. 262 and 285.
95. 1, 2 and 9 July 1919, Pedroncini, op. cit., pp. 317–9.
96. Debeney, op. cit., pp. 4–5.
97. Bourachot, op. cit., p. xiv.
98. Ibid., p. xii. Joffre has been the subject of many biographies and studies, and it is beyond the scope of this chapter to discuss his historical reputation.
99. Philpott, *Anglo-French Relations*, p. 18.
100. 'Situation générale fin octobre 1917' and 'Observations approuvées par le maréchal', May 1918, Pedroncini, op. cit., pp. 233–5 and 269–70.

**Chapter 2**

1. John Dos Passos, *Mr Wilson's War* (New York: Doubleday, 1962), p. 402.
2. For recent general works on Foch see Michael S. Neiberg, *Foch: Supreme Allied Commander in the Great War* (Dulles, Va.: Potomac Books, 2003); Elizabeth Greenhalgh, *Foch in Command: The Forging of a First World War General* (Cambridge: Cambridge University Press, 2011); Jean Autin, *Foch, ou le triomphe de la volonté* (Paris: Perrin, 1987); and Jean-Christophe Notin, *Foch* (Paris: Perrin, 2008).
3. Ferdinand Foch, *The Memoirs of Marshal Foch*, trans. T. Bentley Mott (Garden City, NY: Doubleday, Doran, and Company, 1931), p. 211.
4. Robert Doughty, *Pyrrhic Victory: French Strategy and Operations in the Great War* (Cambridge, Mass.: The Belknap Press, 2005), p. 196.
5. Ibid., pp. 201–2.
6. This quotation has been attributed to several French generals during the war, including Maurice Sarrail, who led the coalition campaign at Salonika. 'Preface', in *Coalition Warfare: An Uneasy Accord*, ed. Keith Neilson and Roy Prete (Waterloo, Ont.: Wilfred Laurier University Press, 1983), p. xii.
7. 25 March 1918, in *Douglas Haig: War Diaries and Letters, 1914–1918*, ed. Gary Sheffield and John Bourne (London: Orion, 2005), p. 393.
8. Greenhalgh, op. cit., p. 57.
9. Quoted in Joseph Monteilhet, *Les Institutions militaires de la France* (Paris: Alcan, 1926), p. 262.
10. For more, see Keith Jeffery, *Field Marshal Sir Henry Wilson: A Political Soldier* (Oxford: Oxford University Press, 2006), pp. 73–4.
11. Quoted in Barbara Tuchman, *The Guns of August* (New York: Random House, 1962), p. 58.
12. For more see Michael Neiberg, 'The Evolution of Strategic Thinking in World War I: A Case Study of the Second Battle of the Marne', *Journal of Military and Strategic Studies*, 13 (2011), available online at https://jmss.org/article/view/57990
13. Foch to Joffre, 6 and 10 November and 6 December 1915, AFGG, tome III, *Les Offensives de 1915. L'Hiver de 1915–1916 (1 mai 1915–21 février 1916)* (Paris: Imprimerie Nationale, 1923), annexes vol. 4, annexes 3056, 3064 and 3122, pp. 206–13, 232–41 and 382–90.

14. Michel Goya, *La Chair et l'acier: L'Invention de la guerre moderne, 1914–1918* (Paris: Tallandier, 2004), p. 261.
15. Nick Lloyd, *The Western Front: A History of the First World War* (London: Penguin, 2021), p. 456 and William Philpott, *Bloody Victory: The Sacrifice on the Somme and the Making of the Twentieth Century* (London: Little, Brown, 2009), pp. 441–2.
16. As an army group commander, Foch did not attend this meeting.
17. Philpott, op. cit., p. 128.
18. Ibid.
19. Ibid., p. 210.
20. Basil Liddell Hart, *Foch: The Man of Orleans* (London: Eyre and Spottiswode, 1931), p. 224.
21. Greenhalgh, op. cit., p. 191.
22. Doughty, op. cit., p. 310.
23. Maxime Weygand, *Foch* (Paris: Flammarion, 1947), p. 147. Foch was facing health problems, probably related to his prostate, but he was obviously well enough to assume command the following year and live another decade.
24. Greenhalgh suggests that Joffre's willingness to sell out Foch stemmed from Foch's complaints to the president of the Senate army commission, none other than Georges Clemenceau, about Joffre's conduct of the war. She calls those complaints 'nails into Joffre's coffin'. See Greenhalgh, op. cit., p. 201.
25. Weygand, op. cit., pp. 154–5.
26. Leonard Smith, *Between Mutiny and Obedience: The Case of the French Fifth Infantry Division during World War I* (Princeton: Princeton University Press, 1994).
27. Notin, op. cit., p. 270.
28. Mario Morselli, *Caporetto, 1917: Victory or Defeat?* (London: Frank Cass, 2001), p. 109. Diaz replaced Cadorna on 8 November.
29. Liddell Hart, op. cit., p. 263. Clemenceau was quite correct. In fact, while he attended some of its meetings, Foch was never formally a member of the SWC.
30. David Zabecki argues forcefully that the Germans were, in fact, not trying to create such a wedge. See his informative *The German 1918 Offensives: A Case Study in the Operational Level of War* (London: Routledge, 2006).
31. John Paul Harris, *Douglas Haig and the First World War* (Cambridge: Cambridge University Press, 2008), p. 460.
32. David Stevenson, *With Our Backs to the Wall: Victory and Defeat in 1918* (Cambridge, Mass.: The Belknap Press, 2011), p. 62.
33. Quoted in Rod Paschall, *The Defeat of Imperial Germany, 1917–1918* (Chapel Hill, NC: Algonquin Books, 1989), p. 145.
34. Maxime Weygand, *Mémoires: Idéal veçu* (Paris: Flammarion, 1953), p. 487.
35. General Sir Charles Grant, 'Some Notes Made at Marshal Foch's Headquarters, August to November, 1918', Liddell Hart Centre for Military Archives, King's College London, Grant Papers, 3/1. Ludendorff may well not have known his craft as he explained his strategic goals for 1918 thus: 'We will punch a hole. For the rest, we shall see.' Quoted in Williamson Murray and Mark Grimsley, 'Introduction: On Strategy', in *The Making of Strategy: Rulers, States, and War*, ed. Williamson Murray, MacGregor Knox, and Alvin Bernstein (Cambridge: Cambridge University Press, 1994), p. 3. Zabecki, op. cit., is especially critical of Ludendorff as a strategist. See also Jay Lockenour, *Dragonslayer: The Legend of Erich Ludendorff* (Ithaca, NY: Cornell University Press, 2021), chapter 3.
36. Greenhalgh, op. cit., p. 355.
37. For more see Michael Neiberg, *The Second Battle of the Marne* (Bloomington: Indiana University Press, 2008).
38. 'The Memorandum of July 24th', by Foch, reproduced in Foch, *Memoirs*, pp. 425–9: 427.
39. Neiberg, op. cit., pp. 155–6; Philpott, op. cit., pp. 518–20.

40. For a brief introduction see Michael Neiberg, 'The Battle of the Meuse–Argonne, 1918: Harbinger of American Great Power on the European Continent?', *Foreign Policy Research Institute*, 9 May 2012, available online at: https://www.fpri.org/article/2012/05/the-battle-of-the-meuse-argonne-1918-harbinger-of-american-great-power-on-the-european-continent/
41. For more on the SWC see Meighen McCrae, *Coalition Strategy and the End of the First World War: The Supreme War Council and War Planning, 1917–1918* (New York: Cambridge University Press, 2019).
42. The best study of this period is Jere Clemens King, *Foch versus Clemenceau: France and German Dismemberment, 1918–1919* (Cambridge, Mass.: Harvard University Press, 1960).
43. Sharon Korman, *The Right of Conquest: The Acquisition of Territory by Force in International Law and Practice* (Oxford: Oxford University Press, 1996), p. 145.
44. Winston Churchill, *The Gathering Storm* (New York: Houghton Mifflin, 1948), p. 6.
45. Raymond Recouly, *Foch: My Conversations with the Marshal* (New York: D. Appleton, 1929).

## Chapter 3

1. Nicholas Atkin, *Pétain* (London: Addison Wesley Longman Limited, 1988), p. 1.
2. Paul Gaujac, *Les Généraux de la victoire, 1914–1918* (Paris: Histoire & Collections, vol. 2, 2007), p. 46.
3. Richard Griffiths, *Marshal Pétain* (London: Constable & Co., 1970), p. xv.
4. Ibid., p. xvi; http://www.ecole-superieure-de-guerre.fr/promotion/14/ (accessed 24 August 2021).
5. Gaujac, op. cit., p. 46.
6. Atkin, op. cit., p. 5.
7. Gaujac, op. cit., p. 46.
8. Griffiths, op. cit., p. xvi.
9. Michel Goya, *La Chair et l'acier: L'Invention de la guerre moderne, 1914–1918* (Paris: Tallandier, 2004), p. 29.
10. Untitled letter, 30 October 1904, *Service historique de la défense* [SHD], 1K188.
11. Ibid.
12. Ibid.
13. Atkin, op. cit., p. 5.
14. Griffiths, op. cit., p. xvii.
15. Gaujac, op. cit., p. 46.
16. Griffiths, op. cit., p. xix.
17. Gaujac, op. cit., p. 46.
18. Robert Doughty, *Pyrrhic Victory: French Strategy and Operations in the Great War* (Cambridge, Mass.: Belknap Press of Harvard University Press, 2005), p. 70.
19. Ibid., pp. 73–4.
20. Gary Sheffield, *Forgotten Victory: The First World War: Myths and Realities* (London: Headline, 2001), p. 107.
21. Griffiths, op. cit., p. 3.
22. Ibid.
23. His predecessor, General Victor D'Urbal, took command of the newly created Eighth Army after four weeks leading XXXIII CA.
24. AFGG, Tome X, *Ordres de bataille des grands unités*, vol. 1, *Grands quartiers généraux, groupes d'armées, armées, corps d'armée* (Paris: Imprimerie Nationale, 1923), p. 839.
25. AFGG, Tome II, *La Stabilisation du front. Les Attaques locales (14 novembre 1914–1 mai 1915)* (Paris: Imprimerie Nationale, 1931), pp. 177–8.
26. Doughty, op. cit., p. 163.
27. Basil Liddell Hart *Foch: The Man of Orleans* (London: Penguin, 1937), p. 192.

28. Michel Goya, *Le Processus d'evolution tactique de l'armée française de 1871 à 1918* (doctoral thesis: University of Paris IV, 2008), p. 271.
29. Jonathan Krause, *Early Trench Tactics in the French Army: The Second Battle of Artois, May–June 1915* (Farnham: Ashgate, 2012), pp. 120–3.
30. Griffiths, op. cit., p. 12.
31. AFGG, Tome III, *Les offensives de 1915. L'hiver de 1915–1916 (1 mai 1915–21 février 1916)* (Paris: Imprimerie Nationale, 1923), p. 180.
32. 'Instruction préparatoire aux opérations de la Nème armée', GAC, 6 August 1915, SHD, 19N735.
33. Doughty, op. cit., p. 185.
34. Ibid., p. 190.
35. Alain Denizot, *Verdun, 1914–1918* (Paris: Nouvelle Éditions Latines, 1996), p. 79.
36. Ibid., p. 82.
37. Alistair Horne, *The Price of Glory: Verdun 1916* (London: Macmillan, 1962), p. 132.
38. Ibid., p. 133.
39. Marshal Henri Phillipe Pétain, *Verdun*, trans. Margaret MacVeagh (London: Elkin Mathews & Marrot Ltd, 1930), p. 77.
40. Doughty, op. cit., p. 273.
41. Denizot, op. cit., p. 94.
42. Ibid.
43. Horne, op. cit., p. 148.
44. Ibid., p. 229.
45. William Philpott, *Bloody Victory: The Sacrifice on the Somme and the Making of the Twentieth Century* (London: Little, Brown, 2009), p. 80.
46. 'Untitled letter', 9 May 1916, SHD, 1K188.
47. Philpott, op. cit., p. 82.
48. Doughty, op. cit., p. 278.
49. Denizot, op. cit., p. 96.
50. Horne, op. cit., p. 234.
51. Doughty, op. cit., pp. 284–5.
52. Ibid., p. 299.
53. Horne, op. cit., pp. 319–21.
54. Lt-Colonel Henri Carré, *Les Grandes heures du Général Pétain 1917 et la crise du morale* (Le Mans: Editions du Conquistador, 1952), p. 11.
55. Doughty, op. cit., p. 345.
56. Ibid., pp. 338–9.
57. Ibid., p. 354.
58. Denis Rolland, *La Grève des tranchées: Les Mutineries de 1917* (Paris: Éditions Imago, 2005), p. 365.
59. Ibid., pp. 148 and 359.
60. Guy Pedroncini, *Les Mutineries de 1917* (Paris: Presses Universitaires de Paris, 1967), p. 57.
61. Rolland, op. cit., pp. 407–12.
62. Carré, op. cit., p. 133.
63. Ibid., p. 120.
64. 'Directive no. 1: Pour les commandants de groupes d'armées et armées seulement', by Pétain, 19 May 1917, in AFGG, tome V, *L'Offensive d'avril 1917. Les Opérations à objectifs limités (1 novembre 1916–1 novembre 1917)*, vol. 2, *Les Opérations à objectifs limités (15 mai –1 novembre 1917)* (Paris: Imprimerie Nationale, 1936), annexes vol. 1, annexe 235, pp. 391–2.
65. Rolland, op. cit., p. 363.
66. Quoted ibid.
67. Pedroncini, op. cit., p. 194.

68. Ibid., p. 211.
69. Goya, *La Chair*, p. 233.
70. Griffiths, op. cit., p. 50.
71. Goya, op. cit., p. 238.
72. Ibid., p. 241.
73. Ibid., p. 240.
74. 'Directive no. 4 pour les groupes d'armées et les armées', by Pétain, 22 December 1917, in AFGG, tome VI, *L'Hiver 1917–1918: L'Offensive allemande (1 novembre 1917–18 juillet 1918)*, vol. 1, *La Préparation de la campagne de 1918: L'Offensive allemand de l'Oise à la Mer du Nord (1 novembre 1917–30 avril 1918)* (Paris: Imprimerie Nationale, 1931), annexes vol. 1, annexe 202, pp. 359–62.
75. Griffiths, op. cit., p. 52.
76. Goya, op. cit., p. 225.
77. Elizabeth Greenhalgh, *Foch in Command: The Forging of a First World War General* (Cambridge: Cambridge University Press, 2011), p. 276. See also 'La Bataille de 1918', 9 October 1917, by General de Barescut, 3rd Bureau, GQG, AFGG VI/1, annexes vol. 1, annexe 7, pp. 11–19.
78. Greenhalgh, op. cit., p. 331.
79. Robert Bruce, *Pétain: Verdun to Vichy* (Washington DC: Potomac Books, 2008), p. 60.
80. Ibid.
81. Griffiths, op. cit., p. 71.
82. It is effectively deconstructed in Elizabeth Greenhalgh, 'Myth and Memory: Sir Douglas Haig and the Imposition of Allied Unified Command in March 1918', *The Journal of Military History*, 68 (2004), pp. 771–820.
83. Quoted in Griffiths, op. cit., p. 69.
84. Greenhalgh, op, cit., pp. 786–7.
85. Greenhalgh, *Foch in Command*, pp. 373–4.
86. Bruce, op. cit., p. 66.
87. Michael Neiberg, *The Second Battle of the Marne* (Indianapolis: Indiana University Press, 2008), p. 117.
88. 26 August 1918, Maréchal Fayolle, *Cahiers secrets de la grande guerre*, ed. Henry Contamine (Paris: Plon, 1964), p. 299.
89. Ibid.
90. Major-General Sir Edward Spears, *Two Men Who Saved France: Pétain 1917; de Gaulle 1940* (London: Eyre & Spottiswoode, 1966), p. 140.

## Chapter 4

1. Denis Rolland, *Nivelle: L'Inconnu du Chemin des Dames* (Paris: IMAGO, 2012), p. 21. Rolland's volume is a major contribution to the historiography of the French Army in the First World War but, as the author admits, he tends to skip over operational details.
2. http://www.ecole-superieure-de-guerre.fr/promotion/13/
3. Rolland, op. cit., p. 28.
4. Ibid., p. 32.
5. Robert Nivelle 'Chez l'empereur de Corée', *Revue de Paris*, July–August 1903, pp. 523–47. This article is a fascinating insight into Nivelle's introduction to French diplomacy in the Far East – Nivelle used English and not French to converse with some of the senior Korean officers.
6. Rolland, op. cit., p. 38.
7. Ibid.
8. Robert Nivelle, *Manœuvres d'artillerie divisionnaire* (Paris: Charles-Lavauzelle, 1913).
9. Roy MacLeod, 'Sight and Sound on the Western Front: Surveyors, Scientists and the Battlefield Laboratory, 1915–1918', *War and Society*, 18 (2000), pp. 34–9; Charles

Nordmann, À *coups de canon: Notes d'un combattant (avec une lettre du Général Nivelle)*, (Paris: Perrin, 1917).
10. Rolland, op. cit., pp. 52–4.
11. Rémi Hebert, *La 1ère de Nivelle: La bataille de Quennevières – juin 1915* (Paris: Éditions Le Manuscrit, 2005); Rolland, op. cit., p. 59.
12. Quoted in Hebert, op. cit., p. 59.
13. Rolland, op. cit., p. 64.
14. Paul Strong and Sanders Marble, *Artillery in the Great War* (Barnsley: Pen & Sword, 2011); Rolland, op. cit., p. 65.
15. Strong and Marble, op. cit., p. 86.
16. See Malcolm Brown, *Verdun, 1916* (London: Tempus, 2000), chapter 15 for an excellent description of this phase of the battle.
17. Rolland, op. cit., p. 70.
18. Pascal Lucas, *The Evolution of Tactical Ideas in France and Germany During the War of 1914–1918*, trans. F.A. Kieffer (US Army, 1925), pp. 86–7.
19. Ian Ousby, *The Road to Verdun* (London: Pimlico, 2003), p. 5.
20. Strong and Marble, op. cit., pp. 84–9.
21. Quoted in Rolland, op. cit., pp. 74–5. Rolland suggests that the battle was won by 'the impetuous Mangin, supported by the organizational skills of Nivelle and tempered by the pessimism of Pétain'.
22. Elizabeth Greenhalgh, *The French Army and the First World War* (London: Cambridge University Press, 2014), p. 171. See also Edward Spears, *Prelude to Victory* (London: Jonathan Cape, 1939), p. 463.
23. Rolland, op. cit., p. 83.
24. Ibid., p. 82.
25. Jack Sheldon, *The German Army on Vimy Ridge, 1914–1917* (Barnsley: Pen & Sword, 2008), p. 230.
26. Anon, 'The Principles of Command in the Defensive Battle in Position Warfare' (Grundsätze für die Führung in der Abwehrschlacht im Stellungskrieg): issued by the Chief of the German General Staff in March 1917 and translated by British General Staff (Intelligence) in May 1917.
27. Anthony Clayton, 'Robert Nivelle and the French Spring Offensive, 1917', in *Fallen Stars: Eleven Studies of Twentieth Century Military Disasters*, ed. Brian Bond (London: Brassey's, 1991), pp. 52–65: 58–9. Clayton notes the Mebu (improved caves) that the Germans used as bunkers and it is notable that Nordmann describes discussing the defensive advantages conferred by these caves with Nivelle in 1914: Nordmann, op. cit., p. 238.
28. Paul Cornish, *Machine Guns and the Great War* (Barnsley: Pen & Sword, 2007), pp. 70 and 98.
29. Jack Sheldon, *The German Army at Passchendaele* (Barnsley: Pen & Sword, 2007), p. 11.
30. Jean de Pierrefeu, *French Headquarters: 1915–1918* (General Books reprint of the translation of the 1920 edition), p. 61. See also Spears, op. cit., p. 32.
31. Robert Doughty, *Pyrrhic Victory: French Strategy and Operations in the Great War* (Cambridge Mass.: The Belknap Press, 2005), pp. 322–5.
32. Timothy Lupfer, *Dynamics of Doctrine: The Changes in German Tactical Doctrine During the First World War* (Fort Leavenworth, Kan.: Combat Studies Institute, U.S. Army Command and General Staff College, 1981), p. 25. Lupfer notes that German offensive tactics shared many tactical concepts with Nivelle's tactical innovations but suggests that the Germans were more successful in executing them. See also Lucas, op. cit.
33. Pierrefeu, op. cit., p. 76.
34. Spears op. cit., pp. 130–1. Spears, a British liaison officer, described d'Alençon as a 'morose giant' (p. 252). Spears worked with most of Nivelle's staff officers but clearly shared Pierrefeu's views on their ability.

35. Pierrefeu, op. cit., pp. 62–4.
36. Ibid., p. 83. The simple truth is that Pierrefeu liked and admired Renouard but disliked d'Alençon, who he described as 'a Napoleon but devoid of genius'.
37. Rolland, op. cit., pp. 88–9.
38. Ibid., pp. 64–9 and 74.
39. Ibid., 62.
40. William Philpott, *Anglo-French Relations and Strategy on the Western Front, 1914–18* (London: Macmillan, 1996), pp. 100–2.
41. Robertson was also wary of Nivelle's claim that he could achieve a decisive success in 1917.
42. 24 March 1917, in Robert Blake, *The Private Papers of Sir Douglas Haig* (London: Eyre and Spottiswoode, 1952), p. 215.
43. Rolland, op. cit., pp. 125–6.
44. Spears, op. cit., p. 477.
45. John Paul Harris, *Douglas Haig and the First Word War* (Cambridge: Cambridge University Press, 2008), p. 300.
46. Ian Sumner, *They Shall Not Pass: The French Army on the Western Front 1914–1918* (London: Pen & Sword, 2012), pp. 143–4.
47. Stephen Yunker, '"I Have the Formula": The Evolution of the Tactical Doctrine of General Robert Nivelle,' *Military Review*, 54 (1974) pp. 11–25: 19.
48. Ibid., p. 22; Rolland op. cit., p. 135.
49. Clayton, op. cit., p. 56.
50. Rolland, op. cit., p. 131.
51. 24 March 1917, *Douglas Haig: War Diaries and Letters, 1914–1918*, ed. Gary Sheffield, and John Bourne (London: Weidenfeld & Nicholson, 2005), p. 277.
52. Rolland, op. cit., p. 150. By carrying this missive Messimy was probably operating on behalf of two masters, Poincaré and Micheler. It is notable that the account of the letter in Jean de Pierrefeu, *L'Offensive du 16 avril: La Vérité sur l'affaire Nivelle* (Paris: Cahiers de la Victoire, 1919), pp. 61–5, omits the sections where Micheler stated that an offensive of some kind was essential. See also 3 April 1917, Raymond Poincaré, *Au service de la France: neuf années de souvenirs*, vol. 9, *L'Année trouble, 1917* (Paris: Librairie Plon, 1932), pp. 101–2 and Spears, op. cit., pp. 356–8.
53. Henri Galli[chet], *L'Offensive française de 1917* (Paris: Librairie Garnier Frères, 1919), p. 87.
54. 'Rapport de Galli', no date and 'notes Helbronner', 7 April 1917, fonds Painlevé, *Archives nationales*, Paris, 313AP121 and 313AP122. See also Rolland, op. cit., p. 158.
55. Rolland, op. cit., pp. 155–60. Rolland suggests that de Castelnau's version of events is the most plausible. Nivelle actually handed over the letter that gave him authority as commander-in-chief – a subtle distinction but an important one.
56. Ibid., pp. 106–10; Pierrefeu, *French Headquarters*, p. 61.
57. Rolland, op. cit., p. 169; Carnets Tournés, 7 April 1917, SHD, 1K860/3.
58. Rolland, op. cit., p. 168.
59. Lupfer, op. cit., p. 23. See also Tony Cowan, 'Germany's Strategy in 1917 and Genius for War? The Introduction of New German Defensive Tactics in Early 1917', doctoral thesis, King's College London (2017).
60. Doughty, op. cit., p. 349.
61. Quoted in Spears, op. cit., p. 346.
62. Lupfer, op. cit., p. 25.
63. Ibid., p. 24. See also Spears, op. cit., pp. 93, 490 and 492 and Richard Watt, *Dare Call It Treason: The True Story of the French Army Mutinies of 1917* (London: Chatto & Windus, 1964), p. 136.
64. Wilhelm Balck, *Development of Tactics – World War*, trans. Harry Bell (Fort Leavenworth, Kan.: General Service School's Press, 1922), pp. 101–2.

65. 21 April 1917, in Maréchal Fayolle, *Cahiers secrets de la grande guerre*, ed. Henry Contamine (Paris: Plon, 1964), p. 217.
66. Spears, op. cit., pp. 494–5.
67. Rolland, op. cit., p. 192.
68. 24, 26 and 29 April 1917, Sheffield and Bourne, op. cit., pp. 286–8.
69. 24 April 1917, Poincaré, op. cit., p. 120.
70. William Philpott, *Attrition: Fighting the First World War* (London: Little, Brown, 2014), pp. 270–1.
71. Rolland, op. cit., p. 200.
72. Balck, op. cit., p. 112. Balck coldly dismisses Nivelle's removal as a purely 'political' act.
73. Colonel Émile Herbillon, *Souvenirs d'un officier de liaison pendant la guerre mondiale. Du général en chef au gouvernement*, vol. 2, *Sous les commandements des généraux Nivelle et Pétain* (Paris: Tallandier, 1930), p. 88.
74. Rolland, op. cit., p. 202.
75. Pierrefeu, op. cit., p. 81, supposedly quoting 'indisputable authority'.
76. Ibid.
77. Rolland, op. cit., p. 209, scathingly summarized in a letter to Painlevé.
78. Yunker, op. cit. Pétain's limited offensives in summer and autumn 1917 certainly utilized the tactical and operational precepts of Nivelle's notorious self-proclaimed 'formula'.
79. The enquiry's proceedings can be found in 'Offensive dans la région de l'Aisne pendant la semaine du 16 au 23 avril 1917', SHD, 5N255.
80. Yunker, op. cit., p. 23, suggests the unnecessarily high German casualties were partly ascribed to deploying far too many men in the first position.
81. Erich Ludendorff, *Ludendorff's Own Story, August 1914–November 1918: The Great War from the Siege of Liège to the Signing of the Armistice, As Viewed from the Grand Headquarters of the German Army* (London: Palala, 2016), p. 29.
82. French casualty figures are discussed in J. F. Jagielski, 'Le Choc de l'offensive Nivelle au Chemin des Dames', *Dossier: Les Chemins de la mémoire*, 176, October 2007, pp. 7–10, http://crid1418.org/doc/textes/ChMem/JFJ_CDD.pdf.
83. Rolland, op. cit., p. 237.
84. Quoted in Basil Liddell Hart, *Foch: The Man of Orleans* (London: Eyre and Spottiswoode, 1931), p. 250.
85. Greenhalgh, op. cit., pp. 216–9.
86. Cyril Falls, *The First World War* (Barnsley: Pen & Sword, 2014, reprint of 1960 original), p. 261.
87. Rolland, op, cit., p. 291.
88. Ibid., p. 240; Watt, op. cit., pp. 133–4.
89. Anthony Clayton, *Paths of Glory: The French Army 1914–18* (London: Cassell, 2003), pp. 130–1. See also David Murphy, *Breaking Point of the French Army: The Nivelle Offensive of 1917* (Barnsley: Pen & Sword, 2015).
90. Paul Painlevé, *Comment j'ai nommé Foch et Pétain: La Politique de guerre de 1917. Le Commandement unique interallié* (Paris: Alcan, 1923).
91. Pierrefeu, op. cit., p. 153; Lupfer, op. cit., p. 24.
92. Greenhalgh, op. cit., p. 218.
93. Clayton, 'Robert Nivelle', p. 63.

## Chapter 5

1. The dignity of Marshal of France was a legacy of the Bonapartist empires, and had been suspended during the Third Republican regime, before its reinstatement as an empty honour for Joffre after his removal from active command in December 1916.
2. The promotion of First World War marshals is discussed in Rémy Porte, 'Les Maréchaux de la Grande Guerre, entre mérites militaires, querelles de chapelle et instrumentalisation politique', *Revue historique des armées*, 292 (2018), pp. 29–40.

3. Generals removed from their commands were posted to a holding depot at Limoges, hence the slang term for sacking. The contemporaneous British army equivalent was Stellenbosched, after the South African War depot.
4. Henry Bordeaux, *Le Maréchal Fayolle* (Paris: Les Éditions G. Crès et Cie, 1921), p.28; the anecdote is recorded in a diary entry for 19–20 December 1918, in Henry Bordeaux, *Histoire d'une vie* (Paris: Librairie Plon, 13 vols, 1951–73), vol. 7, *La Victoire et le traité de Versailles, 21 mars 1918–1 août 1919* (1960), pp. 230–1.
5. 30 August 1914, in Maréchal Fayolle, *Cahiers secrets de la grande guerre*, ed. Henry Contamine (Paris: Plon, 1964), p. 27.
6. Ibid., p. 10.
7. Marshal Ferdinand Foch, *The Memoirs of Marshal Foch*, trans. T. Bentley Mott (London: William Heinemann, 1931), pp. xxi–xxii.
8. Bordeaux, *Fayolle*, pp. 9–10.
9. It was a recurring refrain during the German spring 1918 offensive: 31 March, 9 June and 31 July 1918, Contamine, op. cit., pp. 267, 282 and 292.
10. Bordeaux, op. cit., pp. 22–3. His colleague Pierre Ruffey, who had taught the artillery course alongside him at the ESG, was an army commander in 1914, although his tenure of Third Army was brief, being quickly dismissed after his failure in the Battle of the Ardennes.
11. Maurice Duval, 'Le Maréchal Fayolle', *Carnets de la sabretache: revue militaire retrospective*, 370 (1934), pp. 224–38: 225.
12. Bordeaux, op. cit., p. 26.
13. Ibid., p. 27. This may be creative embellishment on Bordeaux's part. Fayolle's own diary suggests after visiting some of his artillery batteries he spent much of the day at his command post. Modesty, lack of time to record the detail of events, or the simple belief that he was just doing his job may have prevented him outlining his own actions in any detail: 20 August 1914, Contamine, op. cit., pp. 21–2. One of his staff officers recollected his doing something similar a few days afterwards and Bordeaux may have collated several incidents: 19–20 December 1918, Bordeaux, *La Victoire*, pp. 230–1.
14. Bordeaux, *Fayolle*, pp. 14–15; www.ecole-superieure-de-guerre.fr/ (accessed 12 Janaury 2022).
15. Général Amédé Thierry, 'Souvenirs de la Somme', *Service historique de la défense*, Vincennes [hereafter SHD], 1K1698, p. 34.
16. Général Léon Godfroy, 'Souvenirs militaires, 1894–1945', Papiers Léon Godfroy, SHD, 1K534, p. 47.
17. Ibid., p. 50.
18. 'Discourse prononcé par Monsieur le Maréchal Pétain dans l'Amphitheâtre Louis', 6 April 1935, reproduced at www.ecole-superieure-de-guerre.fr/de-1919-a-1939.html (accessed 25 May 2021).
19. Duval, op. cit., p. 226; Douglas Porch, *The March to the Marne: The French Army, 1871–1914* (Cambridge: Cambridge University Press, 1981), p. 219.
20. Général Marie-Émile Fayolle, *Concentration des feux et concentration des moyens* (Paris: Lavauzelle, 1913).
21. Discussed in Simon House, *Lost Opportunity: The Battle of the Ardennes, 22 August 1914* (Solihull: Helion, 2017), pp. 162–71.
22. Marshal Joseph Joffre, *The Memoirs of Marshal Joffre*, trans. T. Bentley Mott (London: Geoffrey Bles, 2 vols, 1932), i, pp. 33–5.
23. Ibid., ii, p. 470.
24. Bordeaux, op. cit., p. 25.
25. Ibid., p. 12.
26. Ibid., pp. 16–17.
27. Contamine, op. cit. This edition was published fifty years after the war, but the original manuscript diary has not been traced.

28. Bordeaux, op. cit., p. 7.
29. Porte, op. cit., p. 34.
30. Bordeaux, *Histoire d'une vie*, op. cit.
31. 11 January 1917, ibid., vol. 6, *L'Année ténébreuse, 3 janvier 1917–21 mars 1918* (1959), p. 14. Fayolle's note of their first meeting was more matter of fact. 'Dinner with General Bordeaux, whose brother, the novelist, I met yesterday. The latter seems better than the general who is rather dull.' 12 January 1917, Contamine, op. cit., p. 201.
32. 21 January 1921, Bordeaux, op. cit., vol. 8, *L'Enchantement de la victoire: 1er août 1919–31 décembre 1923* (1962), p. 39. This meeting may have encouraged Bordeaux to write the biography, although he does not mention writing it in his diary. It was a long-conceived plan as he recorded his intention to prepare notes for such a biography after a meeting with Fayolle in May 1918: 26 May 1918, Bordeaux, *L'Année ténébreuse*, p. 76. He would also write the only biography of Maistre: Henry Bordeaux, *Le Général Maistre* (Paris: Les Éditions G. Crès et Cie, 1923).
33. Bordeaux, *Fayolle*, pp. 10–11.
34. 25 April 1916, Contamine, op. cit., p. 159.
35. Joffre, *Memoirs*, ii, p. 470.
36. 19–20 December 1918, Bordeaux, *La Victoire*, p. 230.
37. 20 and 21 August 1914, Contamine, op. cit., p. 22. He may have been apprehensive beforehand, complaining a few days earlier of a stomach upset and loss of appetite: 17 August 1914, idem, p. 20. This may have been a long-term condition that ultimately killed him. On this occasion he treated it, unsuccessfully, with Champagne! Duval, op. cit., p. 228.
38. 25 August 1914, Contamine, op. cit., p. 24.
39. 26 August 1914, ibid., pp. 24–5.
40. 27 August 1914, ibid., pp. 25–6.
41. 30 August 1914, ibid., p. 27.
42. 1 September 1914, ibid., p. 27.
43. Noël de Castelnau, 'Ordre particulier à la 70[e] division de réserve', 14 September 1914, quoted in Bordeaux, *Fayolle*, p. 29.
44. 4–9 September 1914, Contamine, op. cit., pp. 28–9.
45. Duval, op. cit., pp. 231–2.
46. Bordeaux, op. cit., pp. 30–8.
47. For an overview of this early phase of trench warfare see Jonathan Krause, *Early Trench Tactics in the French Army: The Second Battle of Artois, May–June 1915* (Farnham: Ashgate, 2013). The battle was a forming ground for successful French commanders. As well as Foch, Pétain and Fayolle, Maistre, who would command the other French offensive army group alongside Fayolle in 1918, commanded an army corps in Artois.
48. 23 August 1915, Contamine, op. cit., p. 127.
49. 5 March 1915, ibid., p. 89.
50. Ibid. Fayolle used the term '*la guerre actuelle*' ('the current warfare'), one of Foch's favourite aphorisms, suggesting a similar approach to problem solving.
51. 6 April 1915, Contamine, op. cit., p. 97.
52. 21 April 1915, ibid., pp. 97–8.
53. 30 April 1915, ibid., p. 99.
54. 7 May 1915, ibid., p. 100.
55. Krause, op. cit., pp. 73–4.
56. 9–13 May 1915, Contamine, op. cit., pp. 102–4.
57. 13 and 17 May 1915, ibid., p. 105.
58. Another stroke of fortune for Fayolle, General Ernest Barbot, who commanded the equally good 77 DI in the corps and who perhaps had a stronger claim to be promoted, had been killed by a shell on 10 May.

59. 20 April 1915, Contamine, op. cit., p. 97.
60. 18 May 1918, ibid., p. 106.
61. 6 August 1915, ibid., p. 124.
62. 12, 16, 17 and 21 September 1915, ibid., pp. 128–30.
63. 14 August 1915, ibid., p. 125.
64. 17 August 1915, ibid., p. 125.
65. 13 November 1915, ibid., p. 138.
66. 2 October 1915, ibid., p. 133.
67. 5 October 1915, ibid., p. 133.
68. 21 January 1916, ibid., p. 142.
69. Thierry, op. cit., p. 34. Dubois was sent to command the fortress at Verdun, a pivotal role at that moment in which he did not last long.
70. Duval, op. cit., pp. 233–4.
71. Brigadier-General Edward Spears, *Prelude to Victory* (London: Jonathan Cape, 1939), p. 127.
72. Duval, op. cit., p. 232.
73. 7 April 1917, Bordeaux, *L'Année ténébreuse*, p. 53.
74. 9 April 1917, ibid., p. 56.
75. Spears, op. cit., p. 127.
76. Duval, op. cit., p. 235.
77. Fayolle's role in the battle is examined in detail in William Philpott, *Bloody Victory: The Sacrifice on the Somme* (London: Little, Brown, 2009).
78. Duval, op. cit., p. 234.
79. Fayolle to Foch, 5 June 1916, in AFGG, tome IV, *Verdun et la Somme*, vol. 2, *La Bataille de Verdun et les offensives des alliés (1 mai 1916–3 septembre 1916)* (Paris: Imprimerie Nationale, 1933), annexes vol. 1, annexe 944, pp. 1274–7.
80. Philpott, op. cit., pp. 175–8 and 219–21. Duval, op. cit., p. 237.
81. This was actually shortly before Fayolle's sixty-fourth birthday. Rawlinson diary, 26 April 1916, Field Marshal Lord Rawlinson of Trent Papers, Churchill College Archives Centre, Cambridge, RWLN 1/5.
82. Spears, op. cit., p. 126.
83. Explored in detail in Elizabeth Greenhalgh, 'The Experience of Fighting with Allies: The Case of the Capture of Falfemont Farm during the Battle of the Somme, 1916', *War in History*, 10 (2003), pp. 157–93.
84. For example, 4 August 1916, Contamine, op. cit., pp. 170–1.
85. 23 and 30 September 1916, ibid., pp. 180 and 181.
86. Spears, op. cit., p. 127.
87. Brigadier-General Edward Spears, *Liaison, 1914* (London: William Heinemann, 1930), p. 32.
88. 12 September 1916, Contamine, op. cit., p. 178.
89. 14 and 15 September 1916, ibid., p. 178.
90. Philpott, op. cit., pp. 395–400.
91. 8 January 1917, Contamine, op. cit., p. 198.
92. 11 January 1917, Bordeaux, *L'Année ténébreuse*, p. 15.
93. Maréchal Fayolle and Général Dubail, *La Guerre racontée par nos généraux* (Paris: Libraire Schwartz, 3 vols, 1921), vol. 2, *De la Somme au Rhin*, p. 167.
94. 26 November 1916, Contamine, op. cit., p. 190.
95. 8 January 1917, ibid., pp. 197–8.
96. 8 May 1917, ibid., p. 223.
97. 5 January 1917, ibid., p. 197.
98. 6 January 1917, ibid., p. 197. D'Esperey was another 'colonial' who had moved from the relatively passive eastern end of the front. He would win laurels at Salonika at the end of the war and like Fayolle would become a Marshal of France.

99. 9 January 1917, Contamine, op. cit., p. 199.
100. 8 January 1917, ibid., p. 198.
101. 31 December 1916, ibid., p. 196.
102. 8 March–10 April 1917, ibid., pp. 205–10 passim.
103. Godfroy, op. cit., p. 186.
104. 28 April 1917, Contamine, op. cit., p. 219.
105. 1 May 1917, ibid., p. 222.
106. 15 May 1917, ibid., p. 225.
107. 2 and 17 May 1917, ibid., pp. 222 and 225.
108. 26 April 1917, Bordeaux, *L'Année ténébreuse*, p. 73. See also 21 April 1917, Contamine, op. cit., p. 217.
109. 2 May 1917, Contamine, op. cit., p. 222.
110. 3 May 1917, Bordeaux, op. cit., p. 77.
111. 6 and 7 June 1917, Contamine, op. cit., p. 228. Barthélémy had been one of Fayolle's students, passing out second in his year from the ESG. He commanded a division before and after his appointment.
112. 13, 19 and 23 May 1917, ibid., pp. 224 and 226.
113. 9 May 1917, ibid., pp. 223–4. Anthoine was moved to command First Army in Flanders to support the British army's northern flank in the Third Battle of Ypres. His light casualties in the initial attack Fayolle judged, perhaps unfairly, to be the result of the enemy's evacuation of the ground in front of him rather than the effective application of 'Somme-style' bite and hold tactics. 5 August 1917, ibid., p. 232.
114. 7 June 1917, ibid., p. 228. Gouraud had lost an arm at the Dardanelles.
115. 10 August 1916, in *Correspondence de guerre du Général Guillaumat*, ed. Paul Guillaumat (Paris: L'Harmattan, 2006), p. 135.
116. 26 August 1916, ibid., p. 140.
117. 11 October 1916, ibid., p. 151.
118. 29 June and 1 July 1917, Contamine, op. cit., pp. 229 and 230; 30 June 1917, Bordeaux, op. cit., p. 120.
119. 23 May and 20, 21 and 28 June 1917, and 'Extraits d'une lettre (d'un projet de letter?) de Guillaumat au Général Pétain, 27 June 1917', Guillaumat, op. cit., pp. 210 and 216–19.
120. 28 August and 9 September 1917, Contamine, op. cit., pp. 235 and 236.
121. 30 April 1916 and 7 November 1917, Guillaumat, op. cit., pp. 113–4 and 245.
122. 20 August 1917, Contamine, op. cit., p. 234.
123. 18 July 1917, ibid., p. 231.
124. 27 and 30 August and 9 September 1917, ibid., pp. 235 and 236.
125. 4 November 1917, ibid., p. 243.
126. 28 November and 8 December 1917, ibid., pp. 246 and 248.
127. 23 November and 11 and 12 December 1917, ibid., pp. 244 and 246. Fayolle's judgment of Duchêne proved insightful. He was to lose his army command in June after his poorly organized defences on the Chemin de Dames were overwhelmed during the German offensive.
128. 18 and 20 November 1917, ibid., p. 245.
129. 20 November 1917–15 February 1918, ibid., pp. 245–59 passim.
130. Bordeaux, *Fayolle*, pp. 78–9. A view endorsed by the parliamentary deputy Abel Ferry, cited in Contamine, op. cit., p. 249.
131. 20 November 1917, Contamine, op. cit., p. 245.
132. Fayolle to Foch, 23 December 1917, cited in AFGG, tome VI, *'L'hiver 1917–1918: L'offensive allemande (1 novembre 1917–18 juillet 1918)*, vol. 1, *La Préparation de la campagne de 1918: L'Offensive allemand de l'Oise à la Mer du Nord (1 novembre 1917–30 avril 1918)* (Paris: Imprimerie Nationale, 1931), p. 117.
133. 1 and 6 December 1917 and 2 January 1918, Contamine, op. cit., pp. 247 and 250.

134. 11 and 14 February 1918, ibid., pp. 253–4.
135. 31 December 1917 and 26 January 1918, ibid., pp. 249 and 252.
136. 20 March 1918, ibid., p. 259.
137. 22 March 1918, ibid., p. 261.
138. Godfroy, op. cit., p. 243.
139. 23–30 March 1918, Contamine, op. cit., pp. 261–6.
140. Henry Bordeaux, *Le-Plessis-de-Roye (2 août 1914–1 avril 1918): Un coin de France pendant la guerre* (Paris: Librairie Plon, 1920), p. 235.
141. 13 April 1918, Bordeaux, *La Victoire*, p. 42.
142. 30 March 1918, Contamine, op. cit., p. 266. The same sentiment war repeated on 26 August 1918, ibid., p. 299.
143. 29 August 1914, ibid., p. 27.
144. 30 September 1916, ibid., p. 181.
145. 12 January 1918, ibid., pp. 251–2.
146. 27 August 1917, ibid., p. 235.
147. 23 November 1917, ibid., p. 246.
148. Foch's memoirs are silent on the abilities and achievement of his subordinate.
149. 28 May 1918, Contamine, op, cit., p. 276. The bulk of the artillery and the supporting arms were provided by the French to ensure that the inexperienced Americans had a walkover.
150. 3 and 5 June 1918, ibid., p. 281.
151. 10 June 1918, Bordeaux, op. cit., pp. 97–8.
152. 30 July and 2 and 3 August 1918, Contamine, op. cit., p. 292.
153. For example, 4 July, 23 August, 8 and 26 September 1918, Contamine, op. cit., pp. 285, 298, 301 and 303. Debeney's role in 1918 is discussed elsewhere in this volume.
154. Contamine, op. cit., p. 298.
155. 24 August 1918, ibid., p. 298.
156. 8 August 1918, ibid., p. 294.
157. Duval, op. cit., p. 226.
158. 13 and 14 December 1918, Contamine, op. cit., p. 320.
159. 27 November and 10, 11, 20 and 26 December 1918, ibid., pp. 317, 319 and 321–2.
160. 23 June 1919, ibid., p. 332.
161. 14 July 1919, ibid., p. 333.
162. 28 January, 2 May, 14 July, 17 and 18 October 1919, 27 February 1920, ibid., pp. 324, 327–8, 333–6 and 338.
163. 27 October 1919, ibid., p. 338.
164. 5 September 1919, ibid., pp. 334–5.
165. Porte, op. cit., pp. 34–6.
166. 'Le Général Émile Fayolle', in Paul Gaujac, *Les Généraux de la victoire* (Paris: Histoire & Collections, 2 vols, 2007), i, pp. 46–7. It is possible that Duval, who ended the war as head of France's strategic air force, might have had some influence in the nomination.
167. Fayolle and Dubail, op. cit. Internal matter indicates that Dubail was responsible for most of the first and second volumes. It is likely that the narrative chapters were ghost-written. The clear explanation of 'the doctrine of the Somme' – the methodical tactics and techniques that would be used on the battlefield, as well as an explanation of why trying to 'break through' was misguided – bears Fayolle's imprint.
168. 3 August 1914, Contamine, op. cit., p. 14.
169. 9 May 1917, Bordeaux, *L'Année ténébreuse*, p. 81.
170. 20 August 1914, Contamine, op. cit., p. 22.
171. 9 May 1917, Bordeaux, op. cit., p. 81.
172. 29 August 1917, ibid., p. 183.
173. Spears, *Prelude to Victory*, p. 127.

174. 9 May 1917, Bordeaux, op. cit., p. 81.
175. 8 May 1915, Contamine, op. cit., p. 100.
176. 26 May 1918, Bordeaux, *La Victoire*, pp. 76–7.
177. Duval, op. cit., p. 227.

**Chapter 6**
1. Guy le Mouel and Henri Ortholan, *Le Général de Langle de Cary* (Janzé: Éditions Charles Hérissey, 2014), passim.
2. Ibid., pp. 13–27.
3. Ibid., pp. 27–34.
4. Ibid., pp. 35–50.
5. Ibid., pp. 51–70.
6. Roger Fraenkel, *Joffre: L'Âne qui commandait des lions* (Paris: Éditions Italiques, 2004), p. 88.
7. AFGG, tome I, *La Guerre de mouvement (opérations antérieures au 14 novembre 1914)*, vol. 1, *L'Avant-guerre. La Bataille des frontières* (Paris: Imprimerie Nationale, second edn, 1936), p. 78.
8. Ibid., pp. 53–91.
9. The same route would be taken by von Kleist's Panzer Group in May 1940.
10. Simon House, *Lost Opportunity: The Battle of the Ardennes 22 August 1914* (Solihull: Helion & Co., 2017), passim.
11. Ibid., pp. 29–49.
12. Ibid., pp. 53–60
13. Ibid., p. 111.
14. Ibid., pp. 136–7.
15. Ibid., p. 47.
16. Marshal Joseph Joffre, *The Memoirs of Marshal Joffre*, trans. T. Bentley Mott (London: Geoffrey Bles, 2 vols, 1932), i, p. 181.
17. Mouel and Ortholan, op. cit., p. 122.
18. Ibid., pp. 123–4.
19. Ibid., p. 125.
20. Joffre, op. cit., i, p. 211.
21. Le Mouel and Ortholan, op. cit., pp. 144–6.
22. 'Instruction générale n° 8 pour les généraux commandant les armées', by GQG, 8 December 1914, AFGG, tome II, *La Stabilisation du front. Les Attaques locales (14 novembre 1914–1 mai 1915)* (Paris: Imprimerie Nationale, 1931), annexes vol. 1, annexe 280, pp. 375–7; AFGG II, pp. 145–54.
23. Joffre, op. cit., ii, p. 335.
24. See for example, Jonathan Krause, *Early Trench Tactics in the French Army: The Second Battle of Artois, May–June 1915* (Farnham: Ashgate, 2013), p. 51.
25. AFGG II, p. 236.
26. Robert Doughty, *Pyrrhic Victory: French Strategy and Operations in the Great War* (Cambridge Mass.: The Belknap Press, 2005), pp. 130–4.
27. 20 February 1916, Raymond Poincaré, *Au service de la France: Neuf années de souvenirs*, vol. 7, *Verdun, 1916* (Paris: Librairie Plon, 1931), p. 77.
28. AFGG, tome III, *Les Offensives de 1915. L'Hiver de 1915–1916 (1 mai 1915–21 février 1916)* (Paris: Imprimerie Nationale, 1923), pp. 231–7.
29. Ibid., pp. 362–3.
30. Ibid., pp. 231–7.
31. Doughty, op. cit., pp. 190–5.
32. AFGG, tome IV, *Verdun et la Somme*, vol. 1, *Les Projets offensifs pour 1916 et la bataille de Verdun (21 février 1916–1 mai 1916)* (Paris: Imprimerie Nationale, 1926), pp. 134–8.

33. 'Compte rendu de renseignements n°112', RFV, 7 February 1916, ibid., annexes vol. 1, annexe 162, p. 338.
34. 'Message téléphoné', by GQG, 10 February 1916, ibid., annexes vol. 1, annex 185, p. 383.
35. Joffre, op. cit., ii, pp. 442–51.
36. Malcolm Brown, *Verdun 1916* (Stroud: Tempus, 1999), p. 82.
37. Doughty, op. cit., pp. 270–2.
38. Jere Clemens King, *Generals and Politicians: Conflict Between France's High Command, Parliament and Government, 1914–18* (Berkeley: University of California Press, 1951 & Westport Conn.: Greenwood Press, 1971), pp. 97–100.
39. Joffre, op. cit., ii, p. 446.
40. Ibid.
41. Doughty, op. cit., p. 272.
42. Joffre, op. cit., ii, p. 447.
43. Ibid.
44. King, op. cit., p. 100.
45. Richard Griffiths, *Marshal Pétain* (London: Constable, 1970), pp. 18–19.
46. Joffre, op. cit., ii, p. 446.
47. Doughty, op. cit., p. 285.
48. De Castelnau to Joffre, 26 February 1916, AFGG IV/1, annexes vol. 1, annexe 753, pp. 834–5.
49. 'Dispositions prises dans la RFV en vue d'une attaque ennemie sur Verdun', de Langle to de Castelnau, 3 March 1916, AFGG IV/1, annexes vol. 2, annexe 966, pp. 65–75.
50. Ibid.
51. Joffre, op. cit., ii, p. 522.
52. Général Fernand de Langle de Cary, *Souvenirs de commandement 1914–1916* (Paris: Payot, 1935).

## Chapter 7

1. Henry Bordeaux, *Le Général Maistre* (Paris: Les Éditions G. Crès & Cie, 1923).
2. Ibid., pp. 1–2.
3. Paul Gaujac, *Les Généraux de la victoire* (Paris: Histoire & Collections, 2 vols, 2007).
4. 20 September 1918, Henry Bordeaux, *Histoire d'une vie* (Paris: Libraire Plon, 13 vols, 1951–73), vol. 7, *La Victoire et le traité de Versailles, 21 mars 1918–1 août 1919* (1960), p. 150.
5. Bordeaux, *Maistre*, pp. 7–8 and 25–7; Guy Le Mouel and Henri Ortholan, *Le Général de Langle de Cary (1849–1927): Un breton dans la grande guerre* (Janzé; Éditions Charles Hérissey, 2014), p. 84; http://www.ecole-superieure-de-guerre.fr/ (accessed 29 June 2021). Céleste Déprez, who passed out second, would rise to command an army during the war. Antonin Jaquin de Margerie, who passed out top of his class, was killed in action in November 1914.
6. Fayolle lectured on artillery tactics from 1898–1908; Pétain on infantry tactics from 1902–1911: http://www.ecole-superieure-de-guerre.fr/ (accessed 29 June 2021).
7. Bordeaux, op. cit., pp. 37 and 41.
8. Ibid., pp. 32–5, quoting Paul Maistre, *Spicheren, 6 août 1870* (Paris: Berger-Levrault, 1908).
9. Ibid., p. 47.
10. Lt-Col. Paul Maistre, 'Compte rendu d'un manoeuvre à simple action sur la carte', *Revue militaire générale*, 2 (1908), pp. 526–55.
11. Bordeaux, op. cit., pp. 47–9; Le Mouel and Ortholan, op. cit, p. 84.
12. Simon House, *Lost Opportunity: The Battle of the Ardennes 22 August 1914* (Solihull: Helion & Co, 2017).
13. In contrast to Fifth Army commander General Charles Lanrezac whose anxiety about turning to fight the pursuing enemy was soon to cost him his command. Marshal Joseph

Joffre, *The Memoirs of Marshal Joffre*, trans. T. Bentley Mott (London: Geoffrey Bles, 2 vols, 1932), i, pp. 201–2.
14. House mentions him only once, passing a situation report back to GQG on 20 August: op cit., pp. 55–6.
15. Le Mouel and Ortholan, op. cit., p. 142; 11 September 1914, in Général Fernand de Langle de Cary, *Souvenirs de commandement, 1914–1916* (Paris: Payot, 1935), p. 162.
16. Ibid., p. 126.
17. Marshal Ferdinand Foch, *The Memoirs of Marshal Foch*, trans. T. Bentley Mott (London: William Heinemann, 1931), pp. 114–23 passim.
18. Dates and details of commands here and elsewhere in this chapter are collated from AFGG, tome X, *Ordres de bataille des grands unités*, vol. 1, *Grands quartiers généraux, groupes d'armées, armées, corps d'armée*, and vol. 2, *Divisions d'infanterie, divisions de cavalerie* (Paris: Imprimerie Nationale, 1923 and 1924).
19. The author assumes this refers to Joffre, the only active marshal of France at that time. 27 October 1917, in *Correspondence de guerre du Général Guillaumat*, ed. Paul Guillaumat (Paris: L'Harmattan, 2006), p. 240.
20. William Philpott, *Bloody Victory: The Sacrifice on the Somme and the Making of the Twentieth Century* (London; Little, Brown, 2009), p. 350.
21. Bordeaux, op. cit., pp. 1–2.
22. Ibid., p. 3.
23. Maistre himself had conceived a memorial for his troops, but did not live long enough to see its realization: ibid., pp. 66–7.
24. *Mémoires de pierre: Les Lieux de mémoire dans le Pas-de-Calais*: Ablain-Saint-Nazaire, https://memoiresdepierre.pagesperso-orange.fr/alphabetnew/l/lorette.html (accessed 29 June 2020).
25. Bordeaux, op. cit., p. 3.
26. Yves Buffetaut, *Notre-Dame-de-Lorette: Les Battailes d'Artois*, vol. 1, *1914* (Louviers: Ysec Éditions, 2007) and vol. 2, *1915* (Louviers: Ysec Éditions, 2015) provides a short summary.
27. Foch, op. cit., p. 216.
28. Jonathan Krause, *Early Trench Tactics in the French Army: The Second Battle of Artois, May–June 1915* (Farnham: Ashgate, 2013), pp. 28–9.
29. For early reflections on the emerging tactical challenges see Maistre to Maud'huy, 12 November 1914 and Maistre's report to Maud'huy, 21 December 1914, AFGG, tome II, *La Stabilisation du front. Les Attaques locales (14 novembre 1914–1 mai 1915)* (Paris: Imprimerie Nationale, 1931), annexes vol. 1, annexes 109 and 438, pp. 117–18 and 620–1.
30. Krause, op. cit., pp. 69–70, 107–8 and 131–2.
31. Ibid., p. 142.
32. Général Léon Godfroy, 'Souvenirs militaires, 1894–1945', Papiers Léon Godfroy, *Service historique de la défense*, Vincennes [SHD], 1K534, p. 184. Godfroy's divisional commander had appealed against his division being permanently attached to Maistre's army corps at the end of the Battle of the Somme.
33. It is possible that the rumoured German counter attack was never actually launched. Bordeaux, op. cit., pp. 61–4.
34. 13 March 1916, Bordeaux, *Histoire d'une vie*, vol. 5, *Douleur et gloire de Verdun, 21 février 1916–2 janvier 1917* (1959), p. 34.
35. 14 March 1916, ibid., p. 40.
36. 14 March 1916, ibid., pp. 37–8.
37. 17 March 1916, ibid., p. 46.
38. 'Héröique épopée du 86ᵉ RI: glorieux régiment de Velay, sur le champs de bataille de la Somme', SHD, 1Kt70.
39. Joffre, op. cit., ii, p. 484.

40. 'Denis Duchêne', in Gaujac, op. cit., i, pp. 36–7.
41. 28 May 1917, Bordeaux, op. cit., vol. 6, *L'Année ténébreuse, 3 janvier 1917–21 mars 1918* (1959), p. 89.
42. Godfroy, op. cit., p. 217.
43. Ibid., p. 218.
44. Tim Gale, *French Tanks of the Great War: Development, Tactics and Operations* (Barnsley: Pen & Sword, 2016), pp. 31–6.
45. Godfroy, op. cit., p. 222.
46. Cyril Falls, *The First World War* (London: Longmans, 1960), p. 285.
47. 4 October 1917, Bordeaux, op. cit., p. 200.
48. Bordeaux, *Maistre*, p. 39.
49. 12 October 1917, Bordeaux, *L'Année ténébreuse*, pp. 204–5.
50. René-Gustave Nobécourt, *Les Fantassins du Chemin des Dames* (Paris: Robert Laffont, 1965), p. 307.
51. Gale, op. cit., pp. 54–76.
52. William Philpott, 'France Leads the Way to Victory', in *Britain and Victory in the Great War*, ed. Peter Liddle (Barnsley: Pen and Sword, 2018), pp. 185–203: 190–1.
53. He was not the only one. His army group commander General Louis Franchet d'Esperey had to be stopped from mounting a potentially disastrous cavalry thrust against the St Gobain Massif: Godfroy, op. cit., pp. 224–5.
54. Bordeaux, *Maistre*, p. 84 note.
55. 27 October 1917, Guillaumat, op. cit., pp. 241–2.
56. 14 November 1917, Bordeaux, *L'Année ténébreuse*, pp. 238–9.
57. Godfroy, op. cit., p. 224.
58. 23 November and 11 December 1917, Maréchal Fayolle, *Cahiers secrets de la grande guerre*, ed. Henry Contamine (Paris: Plon, 1964), pp. 246 and 248.
59. AFGG, tome VI, *L'Hiver 1917–1918: L'Offensive allemande (1 novembre 1917–18 juillet 1918)*, vol. 1, *La Préparation de la campagne de 1918. L'Offensive allemande de l'Oise à la Mer du Nord (1 novembre 1917–30 avril 1918)* (Paris: Imprimerie Nationale, 1931), p. 118.
60. Godfroy, op. cit., p. 224.
61. AFGG VI/1, p. 119. The 47 DI plan of operations (26 December 1917) is at AFGG VI/1, annexes vol. 1, annexe 216, pp. 386–92 and the after-battle report (1 January 1918) at annexe 228, pp. 414–6.
62. Fayolle to Foch, 5 January 1918, ibid., annexe 236, pp. 434–5.
63. See for example, Maistre to *Ministre de la guerre*, 28 February 1918, ibid., annexe 411, pp. 923–6.
64. Godfroy, op. cit., pp. 277–8.
65. Bordeaux, *Maistre*, pp. 96–7.
66. 26 August 1918, Contamine, op. cit., pp. 298–9.
67. Bordeaux, op. cit., p. 107.
68. Ibid., pp. 98–103.
69. Ibid., pp. 105–6. Maistre's defensive principles are discussed in AFGG, tome VI, vol. 2, *L'Offensive allemande contre les armées françaises (1 mai–18 juillet 1918)* (1934), pp. 450–2, and set out in 'Note pour les armées', GAC, 9 July 1918, AFGG VI/2, anexes vol. 3, annexe 1871, pp. 387–9.
70. Berthelot's arguments with Maistre and his superior Pétain are discussed in Glenn Torrey, *Henri Mathias Berthelot: Soldier of France, Defender of Romania* (Iași and Oxford: The Centre for Romanian Studies, 2001), pp. 245–53. Torrey explains that under protest Berthelot accepted the principles of the new defensive arrangements while insisting on holding important positions in strength. His defensive adjustments were not completed before the German attack struck. In Berthelot's defence, with only ten days between his taking over Fifth Army and the German attack, several of which he spent arguing with his superiors, he did not have adequate time to prepare.

71. For an up-to-date account of the battle see Michael Neiberg, *The Second Battle of the Marne* (Bloomington, Ind.: Indiana University Press, 2008).
72. 'N'a rien des augures constipés': the comment was made in contrast to Foch, Pétain and Fayolle, the other responsible senior commanders. 22 July 1918, Guillaumat, op. cit., p. 346. Guillaumat was 'joyful' to be assigned to command Fifth Army under Maistre's direction in the final weeks of the war: 2 October 1918, ibid., p. 368.
73. Torrey, op. cit., pp. 256–61.
74. For example, Robert Doughty, *Pyrrhic Victory: French Operations and Strategy in the Great War* (Cambridge, Mass.: The Belknap Press, 2005) whose account of the final 1918 campaign largely focuses on coordinating operations with France's Anglo-Saxon allies. For a corrective see Philpott, op. cit., pp. 195–9.
75. Two recent studies of this final stage of the war by American historians fail to acknowledge Maistre's presence in the chain of command except in his sometimes fraught relations with US senior commanders with whom he was trying to coordinate operations. David Zabecki, *The Generals' War: Operational Level Command on the Western Front in 1918* (Bloomington, Ind.: Indiana University Press, 2018), pp. 267–8 and Doughty, op. cit.
76. Formally, Maistre was instructed to coordinate the preparation of operations with Pershing, leaving the execution to the American commander. 'Instruction personelle et secrète pour le général commandant le GAC, le général commandant la 1$^{re}$ armée américaine', 6 September 1918, AFGG, tome VII, *La Campagne offensive de 1918 et la marche au Rhin (18 juillet 1918–28 juin 1919)*, vol. 1, *Les Offensives de dégagement et la préparation des offensives générales (18 juillet 1918–25 septembre 1918)* (Paris: Imprimerie Nationale, 1923), annexes vol. 2, annexe 998, pp. 321–4: 323.
77. Maistre instructed his army commanders to limit follow-up advances to within artillery range to ensure that the infantry did not suffer unnecessary casualties from enemy rearguards. Maistre to Berthelot, 6 September 1918, AFGG VII/1, annexes vol. 2, annexe 1001, p. 326.
78. Maxime Weygand, *Memoires: Idéal vécu* (Paris: Flammarion, 1953), p. 616.
79. General John J. Pershing, *My Experiences in the World War* (London: Hodder and Stoughton, 1931), pp. 664–5.
80. Ibid., pp. 617–8.
81. Donald Smythe, 'A.E.F. Snafu at Sedan', *Prologue: The Journal of the National Archives*, 5/3 (1973), pp. 135–149. Smythe's assertion, based on an American source, that no one retook the city (p. 145), is incorrect. See Bordeaux, *Maistre*, p. 111.
82. 24–25 January 1919, Guillaumat, op. cit., p. 398.
83. Bordeaux, op. cit., pp. 120–2, quoting an unattributed report on Maistre's work as inspector of infantry.
84. Ibid., pp. 123–7.
85. Bordeaux paints a vivid death scene, the declining general surrounded by his loving family and mourned by his loyal soldier chauffeur: ibid., pp. 133–5.
86. Ibid., p. 122. A second statue, unveiled in 1928, stands in the town he was born, Joinville. 'À nos grand hommes', https://anosgrandshommes.musee-orsay.fr/index.php/Detail/objects/3569 (accessed 12 Janaury 2022).
87. Le Mouel and Ortholan, op. cit., p. 85.
88. Bordeaux, op.cit., p. 6.
89. Ibid., pp. 40–1.
90. Ibid., p. 78.
91. 22 July 1918, Guillaumat, op. cit., p. 346. His portrait would appear, alongside that of his counterpart Fayolle, on the cover of the illustrated periodical *Le Petit journal* as 'Nos chefs victorieux' on 18 August 1918.
92. Quoted in Bordeaux, op. cit., p. 117.
93. Ibid., pp. 114–17.

## Chapter 8

1. Simon House, *Lost Opportunity: The Battle of the Ardennes 22 August 1914* (Helion: Solihull, 2017), passim.
2. Edmund Burke III, *Prelude to Protectorate in Morocco: Precolonial Protest and Resistance, 1860–1912* (Chicago: University of Chicago Press, 1976), p. 29.
3. *Annuaire officiel de l'armée de France pour l'année 1884–1911* (Paris: Berger-Levrault, 1884–1911).
4. Pierre Rocolle, *L'Hécatombe des généraux* (Paris: Lavauzelle, 1980), p. 143.
5. *Annuaire officiel de l'armée de France pour l'année 1886–1888* (Paris: Berger-Levrault, 1888).
6. Claude Carlier, *Sera maître du monde, qui sera maître de l'air: La Création de l'aviation militaire française* (Paris: Economica, 2004), p. 24.
7. Ibid., pp. 63–75.
8. 'Le Général Pierre Roques', in Paul Gaujac, *Les Généraux de la victoire* (Paris: Histoire & Collections, 2 vols, 2007), ii, p. 53.
9. Carlier, op. cit., pp. 137–40.
10. Ibid., p. 135.
11. Ibid., p. 171.
12. Ibid.
13. Ibid., p. 148; House, op. cit., pp. 202–5.
14. Gérard Hartmann, *Le Grand concours d'aviation militaire de Reims 1911*, http://www.hydroretro.net/etudegh/grand_concours_d_aviation_militaire__reims_1911.pdf, (accessed 31 May 2012).
15. Carlier, op. cit., pp. 230–40.
16. Ibid., pp. 219–21.
17. Ibid., p. 231.
18. House, op. cit., p. 106.
19. Ibid., pp. 37–8.
20. Ibid., pp. 38–9.
21. Ibid., pp. 39-40.
22. Ibid., pp. 53–9.
23. Ibid., pp. 42, 44 and 50–3.
24. Ibid., pp. 86–7.
25. Ibid., pp. 94–102.
26. Ibid., pp.91–4.
27. Ibid., pp. 141–9 and 175–86.
28. Ibid., pp. 178–9.
29. Rocolle, op. cit., p. 144.
30. Robert Doughty, *Pyrrhic Victory: French Strategy and Operations in the Great War* (Cambridge Mass.: The Belknap Press, 2005), p. 59.
31. House, op. cit., pp. 124–38.
32. 4 February 1915, Henry Bordeaux, *Histoire d'une vie* (Paris: Libraire Plon, 13 vols, 1951–73), vol. 4, *La Guerre incertaine, de la Marne à Verdun, 2 août 1914–21 février 1916* (1957), p. 158.
33. House, op. cit., pp. 93–4 and 101.
34. Ibid., pp. 94–6.
35. Ibid., pp. 99–100.
36. House, op. cit., p. 107, including n. 115, citing AFGG, tome I, *La Guerre de mouvement (opérations antérieures au 14 novembre 1914)*, vol. 1, *L'Avant-guerre. La Bataille des frontières* (Paris: Imprimerie Nationale, first edn, 1922), p. 396.
37. AFGG I/1, p. 424.
38. 'Ordre général d'opérations n° 22 pour la journée du 25 août', Fourth Army, 24 August 1914, 20.00, AFGG I, vol. 2, *La Manoeuvre en retraite et les préliminaires de la bataille de la Marne* (Paris: Imprimerie Nationale, 1925), annexes vol. 1, annexe 225, pp. 165–7.

39. AFGG I/2, p. 174.
40. Ibid., p. 179.
41. 'Compte rendu de la situation de la IV$^e$ armée, le 25 au matin', Fourth Army, 25 August 1914, ibid., annexes vol. 1, annexe 453, p. 312.
42. Roques to de Langle, four telegrams, 24 August 1914 and 'Compte rendu officieux du 12$^e$ corps. Journée du 24 aôut 1914, 23 heures, raporté par officier liaison', ibid., annexes 292–6 and 298, pp. 208–12.
43. AFGG I/2, pp. 215–25.
44. Rocolle, op. cit., p. 143.
45. '*Chefferie*', noun (per *Nouveau petit Larousse 1970*): in a military context, a French colonial term for an administrative division of engineers.
46. Rocolle, op. cit., pp. 143–4.
47. AFGG, tome III, *Les Offensives de 1915. L'Hiver de 1915–1916 (1 mai 1915–21 février 1916)* (Paris: Imprimerie Nationale, 1923), p. 128.
48. Ibid., p. 131.
49. Ibid., p. 130.
50. Ibid., p. 208.
51. Ibid., pp. 359–61 and 429–30.
52. Henry Contamine, *La Victoire de la Marne* (Paris: Éditions Gallimard, 1970), p. 122.
53. Rocolle, op. cit., p. 144, citing René Pichot-Duclos, *Au GQG de Joffre: Réflexions sur ma vie militaire* (Grenoble: Archaud, 1947), pp. 253–4.
54. 4 February 1915, Bordeaux op. cit., p. 158.
55. 15 March 1915, ibid., p. 183.
56. An undated note in the margin, between 27 and 28 March 1915, ibid., p. 197.
57. 22 August 1915, ibid., pp. 299–300. The book was Henry Bordeaux, *Le-Plessis-de-Roye (2 août 1914–1 avril 1918): Un coin de France pendant la guerre* (Paris: Librairie Plon, 1920).
58. 4 November 1915, Bordeaux, *La Guerre incertaine*, pp. 334–5.
59. Sewell Tyng, *The Campaign of the Marne* (London: Forgotten Books, 2017 reprint of 1935 original), pp. 198, 217–8 and 343–5; Elizabeth Greenhalgh, *The French Army and the First World War* (Cambridge: Cambridge University Press, 2014), pp. 44–5 and 49. Joffre and Gallieni's fractious relationship is analysed in André Bourachot, *Marshal Joffre: The Triumphs, Failures and Controversies of France's Commander-in-Chief in the Great War*, trans. Andrew Uffindell (Barnsley, Pen & Sword, 2013), pp. 112–36.
60. Greenhalgh, op. cit., p. 100.
61. 26 November 1916, *Correspondance de guerre du Général Guillaumat, 1914-1919*, ed. Paul Guillaumat (Paris: L'Harmattan, 2006), p. 157.
62. Jere Clemens King, *Generals and Politicians: Conflict between France's High Command, Parliament and Government, 1914–1918* (Berkeley: University of California Press, 1951), p. 107.
63. Ibid., p. 108, citing Charles Bugnet, *Rue St Dominique et GQG, ou les trois dictatures de la guerre* (Paris: Librairie Plon, 1937), p. 138.
64. Joseph Joffre, *Mémoires du Maréchal Joffre* (Paris: Libraire Plon, 2 vols, 1923), ii, p. 560.
65. Doughty, op. cit., pp. 284–6.
66. Anthony Clayton, *Paths of Glory: The French Army, 1914–18* (Cassell, London, 2003), pp. 103–10. In practice, through the *Noria* (waterwheel) system of reinforcing the battle, divisions were pulled out before their losses made them operationally ineffective.
67. Charles Chinchole, *Le Général Boulanger* (Paris: Nouvelle Libraire Parisienne, 1889), passim.
68. 13 May 1916, Bordeaux, *Histoire d'une vie*, vol. 5, *Douleur et gloire de Verdun, 21 février 1916–2 janvier 1917* (1959), p. 112.
69. William Philpott, *Anglo-French Relations and Strategy on the Western Front, 1914-18* (Basingstoke: Macmillan, 1996), pp. 92–3 and 120–4.

70. Malcolm Brown, *Verdun, 1916* (Stroud: Tempus, 1999), p. 143.
71. Doughty, op. cit., p. 277.
72. 13 December 1916, Bordeaux, op. cit., p. 276.
73. 13 May 1916, ibid., pp. 112–13.
74. 21 March 1916 and 22 July 1917, Guillaumat, op. cit., pp. 106 and 224.
75. Joffre to Roques, 21 March 1916 and Roques to Joffre, 6 April 1916, AFGG, tome IV, *Verdun et la Somme*, vol. 1, *Les Projets offensifs pour 1916 et la bataille de Verdun (21 février 1916–1 mai 1916)* (Paris: Imprimerie Nationale, 1926), annexes vol. 2, annexe 1386, p. 598 and annexes vol. 3, annexe 1761, pp. 135–8; Roques to Joffre, 12 May 1916, AFGG, tome IV, vol. 2, *La Bataille de Verdun et les offensives des alliés (1 mai 1916–3 septembre 1916)* (Paris: Imprimerie Nationale, 1933), annexes vol. 1, annexe 260, pp. 378–9.
76. Roques to Joffre, 22 May 1916, Joffre to Roques, 29 May 1916 and Roques to Joffre, 8 June 1916, AFGG IV/2, annexes vol. 1, annexes 456, 664 and 1009, pp. 676–7, 929 and 1356–7.
77. King, op. cit., pp. 108–9.
78. Bourachot, op. cit., pp. 150–1.
79. King, op. cit., p. 109.
80. Ibid., pp. 110–11.
81. Pierre Miquel, *La Grande Guerre* (Paris: Fayard, 1983) p. 260. By 'secret' it meant that the parliamentary deputies met in closed session without secretaries, journalists, or members of the public in attendance. Such secrecy did not of course prevent deputies talking freely about the proceedings once they were over.
82. King, op. cit., pp. 109–13.
83. Miquel, op. cit., p. 375.
84. 12 June 1916, Bordeaux, op. cit., p. 133.
85. 3 July 1916, ibid., p. 155.
86. 1 June and 3 July 1916, ibid., pp. 128 and 155–6.
87. King, op. cit., pp. 115–22.
88. 3 July 1916, Bordeaux op. cit., pp. 155–6. By the day of the vote the Austrian offensive in the Alps that had been launched in mid-May had largely been contained.
89. King, op. cit., pp. 127–9.
90. 4 August 1916, Bordeaux, op. cit., p. 176.
91. King, op. cit., p. 131.
92. 28 August and 2 September 1916, Bordeaux, op. cit., pp. 186 and 189.
93. House, op. cit., pp. 67–9.
94. Doughty, op. cit., pp. 185–7.
95. Ibid., pp. 211–12; King, op. cit., pp. 67–88.
96. 9 September and 9 and 18 October 1916, Bordeaux, op. cit., pp. 198, 222 and 225–6; King, op. cit., pp. 131–5.
97. Philpott, *Bloody Victory: The Sacrifice on the Somme and the Making of the Twentieth Century* (London; Little, Brown, 2009), pp. 316–43, 346, 411 and 421. Among the allied politicians desire for quick victory with fewer casualties was increasingly at odds with a military strategy rooted in attritional warfare; therefore, progress on the Somme was perceived to be too slow by politicians.
98. 18 October 12916, Bordeaux, op. cit., pp. 225–6; King, op. cit., pp. 133–7.
99. King, op. cit., pp. 137–8.
100. 28 August 1916, Bordeaux, op. cit., p. 186.
101. 2 September 1916, ibid., p. 189.
102. 9 September 1916, ibid., p. 198.
103. 20 September 1916, ibid., p. 210.
104. 18 October 1916, ibid., p. 225.
105. 18 October 1916, ibid., pp. 225–6.
106. 15 November 1916, ibid., p. 253.

107. 23 November 1916, ibid., p. 258.
108. 12 December 1916, ibid, p. 276.
109. Doughty, op. cit., pp. 319–21.
110. Gaujac, op. cit., p. 53.
111. Ibid.

## Chapter 9

1. Général Léon Godfroy, 'Souvenirs militaires, 1894–1945', Papiers Léon Godfroy, *Service historique de la défense*, Vincennes [SHD], 1K534, pp. 2–3.
2. Général Marie-Eugène Debeney, *La Guerre et les hommes: Réflexions d'après-guerre* (Paris: Libraire Plon, 1937), pp. 3–4.
3. Godfroy, op. cit.
4. 8 August 1918, in *The Private Papers of Douglas Haig, 1914–1919*, ed. Robert Blake (London: Eyre & Spottiswoode, 1952), p. 323. Here Haig altered the text of his diary to make the French appear in a less favourable light. His original manuscript diary stated Debeney was 'pleased with himself' despite the defeat of the colonials: *Sir Douglas Haig: War Diaries and Letters, 1914–1918*, ed. Gary Sheffield and John Bourne (London: Weidenfeld & Nicholson, 2005), p. 440 and n. 2.
5. John Terraine, *To Win a War: 1918, the Year of Victory* (London: Papermac, 1986), pp. 112–3. While Terraine acknowledges that Haig's remark was 'possibly a sardonic over-statement', he concludes from it that 'it is clear that the French First Army was not performing well'.
6. Discussed in William Philpott, 'Sir Douglas Haig's Command? The Image of Alliance in Douglas Haig's Record of the War', *The Douglas Haig Fellowship Records*, 15 (2011), pp. 3–13.
7. 9 August 1918, Maréchal Fayolle, *Cahiers secrets de la grande guerre*, ed. Henry Contamine (Paris: Librairie Plon, 1964), p. 295. Debeney's army was operating west of Montdidier.
8. 2 June 1917, in Blake, op. cit., pp. 234–5.
9. http://www.ecole-superieure-de-guerre.fr/ (accessed 23 August 2021).
10. 'Le Général Marie Debeney', in Paul Gaujac, *Les Généraux de la victoire* (Paris: Histoire & Collections, 2 vols, 2007), i, pp. 30–1: 30; Claude Franc, *Le Haut commandement français sur le front occidental, 1914–1918* (Paris: SOTECA, Éditions 14–18, 2012), pp. 34–6; Michel Goya, *La Chair et l'acier: L'Armée française et l'invention de la guerre moderne (1914–1918)* (Paris: Tallandier, 2004), pp. 29, 58 and 66–7; Debeney, op. cit., p. 12.
11. Dubail to Joffre, [10 August 1914], AFGG, tome I, *La Guerre de mouvement (opérations antérieures au 14 novembre 1914)*, vol. 1, *L'Avant-guerre. La Bataille des frontières* (Paris: Imprimerie Nationale, 2nd edn, 1936), annexes, annexe 163, pp. 174–5.
12. Godfroy, op, cit., p. 89.
13. Debeney, op. cit., p. 14.
14. 'Instruction du Général Dubail, commandant la 1re Armée, au sujet des procédés de combat à employer vis-à-vis les Allemands', 3rd Bureau, First Army, 11 September 1914, reproduced in Général Augustin Dubail, *Quatre années de commandement, 1914–1918: Journal de campagne* (Paris: Imprimerie-librairie Militaire Universelle, 3 vols, 1920), i, pp. 106–7.
15. Debeney, op. cit., p. 14.
16. 'Note sur l'organisation d'une artillerie lourde d'armée' and 'Note complémentaire à la note sur l'artillerie lourde et à l'instruction particulière d'opérations n° 11', First Army, 18 September 1914, AFGG, tome I, vol. 4, *La Bataille de l'Aisne, la course à la mer, la bataille des Flandres, les opérations sur le front stabilisé (14 septembre–14 novembre 1914)* (Paris: Imprimerie Nationale, 1933), annexes vol. 1, annexes 411 and 412, pp. 382–6.
17. 17 September 1914, Dubail, op. cit., i, p. 121.
18. For example, 8 August, 13–14 September and 20 November 1914, Dubail, op. cit., i, pp. 20, 113–14 and 242.

19. 8 and 15 May 1915, ibid., ii, pp. 213 and 222.
20. Godfroy, op. cit., p. 136.
21. Debeney, op. cit., pp. 14–15.
22. Godfroy, op. cit., p. 136.
23. Alistair Horne, *The Price of Glory: Verdun 1916* (London: Macmillan, 1962), p. 161.
24. Debeney, op. cit., pp. 15–16.
25. Ibid., p. 16.
26. Quoted in Franc, op. cit., p. 283.
27. Debeney, op. cit., p. 16.
28. Jonathan Boff, *Haig's Enemy: Crown Prince Rupprecht and Germany's War on the Western Front* (Oxford: Oxford University Press, 2018), pp. 129–30.
29. 25 September 1916, 'Carnets de Guerre d'André l'Huillier', SHD, 1Kt185; 'Compte-rendu des 24 heures, 25–26 Septembre 1916', 42 DI, 26 September 1916, SHD, 24N992.
30. Colonel Bourgoin [151ᵉ RI], 'Souvenirs', 12 August 1969, SHD, 1Kt85.
31. 'Rapport du Général Meunier, Commandant l'artillerie du 32ᵉ Corps d'armée, sur l'emploi de l'artillerie au cours des opérations au Nord de la Somme, du 20 Septembre au 17 Novembre 1916 inclus', 23 November 1916, SHD, 22N1714/3.
32. Bourgoin, op. cit.
33. Sixth Army note, 24 September 1916, SHD, 24N992.
34. Bourgoin, op. cit.
35. l'Huillier, op. cit.
36. XXXII CA's operations are summarized in William Philpott, *Bloody Victory: The Sacrifice on the Somme and the Making of the Twentieth Century* (London: Little, Brown, 2009), pp. 398–9.
37. 4 November 1916, Fayolle, op. cit., p. 185.
38. 'Rapport du Général Meunier', op. cit.
39. Debeney, op, cit., pp. 17–18.
40. 21 October 1916, Fayolle, op. cit., p. 182.
41. Debeney to Fayolle, 1 November 1916, 'XXXII CA, Somme, 1916', SHD, 22N1714/1.
42. 'Historique', 40 DI, 19 October 1916, SHD, 22N1714/4.
43. 27 July 1917, in Henry Bordeaux, *Histoire d'une vie* (Paris: Libraire Plon, 13 vols, 1951–73), vol. 6, *L'Année ténébreuse, 3 janvier 1917–21 mars 1918* (1959), p. 133.
44. Debeney, op. cit., pp. 17–18.
45. 'Rapport du Général Meunier', op. cit.
46. Debeney, op. cit., p. 20.
47. 20 December 1916, in *Correspondance de guerre du Général Guillaumat*, ed. Paul Guillaumat (Paris: L'Harmattan, 2006), p. 168.
48. 24 December, ibid., p. 170.
49. Debeney, op. cit., p. 18.
50. 'Speech on the unveiling of the statue of General Foch', by Debeney, 1926, Foch papers (don Fournier-Foch), SHD, 1K129/3.
51. Jean de Pierrefeu, *GQG secteur 1: Trois ans au grand quartier général* (Paris: L'Édition Français Illustrée, 2 vols, 1920), i, pp. 269–70.
52. 1 and 23 May 1917, Guillaumat, op. cit., pp. 202 and 210.
53. Debeney, op. cit., pp. 21–2.
54. Pierrefeu, op. cit., ii, pp. 54–6.
55. 1 May 1917, Général Edmond Buat, *Journal, 1914–1923*, ed. Frédéric Guelton (Paris: Perrin, 2015), p. 387.
56. Godfroy, op. cit., p. 232.
57. Diary, early May 1917, in Elizabeth Greenhalgh, *Liaision: General Pierre des Vallières at British General Headquarters, 1916–1917* (Stroud: The History Press for the Army Records Society, 2016), p. 257.
58. Goya, op. cit., pp. 238–40.

59. Godfroy, op. cit., pp. 219–20.
60. Pierrefeu, op. cit., ii, p. 46.
61. 8–12 June, 3 July and 30 October 1917, Buat, op. cit., pp. 401, 405–6 and 452. Buat himself had divided loyalties. He was an artilleryman in command of the general reserve of heavy artillery at this point, but also one of Debeney's pre-war ESG colleagues.
62. Godfroy, op. cit., pp. 196 and 203.
63. Debeney, op. cit., p. 23.
64. Ibid., p. 24.
65. 22 December 1917, Bordeaux, op. cit., p. 247.
66. 'Huge, majestic, arrogant, very intelligent, hard on the troops, excellent gunner, lacking in goodwill and charm, responding to any call thinking only of himself. All the same this allows him to think big', was Bordeaux's assessment of his replacement, Anthoine: ibid. Anthoine, nicknamed 'the satrap', proved overbearing and unpopular at GQG and was replaced in the summer at Foch's and prime minister Georges Clemenceau's behest: Pierrefeu, op, cit., ii, pp. 165–7 and 224–7.
67. Debeney, op. cit., pp. 24–5.
68. Ibid., p. 26.
69. Maxime Weygand, *Mémoires: Idéal vécu* (Paris: Flammarion, 1953), p. 498.
70. Ibid.
71. Godfroy, op, cit., p. 242.
72. Debeney, op. cit., p. 26.
73. Godfroy, op, cit., pp. 232–3 and 243.
74. Debeney, op. cit., p. 27.
75. Ibid., p. 29.
76. Godfroy, op, cit., p. 244.
77. Debeney was receiving orders from Fayolle, Pétain and soon afterwards the new generalissimo Foch, had to coordinate operations with fellow army commanders Hubert Gough (British Fifth Army) and Humbert, and to give directions to army corps commanders arriving into the battle.
78. It was suggested at the time that the Germans found orders that indicated the arrival of the whole of First Army in the vicinity of Montdidier on the body of a dead staff officer (Commandant de Banville of the operations bureau who was killed on 27 March while on reconnaissance: Godfroy, op. cit., pp. 252–3): 14 April 1918, reporting a conversation with General Huchet [actually General Hucher], Debeney's chief of staff, in Bordeaux, op. cit., vol. 7, *La Victoire et le traité de Versailles, 21 mars 1918–1 août 1919* (1960), pp. 43–4. Hucher's explanation of cause and effect is improbable. German commander Erich Ludendorff had already ordered such a reorientation late on 26 March in response to reports of French reinforcements arriving in the Noyon region, suggesting he had decided to exploit the gap that Debeney was trying to close: David Zabecki, *The German 1918 Offensives: A Case Study in the Operational Level of War* (London: Routledge, 2006), pp. 150–3.
79. Cited in Godfroy, op cit., p. 263. Recent evaluation of the German spring offensive endorses this judgement: Zabecki, op. cit., pp. 161–4.
80. 27 March 1918, in Raymond Poincaré, *Au Service de la France: Neuf années de souvenirs*, vol. 10, *Victoire et armistice* (Paris: Libraire Plon, 1933), p. 93; Weygand, op, cit., p. 499. The Germans, with limited artillery support also, suffered heavily while making progress against the French outposts: Godfroy, op. cit., p. 251.
81. Ibid., pp. 257–8; Debeney, op. cit., pp. 28–34.
82. 8 April 1918, Poincaré, op. cit., p. 116.
83. Godfroy, op. cit., pp. 264–5, 267–8 and 281.
84. These were akin to the 'peaceful penetration' operations being mounted by the Australian Corps on First Army's left.

85. 28 May 1918, Fayolle, op. cit., p. 276. For an account of the Cantigny operation that acknowledges the significance of French artillery support see David Woodward, *The American Army and the First World War* (Cambridge: Cambridge University Press, 2014), pp. 224–31.
86. Debeney, op. cit., pp. 35–6.
87. Godfroy, op. cit., pp. 277–8 and 280.
88. 23 July 1918, Fayolle, op. cit., p. 290.
89. 8 April 1918, Poincaré, op. cit., p. 114.
90. '"The Absolute Limit": British Divisions at Villers-Bretonneux', in Peter Simkins, *From the Somme to Victory: The British Army's Experience on the Western Front, 1916–1918* (Barnsley: Pen & Sword, 2014), pp. 121–55: 148–9.
91. Godfroy, op. cit., pp. 259–62.
92. Ibid., p. 284: 29 July 1918, Sheffield and Bourne, op. cit., p. 436.
93. Basil Liddell Hart, *Foch: The Man of Orleans* (London: Eyre and Spottiswoode, 1931), p. 346. Liddell Hart took the reference from Haig's unofficial ghost-written account of his campaign, George Dewar and Lieutenant-Colonel John Boraston, *Sir Douglas Haig's Command* (London: Constable and Co., 2 vols, 1922), ii, p. 322n. Dewar and Boraston suggest Debeney's skill at manoeuvre warfare was a way to avoid hard fighting and to preserve the French army's strength until the end of the war. This interpretation cemented an enduring perception that British rather than French effort was decisive in the final campaign, one which Haig had written into his own narrative of 1918: 'During all this period from the 8th August onwards much difficulty had been experienced by the Fourth Army on its right by the tendency of the French to hang back, thus exposing a long defensive right flank. Many verbal expostulations were made both to General Debeney and Marshal Foch on the subject...': 'Summary of Operations on the Western Front, 1916–1918', in Field Marshal Earl Haig of Bemersyde papers, National Library of Scotland, Edinburgh, 213/a, p. 74. This narrative is challenged in William Philpott, 'France Leads the Way to Victory', in *Britain and Victory in the Great War*, ed. Peter Liddle (Barnsley: Pen & Sword, 2018), pp. 185–203: 197–8.
94. 28 October 1918, Blake, op. cit., p. 338.
95. Elizabeth Greenhalgh, *Victory Through Coalition: Britain and France during the First World War* (Cambridge: Cambridge University Press, 2005), p. 254.
96. 'Speech on the unveiling of the statue of General Foch', by Debeney, op. cit.
97. Godfroy, op. cit., pp. 291–2.
98. Philpott, *Bloody Victory*, pp. 522–7; Robert Doughty, *Pyrrhic Victory: French Strategy and Operations in the Great War* (Cambridge, Mass.: The Belknap Press, 2005), pp. 476–8.
99. Debeney, op. cit., pp. 31–3.
100. 'Bataille de Montdidier', First Army general order, 20 August 1918, in ibid., p. 380.
101. Haig to Debeney, [16] August 1918, in Godfroy, op. cit., pp. 293–4.
102. Ibid., p. 295.
103. Ibid.
104. Debeney, op. cit., p. 38.
105. Marshal Ferdinand Foch, *The Memoirs of Marshal Foch*, trans. T. Bentley Mott (London: William Heinemann, 1931), pp. 483–4. In accounts of the breaking of the Hindenburg Line the attack on St Quentin is presented as a supporting operation to enable the Fourth Army to cross the St Quentin canal to the north: for example, David Zabecki, *The Generals' War: Operational Level Command on the Western Front in 1918* (Bloomington, Ind.: Indiana University Press, 2018), pp. 244–7.
106. 'Bataille de Saint-Quentin', First Army general order, 10 October 1918, in Debeney, op. cit., p. 381.
107. 1 October 1918, Sheffield and Bourne, op, cit., p. 468.
108. Debeney, op. cit., p. 40.

109. Ibid., pp. 39–40.
110. Recommended by Fayolle, to which GQG acquiesced with ill-grace: Godfroy, op. cit., pp. 307–8.
111. 13 September 1918, Bordeaux, op. cit., p. 145.
112. 15 April, 14 May, 4 July, 8 and 15 September 1918, Fayolle op. cit., pp. 271, 273, 285, 301 and 302.
113. Godfroy, op. cit., p. 3.
114. Ibid.
115. Ibid., p. 227.
116. Robert Doughty, *The Seeds of Disaster: The Development of French Army Doctrine, 1919–1939* (Hamden, Conn.: Archon Books, 1985), p. 77.
117. Gaujac, op. cit., p. 31.
118. Godfroy, op. cit., pp. 322 and 330.
119. Goya, op. cit., p. 405 suggests Montdidier was the 'model battle' for post-war training. Franc, op. cit., p. 388 suggests Pètain and Debeney's legacy was that the set-piece battles of 1917 were the models for post-war doctrine and training. Doughty, op. cit., pp. 81–3, identifies that both Montdidier and the 1917 Battle of Malmaison became models for the 'methodical battle' and the 'attack with limited objectives' respectively, and suggests that the former was selected by Debeney to strengthen the influence he had over the ESG's students. It would seem that wartime experience changed but did not end doctrinal debates between advocates of firepower and shock action in the French army.
120. Commandant Bouchacourt, *L'Infanterie dans la bataille* (Paris: Charles-Lavauzelle, 2nd edition, 1931 [first edition 1927]), pp. 14–122 and 181–200. Bouchacourt had fought with the 94e RI in 42 DI in these actions and was posted as an instructor to the army's infantry school after the war. Louis Edouard Joseph Bouchacourt, https://www.leonore.archives-nationales.culture.gouv.fr/ui/notice/45686#show (accessed 28 October 2021). Debeney had congratulated the division on its success at the time: 'Your division has opened the doors of victory…If the battle now expands beyond expectations, it is due to 42 DI's rapid breakthrough.' Quoted Bouchaucourt, op. cit., p. 81.
121. Louis Émile Mangin, *Les Chasseurs dans la bataille de France. 47e division, juillet–novembre 1918* (Paris: Payot, 1935); Godfroy, op, cit., p. 350.
122. Marius Daille, *La Bataille de Montdidier* (Paris: Berger-Levrault, 1922); Lieutenant-Colonel Alphonse Grasset, *Montdidier: Le 8 août 1918 à la 42e division* (Paris: Éditions Berger-Levrault, 1930).
123. Debeney note, 11 May 1919, in Daille, op. cit., pp. 21–5.
124. Debeney, op. cit., p. 45. Maurice Gamelin, appointed in 1931, would serve for nine years.
125. He reported clearing out his private papers in 1935, even to the point of losing his nomination to the Légion d'honneur: Debeney to Grand-chancelier de la Légion d'honneur, 3 December 1935: https://www.leonore.archives-nationales.culture.gouv.fr/ui/notice/103117 (accessed 28 October 2021).
126. Debeney, op. cit., pp. 3–7.
127. 20 December 1916, Guillaumat, op. cit., p. 168.
128. Debeney, op. cit., p. 46.
129. Marie-Eugène Debeney, *Sur la sécurité militaire de la France* (Paris: Payot, 1930).
130. Gaujac, op. cit., p. 31.
131. Franc, op. cit., p. 384.
132. Debeney, *La Guerre*, p. 9.
133. Weygand, op. cit., p. 374.
134. Godfroy, op. cit., p. 3.
135. Ibid., pp. 384–5.
136. At the time his support was acknowledged by being appointed Knight Commander of the Order of the Bath (KCB), in October 1918 https://www.leonore.archives-nationales.culture.gouv.fr/ui/notice/103117 (accessed 28 October 2021).

## Chapter 10

1. 15 August 1918, Maréchal Fayolle, *Cahiers secrets de la grande guerre*, ed. Henry Contamaine (Paris: Plon, 1964), p. 297.
2. Charles Bugnet, *Mangin* (Paris: Plon, 1934), pp. 1–2.
3. On the colonial army's bad reputation see Marc Michel, *Les Africains et la grande guerre* (Paris: Éditions Karthala, 2014), p. 27. Both of Mangin's brothers were killed in action in the colonies.
4. Elizabeth Greenhalgh, *The French Army and the First World War* (Cambridge: Cambridge University Press, 2014), p. 32.
5. Mali was then called French Soudan. The village complex was roughly 200 miles northeast of Bamako.
6. Mangin to his aunts, 1 March 1891, in Charles Mangin, 'Lettres de Jeunesse', *Revue des Deux Mondes*, 55 (1930), pp. 101–125: 107–8.
7. Ibid., p. 109.
8. Ibid., p. 111.
9. Louis-Eugène Mangin, *Le Général Mangin, 1866–1925* (Paris; Éditions Fernand Lanore, 1986), p. 34.
10. Charles Mangin, *Regards sur la France d'Afrique* (Paris; Plon, 1924), p. 142.
11. Ibid., pp. 143–4.
12. Douglas Porch, *The Conquest of Morocco* (London; Jonathan Cape, 1986), pp. 266–7.
13. Ibid., p. 268.
14. Jean Martet, *Clemenceau – The Events of his Life as Told by Himself to his Former Secretary*, trans. Milton Waldman (London; Longmans, 1930), p. 154.
15. See Michael Finch, *A Progressive Occupation? The Gallieni–Lyautey Method and Colonial Pacification in Tonkin and Madagascar, 1885–1900* (Oxford: Oxford University Press, 2013).
16. Porch, op. cit., p. 283.
17. Ibid., p. 284.
18. Charles Mangin, *La Force noire* (Paris: Hachette, 1910).
19. Richard Fogarty, *Race & War in France: Colonial Subjects in the French Army, 1914–1918* (Baltimore: John Hopkins University Press, 2008), p. 21 and Michel, op. cit., pp. 15–29.
20. Porch, op. cit., p. 264.
21. See Michel, op. cit., pp. 81–130 for details on the Senegalese troops in combat.
22. Ibid., p. 249.
23. Bugnet, op. cit., p. 144.
24. 28 March 1918, Henry Bordeaux, *Histoire d'une vie* (Paris: Libraire Plon, 13 vols, 1951–73), vol. 7, *La Victoire et le traité de Versailles, 21 mars 1918–1 août 1919* (1960), p. 18.
25. Charles Mangin, *Lettres de guerre, 1914–1918* (Paris: Arthème Fayard, 1950), pp. 78–9.
26. 8 BI *Journal de marche et opérations* (JMO), *Service historique de la défense* [SHD], 26N497/13, available at Journaux des unités engagées dans la première guerre mondiale - Mémoire des hommes (defense.gouv.fr). See also Leonard Smith, *Between Mutiny and Obedience: The Case of the French Fifth Infantry Division during World War 1* (Princeton: Princeton University Press, 1994), pp. 39–58.
27. Quoted in Nick Lloyd, *The Western Front* (London: Viking, 2021), p. 34.
28. 8 BI JMO, op. cit.
29. Henri Dutheil, *De Sauret la honte à Mangin le boucher* (Paris: Nouvelle Librairie Nationale, 1923), p. 88.
30. Ibid., p. 90; see also 20 August 1914, Mangin, *Lettres*, p. 15.
31. 22 September 1914, ibid., p. 27.
32. 36ᵉ RI JMO, SHD, 26N612/1.
33. Bugnet, op. cit., p. 146.
34. 5 DI JMO, SHD, 26N268/1.

35. Smith, op. cit., p. 63.
36. 13 November 1914, Mangin, op. cit., pp. 32–3.
37. 27 August 1918, Contamine, op. cit., p. 299.
38. 22 September 1914, Mangin, op. cit., pp. 27–30.
39. Ibid.
40. Jonathan Krause, *Early Trench Tactics in the French Army: The Second Battle of Artois, May–June 1915* (Farnham: Ashgate, 2013). p. 55.
41. Commandant Lefranc, 'La Prise de Neuville-Saint-Vaast', *Revue militaire française*, September 1929, pp. 331–349: 340.
42. 9 June 1915, Mangin, op. cit., pp. 51–2.
43. 5 DI JMO, op. cit.
44. Smith, op. cit., p. 110.
45. 4 January 1916, Mangin, op. cit., p. 83.
46. 129ᵉ RI JMO and 74ᵉ RI JMO, SHD, 26N686/14 and 26N660/13.
47. Figures from Mangin's report quoted in Smith, op. cit., p. 144.
48. 29 May 1916, Mangin, op. cit., p. 115.
49. Bugnet, op. cit., pp. 177–8.
50. III CA JMO, SHD, 26N106/5.
51. 8 May 1916, Mangin, op. cit., p. 112.
52. Bugnet, op. cit., p. 180.
53. Nivelle to Mangin, 7 October 1916 and Pétain to Nivelle, 9 October 1916, AFGG, tome IV, *Verdun et la Somme*, vol. 3, *Bataille de la Somme (fin). Offensives françaises à Verdun (3 septembre–fin décembre 1916)* (Paris: Imprimerie Nationale, 1935), annexes vol. 1, annexes 883 and 913, pp. 1261–4 and 1309–10.
54. 'Artillerie, note sur la lutte d'artillerie pendant les combats du 20–25 octobre 1916', Second Army, [30] October 1916, AFGG IV/3, annexes vol. 2, annexe 1395, pp. 443–5.
55. AFGG IV/3, pp. 486–7.
56. Excellent short account in Robert Doughty, *Pyrrhic Victory: French Strategy and Operation in the Great War* (Cambridge Mass.: The Belknap Press, 2005), pp. 318–45.
57. GAR, 'Ordre général pour les Vᵉ et VIᵉ armées', 5 February 1917, AFGG, tome V, *L'Offensive d'avril 1917. Les Opérations à objectifs limités (1 novembre 1916–1 novembre 1917)*, vol. 1, *L'offensive d'avril 1917 (1 novembre 1916–15 mai 1917)* (Paris: Imprimerie Nationale, 1931), annexes vol. 2, annexe 603, pp. 1086–9.
58. Général Hellot, *Histoire de la guerre mondiale: Le Commandement des généraux Nivelle et Pétain, 1917* (Paris: Payot, 1936), pp. 153–4.
59. Émile Herbillon, *De la Meuse à Reims: Le Général Alfred Micheler* (Paris: Librairie Plon, 1934), pp. 133–4.
60. AFGG V/1, p. 281.
61. Herbillon, op. cit., p. 136.
62. Quoted in Edward Spears, *Prelude to Victory* (London: Jonathan Cape, 1939), p. 343.
63. Herbillon, op. cit., pp. 137–8.
64. Spears, op. cit., pp. 120 and 326.
65. De Mitry to Mangin, 6 April 1917, AFGG V/1, annexes vol. 3, annexe 1218, p. 636.
66. Spears, op. cit., p. 472.
67. 'Note pour les CA', Sixth Army, 17 April 1917, AFGG, tome V, vol. 2, *Les Opérations à objectifs limités (15 mai–1 novembre 1917)*, annexes vol. 1, annexe 55, pp. 92–3.
68. Général Jean Rouquerol, *Le Chemin des Dames, 1917* (Paris: Payot, 1934), p. 145.
69. Ibid., pp. 148–57.
70. Micheler to Nivelle, 29 April 1917, quoted in Herbillon, op. cit., p. 186.
71. Rouquerol, op. cit., p. 177.
72. 7 May 1917, Raymond Poincaré, *Au service de la France, Neuf années de souvenirs*, vol. 9, *L'Année trouble, 1917* (Paris: Librairie Plon, 1932), p. 130.

73. 7 and 10 May 1917, Poincaré op. cit., pp. 131 and 135.
74. 'Rapport du conseil d'enquête instituée par lettre ministérielle no. 18.194 du 14 juillet 1917', SHD, 5N255.
75. 26 April 1917, Bordeaux, op. cit., vol. 6: *L'Année ténébreuse, 3 janvier 1917–21 mars 1918* (1959), p. 73.
76. 10 June 1918, Mangin, op. cit., pp. 268–9.
77. Ibid.
78. 'Ordre de contre-attaque', GAR, 10 June 1918, 16.00, AFGG, tome VI, *L'Hiver 1917–1918: L'Offensive allemande (1 novembre 1917–18 juillet 1918)*, vol. 2, *L'Offensive allemande contre les armées françaises (1 mai–18 juillet 1918)* (Paris: Imprimerie Nationale, 1934), annexes vol. 2, annexe 1390, p. 564. An eyewitness account can be found in Commandant Laure, *Au 3ème bureau du troisième G.Q.G. (1917–1919)* (Paris: Librairie Plon, 1921), p. 145.
79. 'Ordre général no. 1', by Mangin, 10 June 1918, AFGG VI/2, annexes vol. 2, annexe 1431, pp. 609–11.
80. AFGG VI/2, p. 322.
81. Ibid.
82. 11 June 1918, Contamine, op. cit., p. 283.
83. Jean Perré, Commandant Aussenac and Capitaine Suire, *Batailles et combats des chars français: La Bataille défensive, avril–juillet 1918* (Paris: Lavauzelle, 1940), p. 138.
84. Foch to Pétain, 16 June 1918, AFGG, tome VII, *La Campagne offensive de 1918 et la marche au Rhin (18 juillet 1918–28 juin 1919)*, vol. 1, *Les Offensives de dégagement et la préparation des offensives générales (18 juillet 1918–25 septembre 1918)* (Paris: Imprimerie Nationale, 1923), annexes vol. 1, annexe 2, p. 2.
85. Mangin to Fayolle, 20 June 1918, AFGG VII/2, annexes vol. 1, annexe 4, pp. 4–7.
86. AFGG, tome X, *Ordres de bataille des grands unités*, vol. 2, *Divisions d'infanterie, divisions de cavalerie* (Paris: Imprimerie Nationale, 1924), pp. 938–9.
87. AFGG VII/1, p. 54.
88. Général François Boullaire, *Historique du 2$^e$ corps de cavalerie du 1 octobre 1914 au 1 janvier 1919* (Paris: Charles-Lavauzelle & Co., 1923), p. 376.
89. AFGG VII/1, p. 54.
90. See AEF, General Staff, *Histories of the 251 Divisions of the German Army which participated in the War (1914–1918)* (Washington: US War Office, 1920: reprint, London Stamp Exchange 1989). Much of this work is based on French military intelligence reports, particularly for information on German units prior to 1918.
91. 'Emploi tactique des chars d'assaut', GQG, 20 August 1916, AFGG tome IV, vol. 2, *La Bataille de Verdun et les offensives des alliés (1 mai 1916–3 septembre 1916)* (Paris: Imprimerie Nationale, 1933), annexes vol. 3, annexe 3002, pp. 784–5.
92. 'Renseignements complémentaires de détail au sujet de l'emploi des *tanks* à Cambrai', 6 March 1918, SHD, 16N2142.
93. AFGG VII/1, p. 52.
94. 'Annexe au rapport sur les opérations du 18 au 23 Juillet 1918', groupement 1, undated, SHD, 16N2162.
95. Mark Grotelueschen, *The AEF Way of War: The American Army in Combat in World War 1* (Cambridge: Cambridge University Press, 2007), p. 84.
96. Leonard Boyd, *Infantry in Battle* (Washington: The Infantry Journal, 1939), p. 236.
97. *Régiment du marche de la Légion étrangère* JMO, 18 July 1918, SHD, 26N862/9.
98. War Diary, Group of Armies German Crown Prince, 18 July 1918. *United States Army in the World War 1917–1919*, vol. 5, *Military Operations: Champagne–Marne, Aisne–Marne* (Washington, 1948), p. 677.
99. Boyd, op. cit., p. 238. The author commanded the company.
100. AFGG VII/1, pp. 74–5.

101. Boullaire, op. cit., pp. 377–8.
102. AFGG VII/1, p. 74. Although Laure, who was at Mangin's HQ, says that this order was made much earlier: Laure, op. cit., p. 178.
103. AFGG VII/1, pp. 376 and 379.
104. 'Ordre d'opérations no. 301', Tenth Army, 18 July 1918, AFGG VII/1, annexes vol. 1, annexe 154, p. 196.
105. Boullaire, op. cit., p. 380.
106. Tenth Amry JMO, SHD, 26N51/11.
107. 'Intervention du Général Pétain et du Général Fayolle dans la soirée du 18 juillet 1918', in ibid., and Laure, op. cit., pp. 179–81.
108. Laure, op. cit.
109. 18 July 1918, Contamine, op. cit., p. 290.
110. René Tournès, *Foch et la victoire des allies, 1918* (Paris: Payot, 1936), p. 208.
111. AFGG VII/1, p. 228 and Tenth Army JMO.
112. Tournès, op. cit., p. 209.
113. Georges Clemenceau, *Grandeur and Misery of Victory*, trans. F. M. Atkinson (New York: Harcourt, Brace & Co, 1930), p. 217.
114. See Fogarty pp. 274–282 for the reaction from German nationalists to the use of non-white soldiers in the Rhineland occupation.
115. L. Mangin, op. cit., p. 303.
116. Ibid., p. 293.
117. Bugnet, op. cit., gives a fair appraisal of Mangin's career but there is no criticism of its subject. For an assessment of Mangin viewed mainly as a colonial soldier, see Paul Moreau-Vauthier, *Un chef, le Général Mangin, 1866–1925* (Paris: Les Publications Coloniales, 1936), in which over half the book is devoted to Mangin's colonial career.
118. Bugnet, op. cit., p. 320.
119. Quoted in Alistair Horne, *The Price of Glory: Verdun 1916* (London: St Martin's Press, 1963), p. 233.

## Chapter 11

1. Edouard Daladier, *Prison Journal, 1940–1945*, ed. Jean Daladier and Jean Daridan (Boulder, Col.: Westview, 1995), p. 106.
2. Martin S. Alexander, 'Maurice Gamelin and the defeat of France, 1939–40', in *Fallen Stars: Eleven Studies in Twentieth Century Military Disaster*, ed. Brian Bond (Oxford: Brassey's, 1991), pp. 107–40.
3. Pierre le Goyet, *Le Mystère Gamelin* (Paris: Presses de la Cité, 1976), pp. 14–16.
4. Quoted in Maurice Percheron, *Gamelin* (Paris: Éditions Documentales Françaises, 1939), p. 15.
5. Général Maurice-Gustave Gamelin, *Manœuvre et victoire de la Marne* (Paris: Grasset, 1954), p. 20.
6. Pierre Varillon, *Joffre* (Paris: Fayard, 1956), p. 53.
7. Gamelin, op. cit., p. 21; Général Georges-René Alexandre, *Avec Joffre d'Agadir à Verdun* (Paris: Berger-Levrault, 1932).
8. Gamelin, op. cit., p. 42.
9. Joseph Joffre, *The Memoirs of Marshal Joffre*. trans. T. Bentley Mott (London: Geoffrey Bles, 2 vols, 1932), i, p. 15.
10. Gamelin's influence is discussed in Glenn Torrey, *Henri Mathias Berthelot: Soldier of France, Defender of Romania* (Iași and Oxford: The Centre for Romanian Studies, 2001), pp. 62–6.
11. For such a study on the British army see Andy Simpson, *Directing Operations: British Corps Command on the Western Front 1914-18* (Stroud: Spellmount, 2006).
12. Lieutenant-Colonel François de La Rocque, *Service public* (Paris: Grasset, 1934), pp. 194–5.

13. Pierre Rocolle, *L'Hécatombe des généraux* (Paris: Charles-Lavauzelle, 1980); Martin S. Alexander, The *Republic in Danger: General Maurice Gamelin and the Politics of French Defence, 1933–40* (Cambridge: Cambridge University Press, 1993), pp. 21–2, 88–96, 202–6, 218–25 and 247–8.
14. Elizabeth Greenhalgh, *The French Army and the First World War* (Cambridge: Cambridge University Press, 2014), p. 67.
15. Lieutenant-Colonel François de La Rocque, *Au service de l'avenir: Réflexions en montagne* (Paris: Société d'Éditions et Abonnement, 1946), p. 24.
16. René-Gustave Nobécourt, 'Gamelin 14–18' (unpublished typescript kindly provided to the author by M. Nobécourt), p. 190.
17. Robert Doughty, *Pyrrhic Victory: French Strategy and Operations in the Great War* (Cambridge, Mass.: Belknap Press, 2005), pp. 78–97; idem, 'French Strategy in 1914: Joffre's Own', *Journal of Military History*, 67 (2003), pp. 427–54.
18. Gamelin, op. cit.; Général Maurice-Gustave Gamelin, *Servir* (Paris: Plon, 3 vols, 1946–7), vol. 2, *Le Prologue du drâme*, pp. xiv–xvi; Le Goyet, op. cit., pp. 22–34; Joseph Jacques Césare Joffre, *Mémoires du Maréchal Joffre, 1910–1917* (Paris: Librairie Plon, 2 vols, 1932), ii, pp. 141–50, 386–8 and 390–3; Varillon, op. cit., pp. 365–83; Henry Bordeaux, *Joffre, ou l'art de commander* (Paris: Grasset, 1933), esp. pp. 62–95.
19. *Historique du 11ᵉ BCA* (Étampes: Imprimerie M. Dormann, 1920).
20. Nobécourt, op. cit., pp. 192–4; History of 30ᵉ BCA at http://gallica.bnf.fr/ark:/12148/bpt6k63166056/texteBrut (accessed 25 May 2016). The strong fortifications, dense woods and rocky outcrops of the Vosges are apparent in a photographic report at: www.lieux-insolites.fr/cicatrice/14-18/sundgauf/sundgauf.htm (accessed 25 May 2016).
21. Doughty, op. cit., pp. 188–9.
22. 'Note pour le 1ᵉ bureau', by Gamelin, 24 January 1916, in AFGG, Tome III, *Les Offensives de 1915. L'Hiver de 1915–1916 (1er mai 1915–21 février 1916)* (Paris: Imprimerie Nationale, 1923), annexes vol. 4, annexe 3292, p. 677.
23. Julie d'Andurain, 'Verdun, ou le tournant de la doctrine française', *Revue défense nationale*, 787 (2016), pp. 37–45; Allain Bernède, 'Verdun 1916: un choix stratégique, un équation logistique', *Revue historique des armées*, 242 (2006), pp. 48–59.
24. See Jonathan Krause, *Early Trench Tactics in the French Army: The Second Battle of Artois, May–June 1915* (Farnham: Ashgate, 2013).
25. Quoted in Michel Goya, 'Transformation 1916: Le Processus d'innovation de l'armée française de l'hiver 1915 à la bataille de la Somme', at http://lavoiedelepee.blogspot.co.uk/2016/02/transformation-1916-le-processus.html (accessed 9 August 2016).
26. Ibid.
27. 'Étude comparative et évolution des armes légères offensives et défensives au cours de l'année 1916 (Bataille de Verdun)', in *Verdun 1916: Actes du colloque international sur la bataille de Verdun. 6–7–8 juin 1975*, preface and postscript by Maurice Genevoix (Nancy: Édition ANSBV Imprimerie Maisonneuve, 1976), pp. 356–72.
28. Doughty, op. cit., pp. 306, 315–17, 366–7 and 369; Nobécourt, op. cit., p. 195; Michel Goya, *La Chair et l'acier. L'Armée française et l'invention de la guerre moderne (1914–1918)* (Paris: Tallandier, 2004).
29. William Philpott, *Bloody Victory: The Sacrifice on the Somme and the making of the Twentieth Century* (London, Little, Brown, 2009), pp. 259–60.
30. Ibid., p. 259; XX CA war diary ['Journal de marche et opérations' – hereafter JMO], SHD, 26N193/6.
31. Stephen Westmann, *Surgeon with the Kaiser's Army* (Glasgow: William Kimber, 1968), pp. 101–5.
32. See for example the cover illustration of *Le Pays de France* (8 August 1918), Gamelin wearing a helmet with the three stars of a corps commander, at https://fr.wikipedia.org/wiki/Fichier:Maurice_Gustave_Gamelin.jpg (accessed 25 May 2016).

33. Maud Sutton-Pickard, *France in Wartime, 1914–1915* (London: Methuen, 1915), p. 89.
34. Quoted in Philpott, op. cit., p. 260.
35. 11 August 1916, Marshal Marie-Émile Fayolle, *Cahiers secrets de la grande guerre*, ed. Henri Contamine (Paris: Librairie Plon, 1964), p. 173.
36. J. E. B. Seely, *Fear, And Be Slain: Adventures by Land, Sea and Air* (London: Hodder & Stoughton, 1931), p. 176; cf. comments on Seely as a brigade commander in Brigadier-General Archibald Fraser Home, *The Diary of a World War I Cavalry Officer*, ed. Diana Briscoe (Costello: Tunbridge Wells, 1985), pp. 125–27 and 141. Thanks to Dr John M. Bourne for elucidating this point.
37. 24 September 1915, in Captain Ferdinand Belmont, *A Crusader of France*. Lettres d'un officier de chasseurs alpins, *Killed in Action, December 1915*, trans. G. Frederick Lees (London: Andrew Melrose, 1917), p. 307.
38. See Greenhalgh, op. cit., pp. 147–57 and 163–7.
39. Nobécourt, op. cit., p. 235; even before the recent archive-based new work that underpins this collection, one historian thought 'perhaps most' French generals 'proved more imaginative and adaptable than their British colleagues'. Douglas Porch, 'The French Army in the First World War', in *Military Effectiveness*, vol. 1, *The First World War*, ed. Allan Millett and Williamson Murray (London: Unwin Hyman, 1988), 190–228: p. 191.
40. Doughty, op. cit., pp. 293–6.
41. Peter Simkins, *From the Somme to Victory. The British Army's Experience on the Western Front 1916–1918* (Barnsley: Pen & Sword, 2014), pp. 56–8.
42. Christopher Duffy, *Through German Eyes: The British and the Somme 1916* (London: Phoenix, 2007), pp. 167–8, quoting Albrecht Stosch, 'Somme Nord: Die Brennpunkteder Schlacht im Juli 1916' (part 1 of 11), vols XX and XXI (1927) of *Reichsarchiv, Schlachten des Weltkrieges in Einzeldarstellungen* (Berlin: 1921–30, 37 vols). See also Jack Sheldon, *The German Army on the Somme, 1914–1916* (Barnsley: Pen & Sword, 2005).
43. 'La Bataille de l'Aisne (avril–juin 1917): La 9ᵉ division d'infanterie', http://crid1418.org/doc/bdd_cdd/unites/DI9.html (accessed 26 May 2016); 9ᵉ DI (France), p.5, at http://fr.wikipedia.org/wiki/9e_division_d'infanterie_(France) (accessed 9 March 2012).
44. *Historique du 66ᵉ bataillon chasseurs à pied en campagne, 1914–1918* (Paris: Imprimerie-Librairie Militaire Universelle L. Fournier, 1920) at http://gallica.bnf.fr/ark:/12148/bpt6k63228018/texteBrut (accessed 29 December 2021); four officers won the Légion d'honneur for their actions on 16–17 April 1917, two other soldiers were awarded the Médaille Militaire and three received army commendations.
45. Ibid.
46. Ibid. However, at an open-air concert for 151 DI (General Pierre des Vallières), in reserve near Noyon on 19 July 1917, the actress Marie Delna closed the show by mounting the stage with the Tricolour flag to sing *La Marseillaise*. 'When she had finished, the applause was mixed with an outburst of hissing from the mass of soldiers. …the incident proved that the evil virus which had appeared in the army after the set-back of 16 April had not completely vanished and that it was still necessary to handle the men with care.' René Arnaud, Tragédie bouffe: *A Frenchman in the First World War* (London: Sidgwick & Jackson, 1966), pp. 131–3.
47. 'La Bataille de l'Aisne', op. cit.; Guy Pédroncini, *Les Mutineries de 1917* (Paris: Presses Universitaires de France, 1967), pp. 127–8; Denis Rolland, *La Grève des tranchées: Les Mutineries de 1917* (Paris: Éditions Imago, 2005), pp. 99–101; Anthony Clayton, 'Robert Nivelle and the French Spring Offensive of 1917', in *Fallen Stars*, pp. 52–64.
48. Arnaud, op. cit., p. 149.
49. Doughty, op. cit., p. 364.
50. 9 DI Order No. 228, 9 November 1917, https://gallica.bnf.fr/ark:/12148/bpt6k63228018/texteBrut.
51. *Historique du 66ᵉ bataillon de chasseurs*, op. cit.

52. '9ᵉ division d'infanterie (France)', http://fr.wikipedia.org/wiki/9e_division_d'infanterie_ (France) (accessed 9 March 2012)
53. Percheron, op. cit., pp. 21–2.
54. 29 March 1918, Henry Bordeaux, *Histoire d'une vie* (Paris: Libraire Plon, 13 vols, 1951–73), vol. 7, *La Victoire et le traité de Versailles, 21 mars 1918–1 août 1919* (1960), p. 22; Nobécourt, op. cit., pp. 361–73.
55. Jean Petibon, *Le 9ᵉ division en 1918: Étude tactique. Préface et annotations du général Gamelin* (Nancy: Berger-Levrault, 1931); Petibon became Gamelin's chief of staff from 1937–40.
56. 'Rapport sommaire sur les opérations effectuées sous le commandement du général Gamelin du 22 mars au 30 mars 1918', SHD, 19N1101, no. 1292/3/B.
57. Author's emphasis. AFGG, tome VI, *L'Hiver 1917–1918. L'Offensive allemande* (1 novembre 1917–18 juillet 1918), vol. 1, *La Préparation de la campagne de 1918. L'Offensive allemande de l'Oise à la Mer du Nord (1novembre 1917–30 avril 1918)* (Paris: Imprimerie Nationale, 1931), pp. 142–5.
58. Petibon, op. cit.
59. AFGG VI/1, op. cit.
60. Nobécourt, op. cit., pp. 366–9.
61. Le Goyet, op. cit., p. 37.
62. 'Rapport sommaire', op. cit.
63. See 'X' [anon.], 'La Bataille de France de 1918. La Bataille entre Somme et Oise 21 Mars– 6 Avril', *Revue des deux mondes (1829–1971)*, Sixième Période, 46/2 (15 Juillet 1918), 241–302: pp. 254–5 and 258–79.
64. Le Goyet, op. cit., p. 37.
65. 'R.M.', review of Petibon, *La 9ᵉ division en 1918*, in *Revue militaire suisse. Bulletin bibliographique*, 77 (1932), p. 426.
66. 'La Bataille de France de 1918', op. cit., p. 279.
67. 30 March 1918, Bordeaux, op. cit., p. 23.
68. 'Rapport sommaire', op. cit.
69. La Rocque, *Au service de l'avenir*, p. 25.
70. Patrick Takle, *Nine Divisions in Champagne: The Second Battle of the Marne* (Barnsley: Pen & Sword, 2015), p. 142 (kindly drawn to my attention by Mr Keith Brame of the Western Front Association).
71. Ibid., p. 148.
72. See Michael S. Neiberg, *The Second Battle of the Marne* (Bloomington, Ind.: Indiana University Press, 2008).
73. Herbert Sulzbach, *With the German Guns. Four Years on the Western Front* (London: Leo Cooper, 1998), p. 183.
74. *Historique sommaire du 4ᵉ régiment d'infanterie pendant la guerre 1914–1918* (Nancy: Berger-Levrault, n.d.d), pp. 14–15, at http://tableaudhonneur.free.fr/RI-004.pdf (accessed 10 July 2016).
75. Goya, *La Chair et l'acier*, pp. 410–11; Lieutenant-Colonel Barrand, *Tactique d'infanterie. Quatre cas concrets vécus avec le 2ᵉ bataillon du 82ᵉ régiment d'infanterie en cours de la guerre de mouvement (mars–octobre 1918)*, preface by Maurice Gamelin (Paris: Lavauzelle, 1932).
76. Leonard V. Smith, Stéphane Audoin-Rouzeau and Annette Becker, *France and the Great War 1914–1918* (Cambridge: Cambridge University Press, 2003), pp. 127–31.
77. 'Meilleure utilisation de l'aviation d'observation au cours de la guerre de mouvement: rapport du 10ᵉ CA', 12 September 1918; and 'Aviation d'observation en campagne: étude du commandant Jauneaud', 10 August 1918, SHD, 1A 89/2; Goya, op. cit,, pp. 390–3, 402–3 and 410–11.
78. Sulzbach, op. cit., p. 205.

79. 82ᵉ RI JMO, https://www.memoiredeshommes.sga.defense.gouv.fr/fr/arkotheque/inventaires/ead_ir_consult.php?fam=3&id_ark_ead_les_irs=6 (accessed 11 January 2022).
80. Cabinet particulier du général Gamelin JMO, 18 October 1939, SHD 1K224/9; also http://jacques.pingot.free.fr/chronique/Ernestpingot/82RI.htm (accessed 1 January 2016).
81. 14 September 1915, in Belmont, op. cit., pp. 302–3; William Philpott, *Attrition: Fighting the First World War* (London: Little, Brown, 2014), pp. 327–38.
82. Doughty, op. cit., p. 511. For French industrial mobilization see Alain Hennebicque, 'Albert Thomas and the War Industries', in *The French Home Front 1914-1918*, ed. Patrick Fridenson (Oxford: Berg, 1992), pp. 89–132; Louis Loucheur, *Carnets secrets, 1908–1932* (Brussels & Paris: Brepols, 1962); John Godfrey, *Capitalism at War: Industrial Policy and Bureaucracy in France, 1914–1918* (Leamington Spa: Berg, 1987).
83. 82ᵉ RI JMO, op. cit.
84. See Général Andréa, *La Révolte Druze et l'insurrection de Damas, 1925–1926* (Paris: Payot, 1937); Alexander, *Republic in Danger*, p. 224.
85. 27 October 1918, Général Edmond Buat, *Journal, 1913–1923*, ed. Frédéric Guelton (Paris: Ministère de la Defense, Perrin, 2015), p. 681.
86. Charles Delvert, *From Marne to Verdun. The War Diary of Captain Charles Delvert 1914–1916*, trans. Ian Sumner (Barnsley: Pen & Sword, 2016), pp. 204–5; Général Marie-Eugène Debeney, *La Guerre et les hommes: Réflexions d'après-guerre* (Paris: Librairie Plon, 1937), pp. 39–40.
87. Arden Bucholz, review of Michael S. Neiberg, *The Second Battle of the Marne*, in *Central European History*, 42 (2009), pp. 565—567.
88. 26 October 1918, Buat, op. cit., p. 680.

## Chapter 12

1. Preface to Général Paul-Alexandre Bourget, *Le Général Estienne* (Paris: Berger-Levrault, 1956), p. 8.
2. Ferdiand Deygas, *Les Chars d'assaut: Leur passé, leur avenir* (Paris: Charles-Lavauzelle, 1937), p. 78.
3. Bourget, op. cit., p. 36.
4. Ibid., p. 90.
5. Colonel E. Ramspacher, *Le Général Estienne: Père des chars* (Paris: Editions Lavauzelle, 1983), p. 26.
6. 'L'Aéroplane, oeil de l'artillerie, note publiée le 1ᵉʳ février 1912 par le Lieutenant-colonel Estienne', reproduced in Lieutenant-colonel F. L. E. Rimailho, *Artillerie de campagne* (Paris: Gauthier-Villars, 1924), pp. 496–7.
7. 'Projet d'organisation, de règlement de manœuvre et de service en campagne de l'aviation d'artillerie', 1 May 1914, partially reproduced in ibid., pp. 498–502.
8. Ramspacher, op. cit., p. 30.
9. *Historique du 22ᵉ régiment d'artillerie pendant la campagne contre l'Allemagne* (Paris: Charles-Lavauzelle, 1920), p. 2.
10. Ibid., p. 3. His writing on morale and leadership before the war illustrates how simplistic the idea that pre-war French military thought split exclusively along the lines of morale and an offensive spirit versus firepower is.
11. Eyewitness account quoted in Leonard Smith, *Between Mutiny and Obedience: The Case of the French Fifth Infantry Division during World War 1* (Princeton: Princeton University Press, 1994), p. 50.
12. Quoted in Bourget, op. cit., p. 44.
13. *22ᵉ régiment d'artillerie de campagne, journal de marche et opérations* (JMO), 6 and 7 September 1914. See also Bourget, op. cit., pp. 36–9.

14. Estienne to Joffre, 1 October 1915, *Service historique de la défence*, Vincennes [SHD], 16N2120.
15. Estienne to Joffre, 1 December 1915, SHD, 16N2121.
16. Joffre to Dubois, 6 December 1915, SHD, 16N2121.
17. 'Sommaire de l'exposé verbal du Colonel Estienne, le 12 décembre 1915 à Chantilly au Général commandant en chef', SHD, 16N2121.
18. 'Exécution de la notification 31.786 du 28 Janvier 1916 au Général commandant l'AS', by Estienne, SHD, 16N2120, p. 9.
19. Estienne to Joffre, op. cit.
20. 'Note pour le 1$^{er}$ bureau', by Gamelin, 24 January 1916, AFGG, tome III, *Les Offensives de 1915. L'Hiver de 1915–1916 (1 mai 1915–21 février 1916)* (Paris: Imprimerie Nationale, 1923), annexes vol. 4, annexe 3292, p. 677.
21. 'Note pour M. le Sous-Secrétaire d'État', 13 February 1916, SHD, 16N2120.
22. Gilbert Hatry, *Renault, usine de guerre 1914–1918* (Paris: Éditions Lafourcade, 1978), p. 8.
23. Estienne to Joffre, 28 December 1915, SHD, 16N2121. On prior experimentation with armoured vehicles in France, see Deygas, op. cit., pp. 51–70.
24. 'Note pour M. le Sous-Secrétaire d'État', op. cit.
25. Thomas to Joffre, 27 February 1916, SHD, 16N2121.
26. Jean-Claude Devos, Jean Nicot, Philippe Schillinger, Pierre Waksman and Josette Ficat, *Inventaire sommaire des archives de la guerre série N 1872–1919: 1N–14N* (Troyes: Imprimerie La Renaissance, 1974), p. 67.
27. Thomas to Joffre, 30 September 1916, SHD, 16N2121.
28. Ibid.
29. Thomas to Joffre, 27 April 1916, AFGG, tome IV, *Verdun et la Somme*, vol. 2, *La Bataille de Verdun et les offensives des alliés (1 mai 1916–3 septembre 1916)* (1933), annexes vol. 1, annexe 3, pp. 54–6.
30. Léon Dutil, *Les Chars d'assaut: Leur création et leur rôle pendant la guerre (1915–1918)* (Paris: Berger-Levrault, 1919), pp. 11–12.
31. Thomas to Joffre, op. cit.
32. This was an engineer's remark upon seeing a St Chamond for the first time, quoted in Ramspacher, op. cit., p. 46.
33. Estienne to Joffre, 1 November 1916, AFGG, Tome V, *L'Offensive d'avril 1917. Les Opérations à objectifs limités (1 novembre 1916–1 novembre 1917)*, vol. 1, *L'offensive d'avril 1917 (1 novembre 1916–15 mai 1917)* (Paris: Imprimerie Nationale, 1931), annexes vol. 1, annexe 74, pp. 128–9.
34. *Historique du 22$^e$ régiment d'artillerie*, op. cit., p. 5.
35. 'Compte-rendu d'une mission en Angleterre les 25 et 26 juin 1916', III CA artillerie, 26 June 1916, SHD, 16N2121.
36. Joffre to Estienne 25 October 1916, SHD, 16N2121.
37. Joffre to Humbert, 30 September 1916, SHD, 16N2121.
38. 'Comité consultatif de l'artillerie d'assaut, procès-verbal 1$^{ère}$ réunion', *Ministère de l'armement*, 17 December 1916, SHD, 16N2129. The representatives changed over time but the organizations sending delegates to the *Comité* were fairly constant.
39. Ibid.
40. Des Vallières to GQG, 1 August 1916, AFGG, IV/2, annexes vol. 3, annexe 2665, p. 341.
41. Quoted in Elizabeth Greenhalgh, 'Technology Development in Coalition: The Case of the First World War Tank', *The International History Review*, 22 (2000), pp. 806–36: 811.
42. 'Compte-rendu d'une mission en Angleterre', op. cit.
43. Albert Stern, *Tanks, 1914–1918: The Log Book of a Pioneer* (London: Hodder & Stoughton, 1919), pp. 87–90.
44. 'Note sur l'emploi des C[uirassés] T[errestres] le 15 Septembre', des Vallières to Joffre, 17 September 1916, AFGG IV, vol. 3, *Bataille de la Somme (fin). Offensives françaises à*

*Verdun (3 septembre–fin décembre 1916)* (Paris: Imprimerie Nationale, 1935), annexes vol. 1, annexe 463, pp. 643–4.
45. Joffre to Thomas, 20 November 1916, SHD, 16N2121.
46. 'Bases générales de l'organisation et de la tactique de l'artillerie d'assaut (A.S.)', Estienne to Joffre, 9 October 1916, AFGG, tome V, *L'Offensive d'avril 1917. Les Opérations à objectifs limités (1 novembre 1916–1 novembre 1917)*, vol. 1, *L'offensive d'avril 1917 (1 novembre 1916–15 mai 1917)* (Paris: Imprimerie Nationale, 1931), annexes vol. 1, annexe 49, pp. 88–9.
47. Ibid. This was a pre-war French infantry slogan.
48. 'Rapport au sujet de la participation aux opérations de la V armée des groupements Bossut et Chaubès de l'artillerie d'assaut, 23 avril 1917, tableau no. 2', by Estienne, SHD, 16N2120.
49. 'Projet pour l'emploi tactique des chars d'assaut', GQG, 1 May 1917, SHD, 16N2120.
50. 'Emploi des tanks le 16 avril 1917', undated note, SHD, 16N2120, p. 3.
51. Ibid., pp. 4–5.
52. 'Rapport au sujet de la participation du groupement Lefebvre et du 17ᵉ BCP aux opérations de la VIᵉ armée, les 5 et 6 mai 1917', by Estienne, 18 May 1917, SHD, 16N2120.
53. Ibid.
54. Fernand Pellegrin, *La Vie d'une armée pendant la grande guerre* (Paris: Flammarion, 1921), pp. 172–3.
55. 'Instruction provisoire sur l'emploi des chars d'assaut', GQG, 29 December 1917, SHD, 16N2142.
56. 'Instruction sur l'emploi des chars d'assaut', 14 July 1918, SHD, 16N2142.
57. 'Compte-rendu d'une mission en Angleterre', op. cit.
58. Ibid.
59. Estienne to Joffre, 27 November 1916, SHD, 16N2121.
60. Ibid.
61. Thomas to Joffre, 13 December 1916, SHD, 16N2121.
62. 'Comité consultatif de l'artillerie d'assaut, procès-verbal', 30 December 1916, SHD, 16N2129.
63. Ibid.
64. Thomas to Estienne, 17 March 1917, SHD, 16N2121. A copy of this letter was sent to Nivelle.
65. Estienne to Thomas, 21 March 1917, SHD, 16N2121. This letter was sent via Nivelle.
66. Nivelle to Thomas, 13 April 1917, SHD, 16N2120.
67. Ibid.
68. Pétain to Thomas, 10 May 1917, SHD, 16N2120. This order was in addition to the 150 Renaults initially ordered.
69. Jean Perré, 'Chars et statistique: Les constructions et les pertes', *La Revue d'infanterie*, July 1935, pp. 75–113, tableau no. 1.
70. 'Note sur les unités d'AS formées ou à former en 1917', GQG, 12 June 1917, AFGG V, vol. 2, *Les Opérations à objectifs limités (15 mai–1 novembre 1917)*, annexes vol. 1, annexe 492, pp. 809–12.
71. Estienne to Pétain 22 July 1917, SHD, 16N2120.
72. Estienne to Pétain, 1 December 1917, SHD, 16N2121.
73. 'Note sur la sortie des chars légers', GQG 3ᵉ Bureau, 22 April 1918, SHD, 16N2120. Defects ranged from engine problems to badly fitting turrets.
74. 1 April 1918, Raymond Poincaré, *Au service de la France: Neuf années de souvenirs*, vol. 10, *Victorie et armistice, 1918* (Paris: Plon, 1933), p. 104.
75. Estienne to GQG, 27 November 1916, SHD, 16N2121.
76. Estienne to Thomas, 22 May 1917, SHD, 16N2121.

77. 'Situation des groupes d'AS au point de vue disponibilité à la date du 15 novembre 1917', 16 November 1917, SHD, 16N2120.
78. Estienne to Pétain, 12 June 1917, SHD, 16N2120. Estienne said that military aviation 'presents numerous technical analogies', one being that there would be as many tanks in service as there were aircraft by the end of 1917.
79. 'Renseignements complémentaires de détail au sujet de l'emploi des tanks à Cambrai', 6 March 1918, GQG, SHD, 16N2142.
80. 'Compte rendu de l'opération du 9 Juillet (Fermes Portes et des Loges)', *Groupement* Chanoine, 11 July 1918, SHD, 16N2163.
81. 'Annexe au rapport sur les opérations du 18 au 23 Juillet 1918', *Groupement* I, undated note, SHD, 16N2162.
82. Tenth Army JMO, 14 July 1918, SHD, 26N51/11.
83. Estienne to Pétain, 3 September 1918, SHD, 16N2142.
84. 'Note pour les armées: Enseignements tirés des combats récents en ce qui concerne l'artillerie d'assaut', 9 September 1918, SHD, 16N2142. This note was addressed to all commanders, down to the level of infantry battalion and artillery *groupe*.
85. See Francois-André Paoli, *L'Armée francaise de 1919 à 1939: La Reconversion* (Paris: Ministère des Armées, État-major de l'Armée de Terre, Service Historique, circa 1970), pp. 163–5 and 167.
86. Quoted in Arlette Estienne-Mondet, *Le Général J. B. E. Estienne: Père des chars* (Paris: L'Harmattan, 2010), p. 315.

# Index

Ablaincourt, engagement at, 1916, 154–5
Ablain-Saint-Nazaire, 112–3, 150
*Affaire des fiches*, 20
André, Gen. Louis, 20
Aisne river and region, 5, 6, 28, 68, 92, 96, 101, 137, 160, 217, 232, 238
Albert, King of the Belgians, 50
d'Alencon, Lt.-Col. Marcel, 91, 93, 95, 98
Alexandre, Maj. Georges-René, 227
Alexeieff, Gen. Mikhail, 37, 41
America, 43, 44, 57, 62, 78–9, 97, 120
  army, 159
  in battle, 125, 160–1, 198
  and coalition command, 58, 60
  in Meuse–Argonne offensive, 1918, 162–3
  in Second Battle of the Marne, 1918, 220–2
Amiens, 27, 59–60, 124, 126, 158, 196–8, 205, 227, 236
  Battle of, 1918, 61, 157, 186, 199–200
Anthoine, Gen. François, 20, 21, 99, 121, 194, 196
Archinauld, Col. Louis, 207–8
Ardennes, Battle of the, 1914, 130, 134–6, 149
  French army in, 26
Ardre river, 237
Arnaud, René, 233
Arras, 92, 97, 101, 111, 150
Artois, 5–6, 9, 11, 21, 23, 31, 53, 70, 137–8, 139, 142, 147, 154, 173
  First Battle of, 1914, 68
  Second Battle of, 1915, 10, 32, 49, 68–9, 152, 212–3
  Third Battle of, 1915, 10, 71, 113–4, 152–3, 229
Asquith, Herbert, 178
Austria–Hungary, 32, 36–7, 41, 43
  army, 157–8
Avre river and sector, 118, 187, 196, 198, 201

Balkans, 33, 42
  Balkan Wars, 241–2
Balfourier, Gen. Maurice, 231
Bapaume, 89
  Bapaume–Péronne road, 117, 191

Bapst, Gen. Étienne, 144
Barbot, Gen. Ernest, 229
de Barescut, Gen. Maurice, 87, 195
Bar-le-Duc, 72
Barthélemy, Gen. Joseph, 120, 123
*Bataille générale*, 61–2
Beauvais Agreement, 1918, 60
Belgium, 132–3
  army, 28, 49
Bernède, Allain, 229
Berthelot, Gen. Henri, 25, 41, 43, 160, 191, 237, 238
Bertrix, action at, 1914, 134
Blondlat, Gen. Ernest, 141
Blondlat, Max, 151
Boff, Jonathan, 8
Bois St Pierre Vaast, 117, 191–3
Bonneau, Gen. Louis, 188
de Bonneval, Gen. Léon Deshayes, 144
Bordeaux, Henry, 38, 44, 171, 172, 196, 234
  on Debeney, 201
  on Gamelin, 236
  on Fayolle, 108–10, 120, 123–5, 128–9
  on Maistre, 147–8, 150, 153, 157, 160, 163–4
  on Roques, 174–5, 178, 180–1, 183
Bouchavesnes, 12, 117, 191, 234
Boucheron de Boissoudy, Gen. Antoine, 151, 154, 159, 192–3
Bourachot, André, 46
Breton, Jules-Louis, 246
Briand, Aristide, 34, 38, 42–3, 56, 61, 96, 174
  and Nivelle, 89, 93
  and Battle of Verdun, 1916, 143–4
Brimont, 100
  action at, 1914, 211–12, 214
Britain – see Great Britain
Bruchmüller, George, 88
Brugère, Gen. Joseph, 102–3, 218
Brun, Jean, 167
Brusilov Offensive, 1916, 37
Buat, Gen. Edmond, 20, 194, 202, 239
Bulgaria, 33, 42, 181–2

Cadorna, Gen. Luigi,
  and Joffre, 36, 40, 43, 58

Calais Conference, 1917, 93–4
Cambrai, Battle of, 1917, 252–3
Cantigny, action at, 1918, 125, 198
Caporetto, Battle of, 1917, 58, 122, 157
Carency, 112–13
Casba Kisba, action at, 1913, 209
Casba Tadla, action at, 1913, 208–9
de Castelnau, Gen. Noël de Curières de, 20, 21, 34, 48, 56, 70, 89, 90, 91, 97, 110–11, 140–1, 182, 193
   and Battle of Verdun, 1916, 143–5, 177
*Centre des hautes études militaires* (CHEM), 202
Champagne region, 7, 9, 31, 120, 137, 142, 149, 160, 162, 173–4, 236–7
   First Battle of, 1914–15, 138–9
   Second Battle of, 1915, 10, 23, 33, 70–1, 114, 130, 140–1, 146, 229
Chantilly Conference, 1915, 35, 37
Charteris, John,
   on Joffre, 35–6
Château-Thierry, 61, 169
Chemin des Dames ridge, 6, 16, 17, 57, 75, 78, 80, 92, 98, 99, 102, 104, 125, 147, 154–6, 159, 162, 195, 232, 248
Churchill, Winston, 23
Clausewitz, Karl von, 52, 66
Clayton, Anthony, 105
Clemenceau, Georges, 20, 45, 80, 102, 103, 104–5, 123, 198, 216, 238
   and Foch, 51, 58–9, 60–2
   and Mangin, 208, 218, 224
   and tanks, 252
*Comité consultatif de l'artillerie d'assaut*, 246, 250–1
*Comité de guerre*, 89, 96–7, 105
Compiègne, 62, 96, 218
*Conseil supérieur de la guerre* (CSG), 24, 45, 127, 132, 149, 163, 202, 227
Contamine, Henry, 174
Cordonnier, Gen. Émilien, 41, 81

Daille, Maurice, 202
Daladier, Edouard, 226
Dardanelles campaign, 1915, 32–3
Debeney, Gen. Marie-Eugène, 12, 13, 14, 16, 19, 34, 45, 109, 124, 125, 157, 159
   assassination of, 204
   character, 185–6, 187, 190, 193, 196, 201, 203–5
   as chief of staff, 194–6
   in command of First Army, 196–202, 236
   and Fayolle, 126
   on military education, 21–2, 204
   military ideas, 188, 189, 193, 196, 201, 202–3
   post-war career, 202–3
   pre-war career, 187–8

de Gaulle, Capt. Charles, 74, 82
Dehayes de Bonneval, Gen. Léon, 144
Demange, Gen. Marie-Georges, 188–9
Diaz, Gen. Armando, 58, 123
Diéna, action at, 1891, 207–8, 213
*Direction de service automobile* (DSA), 242–3, 244–6, 250
Dinant, 169
Douaumont, Fort, 14, 72, 74–5, 87–8, 119, 141–3, 145, 177, 213–15
Doughty, Robert, 49, 105, 233
Doullens Agreement, 1918, 59–60
Doumenc, Maj. Aimé, 244, 245
Doumer, Paul, 33, 218
Dreyfus affair, 20, 50–1
Driant, Col. Emile, 37
Dubail, Gen. Augustin, 145–6, 173, 175, 179, 186, 188–9
Dubois, Gen. Pierre, 85, 114
Duchêne, Gen. Denis, 99, 122, 125, 154, 157, 159–60
Dutheil, Henri,
   on Mangin, 210
Duval, Gen. Maurice, 107, 115–17, 119–20, 123, 126, 128, 129

Ebener, Gen. Charles, 85
*École polytechnique*, 107, 166, 176
*École supérieure de guerre* (ESG), 21–2, 49, 77, 114, 121, 166, 167–8, 195, 202, 204, 227
   Fayolle at, 108
   Foch at, 51–2, 108, 148
   Maistre at, 148
   Pétain at, 65, 66–7, 108
Estienne, Gen. Jean-Baptiste, 7, 8, 20, 214
   and artillery, 240–2
   character, 240, 242, 255
   and military aviation, 167, 240–1
   pre-war career, 240–1
   and tanks, 229, 240, 242–54
Eydoux, Gen. Joseph, 135

Falkenhayn, Gen. Erich von, 41, 46
Fallièrs, Armand, 30
Falls, Cyril, 103, 105
Fashoda expedition, 206, 208
Fayolle, Gen. Marie-Émile, 9, 12, 15–17, 19–21, 53, 68, 79, 81, 148, 150, 152, 158–9, 161, 164, 186–7, 191, 198, 199, 218–19, 223, 229, 231, 239
   in Battle of the Somme, 1916, 40, 55, 114–18, 120, 232
   and the British, 116, 117–8, 122–3
   character, 106–10, 112–14, 119–20, 124, 126, 128–9, 151
   in command of 70 DI, 110–13
   in command of Sixth Army, 114–18

in command of XXXIII CA, 113–14
and Foch, 116, 119, 123–6, 129
and Italy, 122–3, 157
made Marshal of France, 106, 109, 126–7
military ideas, 11, 13–14, 31, 106, 110–15, 117–18, 120, 124, 192
and Pétain, 113, 120, 129
post-war career, 126–7, 163
pre-war career, 107–9
reputation, 127–8
and subordinates, 121, 125–6, 198, 201
First World War,
 allied strategy in, 6
 military tactics in, 3–4, 5–6, 9–10
 nature of, 5, 23
 operations in, 3, 4–5, 8, 13, 15–16, 17–19, 21
Flaucourt plateau, 116
Flers–Courcelette, Battle of, 1916, 41, 117
Florenville, 172
Foch, Marshal Ferdinand, 2, 3, 13–16, 19–21, 27–9, 44–6, 64, 70, 89, 101, 105–9, 112, 117, 127, 137, 149, 159, 161, 187, 193, 197, 201, 204, 219, 223, 227, 239
 and armistice negotiations, 62
 in Battle of the Somme, 1916, 18, 36, 39–40, 44, 54–6
 and the British, 52, 55
 character, 48, 50
 as chief of staff, 57–8, 79, 120
 and coalition command, 49–50, 57–8, 59–60, 162
 and doctrine, 10–11, 12, 18, 49–53, 199
 at ESG, 51–2, 108, 148
 in First Battle of Ypres, 1914, 5–6
 as generalissimo, 1918, 18–19, 21, 44–5, 48, 60–2, 80, 158
 and Italy, 58
 memoirs, 203
 and Nivelle Offensive, 1917, 100, 103, 218
 and operations, 3, 17, 18–19, 61–2, 114
 and peace terms, 62–3, 224
 and Pétain, 80
 and politics, 51–2, 56, 58–9, 62–3
 and strategy, 44, 56–7, 60, 61–2, 198, 220
Fournier, Gen. Henri, 1, 22, 163
Franco-Prussian War, 1870–1, 109, 131, 148, 206
French army, 45
 and aircraft, 8, 9, 13, 17, 166–8, 237, 240–1
 armies,
  First Army, 19, 20, 92, 106, 109, 118–19, 123–6, 132, 173–4, 186, 188–9, 201, 203
  Second Army, 10, 14, 20, 38, 42, 48, 69–71, 74, 86–7, 110–11, 121, 140, 143–4, 193, 213

Third Army, 4, 20, 33, 92, 98, 123–5, 132, 137, 144, 181, 186, 197, 234, 252
 in Battle of the Matz, 1918, 218–19
Fourth Army, 4, 7, 26, 71, 99–100, 121, 130, 141, 184
 in Battle of the Ardennes, 1914, 133–5, 149, 168–9
 in First Battle of Champagne, 1914–15, 138–9
 in 1918 battles, 159–60, 162
 in 1914 retreat, 136–7, 172
 in Second Battle of Champagne, 1915, 139–41
Fifth Army, 28, 67–8, 75, 92, 98–9, 121, 141, 159–62, 210, 215–17, 237, 248
Sixth Army, 11, 28, 40, 54, 75, 85, 90, 92, 94, 98–100, 106, 141, 155–7, 159–60, 190–1, 195, 220, 229, 249
 in Battle of the Somme, 1916, 114–18
 in Nivelle Offensive, 1917, 215–18
Seventh Army, 193, 195
Ninth Army, 28, 48, 149, 159–61, 220
Tenth Army, 10, 40, 61, 68–9, 71, 81, 92, 99, 113–14, 117, 125, 150, 153–4, 157–66, 198, 212–13, 215–16, 219–23, 225, 253
army corps – *corps d'armée* (CA),
I, 121, 193
I CAC, 99
II, 24, 154, 175
II CAC, 99, 141
II CC, 220–2
III, 14, 38, 74, 86, 210–14, 241, 245
V, 99, 193, 234
VI, 181, 216
VII, 85, 118
IX, 136, 218
XI, 88, 133–5, 214–15
XII, 133–4, 137, 138
 in Battle of the Ardennes, 1914, 168–71
XIII, 190
XV, 65
XVII, 133–4, 136, 138, 171
XIX, 104
XX, 48, 69, 70, 101, 107, 145, 148, 153, 221–2, 229, 231–2
XXI, 69, 112, 156, 158, 159, 164
 action at Notre-Dame-de-Lorette, 1914–15, 149–52
XXX, 144, 221–2
XXXI, 186
XXXII, 99, 191–3, 202, 203
XXXIII, 68–9, 106, 112, 152
XXXV, 85, 187
XXXVIII, 191

army groups,
  Groupe d'armées du centre (GAC), 70–1, 73, 75, 91, 100, 106, 120–1, 130, 140, 141–2, 144–6, 147, 159–62, 198, 213
  Groupe d'armées de l'est (GAE), 189, 193, 197, 229
  Groupe d'armées du nord (GAN), 70–1, 92, 100
  Groupe d'armées de réserve (GAR), 91–2, 98, 99, 107, 123–4, 159, 215, 219, 232
and artillery, 4, 7–8, 9, 13–14, 26, 29
battalions of *chasseurs d'Afrique*,
  2$^e$, 131
battalions of *chasseurs alpins* (BCA),
  11$^e$, 227, 229
  15$^e$, 227
battalions of *chasseurs à pied* (BCP),
  3$^e$, 65
  8$^e$, 65
  24$^e$, 65
  29$^e$, 65
  60$^e$, 233
brigades,
  2$^e$ brigade d'*artillere spéciale*, 253–4
  *brigades d'infanterie* (BI),
    2$^e$ colonial, 229
    4$^e$, 67
    8$^e$, 210–11
    19$^e$, 107
    27$^e$, 85
    110$^e$, 85
and casualties, 56–7
colonial, 19–20, 119, 206–7
divisions – *divisions d'infanterie* (DI),
  3 colonial, 85–6, 134, 171
  5, 87, 210–14, 224, 242
  6, 68, 227, 241
  7, 167–8
  9, 232–7
  10, 69–70, 233–5
  13, 150, 153
  23, 170
  24, 170
  25, 187–91, 203
  35, 235–6
  38, 220
  39, 212
  40, 191
  42, 191, 202
  43, 150–4, 159
  47, 158, 202, 229, 230–1
  57, 189
  61, 85–6
  62, 153
  66, 191

  70, 68–9, 106, 107–8, 110–13
  77, 68–9, 229
  120, 153
  153, 230
  168, 232
and firepower doctrine, 7–8, 9, 66, 87–8, 108–9, 112, 117, 139, 191–2, 221, 230
generalship debate, 2–3
and logistics, 13, 14, 16, 72–3
and morale, 193
mutinies in, 1917, 16–18, 57, 64, 75–7, 104, 155, 187, 233–4
in 1914, 26–7
and politics, 20, 57, 105, 119, 148
promotion in, 19–20, 150, 154, 165, 171
regiments,
  *régiments d'artillerie*,
    2$^e$ RAC, 241–2
    5$^e$, 85
  *régiments d'infanterie* (RI),
    4$^e$, 232, 237
    20$^e$, 75
    33$^e$, 82
    79$^e$, 148
    82$^e$, 232–4, 238
    89$^e$, 324
    94$^e$, 202
    109$^e$, 149, 153
    313$^e$, 232–3
    329$^e$, 324
  *régiment d'infanterie colonial de Maroc*, 220
and 'scientific battle' doctrine, 11, 17, 53, 114–15
and tactics, 3–4, 7–8, 9–10, 13, 18–19, 26, 30–1, 55, 65–6, 77–8, 110–11, 122, 138–9, 155–6, 194–5, 200–1, 220–1, 229–30, 237–8
and tanks, 8, 16–19, 155–6, 220–2, 229, 238, 242–54
and uniform, 7, 26
Franchet d'Esperey, Gen. Louis, 28, 89, 92, 96–7, 106, 119, 159, 198, 209
  on Mangin, 210
French, F.-M. Sir John, 1, 25–6, 28, 35, 50
Frontiers, Battle of the, 1914, 26–7, 165, 171, 228
Fuller, J.F.C., 240

Gadel, Gen. Joseph, 232
Gallieni, Gen. Joseph, 27, 52, 174, 179, 181
  and Joffre, 33–4, 38, 176–7
Gamelin, Gen. Maurice, 13, 14, 21, 27, 149
  in Battle of the Marne, 1914, 228–9
  in Battle of the Somme, 1916, 230–2
  command style of, 228, 231–2, 236
  in 1918, 234–8
  post-war career, 238

pre-war career, 226–8
in Second World War, 226, 238–9
General Allied Offensive, 1916, 35, 37, 39, 40, 42–3
General Allied Reserve, 79
Gérard, Gen. Augustin, 175, 179
German army, 6, 43
  in Battle of Verdun, 1916, 71, 142–3
  morale, 17
  in 1918, 220–1, 223
  in 1914, 133–4, 169–70
  operational doctrine, 26, 89–90, 139–41
  in spring 1918 offensive, 59–61, 79, 80, 123–4
Givenchy, 152–3
Godfroy, Lt.-Col. Léon, 155, 157, 195–6, 198, 202
  on Debeney, 185–6, 189, 194, 201, 204
Gough, Gen. Hubert, 93
Gouraud, Gen. Henri, 121, 159–60, 162, 218, 239
Goya, Michel, 43, 69, 230
Grand Couronne, defence of, 1914, 28, 110
de Grandmaison, Col. Louis, 3, 108, 188
Grasset, Lt.-Col. Alphonse, 202
Great Britain, 24, 49–50
  army, 25–6, 28, 30, 33, 39–40, 43, 67, 158, 232
  in Battle of the Somme, 1916, 55, 246–7
  Fifth Army, 187, 201, 236
  Fourth Army, 116, 186, 198–9
  generals debate in, 1
  in 1918 campaign, 59, 79, 124, 161, 196–7, 198–200, 234–6
  tank programme, 246–7, 249
Greenhalgh, Elizabeth, 50, 105
Guillaumat, Gen. Adolphe, 67, 176, 178
  on Debeney, 193–4
  and Fayolle, 121–2
  on Maistre, 150, 157, 161, 163–4
Guise,
  Battle of, 1914, 5, 28
  Battle of, 1918, 196, 200–1

Haig, F.-M. Sir Douglas, 1, 11, 50, 57, 59, 61, 98, 126, 178, 199, 247
  and Battle of the Somme, 1916, 54
  and Debeney, 186–7, 199–200
  and Foch, 52, 46, 80
  and Joffre, 35–6, 39–40
  and Nivelle, 92–6, 100–1
  and Pétain, 79–80
  and strategy, 35–6, 38–9
Hangard, action at, 1918, 199
Harris, Paul, 95
Hartmannswillerkopf, 7, 229

Hébert, Rémi, 86
Heer, Gen. Frédéric-Georges, 71, 141–4
Hindenburg, Gen. Paul von, 41, 90, 105
Hindenburg Line, 126, 161, 186
  capture of, 1918, 200–1
  German retreat to, 1917, 15, 56, 75, 90, 94–5, 97, 119
Hitler, Adolf,
  and Mangin, 224
Hoeville, action at, 1914, 110–11
Humbert, Gen. Georges, 98, 125, 144, 286, 197, 218, 234
'Hundred Days' offensive, 1918, 237–8

Italy, 33, 36–7, 39, 43, 58, 95, 106–7, 122–3, 181
  army, 123
Isonzo,
  Fifth Battle of, 1916, 36–7
  Seventh Battle of, 1916, 40
  Sixth Battle of, 1916, 40

Jeanneney, Jean, 224
Joffre, Gen. Joseph, 2, 3, 5, 8, 14–15, 20, 21, 23, 48, 49, 52, 55–6, 67–8, 70, 71, 73–4, 91, 94, 101, 105–6, 108–10, 113, 116–18, 127, 130, 135, 137, 149, 153, 159, 172, 188, 193, 204, 233, 245
  and America, 44
  appointment of, 20, 24
  and artillery, 4
  and Battle of Verdun, 1916, 142–4, 177–8, 180–1, 190, 213–14, 229
  character of, 27, 29, 35–6, 38, 44, 45
  and coalition war, 26, 28, 30–4, 35, 39, 43, 46
  and command, 27, 40, 44–5, 47
  and Gamelin, 227–9
  and Great Britain, 25–6, 29–30, 32–3, 35–6, 38–40
  and Italy, 36–7, 43
  memoirs, 45, 47, 203
  in 1914, 26–8, 132–3, 136
  and Nivelle, 86–8, 213
  and operations, 9, 23–4, 30–1, 139–40
  and politics, 33–4, 37–8, 42–3, 46, 143–5, 176–84
  pre-war career, 24–6
  reputation, 23, 29, 34, 46–7
  and Roques, 165, 171, 173–4, 176–84
  and Russia, 25, 29, 32, 37
  and strategy, 16, 23–4, 30, 34–5, 38–9, 42, 43–4, 46–7, 137–8
  and tanks, 242–3, 245–7, 249–50
Juvincourt, action at, 1917, 232–3, 248

King, Jere Clemens, 176, 180, 182–3
Kitchener, F.-M. Lord Herbert, 29, 30, 46
  and Joffre, 32–3
Krause, Jonathan, 152, 229–30

Laffaux, 98
  action at, 1917, 155, 248–9
La Gallet, Gen., 67
Lake Naroch, Battle of, 1916, 37
de Langle de Cary, Gen. Fernand, 4, 7, 15, 20, 149, 164, 168, 171–3
  in Battle of the Ardennes, 1914, 132–6
  in Battles of Champagne, 1914–15, 138–41
  in Battle of Verdun, 1916, 141–6
  character, 132, 137
  and Joffre, 132, 136, 137, 144–6
  pre-war career, 130–2
  reputation, 130, 136
  retirement, 145–6, 178
  in retreat to the Marne, 1914, 136–7
Lanrezac, Charles, 67, 132, 146
Laon, 157
de La Roque, Lt.-Col. François, 228, 236
Lebrun, Gen. Leoncé, 213–14
Le Cateau, Battle of, 1914, 28
Le Goyet, Pierre, 235–6
Les Invalides, 45, 105, 127, 130, 146, 164, 184
Le Linge, 7, 229
Libramont, 169–70
Liddell Hart, Basil, 63, 69, 199
Liège, 132–3, 142
*Limogéage*, 19
Lloyd, Nick, 53
Lloyd George, David, 29, 42, 55, 57–60, 62–3, 101
  and command, 92–4
London Conference, 1917, 93–4
Loos, Battle of, 1915, 32, 35, 71
Loucher, Louis, 251–2
Ludendorff, Gen. Erich, 41, 60, 62, 75, 90, 102–3, 105, 158, 160–1, 234
  and strategy, 95, 197
Lupfer, Timothy, 105
Lyautey, Gen. Hubert, 20, 95, 106
  minister of war, 43, 52, 90, 181–3
  and Mangin, 208–10, 225

Madelin, Louis, 92
Maginot, André, 202
Maissin, action at, 1914, 134–5
Maistre, Gen. Paul, 9, 13, 14, 17, 19, 22, 27, 38, 84, 109, 112, 122, 190, 198
  and Americans, 162–3
  in Battle of the Somme, 1916, 153–4
  in Battle of Verdun, 1916, 153

character, 147, 149–50, 153, 155, 164
  in command of GAC, 159–64
  in command of Sixth Army, 154–7, 164
  in Italy, 157–8
  at Maubeuge enquiry, 1, 163
  military ideas, 148–9, 152, 155–6, 158, 160, 163–4
  pre-war career, 148–9
  post-war career, 163–4
  reputation, 147
Malmaison, Battle of, 1917, 17, 78, 147, 151, 155–7, 195, 249
Mangin, Gen. Charles, 8, 14–17, 19–20, 61, 90, 92, 95–6, 102–3, 105, 126, 155
  in Battle of the Matz, 1918, 125–6, 198, 218–19
  in Battle of Verdun, 1916, 213–15
  character, 207–10, 218, 225
  in command of Tenth Army, 159–61, 253
  Fayolle on, 118–19, 206, 212
  and Micheler, 94, 98, 100, 215–18
  military ideas, 209–10, 225
  and Nivelle, 213–18
  post-war career, 224
  pre-war career, 206–10
  reputation, 206, 214, 224–5
  in Second Battle of the Marne, 1918, 81, 220–3
Mangin, Gen. Louis Émile, 202
Marchand, Gen. Jean-Baptiste, 206–8
Mareschal, Gen. Henri, 235
Marne,
  First Battle of the, 1914, 5, 28–9, 47, 48, 68, 130, 149
  retreat to, 1914, 171–3
  river, 125, 159–61
  Second Battle of the, 1918, 61–2, 80–1, 159–61, 220–3, 225, 236–7, 253
Matz, Battle of the, 1918, 125, 218–19, 225
de Maud'huy, Gen. Louis, 68, 150, 188
Maunoury, Gen. Michel, 28
Mazel, Gen. Olivier, 98, 102, 121, 218
Messimy, Gen. Adolphe, 27, 67, 96, 176
Messines ridge, 6
Metz, 62, 132
Meuse–Argonne, Battle of, 1918, 62, 147, 159, 161–2
Meuse,
  Crossings, Battle of the, 1914, 28, 136, 172–3
  river, 132–4, 137–8, 142–3, 169, 173, 210
Mezières, 162
Micheler, Gen. Alfred, 84, 95, 102, 118–19, 148, 150, 155, 232
  in Battle of the Somme, 1916, 40, 153–4
  and Mangin, 94, 98, 100, 215–18

in Nivelle Offensive, 1917, 91–2, 96–8, 218
Millerand, Alexandre, 32, 79
de Mitry, Gen. Anthoine, 160, 216
Mollandin, Gen. René, 159
Moltke, Gen. Helmuth von, 5, 27, 28
Monhove, Col. Jean, 245
Montdidier, 196–7, 218
  Battle of, 1918, 126, 157, 186, 199–200, 202
Monte Tomba, action at, 1917, 157–8
Moreuil, 200
Morhange, action at, 1914, 48, 197–8
Morocco, 208–9
Montagu, Edwin, 247
Montgomery, Gen. Archibald, 116
Moronvilliers, 98, 100
Mourret, Gen. Léon, 242–3, 246, 249–50
Mutinies – see French army

Namur, 133, 169
Nancy, 110, 148, 173
Napoleon III, 23
Négrier, Gen., 204
Neufchâteau, 133, 169
Neuville-Saint-Vaast, 212–13
Nevramont, action at, 1914, 134
Nicholas, Grand Duke, 32
Nivelle Offensive, 1917, 16–17, 57, 75–6, 83, 99–100, 154, 215–17, 248
  artillery, 99
  casualties, 75, 100, 103
  plan, 89–90, 92–3, 97–9, 102, 118–19
Nivelle, Gen. Robert, 9, 12–14, 20–1, 23, 38, 40–3, 45, 77, 118, 128, 184, 193–4, 245
  in Battle of Verdun, 1916, 74, 86–8
  commander-in-chief, 15–16, 56, 89–103
  and Haig, 92–6, 100, 101
  and Mangin, 213–18
  military ideas, 56, 75, 84–6, 90–1
  in 1915, 85–6
  in 1914, 85
  in North Africa, 104
  and politics, 95–7, 100–1, 105
  pre-war career, 83–5, 148
  reputation, 83, 105
  and tanks, 250
Nobécourt, René-Gustave, 229
Nordmann, Charles, 85
*Noria* system, 14, 73, 76
Notre-Dame-de-Lorette, 68–9, 71, 111–12, 147, 158, 163–4
  actions at, 1914–15, 150–2
Noyon,
  Battle of, 1918, 234–6
  salient, 137

Oise,
  river, 89, 92, 190, 224, 236
  sector, 118
Onhaye, action at, 1914, 209–10
Ourcq, Battle of the, 1918, 161

Painlevé, Paul, 56, 57, 75, 76, 98, 103, 194, 217–18
  minister of war, 92
  and Nivelle Offensive, 1917, 96–8, 100–2, 105
Paris, 28, 59, 61, 79, 80, 94, 131, 137, 176
  Peace Conference, 62
Passaga, Col. Germain, 229
Passchendaele ridge, 6, 122
Pedroncini, Guy, 76
Pellé, Gen. Maurice, 180, 227, 234
Pershing, Gen. John, 44, 61, 62, 80, 162–3
Perthes-lès-Hurlus, 7, 141
Pétain, Gen. Philippe, 2–3, 9, 13, 19, 20–1, 27, 37, 40, 44, 53, 57, 59–60, 63, 75, 91, 99, 100, 104–6, 119, 121, 140, 146, 151–2, 156–7, 159, 162, 178, 181, 183–5, 195–6, 210, 218–20, 222–5, 233, 239, 255
  in Battle of Verdun, 1916, 14, 38, 71–4, 86–8, 143–4, 153, 177, 213–15
  commander-in-chief, 16, 64, 76–81
  and Debeney, 187–8, 194, 198, 204
  Fayolle on, 113, 124
  and Foch, 80–1
  and Haig, 79–80
  in 1915, 68–71, 150, 152
  in 1914, 67–8
  and Nivelle, 86–7, 95–7, 119
    replaces Nivelle, 76, 100–2, 120, 194–5, 249
  and operations, 76–7, 78–9
  pre-war career, 64–7, 148
  and tactics, 7, 17–18, 65–6, 68, 69–70, 77–8
    defensive, 234–5
  and tanks, 250–2, 254
  and Vichy regime, 82
Petiti, Gen., 41
Piave river, 58, 121, 158
Pierrefeu, Jean de, 91, 97–8, 102, 105
Pinchon, Steven, 62
Plan XVII, 24–7, 132
Plumer, Gen. Sir Herbert, 122
Poincaré, Raymond, 40, 43, 45, 97, 100–1, 140, 177, 181, 198, 218, 251
  on Foch, 2
  on Joffre, 27
Porch, Douglas, 2–3, 22
Pont, Gen. Ferdinand, 194
Pouydraguin, Gen. Gaston d'Armau de, 229, 231–2

Quennevières, action at, 1915, 85–6, 97

Race to the Sea, 1914, 5, 115, 150
Rancourt, 191
Rapallo Conference, 1917, 58
Rawlinson, Gen. Sir Henry, 189
   and Debeney, 198–9
   and Fayolle, 116
Reims, 61, 80–1, 92, 95, 120, 137, 147, 149, 160–1, 162, 168, 191, 212, 220, 236–7, 253
Renault FT 17 tank, 249–51
Renault, Louis, 243, 249–50
Renouard, Col. Georges, 91, 95
Rhineland, 63, 106, 126, 206, 224
Ribot, Alexandre, 96, 97, 101, 218
Rimailho, Col. Émile, 244
Robertson, F.-M. Sir William, 93, 101
Robillot, Gen. Felix, 222
Rocolle, Pierre, 166, 173, 174
Rolland, Denis, 75, 87, 104
Romania, 42–3
   entry into the war, 40–1, 153, 181–3
Roques, Gen. Pierre, 4, 8, 15, 20, 137
   in Battle of the Ardennes, 1914, 134, 165, 168–71
   character, 174–5, 176, 178–9
   in command of First Army, 173–5
   and Joffre, 145–6, 171, 173–4, 176–84
   and military aviation, 166–8
   minster of war, 38, 42–3, 146, 176–84
   post-war career, 184
   pre-war career, 166–8
   reputation, 165, 184
   in retreat to the Marne, 1914, 171–3
Rossignol, action at, 1914, 134
Ruffey, Gen. Pierre, 4, 132, 137, 146, 181
Russia, 24, 28, 29, 32, 34, 37, 39, 40, 41, 43, 57, 63, 79, 120
   army, 25
   revolution, 44, 94, 97, 103
Russo-Japanese War, 1904–5, 66, 241

Sailly-Saillisel, 192, 202
St Chamond tank, 244–5, 246, 247, 249–51
St Cyr, 52, 64–5, 83, 131, 148, 187, 226
St Mihiel, Battle of, 1918, 62, 173, 175
St Quentin, Battle of, 1918, 196, 200–1
Salonika campaign, 33, 41, 159, 181
Santerre plain, 153
Sarrail, Gen. Maurice, 20, 41, 43, 181–3
   *affaire* Sarrail, 33–4
Saussier, Gen. Felix, 65
Schlieffen Plan, 67
Schneider tank, 243–4, 246, 248–51
Sedan, 132, 136, 162–3, 169
Semoy river, 169, 172

Serbia, 33
Serrigny, Bernard, 71, 102
75mm gun, 4, 7–8, 108
Sidi Bou Othman, action at, 1912, 208–9
Smith, Leonard, 213, 224
Smythe, Donald, 163
Soissonais, Battle of the, 1918, 161, 220–1, 225, 253–4
Soissons, 61, 95, 220, 223, 253
Somme,
   Battle of the, 1916, 6, 11–13, 15, 18, 21, 23, 36, 38, 39–41, 43, 55–6, 87, 100, 106, 112, 115–8, 121, 124, 153–4, 181–2, 187, 191–4, 202, 214, 246–9
   planning, 54, 73–4, 114–5, 177
   river, 71, 89, 158, 190, 234
Sordet, Gen. André, 210
Souain, 7, 149–50
Souchez, 112, 152
Souville, Fort, 87
Spears (Spiers), Edward, 105, 115, 116, 128, 217
Spring offensive, 1918 – see German army
Sulzbach, Herbert, 237–8
Supreme War Council (SWC), 58–9, 62

Tahure, 7
Tardenois, Battle of the, 1918, 161
Thiepval ridge, 6, 40
   village, 41
Thomas, Albert, 98, 194, 252
   and tanks, 243–5, 250–1
Trentino, 37
Trochu, Gen. Louis, 131
Tudor, Henry, 88
Turkey, 32

United States – see America
d'Urbal, Gen. Victor, 68, 114, 146, 179

des Vallières, Gen. Pierre, 194, 246
Vauquois, Butte de, 7
Vaux, Fort, 14, 75, 87–8, 119, 141, 153, 215
Verdun, 117, 119–21
   Battle of, 1916, 13, 14–15, 23, 36, 37–8, 39, 40–2, 54, 55–6, 71–4, 83, 86–7, 99, 130, 132, 142–7, 177–82, 187, 190, 193, 213–15, 232
   casualties, 88
   logistics, 72–3
   fortress, 5, 6–7, 28, 141–2
   Second Battle of, 1917, 17, 121–2, 195
Verrier, Gen. Elie, 211
Versailles, Treaty of, 1919, 63
Vesle river, 161, 237
Vichy regime, 2, 82, 204–5
de Villaret, Gen. Étienne, 145

Villers-Bretonneux, 198–9
Vimy ridge, 6, 10, 32, 68–9, 89, 98, 111–12, 113, 150, 152–3, 212
Viviani, René, 33
*Voie sacrée*, 13, 72–3, 244
Vondescheer, Col., 65–6
Vosges mountains, 7
Voyron, Gen. Émile, 84

Weygand, Gen. Maxime, 52, 56, 59
  on Debeney, 196, 204
  on Estienne, 240

William, Crown Prince, 142
Wilson, Gen. Sir Henry, 51–2, 80, 93
Wöevre plain, evacuation of, 1916, 143
Württemburg, Gen. Duke Albrect von, 133–4

Ypres, 6, 29, 49–50, 80
  First Battle of, 1914, 5–6
  Third Battle of, 1917, 20, 195
Yser river, 29, 49–50

Zeller, Lt.-Col. Léon, 195